D0956112

GLORIA & JOE

Also by Axel Madsen

NONFICTION

Billy Wilder

William Wyler: The Authorized Biography

The New Hollywood: American Movies in the 1970s

Malraux: A Biography

*Hearts and Minds: The Common Journey of
Simone de Beauvoir and Jean-Paul Sartre*

John Huston: A Biography·

Living for Design: The Yves Saint Laurent Story

Private Power

Open Road

*60 Minutes: The Power and the Politics of
America's Most Popular TV Show*

Cousteau: A Biography

FICTION

Unisave

Borderlines

GLORIA & JOE

by Axel Madsen

Arbor House · William Morrow · New York

Library of Congress Cataloging-in-Publication Data

Madsen, Axel.
    Gloria and Joe / by Axel Madsen.
        p.   cm.
    Bibliography: p.
    Includes index.
    ISBN 0-87795-946-3
    1. Swanson, Gloria—Relations with men. 2. Kennedy, Joseph P.
(Joseph Patrick), 1888–1969—Relations with women. 3. Actors—
United States—Biography. 4. Ambassadors—United States—
Biography. 5. Kennedy family. I. Title.
PN2287.S9M33 1988
791.43′028′0924—dc19
[B]

Manufactured in the United States of America

Published in Canada by Fitzhenry & Whiteside, Ltd.

10 9 8 7 6 5 4 3 2

Contents

Acknowledgments

I could not thank all the people who took time to help me prepare this book—and not all would want their names to appear. Besides expressing my gratitude to Gloria Swanson herself for the interviews she accorded me in 1974, let me thank at least:

In Los Angeles: Mel Froman, Michael Hargraves, Betty Lasky, Viege Traub, and the librarians at the Academy of Motion Picture Arts and Sciences.

In Paris: Philippe Labrousse, Emmita de la Falaise, and Georges Hoffman.

In New York and Chicago: Harry Parish and Mr. and Mrs. William Petersen.

In Solebury, Pennsylvania: Dr. Edwin Carlin.

AXEL MADSEN

Carversville, Pennsylvania
October 1987

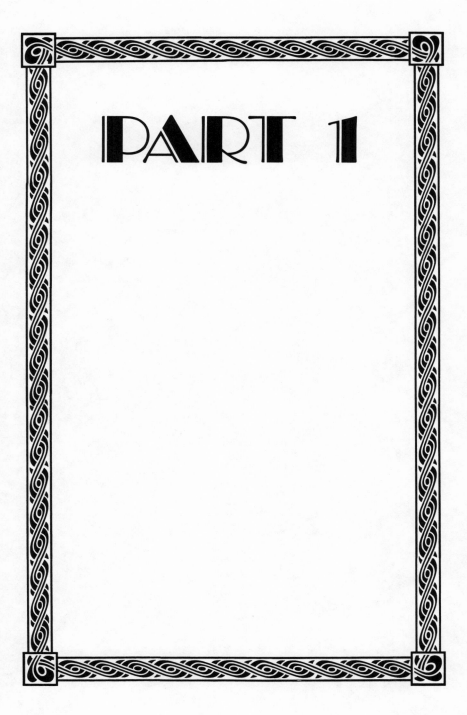

PART 1

The Savoy Plaza

*Lady, lady, should you meet
One whose ways are all discreet,
One who murmurs that his wife
Is the lodestar of his life,
One who keeps assuring you
That he never was untrue,
Never loved another one.
Lady, lady, better run.*

—DOROTHY PARKER

He was surprised at how tiny she was; she thought he didn't look like a banker. She was amused by his Boston accent; he was shocked when she told him her five-year-old adopted son hadn't been christened. She surprised him by ordering steamed string beans, braised celery, and zucchini; he ordered shrimp cocktail to start with, and told her he had three boys and four girls.

Gloria Swanson was staying at the elegant new Savoy Plaza Hotel on Fifth Avenue across from Central Park South. She was in New York this last week of November 1927 to show United Artists sales and distribution chiefs her daring screen adaptation of Somerset Maugham's famous short story that ran on Broadway for eighteen sold-out months as *Rain.* She was convinced—and a sneak preview in California had confirmed her most optimistic expectations—that in this picture, starring Lionel Barrymore and herself, she had a hit. She was hundreds of thousands of dollars in debt, and lawsuits for the nonpayment of bills were piling up, but on the way into the Renaissance Room with her manila envelope under one arm, she had told the maître d' to put the check on her bill. If the gentleman asked for it, the headwaiter should say the lunch was compliments of the management.

Joseph P. Kennedy mentioned a few familiar names. He had looked forward to meeting her. They mentioned the unusually mild weather, the fact that this was the only day they were both free, small worlds. They both knew First National Pictures' Bob Kane, of course. At her time at Paramount, Robert Kane, Sidney Kent, and Sam Katz were known as the front office KKKs.

The maître d' helped them get rid of the oversized menus. She was returning to Hollywood Saturday, she said.

People at nearby tables couldn't take their eyes off her, he noticed. She lit up the room. At twenty-eight, she was the embodiment of the vivacious, secure, and intriguing woman. Her screen image of the new, sophisticated 1920s female, combined with her ambitious, aggressive, managerial nature, had made her the top box-office magnet. Thousands struggled for a glimpse of her at premieres; fans deluged her with 10,000 letters a week. Her flamboyant fashions and innovative hairstyles, even her chin mole, were copied by millions of women. Diminutive (she stood all of 5'1"), she was every inch and every moment the star. Over the long-distance telephone, Kane had asked him if he were free for lunch Thursday. She was looking for financing for her next film, and possibly for a tie-over loan.

She guessed her luncheon partner to be in his late thirties. He was broad-shouldered and athletic in his three-piece pinstripes. His freckled face and toothy smile were still boyish, and the horn-rimmed glasses gave him something of Harold Lloyd's quizzical innocence. If she was on her guard, it was because the name Joseph P. Kennedy had figured among the industry chiefs who had condemned her for filming the Somerset Maugham story. On the phone, Kane had confirmed that Joe Kennedy was a distributor, but also that he was a banker and a consultant to several Wall Street investment houses just starting to get into motion pictures. Maybe he was ready to give Bank of America a little competition. "Since you're going to New York, I'll give him a call." Bob Kane had also told her to relax. Everyone producing pictures was in debt. The money always came in eventually.

"My wife and children were impressed when I told them who I was having lunch with," he said, smiling. He looked across at the face that conformed to no known specifications of beauty but photographed successfully from any angle—the chiseled chin, dished nose, and curious almond-shaped eyes ("blue as splinters of heaven," a fan magazine effused) that somehow blended into a bizarre loveliness. She had an elfin quality and a vivid, lively magnetism that was so arresting that nobody had much to say in her presence. Her daughter's name was also Gloria, he noted. What was her little boy's name?

"Joseph, after my late father. Both Gloria and I have called him Brother for so long the poor boy thinks it's his real name."

He told her his eldest son was named Joseph, too, after him. He couldn't help noticing how the rest of the luncheon guests watched them—watched her—and pretended not to hear what they were saying.

She handed him the contents of her folder and thought he looked relieved to have something to study. At Bob Kane's suggestion, she explained, she had had her accountant prepare a memorandum outlining proposals by United Artists and Bank of America for financing *Rockabye,* her next film. She would be grateful if he would tell her which offer seemed the better, and if he had an alternative proposal of his own.

Behind the movie star's dark, husky voice, determined chin, and regal sparkle, he guessed at a chaotic existence, days tied up in knots with her press agent, script manager, production chief, wardrobe designer, secretaries, maids, and bill collectors. Even though she was going to release *Rain* under the title *Sadie Thompson,* she was playing with dynamite. The Maugham story about a puritanical South Seas missionary who tries to reform a prostitute only to fall prey to her spunky charms was the property every studio had itched to do and every actress with a brain and a figure had dreamed of doing. The two-year-old decency code, however, automatically banned story material that ridiculed the clergy, and it warned producers to be extra careful when depicting women selling their virtue.

He asked about the people running her company, about her accountant. "Irving Wakoff," she said.

He didn't know the accountant to the stars. Scanning the papers, he said nobody in Hollywood knew how to draw up a balance sheet that answered bankers' questions. Certainly nobody knew how to depreciate, to amortize, to capitalize—the very things that in any other business spelled the difference between success and failure.

He didn't tell her Kane had suggested that he look into her affairs with the view of perhaps taking over Gloria Swanson Productions, that she was now prepared to place herself in proper hands and star in pictures instead of trying to be a businesswoman. When he asked about her overseas grosses, she grimaced.

Gloria had her own office in Paris because Paramount distributed her films there, and she didn't trust their figures or their advertising. If Henri, her husband, was in France right now, it was to try and make sure *The Love of Sunya* got booked into the right cinemas. Here, the press had called it a fragile little fantasy of sweetness. Joseph Schenck, the head of United Artists, had said it wasn't exactly dynamite, and Wakoff felt that only foreign revenues could make it break even. The notices were much better in Europe.

The Love of Sunya had inaugurated the Roxy eight months earlier. The biggest night in movie history, the newspapers had called the premiere. U.S. senators and generals; the governor of New Jersey; Mayor Jimmy Walker; the "czar" of the Motion Picture Producers association, Will Hays; Irving Berlin; the Shuberts; the Harold Lloyds; Schenck and his wife, Norma Talmadge; Adolph Ochs; and Mrs. Otto Kahn attended. The crowd almost broke down the doors when Charlie Chaplin tried to sneak in unnoticed. The 100-piece Roxy Symphony preceded the forty-member Roxy Ballet on the stage. Filmed greetings from President Calvin Coolidge, Mayor Walker, and the eighty-year-old Thomas Alva Edison appeared on the giant screen with printed titles before spotlights picked her out in the audience, wearing a scintillating black evening gown, her hair lacquered down flat against her head the way she wore it in several sequences in the film.

"Funny," he said, "I used your picture to illustrate the fact that movies are like green salads, they wilt fast." To inaugurate the Roxy, he explained, her picture might have rented for $50,000 for a ten-day engagement. Nine months later it would rent for $7.50 in Oshkosh, Wisconsin.

Where had he used *Sunya* to show the perishable nature of motion pictures? It was just three days after the Roxy premiere, while speaking at his alma mater, Harvard.

When he said "Hah-vad," she tried to remember whom he reminded her of. She asked where he had learned about the picture business, and he said, "At Harvard. I'm just applying the principles I learned there to the movie industry because I'm convinced most people in pictures don't know how to do that."

To show she knew a few things about figures, she said that, if you believed the newspapers, the only people making any money in movies were the stars; the moguls were all working for nothing. The way she understood the arithmetic, eighty percent of the box office went to exhibitors and distributors, to say nothing of their friends, the butcher, the baker, and half the world, who walked in for free. But how could she as a producer stop that? "Why, not even Mary Pickford's mother can be in twenty thousand theaters every night to count the house."

"Does she do that?" he asked, incredulous.

"That's what they say, but you couldn't prove it by me because she never took me along."

He burst into peals of laughter and whacked his thighs. People at nearby tables shifted in their seats, but he couldn't stop laughing. As she would write more than fifty years later, "he was enjoying himself so unabashedly, so unaffectedly, that I started laughing too."

When he grew businesslike again, he told her that since she knew Sidney

Kent she should ask him for some old Paramount distribution figures for Europe. With those one could work out projected overseas grosses for *Sunya* and *Sadie Thompson.* Upcoming play dates should be counted as income, as accounts receivable. "Otherwise your balance sheet for this entire year will be just an inventory of cost—all red ink."

He said all the right things convincingly, she thought.

As the waiters cleared the plates, she observed him with more interest than she usually accorded businessmen. Behind the bespectacled glance, receding blond hairline, Boston accent, and sonorous laughter, she divined shrewdness, imagination, and an electric and vital temperament. He was fun and spoke with enormous facility. Suddenly she knew who it was he reminded her of. It was Craney Gartz, her millionaire suitor ten years ago. Her success as a funny, impossible girl in crazy clothes in Cecil B. De Mille's "Park Avenue idylls" had made her realize that Craney's money, good looks, and teasing, patrician snobbery were not enough. Craney kissed wonderfully, but she had never allowed him to take her to bed. Like her luncheon guest, Craney knew how to talk passionately, how to be inspired by ideals.

A waiter brought him his pie, ice cream, and coffee. He had heard about the duplicity she and Raoul Walsh, her director, had used to get the Somerset Maugham screen version started, how they had changed the Reverend Davidson into a Mr. Davidson. Since they couldn't use the title of the forbidden play, Walsh opened the picture with a torrential downpour designed to jog people's memory of the stage play that Jeanne Eagles had made memorable on Broadway and Tallulah Bankhead had tried to repeat in London only to be vetoed by Maugham in favor of Olga Lindo. He also knew production money had dried up for her after Will Hays and the Motion Picture Producers had put pressure on United Artists and Joe Schenck. With Kent, Katz, and twelve other studio chiefs and distribution heads, he himself had signed a telegram to Schenck condemning the making of *Rain* under any subterfuge title. Bob Kane had told him that, in order to finish the picture, Gloria Swanson was selling property in New York and California.

Stirring his coffee, he leaned forward and, with a twinkle in his eye, asked how she had managed to get Will Hays to give her the go-ahead in the first place.

For a second she resented the question. She was still smarting from the battle. Then she thought he was paying her the compliment of dealing with her as an equal, producer to producer. "I just invited him to lunch and asked him," she said.

She realized her mistake the moment he burst into laughter. There was something in his mirth that implied she had used her feminine wiles on Hays when in fact she had outsmarted Hollywood's "director of morals" and the rest of them.

Taking out a cigarette, she said in measured tones, "I think I told all you gentlemen as much when I replied to your telegram to Joe Schenck in June. I know you got your copy, Mr. Kennedy, because your secretary or assistant replied."

He reddened.

Fumbling for a match, he said he had understood the issue of defying the decency code to be a mere formality. *Rain* ridiculed a clergyman, therefore no one was supposed to adapt it for the screen. "A number of other signers had done me a favor. I felt I owed them one in return."

A waiter smartly lit her cigarette. When she asked what favor they had done, he told her that, to assist in the industry's rehabilitation, he had persuaded Harvard to sponsor a series of speeches by a dozen top film people last March. Marcus Loew, Adolph Zukor, Jesse Lasky, Harry Warner, Will Hays, William Fox, and a half dozen others had lectured on the film business.

"Adolph Zukor at Harvard," she said. "That's an image to conjure with."

They both smiled.

In any case, she was proud of *Sadie Thompson,* she said. Barrymore was marvelous as the sanctimonious, lustful hypocrite. And so was Raoul, both directing and playing the marine sergeant with whom she runs off in the end.

She couldn't resist telling him that Raoul and she had had a hard time identifying the name Joseph P. Kennedy among the Zukors, Loews, Foxes, and Laskys on the collective telegram. What had he produced?

His answer was mildly defensive. "My most successful picture was *The Gorilla Hunt.*"

"Never heard of it."

"I walked out of it myself, and I can't for the life of me understand why it made money, but it did."

Had she heard of cowboy pictures starring Fred Thomson? Big-city audiences generally had no idea who was Fred Thomson and his spirited gray stallion, Silver King, but in theaters outside large cities their pictures had the widest distribution. Fred Thomson was married to Frances Marion, the writer.

"Frances is a friend of mine, a woman with a talent for picking people."

He called for the bill. The maître d' told him the lunch was on the house.

When he glanced over her accountant's memo one more time and, without making an offer of his own, advised her to accept Joe Schenck's proposal, she realized the luncheon had been a waste of time. His handshake, when they said good-bye in the lobby, was firm; she was sure she wouldn't see him again.

It was turning colder after a record warm autumnal spell (the Weather Bureau thermometer atop the Whitehall Building had touched seventy degrees the previous afternoon, a new high for a November 23). De Mille's *King of Kings* was playing at the Gaiety; John Gilbert and Greta Garbo were opening in *Love,* Metro-Goldwyn-Mayer's adaptation of Tolstoy's *Anna Karenina,* at the Embassy; Michael Curtiz's *Good Time Charley* was at the Roxy; Aileen Pringle and Barrymore were featured in *Body and Soul* at the Loew's Lexington; and at the Warner on Broadway and Fifty-second Street, *The Jazz Singer* was entering its second month ("See and Hear Al Jolson on the Vitaphone," cried the newspaper ads).

Joe Kennedy rushed back to his office at the 1560 Broadway building. These days he spent most of his time at the West Coast studio of Film Booking Office Inc., but like any self-respecting movie company FBO maintained its corporate headquarters in New York. It was less than two years ago that he had strolled into FBO to take charge. If Gloria Swanson wanted to know who he was, it was all in the September issue of *Photoplay*. A feature article described how he had been in his new office all of half an hour when he had sent for one of his vice presidents. The man appeared, expecting to discuss weighty matters of policy. "Kennedy was studiously examining his desk, going through the drawers with systematic efficiency. Then he looked up with an air of great profundity. 'What this corporation needs first and most of all, is a nice box of Havana cigars for the president's office.' After that they proceeded to business." The most influential film journal for the general audience told how just fifteen months after engineering the takeover of FBO, Kennedy had become known as someone who was bringing substance to a picture business that was supposed to work in mysterious ways and be controlled by some deep combination of luck, magic, and genius.

Since he and his group of Boston backers had bought control of FBO, he had not only turned the small, debt-ridden company around, he had also acquired an increasingly ambitious view of motion pictures.

Walking into his office, Kennedy told his secretary to get Sidney Kent in Los Angeles. Kent was Paramount's sales genius and one of the executives Kennedy had persuaded to speak at Harvard. A cool, practical, eternally disapproving watchdog against dangerous expenditures, he was the kind of manager that Joe Kennedy believed every movie company should have. Kent was an elegant easterner like himself, less than happy in California. Their conversation was to the point. Joe had just met Gloria Swanson and wondered if Sid would do him the favor of getting together some figures on her European grosses.

No problem. Kent could have a set of figures by tomorrow. Joe explained that he needed the figures to see if Swanson's future overseas revenues could collateralize a production loan. Sid became personal. He and his wife were in the process of getting a divorce. His lawyer had asked for a postponement, but Milton Cohen, his wife's attorney, was being difficult. Cohen was also Gloria Swanson's lawyer. Did Kennedy think he could ask Gloria to give her lawyer a call?

Swanson didn't go out that afternoon. Telling the hotel operator not to disturb her, she spent the next three hours with UA's heads of sales and distribution. She suggested they screen the picture for the big theater owners while she was in New York and could answer questions.

Gloria had become one of the "united artists" a year ago. Fifty-three feature films had convinced her that studios inevitably became factories of mediocrity and that, however much she was idolized and envied, the public was tiring of the repetitious society pictures she was doing. When Paramount offered her $10,000 a week plus half the profits of any film she appeared in, she began to seek out more substantive roles in independent productions.* She had bought into United Artists Corporation and become an equal owner with D. W. Griffith, Charles Chaplin, Mary Pickford and her husband Douglas Fairbanks, and—UA's real power now—Joseph M. Schenck. Of all the women in the movies, only Pickford and Swanson had their own production units. Mary had the assistance of Doug, the most business-minded and astute of the four founding partners. Swanson's French marquis had a reputation for a reckless taste in spats, but no talent for standing up to Schenck in loan and contract negotiations. She had had to learn fast.

To get the sales and distribution chiefs excited about *Sadie Thompson,* she showed them the cards from the San Bernardino sneak preview. Most were positive to raving. "Splendid, don't cut a scene," said one. "Miss Swanson wonderful. Super picture," commented another. Others read, "First picture I ever saw where Gloria didn't wear a million dollars' worth of clothes." "Wonderful. Way ahead of the play at the Biltmore." The negatives ran from the ambiguous, "A slam on the christian nation" to "Acting was wonderful but as a church member think religion should be left out of pictures" and "Disgusting." The point was that not one was

---

*All figures in this book are given in vintage dollars. To get a sense of Hollywood's Fabulous Twenties, the reader should multiply all figures by approximately 5.5. Thus, $10,000 a week in 1927 is the equivalent of $55,000 in 1988. It should also be kept in mind that federal and state taxes on high incomes averaged a mere three percent in 1928. (Source: Wharton Econometrics Associates)

indifferent. Before they broke up the meeting, she agreed to a series of publicity interviews.

At five o'clock an apologetic hotel operator called her suite. A Mr. Kennedy had been phoning for two hours and was now downstairs asking to see Miss Swanson. Bemused, she told the desk to send him up.

When she opened the door, Joe apologized for disturbing her and came straight to the point. He had called Kent about the European grosses of her films. "He will give us everything we need. He'll be calling back tomorrow."

Before she could say, Who's *us?* he said there was something she could do for Sidney in return. He explained the situation: The Kents were getting a divorce, and Mrs. Kent's lawyer, Milton Cohen, was being stubborn about a postponement. Would she call Cohen and ask him to reconsider?

She felt a little guilty about the way she had deflated his producer's ego at the end of their lunch. All right, she would call Milton and tell him Sidney was helping her out.

"Could you phone him now?" he asked. "I'd like to have an answer when Sid calls me in the morning."

She hated to be pushed, but as she would remember, his urging had an almost playful tone to it, as if he were sharing the fact that it was fun to get things done quickly and efficiently. Chance would have it that Milton was in his office. When she got him on the line, she told him she hated to ask favors, but here she was asking for one anyway.

Hearing her out, Milton agreed to give Sid Kent's lawyer a postponement. "Mr. Kennedy had been standing beside me during the call," she would write in her memoirs. "When I told him Milton would do what I had asked, he smiled as if I had passed a special test of his devising. He called me a good scout and said he wouldn't forget it."

He also said he had found out from the hotel manager that it was Gloria who paid for the luncheon. So now it was his turn. Would she have dinner with him? He had a proposition to discuss with her.

She had an engagement with her old friend Le Roy Pierpont Ward, but had a hunch the dinner with Kennedy might be important. So she phoned Sport, as everybody called the unofficial master of the most fashionable Manhattan set, and changed their dinner date.

Then she accepted Kennedy's invitation. He would call for her at 6:30. It was a bit early, but he wanted to take her to a special place on Long Island.

Gloria

When Adelaide Svensson and her daughter reached Los Angeles in the spring of 1915, sixteen-year-old Gloria was a veteran movie actress. Yet Mrs. Svensson and the flat-chested Gloria, with her bad posture, Illinois twang, and gamine toughness, were no onrushing stage mother and daughter team getting off the train at Union Station. Los Angeles was a mere stopover—at least that was how Gloria understood it—on their way to the Philippines to join Gloria's army father at his new post.

Along with her sister Clara, Adelaide—"Addie" to everybody—had recently inherited a modest sum from her miserly Polish-born father, known to Gloria as Grandpa Klanowski, and was in no hurry to get to San Francisco, the embarkation point for military dependents sailing for Manila. Mother rented an apartment in a two-story house on Cahuenga Boulevard, a tree-lined street running north from Beverly Boulevard through the heart of Hollywood. Gloria's personal world fell apart the day she asked when they'd be moving on. They might not go to Manila, Addie said. The explanation that followed was that Mother was separating from a hopeless alcoholic, a man whose problem was he couldn't face problems. The money from Grandpa gave her breathing space, allowed her to think things over away from Grandma Bertha and Daddy's relatives. If, after all, she decided that no other life was possible, they might still go. In his letters, Daddy begged her to give him another chance.

Through her mother's story, Gloria recognized instances of her childhood, her father's drinking, hearing them argue. She didn't know he gambled, that he had run up debts. She vaguely understood what her mother meant when she said she and Daddy had not been "close" for the past five years, that this last year's living apart had given Mother the idea of a permanent separation.

When Addie finished, Gloria was too shocked to cry. "Don't you really love him?" she asked.

"Not just now," Mother answered, "and I haven't for some time."

Then and there Gloria realized she hardly knew her father, that by upbringing she was more her mother's child than his. But still, she loved her absent father. She would never abandon him.

Gloria was the only child of Joseph Svensson and Adelaide Klanowski. Her father was one of thirteen children of second-generation Swedish emigrants. Jons and Johanna Svensson had taken their brood to Lutheran church every Sunday and allowed no drinking or card playing in their house. People later said this was why several of their sons turned out to be heavy drinkers and gamblers. Joseph's elder brother Charles was an adventurer. He was prospecting for gold in the Canadian Northwest Territories in 1899 and later told everyone how one night he had seen a strange light and dreamed his brother Joe had a baby girl.

Gloria was born March 28, 1899 on the second floor of 341 Grace Street in Chicago. Since it was Holy Week, Joe decided to call the girl Glory. She was christened Gloria May Josephine Svensson—May for her maternal great-grandmother and one of Joe's sisters; Josephine for her father. On her mother's side they spoke German and, besides Grandpa Klanowski, were mostly Alsatians. Gloria would remember her great-grandfather telling her he had been chef at the royal household in Baden-Baden before emigrating to the States in 1852. He loved to talk about the great Chicago fire in 1871. Their house on La Salle Street had burned to the ground. They had saved their children and the clothes on their backs, nothing else.

Grandpa Klanowski was a man of property who lived near Lincoln Park, but he was such a miser that Grandma Bertha divorced him and remarried, giving Gloria a second maternal grandfather, Grandpa Lew. The divorce turned Grandpa Klanowski into such a hater of women that he hired a man to cook and clean for him. Gloria believed he worried about his skinflint reputation because he once started to give her a dime and then, after studying the expression on her face, upped it to a quarter.

An only child, Gloria grew up close to her parents. In her autobiography she would note that in her nightly prayers there were only the three of them. "I used to kneel and say my prayers out loud. They were the same every night. 'Now I lay me down to sleep, I pray the Lord my soul to keep. If I should die before I wake, I pray the Lord my soul to take. God bless Daddy and God bless Mommy and make me a good girl.' After I climbed into bed, I always added a silent prayer that God would somehow find a way for me to get out of going to school without being sick."

She would remember a grade school teacher telling her mother that she didn't pay attention, that instead of copying out arithmetic problems she drew pictures, to which Mrs. Svensson responded that her daughter was obviously artistic. Next thing Gloria knew she was enrolled in the children's drawing class at the Art Institute.

Joe worked in the Chicago office of a congressman. His parents had little regard for politicians and joked that Joe's job could only prepare him to become a lawyer or a crook. They didn't think of government service. Joe anglicized his surname, and when Gloria was eight, the War Department in Washington notified him that it was putting him in charge of transportation for the United States Army, either in the Philippines, Puerto Rico, or Panama, where American ingenuity was building the canal. Gloria thought her prayers for no more school had been answered.

Instead of the Philippines, Puerto Rico, or Panama, Joe Swanson went first to Florida. Mother and daughter followed. The train trip took three days and two nights, and the further south they got, the hotter it got. They opened the windows only to have soot from the locomotive blacken them. By the time they reached Tampa, Gloria's hair was, for the first time in her life, truly dirty. But she wasn't in school.

The house they lived in at the Key West Army Base was in front of the dock where the army kept a launch and several dinghies. The house stood on pillars, to protect it from flooding during the hurricane season, and had a veranda with a beautiful view in every direction. Joe Swanson took his daughter grunt fishing and taught her to tell time by the different bugle calls. Even school wasn't so bad. With four or five other army brats, Gloria was driven to a private school in a buckboard by a soldier. On warm days the teacher took the class outside to sit under the palm trees.

Singing in Sunday school led to Gloria's first contact with show-business people. Venice Hayes, a New York actress spending the winter in Key West with her tubercular father, said Gloria had a pretty voice and was astonished to hear the pretty eight-year-old had never taken singing lessons. The Swansons were invited to meet Frank Hayes, who was also in the theater. Mother told Gloria that tuberculosis was not contagious if windows were kept open and one didn't get too close to the TB sufferer, but Gloria thought the elegant and terribly thin Hayes smelled funny. With the local people, he was helping put together a show in which Venice would play the leading lady. After hearing Gloria sing, Hayes asked her mother if the girl could be part of the soiree.

Mother coached Gloria to sing "As the World Rolls On," made her a new dress, and on the night of the show was backstage, while Daddy and people from the base were in the audience. Gloria, who had never heard grown-ups talk openly and rapturously of love, was so enthralled by Venice playing her love duet she didn't realize the actor in the scene had forgotten his lines. Suddenly, Hayes was next to her, shoving her onstage, and whispering, "Sing your song, Glory, now!"

Walking into the limelight, Gloria looked back toward the wings to make sure there wasn't some mistake, but both Hayes and Mother nodded vigorously. Gloria stood center stage waiting for the note from the piano. None came. Finally, she just sang "As the World Rolls On" a capella. Everyone clapped. She ran offstage. Mother hugged her, Hayes beamed. Gloria couldn't understand why. She had had no piano accompaniment, and during the entire second chorus all she had been able to think of was that she needed to go to the bathroom. She decided her future was in drawing.

Her next stage performance came four years later in San Juan's old opera house. The Swansons transferred to Puerto Rico when Gloria was eleven. Together with Colonel Howes, his wife, and their two children, Bobby and Harriet, the Swansons and five other army families lived in San Juan's Artillery Park. The island had been under American control for only twelve years, and Gloria realized she and the other army families were different—privileged. She loved the feeling. She also loved the smells and sounds of the Caribbean city: the smell of tamarinds, mangoes, and papayas in the open market, the odor of kerosene on the tile floor to repel insects, the music of church bells, street carnivals, and guitars. She was soon playing with a major's son one year younger than herself. They learned to ride together. The boy loved the beach, but she was afraid of water and refused to learn to swim and dive.

Harriet Howes had Gloria persuade her mother to let her change schools so she could be part of *The American Girl,* a musical show set in a girls' school. They rehearsed for weeks. Harriet played the principal because she was the tallest; Gloria played a willful girl who left school and had to be tricked by her friends to go back. Colonel Hayes commandeered the beautiful old rococo opera house in San Juan for the two performances of *The American Girl.* On opening night Gloria found a gold star on her mirror and her name painted under it—in her father's handwriting. She would not record any audience reaction to her performance but remembered telling herself she would be an opera singer.

She learned some of the facts of life at the stable when she and her girlfriend found a newborn colt in a stall and Gloria's best friend told her it was naturally beige because its father was the beige stallion. "Its father? Horses don't get married," Gloria objected.

"Glory, you know what I mean," came the answer.

She didn't really, but by questioning other girls she came to a proximate understanding of what she sensed was an acutely uncomfortable subject for most people.

Addie loved to make dresses for her daughter, and Gloria loved to show off the clothes her mother made. In June 1914 Joe Swanson was temporarily based on Governors Island, the two-square-mile dot in New York harbor, and his wife and daughter went to Chicago for the summer, arranging to stay with Grandma Bertha.

Mother was finishing a dress patterned on one in the wardrobe of the famed dancer-actress Irene Castle when Aunt Inga, Gloria's uncle's sister-in-law, came for a visit. Aunt Inga knew all kinds of interesting people. A trained nurse working for wealthy Lake Shore families, she was the only woman Gloria knew who smoked. To entertain the fifteen-year-old Gloria, she offered to take her to a place on Argyle Street on the North Side where they made motion pictures.

In Puerto Rico, Mother and Gloria had seen moving pictures in a hot little movie house. They had watched people move around on a sheet, waving their arms and making faces. After ten minutes it was all over, and Addie had decided she'd never spend another nickel to see that again. Aunt Inga asked if they had seen *Quo Vadis.* "What's that?" Addie asked, her mouth full of pins. Inga explained that it was an Italian epic that was being shown at the opera house. It cost a dollar to get in, but a live symphony orchestra played all through the picture, which ran for nearly an hour and a half. And on the screen you saw chariot races, slave galleys, and an arena full of lions. Inga wanted to see the movie, but she didn't want to go alone. Which was why she was ready to take a Mr. Spoor up on his invitation to see his motion picture factory on Argyle Street. Maybe the Americans were doing things as exciting as the Italians.

George K. Spoor was the "Ess" to F. M. ("Broncho Billy") Anderson's "ay," in Essanay, a company that made pictures both in Chicago and in Niles Canyon near San Francisco. Anderson made the Broncho Billy movies out in California, while on Argyle Street, Spoor was in charge of two-reel comedies and dramatic pictures. The company's big star was Francis X.

Bushman. The studio also employed a trio of famous stage actresses: Beverly Bayne, Ruth Stonehouse, and Gerda Holmes.

Gloria convinced her mother to let her wear her new Irene Castle dress for the visit to Essanay. Spoor was out of town, but his brother came out to meet Aunt Inga and Gloria, and quickly found a nice young man to take them around.

The guide took them to a cavernous cement basement room, where a man with a pistol in his belt and a whistle around his neck sat on an upturned barrel and yelled, "Kick him! Fall on his face!" to a dozen young men and women piled up in a screaming heap. Occasionally, the visitors could distinguish faces, but most of the time all they saw was arms and legs. Some of the feet had roller skates on them. The man on the barrel shouted, "Funny. Good! Now do it again."

Everybody got off a great big woman in a maid's uniform lying on the floor. The guide explained to Inga and Gloria that the man on the barrel was E. Mason ("Lightning") Hopper, the director. The fat woman turned out to be Wallace Beery in drag. In *Yankee Consul* on Broadway, the tall, good-looking, thirty-year-old Beery had been the understudy for Raymond Hitchcock and was an immediate sensation when he went on for Hitchcock one night. At Essanay he played Sweedie, the dumb Swedish immigrant maid, in the slapstick two-reelers that were making a fortune for the company. Inga and Gloria noticed the camera and the quiet little man fussing over it.

When everybody was ready, the little man started grinding the camera, Hopper started screaming, and the roller skaters fell in a pile on Beery, kicking him and trying to sit on his face. They had to do it one more time because somebody knocked Beery's wig off.

Inga and Gloria didn't get to meet Francis X. Bushman, but the guide took them upstairs to watch the shooting of a wedding scene for another picture. Here, things were a little more sedate, and the guide told them Gerda Holmes played the bride and Richard Travers the groom. Inga knew who Gerda Holmes was. While they watched, a man walked over and introduced himself as Mr. Babile, the Essanay casting director. He wondered if he could have Gloria's address and phone number. She looked at her aunt, who said, "Go ahead." Babile explained that directors were looking for interesting new types all the time. Gloria was sure the reason for Babile's interest was the Irene Castle dress.

Babile called the next morning and asked Gloria to come in at 1 P.M. and be in a picture. She told him she had to ask permission. When Mother said she didn't see anything wrong with it as long as Mr. Spoor was a friend of Aunt Inga's and Gloria was on vacation, Gloria went back to the phone and said yes. Babile told her to wear the same dress as the day before. She knew it.

When she got to the studio, she was taken upstairs, where twenty people were being coached for a continuation of the wedding scene she had watched the day before. Gerda Holmes was expected at any moment. Richard Travers was already there. When the director saw Gloria, he asked his assistant to get her a bouquet of flowers. Holmes arrived, they rehearsed the scene. The director hollered, "Let's go." Gloria came forward with the flowers; Holmes gave her a big smile when she took them from her and then smiled at Travers. The director said, "That's it for this one," and stagehands started taking down the scenery.

An assistant told Gloria and several others to stop by the office on their way out. Each was given a pay envelope. When Gloria opened hers she found an absolute fortune: $3.25. For one hour of doing nothing! No wonder boys and girls were willing to fall in a heap on roller skates. When she got home, she called Aunt Inga and made a date to go shopping at Marshall Field's the next day.

Gloria was called back in her Irene Castle outfit for a scene outside a church. A few days later she went to New York to see her father and a girl she had first met in Key West, and was happy to leave the pictures behind. She was going to be an opera singer after all.

Less than a week into her New York vacation, Mother forwarded a typewritten letter from Essanay, offering Gloria a position as a guaranteed stock player at $13.25 a week for a four-day week or $20 if she worked six days a week. With her own money, Gloria could take classes at the Art Institute and singing lessons with a good teacher. It also meant she wouldn't have to go to school. Her mother had read the offer and hadn't torn it up. That had to mean Mother didn't think it was out of the question.

When Daddy came to dinner at the girlfriend's Staten Island mansion, the parents talked only about the war that had broken out in Europe. America was not involved, but Daddy said all army bases were on permanent alert. He didn't expect to be stationed on Governors Island much longer. There were rumors that his next assignment would be Manila. He seemed a little sad when he took her to Grand Central Station for her return to Chicago. Maybe it was the war, she thought, or just saying good-bye.

Because of the war and the uncertainty of their future, Mother told Gloria she could quit school and work in pictures as long as they stayed in Chicago.

Gloria reported to work at Essanay and was assigned a little cubicle of a dressing room with a girl named Virginia Bowker. The next day they were told to report to Lightning Hopper to play society ladies in another Sweedie comedy with Wallace Beery. Gloria was less than impressed by the world of pictures. Beery looked totally ridiculous playing Sweedie. He told Virginia and Gloria that, to get the laughs, they should act as if they were completely fooled by his disguise. Gloria imagined he hated the Sweedie pictures as much as Virginia and she did, and couldn't wait to escape to screen romance.

Working at the studio got to be like going to school. Gloria worked endless, boring hours playing stuck-up society women in the improvised pratfall two-reelers. *Elvira, Farina and the Meal Ticket* was typical. Gerda Holmes played her mother, Elvira, and the meal ticket was the father who struck it rich and provided enough money for mother and daughter to get stuck-up with highfalutin ideas and eat with finger bowls. Gloria thought the story so exaggerated and so obvious that it was ridiculous.

Beery was a show-off. He had a pretty singing voice and a Stutz Bearcat open roadster to take girls for a spin. Several girls thought he was an exciting catch. He was single and not keeping company with anyone in particular. When he invited Gloria for a ride, he tore through the streets at thriller speeds. He had been a racing driver and wanted everyone to know it.

Suddenly he was gone. A girl's parents had complained to Spoor about Wally and threatened to go to the police because their daughter was a minor. Within a week the payroll department demanded birth records from all the girls, and the men and women were strictly separated. Wally, Gloria was told, had been shipped to California to work on cowboy pictures. One evening Virginia's father stormed into Essanay and dragged her out of the studio, hollering that no daughter of his was going to work in pictures. Looking into the mirror she had shared with Virginia, Gloria realized that under the Psyche-knot hairdo, the heavy eyebrows, and the society getups of the woman she was playing, she was a minor herself, not even seventeen. As she would say, "I was as much a female impersonator as Mr. Beery was."

Joe Swanson was transferred to Manila. Wally sent a postcard from San Francisco. Gloria was assigned to serious pictures and got to meet Louella Parsons and Edmund Lowe, a pair of Essanay writers. Lowe called Gloria "Miss Swanson," and one day invited her to a theater party. They would be going with Ruth Stonehouse, one of Essanay's big stars, and her husband. When Lowe called for Gloria in a chauffeured automobile, Mother explained that her daughter had to be home by midnight. He said he understood perfectly. The play was the George M. Cohan success *Seven Keys to Baldpate.* Gloria had never worked so hard at playing a grown-up. After the play they went to the College Inn to hear Sophie Tucker sing. It was 1:30 when Lowe delivered her to the door. She dreaded the maternal welcome and was surprised to hear her mother simply say, "I thought I had your promise, Mr. Lowe. Good night." The writer was sufficiently mortified to keep his distance after that.

Daddy wrote that he would send for them as soon as possible. Another postcard from Beery asked Gloria why she didn't come out to California to make a few pictures.

Francis X. Bushman, the biggest star in pictures, wore a large amethyst ring on his finger and had a spotlight inside his lavender car that illuminated his famous profile when he drove at night. The big dark secret at the studio was that he was married and had five children. The studio feared that audiences would not find him believable as a romantic lover if they knew he had a wife and kids like everybody else. Beverly Bayne, who had a dressing room next to the one Gloria shared with three other girls, always starred with Bushman, and gossip had it that they were madly in love. Actors were, of course, not supposed to come anywhere near the women's dressing room, but Bushman was a law unto himself. When he was in Bayne's dressing room, Gloria and the other girls got up on dressing tables to try and hear what was going on next door. Once when Gloria was alone, waiting for a seamstress, Bushman came in and stood beside her. Casually, he put his hand on her thigh. She looked up and touched his face. They didn't exchange one word.

In January 1915 Charlie Chaplin arrived from California. Mack Sennett had offered to increase his salary to $1,000 a week to remain the Keystone Company's biggest asset, but Spoor offered the comedian $1,250 a week. Chaplin was dismayed to discover the chilliness of a Chicago January and the fact that the Essanay staff had little or no concern for the quality of their product.

Ben Turpin, a wizened little man with permanently crossed eyes and a prominent Adam's apple, however, proved a delightful comedy partner. Chaplin tried out Gloria and was less than overwhelmed. She proved to be wooden and unresponsive. "All morning I felt like a cow trying to dance with a toy poodle," she would remember. "Moreover, I knew after one hour that I didn't want to spend the next month or so trying to be cute and elfish, so I made very little effort and finally told him I just didn't see the humor in many of the things he was asking me to do."

When Addie announced a month later that they were leaving and making a stop in California on their way to Manila, Gloria suggested she write to Beery to ask if he knew a place they could stay in Los Angeles. Babile told her that since she was going she should look up Mack Sennett. He gave her a letter of introduction, saying, "It might be useful to know someone who knows you've been in pictures."

Before setting out for California, Addie took her daughter to a famous voice teacher, telling him Gloria would never be able to study with him since they were leaving Chicago, but that she would pay him good money for an honest opinion. Gloria sang "The Rosary." The teacher beamed and gave his verdict: Gloria had a lovely voice, a voice good enough to make it worthwhile to invest in lessons.

"Gloria Swanson arrived in Hollywood as a flat-figured extra from Chicago with brilliantined, spit-curled hair," British *Vogue* would write in 1975 in summing up the "reckless twenties" and its film stars. "Her camera-proof face, rather viciously beautiful, suited the most bizarre and exaggerated fashions."

Not quite, as it were. Although baby fat lingered in her face, Gloria was a spindly sixteen-year-old and her bosom was indeed modest, but her hair was long and full in the style of the ideal of 1920s youth, Mary Pickford. Her pixie nose and too wide mouth prevented her from being called a beauty, but the upturned nose gave her a gorgeous profile. What was striking about her was her too large blue eyes. Addie had taught her to wear clothes, and this ability was no small asset, but she was still very much her mother's dutiful but somewhat spoiled only child.

Beery was at Union Station to greet them. To Gloria, he seemed serious and he looked terrific with his California tan. He had driven down from San Francisco. He was charming and on his best behavior. Gloria could see Mother liked him.

At dinner that night he regaled them with stories of picturemaking and with his imitation of his boss, Broncho Billy. It was the boondocks up there in Niles—no bathrooms, squeaky beds. If only someone would hire him. He was appalled when Gloria told him Mr. Babile had written her a letter of introduction to Mack Sennett, but that she wasn't sure she was interested. Turning to her mother, he said, "Addie. Babile is no fool." To Gloria he said she should get out to Edendale with that letter first thing Monday morning. Gloria liked Wally's interest in her. Perhaps the scandal in Chicago had done him good after all. He was serious and ambitious.

Gloria was hired on the spot.

Mack Sennett, to whom the world would owe the discovery of Chaplin, Harry Langdon, Roscoe "Fatty" Arbuckle, W. C. Fields, and Bing Crosby, was a burly thirty-six-year-old Canadian former boxing trainer and bit player discovered by D. W. Griffith. A pair of Griffith backers had financed Sennett's Keystone comedies, and the lavish continuation of custard pies, Ford Model T automobiles, bathing beauties, and knockabout farces that he, his girlfriend Mabel Normand, and their friends had been making in off-the-cuff fashion since 1912 had turned him into the King of Comedy and Mabel into the screen's great comedienne.

For her interview with Sennett, Gloria made herself up to look thirty.

In her memoirs, she would write that Sennett saw through the rouge and the eyeliner and put her in two-reelers with Bobby Vernon, a boy-next-door type. What impressed Sennett at their first meeting was her ambition. "She had a cute nose and beautiful eyes," he would recall in *King of Comedy,* his 1954 autobiography. "The Swanson eyes are indeed magic and beautiful. It isn't a trick of makeup that beams them at you from the screen."

With Teddy the Great Dane and Pepper the Cat, Vernon and Swanson starred in such chase-and-scamper shorts as *Teddy at the Throttle* and *The Nick O'Time Baby.* After Essanay, the Sennett system was actually fun. She was told to act her own age. Her director was Clarence Badger, a former journalist in his early thirties. "You never knew what the person next to you was going to do," she would remember. "Stuntmen and gagmen and comics were all jabbering constantly and struggling to get their ideas accepted. As soon as someone thought of something he would jump on his feet and act it out. 'Look,' he'd say, 'what if Bobby starts to dance close and Gloria backs off?' Then someone else would say, 'Wait! What if *Gloria* starts to dance close and Bobby backs off.' "

Nothing was sacred. To the primitive humor of undress and obesity, Sennett and his people added ridicule of virtue, authority, romantic love, and religion. In Sennett's world all lawyers were shysters, all pious people hypocrites, all sheriffs venal, and in that world everybody was caught with his pants down, including the boss. The way Gloria heard it, Mack and Mabel had been set to be married a month earlier, but then Mabel discovered her fiancé in his long johns and actress Mae Busch stark naked, rehearsing, according to Sennett, for a new picture. Before Mabel could even react to this explanation, Busch apparently struck her with a vase. Somehow, Mabel and Mack made up, although the wedding plans were canceled.

Besides the cross-eyed Ben Turpin from Chicago, Gloria got to know Fatty Arbuckle and his wife, Minta Durfee. A grossly fat man weighing over three hundred pounds, Arbuckle was fantastically coordinated and light on his feet, an unlikely combination that served as the basis for much of his comedy. Audiences adored him, and Sennett teamed him with Chaplin, Mabel, and Buster Keaton. Minta told Gloria the story of the boss and Mabel a little differently. After walking in on Sennett and Busch, Mabel went straight to the Santa Monica pier and jumped off. Some workmen saw her head hit the pilings and fished her out of the water. It just made a taller yarn to say the hole in Mabel's head was caused by another woman.

There were no scripts in Keystone comedies. Actors were recruited from the ranks of vaudevillians and circus clowns. They ran and chased and fell in MacArthur Park and the hilly streets above Glendale Boulevard. They didn't care if every hair was in place.

When the first Bobby Vernon–Gloria Swanson two-reeler was finished and Sennett screened it, he said he didn't like all of it, in fact some of it would have to be done over, but if audiences didn't find it fresh and funny, they were crazy. Badger told Gloria that the boss thought she was a terrific match for Vernon, that a contract was being worked up. In the meantime her salary would be $100 a week.

Mother met new people. With her daughter's earnings adding nicely to her inheritance from her father, Addie found a new apartment for them and announced she was getting a divorce. When Gloria asked if she was going to marry someone else, she said that in California there was something called an interlocutory decree, which meant a divorce couldn't become final for one year. There *was* someone, Gloria found out, a small man with ginger hair and a ginger mustache named Matthew Burns. Gloria was appalled that her mother could dream of leaving her father for this elderly drip. She decided she could never accept him as a stepfather even if she would have to accept him as her mother's husband. She had trouble writing to her father. She couldn't tell him that Mother was looking years younger and having the time of her life, or that at sixteen she was probably making as much money acting silly with Bobby Vernon as her father did. She ended up writing him as little as possible.

Wally drove down on weekends, and Gloria found he was the only person she could talk to. Mother winked and looked the other way when, at seventeen, Gloria eloped with Wally.

A minister in Pasadena interrupted his supper to marry them. In a hotel room afterward, Wally turned off the light and, repeating "You drive me crazy," tore her nightgown and thrust himself into her. When he rolled away she felt blood everywhere. After he fell asleep she turned on the light and crawled to the bathroom, afraid to look at herself. She spent the rest of the night sitting wrapped in towels to stop the pain. All she could think of was following her grandmother's and mother's examples and getting a divorce.

Mack Sennett hired Beery at $50 a week with an option to raise him to $100 a week on January 30, 1917. Gloria quickly learned not to be afraid of Wally's temper and devised ways to keep him from stealing her money. She also accepted the humiliation of letting his folks move in with them. The last straw came when she got pregnant and Wally tricked her into having an abortion. With his mother, Margaret, looking on, Wally forced Gloria to take some pills that he said would cure her morning sickness. The medicine made her keel over in pain and collapse into unconsciousness. When she came to, she was in a hospital bed. A nurse told her she was lucky, she was strong as an ox. "You're young. You're pretty. You've got all the time in the world to have another baby." Beery was only a few months away from stardom—at $10,000 a week. But Gloria had had enough, and after eight weeks of married life she walked out of Alvarado Street and took a trolley back to her mother.

She hated being cast as a Keystone bathing beauty. While rumors flew that Sennett was having money problems and was about to sell out the studio and stock company of comedians and directors to the Triangle Company, he had her join walrus-whiskered Chester Conklin, giant Mack Swain, and the bathing beauties in *A Pullman Bride*. Badger, Bobby Vernon, and the old gang meanwhile went to work for Triangle. Gloria tried to get out of the bathing beauty two-reeler by saying she couldn't swim.

"I could never get the tempo of it and I hated the vulgarity that was just under the surface of it every minute," she would recall. "It was a world of falling planks and banana peels and wet paint and sticky wads of gum, of funny-looking fat men with painted mustaches blowing the foam off beer at each other, of stern battleaxes wielding rolling pins and wearing curlers in their hair, and of cute giggly hoydens getting teased, tickled, and chased." She went to see Sennett and told him she didn't want to be in any more pictures like that. He defied her to stop him from tearing up her contract. She held his stare. On the count of ten he tore it up.

She turned eighteen a week before the United States declared war on Germany. Reaching legal adulthood was an occasion for introspection. Her mother was within months of her divorce and trying to keep steady company with Burns. She didn't need Gloria around. Gloria would not be free of Wally for almost another year and, she realized, the prospects for an eighteen-year-old divorcee with a ninth-grade education were not the brightest. To get out of her own depression, she called Badger at Triangle in Culver City. The director was delighted to hear from her. He, Bobby, and the rest of the old company were making two-reelers. He didn't know what the war would do to pictures, but he was sure he could put her in a one-reeler he was starting in a few days. Why didn't she come out and see him? She realized she would have to change trolleys three times to get to Culver City. To look presentable, she bought a bottle-green suit with a squirrel collar that cost her her remaining savings—$300. A folly, but she had to have it.

Triangle was a studio on its way out. Originally the distribution company for Thomas Ince, the cowboy director-turned-producer, and for Griffith and Sennett, Triangle was desperately trying to find new investors and to retain its stars. Each time a star came up for renewal, the competition, often led by Adolph Zukor and Jesse Lasky of Famous Players–Lasky, ran off with him or her. Zukor and Lasky had lured Mary Pickford away in 1916 with an astronomical $100,000-a-year contract and had since convinced Douglas Fairbanks to follow suit. Triangle's roster still included William S. Hart, Charles Ray, Lillian and Dorothy Gish, Norma and Constance Talmadge, Bessie Love, and such prestigious crossovers from the stage as Billie Burke and Sir Herbert Tree. What it didn't have under the leadership of financiers Roy and Harry Aitken, two Wisconsin brothers who had been in pictures since 1905, was a sense of showmanship.

Triangle had distribution offices in thirty-five cities. While Roy Aitken acquired foreign movies for the company, Harry Aitken presided over the production and release of Triangle's own films. A balding man with a disarmingly open face, Harry was notoriously impatient—even with his own empire-building, insofar as it required him to manage the day-to-day business. Although the story material at Triangle was as spicy as anything Famous Players–Lasky had to offer, the public would have never known that from its "honest" advertising ("delightful" and "pleasing" were typical superlatives). Famous Players–Lasky produced movies with a glossier, far more elaborate look and had no compunction about hyping sex and sensation. Most of Triangle's directorial and performing talent would soon be working for Famous Players–Lasky.

Instead of shooting two-reelers with Badger and Bobby, Gloria got to "go dramatic" and play the leads in a sextet of Triangle features that in less than a year made her as famous as the Gish sisters. Her Svengali was Jack Conway, a tall, lean, blue-eyed director with a marvelous smile who would still be making movies in 1948. Working with Conway, Gloria quickly realized, was like going to an elegant party every day. She had never met a man like Jack. Barely more than ten years her senior, he was sensitive, intelligent, and amusing, the kind of man women in fashion magazines always had on their arms, the kind of man who automatically got a manicure when he got a haircut, and smelled faintly of cologne.

Conway taught her the importance of timing, of playing to the camera, of sustaining a scene. She went out of her way to learn the titles of the sixteen pictures he had directed and the name of his cologne. Gossip quickly let her know he was married and had a little girl. Noticing Gloria's crush on him, he told her his wife was a jealous, vindictive woman who checked up on him. Furthermore, he said to Gloria, as much as he would love to have an affair with her, he didn't want to mess up her blossoming career.

Her first surprise on the Conway set was to be handed a script entitled *Smoke*. At Essanay there had been only one copy of the story outline, and the director had it; at Keystone, scripts hadn't existed. Based on a *Saturday Evening Post* story, *Smoke* was about a good-bad girl who created a scandal by flirting with a married man. In her biggest scene, she'd wear nothing but a "teddy bare"—a snug, sleeveless undergarment—and jump into Los An-

geles harbor to rescue her crippled lover. When it came to shooting the
scene at the Wilmington docks at night, she didn't tell Conway she couldn't
swim, only that she hoped he didn't expect her to be an expert. The sequence
required only one dive, he said. Instinct saved her when she jumped fifteen
feet into the klieg-lit water in her teddy and thrashed around until they
grabbed her.

"We'll shoot it once again just in case, with the double," Conway told
her when they brought her up in towels.

After she got into dry clothes in a car, he came over. "I thought you
were faking," he said.

"I was. I can't swim a stroke."

He grinned. Their lips met.

Theda Bara, a tailor's daughter from Cincinnati née Theodosia Good-
man, was the first screen vamp. She had reached her high-water earnings
mark of $6,000 a week at William Fox's studio playing Carmen, Cleopatra,
Salome, du Barry, Camille, and assorted other femmes fatales (Fox alleged
she had been born in the Sahara, the love child of a French artist and his
Arab paramour). Although the flapper had not been invented yet, the public
was ready for a more sophisticated type, a woman no less predatory perhaps, but not necessarily evil in her primal nature. Playing this kind of
bad-but-good girl was the first Swanson specialty.

Before they were through filming, Harry Aitken had changed the title
of *Smoke* to *You Can't Believe Everything,* decided Gloria should be the
new Triangle star, and told Frank Borzage, who would be Hollywood's
"dream factory" director par excellence in the 1930s, to look for a script
for her. Gloria wanted to work with Conway but did *Society for Sale* with
Borzage. The story was about a fashion model who tries to crash London
society, not knowing she had noble blood all along. Her leading man was
William Desmond, but Borzage had orders to film endless shots of Gloria
in couturier dresses. Desmond, who was twice her age and himself a star,
resented the whole exercise. It took a week and a half to shoot a full-length
"five-reeler," but Gloria couldn't wait to get back with Jack.*

The contract the company was working out for her didn't come
through, but the studio upped her salary to $165 a week. Jack told her that
Aitken wanted her to know that, within reason, she could have anything
she desired. She had fallen in love with the new Kissel Kar Silver Special
Speedster, which had just been unveiled at the auto show. What she wanted,
she told Jack, was a better apartment with enough space for her mother,

---

*Five reels equaled 55 ½ minutes of screening time. The standard length of a feature
remained under an hour and a half until the dawn of television.

a Kissel, and a divorce. Triangle got her into Court Corinne, where many women in the industry lived, and ordered a Kissel coupe. Divorce was another story. Men between eighteen and forty-five were waiting to be called up for war. Married men were automatically deferred, however. Once Wally got his deferment, perhaps Jack's lawyer could start the process.

In the meantime Conway and Swanson made *Her Decision.* She played a private secretary who marries her boss for his money only to fall in love with him. Her leading man was J. Barry Sherry. Jack concentrated on making Gloria stand out and, in the process, managed to make Sherry as angry as Desmond had been in *Society for Sale.*

The magic was somehow gone when they made *Her Decision.* Jack was irritable, and he hurried through the ten days of shooting at breakneck speed. The day they finished, he told Gloria he was leaving Triangle. Aitken had gone back on his word to let Conway have full say over how his pictures were released. And for the duration of the war, Triangle would promote its movies as "Clean pictures for clean people." That catchphrase might be admirable in its patriotic intentions and in its underlying message that going to the pictures was quite respectable, but in people's minds, Jack fumed, it translated into dull pictures for dull people.

Without Jack, Triangle lost a lot of its attraction for Gloria. No contract had come through from the Aitken brothers, but she didn't mind the time off while the company prepared her next picture. If nothing else, she got to know her neighbors at Court Corinne. The social life of the place consisted of movie gossip, girls' parties, and sunbathing. Theda Bara had lived in one of the bungalows, and in another apartment, an unknown young actress had recently died from an abortion, paid for by Griffith. Anything that happened in Hollywood on a given day was common knowledge in Court Corinne by sundown. Gloria and Mother had gotten to know Beatrice La Plante, a Canadian-trained nurse and actress who had played in two white-slavery pictures with Sessue Hayakawa and had not worked since. Bea was intelligent and feisty. Gloria had taken her to work with her in the new Kissel and had introduced her to all the Triangle directors she knew. Nobody wanted to hire Bea, not even Jack. However, he invited the two girls to come duck hunting in the Ventura salt marshes one Sunday with him and a bachelor friend who was almost as unsuccessful as Bea. John Gilbert had been in thirteen Triangle pictures in 1917—not that anybody had noticed, he pointed out—and now wanted to become a director like Jack. Bea found the future MGM star—remembered for his scorching love scenes with Greta Garbo a decade later—to be terribly interesting, but the attraction was not mutual. Still, the foursome spent a marvelous day. "Everywhere, Jack was the perfect teacher," Gloria would recall, "and for the moment, to me, all other men seemed vulgar and dull beside him."

Before Triangle had the next picture ready for her, the casting director at Famous Players–Lasky called and asked her to meet Cecil B. De Mille.

Posterity would not be kind to De Mille, associating his name with incongruous baroque taste and schoolboy megalomania, but during his lifetime this failed actor who came to directing by accident was *the* larger-than-life Hollywood creator. His flair for publicity was unparalleled among directors—men not lacking in the art of self-promotion. Sporting puttees, breeches, and a silver whistle and wearing his baldness as if it were out of the question for him to have hair like ordinary men, he boldly cut the figure of the imperial master.

De Mille was the son of an Episcopalian minister and from a family of Dutch origin. His puritan upbringing might explain his taste for biblical extravaganzas and the quasisadistic undertow of many of his films, but not his keen sense of social fads and fashions. Until he turned his attention to moviemaking, screen characterization had divided the world into heroes and heroines, villains and vamps. But with *The Cheat,* starring Fanny Ward and Sessue Hayakawa, he told the story of a "good" woman forced by the exigencies of the plot to behave for most of the film like a vamp. The first motion picture to be made into a stage play, *The Cheat* evoked a sense of moral unscrupulousness and emotional hysteria never before depicted on the screen. The 1916 public's favorable response to this brew convinced De Mille that a whole new audience was going to the movies, an audience that preferred to see courage and weakness, good and evil in a heady mix of human fallibility. De Mille's peculiar insight was to see that puritanism needed only to be paid the merest lip service to be placated, that people could be shown, at length and in intimate detail, what they ought not to do themselves. The titles he and Lasky put on the films rebuked the plots— *We Can't Have Everything, Don't Change Your Husband, Forbidden Fruit, Feet of Clay, Fool's Paradise*—but De Mille was the first filmmaker to realize he could present five reels of ticket-selling sin provided that in the last reel he trumpeted conventional morality. While Moses received the Law on the mountain in *The Ten Commandments,* De Mille made the most of the bacchanalian revels around the golden calf below.

In 1918, when the thirty-seven-year-old De Mille wanted to meet Gloria Swanson, he had not yet discovered his biblical inspirations but was, with Griffith, the best-known director in the business. He was the premier asset of Zukor and Lasky, a pair of entrepreneurs who in 1913 had merged their successes into Famous Players–Lasky and, two years later, absorbed an association of independent distributors called Paramount Pictures. The Hungarian-born Zukor, who would live to be 103, was the senior partner and the classic incarnation of the immigrant boy of fifteen who made good in the land of opportunity. Diminuitive and soft-spoken—and sometimes known to his later employees as "Creepy"—Zukor was essentially a businessman with only minor interest in the actual creation of movies. He lived in New York and generally steered clear of Hollywood, while Lasky, a natty native Californian with blue-gray eyes behind silver-rimmed pince-nez, was the original bicoastal movie mogul. With his painter-poet wife, Bess, and their three children, Lasky divided his existence between an opulent apartment on New York's Fifth Avenue and a huge beach house in Santa Monica. When Lasky was on the East Coast, he had lunch with Zukor every day, first at Delmonico's and in later times at Sherry's, exchanging ideas and plotting the destiny of their growing empire. They called each other Mr. Zukor and Mr. Lasky and at their lunches engaged in a ritual of offering each other cigars from their breast pockets.

Lasky was one year older than De Mille. The two men were closer than many brothers.

Before De Mille, "love" on the screen had been the exclusive prerogative of the young and single; the married couples that were portrayed were usually fuzzy background figures. In his films, however, husbands and wives were human, all too human, and the plots began where others left off—with the honeymoon over and the man and wife sitting down to decorous dinners to ponder their bargain. De Mille was no cultural agitator, no screen Ibsen, Shaw, or Pirandello, and his last reels always upheld traditional values and ensured the errant partner's return to the marriage fold; but prior to the final fade-out, a wide domain was laid bare.

De Mille discovered the bathroom as a device for exploring domestic life. To a generation brought up never to mention personal sanitation, he introduced the depiction of bathing and the attendant disrobing. In ornate new temples of cleanliness, undressing and partial nudity were so obvious a necessity that even the most pious of audiences could hardly object. De Mille's bathrooms and boudoirs eventually became something of a joke, but to the moviegoers of World War I, of cold-water flats and restrictions, they were riveting images of luxury and beauty. Lingering scenes in which the heroine and, sometimes, the hero washed and anointed themselves in preparation for revels of a magnitude and splendor that surprised even true aristocrats were a prolonged rapture. For the price of a ticket, shopgirls were awakened to dreams of fashion and style. For the males in the audience, the director made Sylvia Ashton, Kathlyn William, Florence Vidor, and Mildred Harris look fetching in a variety of bed and bathtub scenes, or in shipwrecks that managed to show the leading lady as a castoff clutching wet and torn garments on deserted islands.

For public consumption, De Mille liked to fuse all contributions into his own promethean creation. In reality, the stories of marital manners among the rich were usually culled from the pages of William Randolph Hearst's *American Weekly*. The person doing the culling was a remarkable spinster named Jeanie Macpherson. This former actress was a powerful figure in the director's professional life, both dismissive and jealous of actresses and, at production meetings, a furiously obsessive presence. As De Mille's mistress—it was she who began calling him C. B.—she was always either offended, hurt, or sarcastic. She had to tolerate his newest conquest, Julie Faye, a former Mack Sennett trooper who spoke with a southern drawl and utterly fascinated the director with her wit, grace, and style. When Macpherson disagreed with her lover, their language became vividly purple. Still, he imposed Faye as a "studio reader," and members of his staff were fascinated by the tension and surprising unity of the curious ménage à trois.

De Mille's ruthlessness, tantrums and cruelty was confined to the film set. At home with the adorable Constance Adams he was a model of kindness and consideration. He adored Constance and was to remain her spouse, though not an exemplary one, for nearly sixty years.

Women found De Mille physically fascinating. Actresses, female scenarists, and socialites all thought he was an irresistible mix of circus ringmaster, cavalry leader, and man of action forever ready for the heat of epic events. He accentuated his Roman good looks with shirts opened on a muscular throat, well-cut riding breeches, and burnished boots.

When Gloria was let into his paneled office with its tall stained-glass windows and deep polar-bear rug, he stood by his thronelike desk and thanked her for coming. He led her to a large sofa, sat down beside her, and proceeded to see right through her. He had seen her in a Mack Sennett comedy and had never forgotten her, he said. He was preparing a picture in which he wanted to use her.

Once assured she wanted to make a picture with him, he needed to know if she was free to do so, if she had an agent, and whether she was under contract to Triangle. She protested that, at nineteen, she handled her own affairs and was not under contract to anyone.

It was not to be. As soon as Harry Aitken got wind of De Mille's interest in her, he ordered her to work in a new picture. When she balked, he and lawyers for Famous Players–Lasky agreed to quick arbitration. Arbitration was the new management ploy to make sure studios, not actors, had the last word. An arbitrator selected by the two companies quickly ruled that by accepting the raise, Gloria had, in effect, agreed to a verbal contract and therefore belonged to Triangle. She had tears in her eyes when De Mille himself called her with the verdict. Triangle immediately began publicizing her name and put her in wartime melodramas.

Letters from the front told Gloria her father was with the American Expeditionary Force in France. Without a word of warning, her mother married Matthew Burns one weekend and moved out. The girls at Court Corinne took to Gloria's sudden stardom with bitchy envy. If nothing else, Gloria told herself, she was making money and could afford to move. She told Bea to come with her. "You can be my secretary, my dependent, anything you want," she told her. "Just call a real-estate agent and get us out of here." They found a beautiful furnished house for rent on Harper Avenue in West Los Angeles. It was expensive. "Let's take it," said Gloria. "If I run myself into debt, maybe they'll fire me. Get a maid."

She hated Gilbert Hamilton, her director on *Everywoman's Husband,* until she found out that he, too, was serving out his sentence at Triangle. Her next director was Albert Parker, an eccentric Englishman and a shameless flirt who would be energized when associated with Douglas Fairbanks in the 1920s. *Secret Code* was a patriotic spy story in which the villain tries to blackmail Gloria into spying for the Kaiser. Parker sent her flowers and told her his wife was awful. "So's my husband," Gloria answered, "but my divorce isn't final and I don't want him to have any grounds for prolonging it."

One night she told Albert to leave the studio after her and to drive behind her to a quiet spot near the Beverly Hills Hotel where they could talk. They laughed and talked and failed to notice a car pulling up on the other side of the deserted road. Suddenly, Wallace Beery was there, flinging their car door open and punching Albert in the nose. He glowered a moment at Gloria and stormed off.

"My God, who was that?" Albert asked, wiping blood from his face.

"My husband," she groaned. "Now he'll report that he found us together."

Albert wasn't a director for nothing. To make sure charges of adultery wouldn't delay their respective divorces, he dramatically rammed his car into a tree on his way back. With such an alibi to back up his contention that he had been somewhere else that evening, he was sure no one would believe Beery.

Parker and Swanson made another spy drama, *Wife or Country.* This time Gloria played a girl tricked into spying for the enemy and paying for her betrayal by swallowing a bottle of poison pills. She had completed two more pictures, one directed by her first Essanay director, E. Mason Hopper, when Triangle floundered in bankruptcy, eventually to be bought out by Samuel Goldwyn.

Without a day off, Gloria changed employers on November 5, 1918. De Mille wanted the now well-publicized Triangle star for a story of a woman who leaves her busy, neglectful husband to marry another man, discovers her new spouse is a womanizing gambler and drinker, and sets out to win back her first mate. When Gloria reported to work at the studio on Sunset

Boulevard and Vine Street, she was taken to a spacious dressing room with fresh-cut flowers on the dresser, a soft lounging couch, and mirrored wall.

"Gloria was, of course, very young then, but I saw the future that she could have in pictures if her career was properly handled," De Mille would say in his autobiography. "I could name stars, some of them very competent artists, who have ruined their careers or at least suffered serious setbacks because early success has gone to their heads, or a kind of greedy overconfidence or misjudgment of their own talents has led them to take on roles for which they were not suited. . . . But Gloria Swanson suffered no such illusions. I never told her, until after her first few successes under my direction, why I was handling her career in a certain way, but she was intelligent enough to know and patient enough to wait." In reality, De Mille exploited the very young Gloria and, when her second husband blackmailed her, connived with Lasky to make her cave in to extortion.

Being De Mille's leading lady meant more than having an ample dressing room. It meant getting the glamour treatment. Alphareleta Hoffman and Mitchell Leisen, who was later to be a director of elegant Hollywood romances, designed the clothes she wore—and which thousands of women soon copied. De Mille was not as much concerned with being à la mode on the screen as with being sensational, and he instructed his designers to exaggerate fashions. The sky was the limit, he told them, and his heroines were smothered in ostrich plumes and staggered under the weight of couturier collections.

Elliot Dexter, who had starred with Mary Pickford in *A Romance of the Redwood*, was cast as Gloria's first husband; Lew Cody, a stock "cad type" in all studio casting files, played her second spouse.

On the first day of shooting, the hairdresser assigned to Gloria and two wardrobe ladies helped her into a white day dress. A Pinkerton detective knocked on the dressing-room door and came in with a velvet-lined chest of genuine jewels. Mr. De Mille, she was told, always had his actresses pick out the jewelry they wore in his films. An assistant escorted Gloria to the set. A minute later the master entered with his retinue of people. While he scrutinized the set, the assistant whispered to Gloria that the lady behind De Mille was Jeanie Macpherson. The man behind *her* was Sam Wood, the no-nonsense first assistant director. De Mille's eyes beamed when they fell on Gloria. He came over, took her hand, and with an expansive gesture said, "This is your home. Take all the time you need to get acquainted with it. If anything seems wrong, we'll talk about it." When De Mille was ready to sit down, a Filipino boy shoved a director's chair under him. De Mille insisted that nobody talk above a whisper and demanded that hammering on other sets cease the moment he arrived. In the pocket of his breeches he carried a handful of obsolete twenty-dollar pieces which he would jangle as a warning of shortening patience, not unlike the rattle of a poisonous snake. All charm vanished when he fell into one of the sudden insane rages that could overtake him without warning.

Gloria walked through the set, fluffing pillows, touching the keys of the grand piano, opening the French doors leading to a garden, then walked back and rearranged a vase of lilies.

De Mille huddled with his cameraman, came over, and in a voice not much louder than a whisper, said they would begin with a scene where she hurriedly packs a suitcase. He took her into the bedroom set and pointed to the suitcase and to the chest of drawers from which she should select the things she wanted to pack in it. "He didn't tell me why I was packing or where I was going," she would remember. "He didn't even tell me the name of the film. He just said they would start shooting as soon as I was ready." Midway through the filming of the scene, she heard people laugh and whistle, shout and scream. She went right on packing until De Mille walked onto the set, took her arm, and told her they'd stop shooting for the day. Word had just reached the studio that an armistice had been declared. The war was over.

All Gloria could think of was her father in France. She started to cry with happiness.

Dexter initiated her into the idiosyncracies of working for De Mille. Actors had no scripts; the director told them what the story was about and what each scene meant, but never gave specific instructions. He let them watch the daily rushes of the previous day's work so they would catch their own mistakes and see how they could fill out the characters they were playing. For the first time Gloria began to see how small gestures and expressions could be controlled and used to heighten a moment or save a scene. Dexter also introduced Gloria to his wife, the English actress Marie Doro, who had starred in *Oliver Twist* in 1916 and had been brought over by Lasky. Gloria thought that she was a true beauty and that Elliot and Marie were a radiantly happy couple.

The Dexters took Gloria dancing one night at the Ship Cafe, an ocean-side glamour spot in Santa Monica. Marie introduced her to Craney Gartz, a gorgeous-looking millionaire who was heir to the Crane bathroom-fixture fortune. A marvelous dancer, he was the first chic radical Gloria had ever met. He talked about Nietzsche, Isadora Duncan, the Fabians, and the Bolsheviks, and said that the war had been a mockery, that everybody in America was twiddling his thumbs while a few artists and theorists in Europe were destroying the old order. He imagined her dream was to marry a rich man and get out of pictures. Not that he would marry himself. Marriage destroyed people.

"May I kiss you?" he asked when they drove up to the house on Harper

Avenue. She said yes, if he would hurry, because she had to be at work at seven. He kissed even better than he danced.

Zukor and Lasky decide to call the new De Mille production *Don't Change Your Husband.* At the end of the shooting, De Mille gave Gloria a contract to look over. The contract was between the two of them. The $150 a week she was being paid would automatically be raised to $200 a week at the end of four months. In two years she would be making $350 a week. Thrilled, she signed and dated the contract December 30, 1918.

To launch *Don't Change Your Husband,* the new Famous Player was given her first press conference. "I'm not temperamental," Gloria told the *Boston Post.* "I was lucky, Mr. De Mille noticed me. A thousand more talented girls, more attractive girls, more intelligent girls are passed over. I had the good fortune to be picked. . . . Who said I had a big head? I bet it was a woman. Women are awful. They're just cats." To questions about her own desire for wedlock, she cried, "Marry, I? Heavens. I was married. I was married when I was seventeen. I knew nothing. I was full of romance. Now there's little romance left in me."

After New Year's she began fittings for her next picture, which would star Elliot Dexter again, Sylvia Ashton, and Tom Forman. Adapted from a story by Edgar Selwyn, it was the tale of a doctor (Dexter) and a soldier (Forman) in love with the same woman. The picture was called *For Better and for Worse.* Gloria staggered under the weight of jewels, furs, and ostrich plumes. *Vogue* considered her a prime example of movie bad taste, but she was a tremendous hit with the public. Her bosses knew they had made a discovery when *Don't Change Your Husband* was held over after its New York premiere. The film had cost $74,000 to make and grossed just under $300,000 in six months.

Gloria and Craney saw a lot of each other. She revered De Mille. Craney loved to puncture reputations he considered inflated, and he called De Mille's movies "commercial fancy-dress tearjerkers." "You love to criticize Mr. De Mille because he's a great artist and you're not," she snapped. Craney had a way of teasing her to the boiling point, then saying beautiful things when she got angry and hotly denied she was angry. The more he exasperated her, the more she thought she was falling in love with him. He wanted her to run away with him and help him spend his thirty million.

He introduced her to politics and world events. The Russian Revolution was mankind's biggest hope, and he couldn't wait to visit the new Soviet Union. He mentioned Lenin and Trotsky, and told her the latter had been a Russian emigré in New York, writing and speaking for the socialist cause, who had returned to Russia to become president of the Soviet Union.

For their third picture, De Mille turned to the author of *Peter Pan* and adapted James Barrie's 1902 play, *The Admirable Crichton.* The day De Mille made the announcement, he called together some forty actors, cameramen, set and costume designers, animal trainers, and engineers and told them the story. A titled British family with two spoiled daughters sets out on a cruise. Their private yacht is shipwrecked, and on the desert island where they and their servants are washed ashore, the tables are turned. Crichton, the butler, becomes the lord and master by virtue of his common sense and skills in the art of survival, and a snobbish, spoiled Lady Mary falls in love with him. When they return to civilization, they also return to their old upstairs-downstairs social order. As Lady Mary, Gloria would wear the most exotic array of clothes. Thomas Meighan, the stolid, handsome Irish leading man, played Crichton.

De Mille opened the picture with Lady Mary's ritualized rising from bed as a prelude to her ablutions. The still invisible Gloria has her way prepared for her by a maid filling the receptacle above her shower with rosewater and laying out bath crystals and king-sized powder puffs. When Gloria rises, she lets the bed wrap slide off her shoulders while the maids raise a towel to hide the intervening gap of bare flesh. Finally, there is the immersion in bath water artfully colored for the sake of modesty. After the shipwreck, Lady Mary is down to wearing a strategically torn negligée and later a revealing homemade sarong. Cunningly, De Mille developed the image of a haughty beauty turned primitive.

The entire company motored to Santa Barbara in preparation for sailing to uninhabited Santa Cruz Island. They would spend two weeks shooting the Robinson Crusoe stuff on the island. Gloria forbade Craney to visit her on location, which didn't prevent him from driving up to see the shooting of the family embarking on the princely cruise. Gloria told him this was no tearjerker but a story by one of the leading playwrights. To belittle whatever the paltry Barrie had written, Craney gave her a book by Karl Marx to read on the deserted island.

If the Santa Cruz location didn't give Gloria a chance to acquaint herself with Marxism, it gave her a new friend. Lois Wilson was a former Alabama schoolteacher who never stopped working and got her first break in *Miss Lulu Betts,* a "family picture" directed by De Mille's brother, William. Lois was the fiancée of Richard Dix, another De Mille actor, and she was the confidante and best friend of John Gilbert, trying to help him patch up his marriage.

When the company got back, Bea La Plante had a telegram from Captain Swanson announcing his upcoming visit to Los Angeles. Gloria hadn't seen her father in five years. She called her mother, but Addie didn't want to see him. She had only a distracted interest in Gloria's career and, since her marriage, had led a life totally separate from her daughter's. Gloria told Bea that if Daddy showed up while she was at the studio, Bea should bring him over.

De Mille said the picture needed a new title. Nobody could pronounce Crichton, and many thought the title was *Admiral Crichton*. His new title was *Male and Female*. They were shooting a scene with a leopard when Bea brought Daddy to the set. De Mille gave Gloria the rest of the day off.

To his daughter, Joseph Swanson looked ten, not five years older, thin, exhausted. She also measured the distance between them. He had no idea who De Mille was, or Wallace Beery. She realized she couldn't tell him that a brash young snob worth thirty million wanted her to live with him without the benefit of marriage. Daddy told her he would be stationed at Fort McArthur in Los Angeles harbor and asked about Addie. When they got to the house, he had a large drink and excused himself to get ready for dinner. At the table he was polite and attentive. Bea told stories about Court Corinne. When he went upstairs, the trained nurse in Bea diagnosed narcotics in addition to alcoholism. Gloria knew nothing of drug addiction except that she could never mention it to him.

They drove to a flying field out in the San Fernando Valley one Sunday. A smart young lieutenant recognized the movie star and invited her to go up with him in one of the two planes sitting in the middle of the field. She thought it would be fun to be able to tell Craney she had been flying without him, and said yes. She found the flight absolutely thrilling. She motioned to the pilot to do somersaults and turns, like she had seen in war movies, and squealed with joy when he did a loop-the-loop.

When they got down, she ran to Daddy, telling him she'd start taking lessons every Sunday. But her father was pale, twitching. He had tears in his eyes and made her promise never, never to do that again. "You're my little girl," he sobbed. She took him into her arms.

Let's Do It

Joe was at the Savoy Plaza in dinner clothes and with a chauffeured limousine waiting outside on Fifth Avenue on the dot of 6:30. When Gloria, in the smartest evening dress she had brought along on her business trip, got down to the lobby, she saw a man who looked like an aide or detective hand Joe Kennedy something which he put in his overcoat pocket. Then Joe saw her. His face lit up as he dismissed the messenger and came forward. With a big smile he handed her a florist's box.

She opened it and visibly winced. She hated corsages and she hated orchids because they made her look like somebody's visiting aunt or piano teacher. When Joe offered to pin it on her fur coat, she heard herself say she would carry it. That way the flower wouldn't be crushed.

The limo took them over the Queensboro Bridge toward Long Island. The weather was turning colder and the forecast for the Thanksgiving weekend was for occasional rain. Joe asked several times if she was warm enough, indicating that the automobile was heated. After a while the heat was too much and she said the chauffeur could shut it off.

Their conversation during the three-quarter-hour ride was all about motion pictures, with Joe doing most of the talking. She was usually bored with movie talk, but she realized that if he was sticking to this one subject it wasn't for fear she might not be interested in anything else, but because his own interest in the film business was bottomless. He questioned her about various directors and showed interest in budgets, schedules, and publicity.

What he really wanted to know was why she had turned down Jesse Lasky's last offer two years ago. Sidney Kent had told him how Lasky had held an all-night conference with Paramount's New York office on the long-distance telephone before offering her $20,000 a week for two years plus half the profits of any film she appeared in. It had been the fattest offer ever made to any screen star, but it had not been enough. Why hadn't Paramount upped its offer? According to Kent, Lasky had been willing to go higher. Swanson was the company's biggest star; every picture she made was a winner. But Zukor feared the precedent, feared that the rest of the contract players would demand similar raises. "It will ruin us, Mr. Lasky," Zukor had shouted over the telephone.

But Joe had also heard that most Paramount executives now favored Lasky's position, that the loss of Swanson for a paltry million had been a mistake. They were using up their natural resources of stars faster than new ones could be developed, putting promising newcomers in more pictures— six or eight a year. Careers became full-blown in a matter of months instead of years, and film idols lost their luster much faster, too. To give Gloria a rival and keep her demands in check, Lasky had imported Pola Negri. The studio had fanned a fake Negri-Swanson rivalry until fan magazines reported all females on Hollywood Boulevard were either Negri fans with white faces and red lips or Swanson faithfuls, using no mascara and wearing only one earring. The point was that four years later Negri was giving stereotyped performances in pictures that looked as though they were turned out by stamping machines. Perhaps it was the fault of bad scripts and misguided publicity. In any case, exhibitors demanded that Negri's name be removed from the advertising of her pictures.

Turning to the movie queen on the backseat, he asked if she would mind telling him why she had turned down Lasky's last offer. He had heard Paramount's version from Kent, he added; he would love to hear her side of the story.

His question seemed so open and direct that she told him. She had taken a certain pleasure in saying no to a million-plus dollars, first because United Artists and Joe Schenck were waiting for her with open arms and second because it seemed the only way to convince Paramount, and studio executives in general, that their exploitation of their stars was ruthless and intolerable. "I won't deny that I've passed through a few anxious times since

I turned down that million, Mr. Kennedy, but all things being equal, I'm sure I'd do it again. After all, I would have been the second or third person in movie history to sign a million-dollar contract, but I was the first ever to turn one down."

There was more to it than that, but he liked her answer and grinned. He liked to laugh, she discovered. When she said something in a perfect imitation of his Boston accent, he went into long, loud peals of laughter, groaned pleasurably, and asked her to do it again. Behind the propensity to laugh she divined a trigger temper.

The restaurant was elegant, with an orchestra for dining but no dancing. She felt his disappointment when she ordered steamed vegetables, rice, and unbuttered dark bread. He ordered a big meal for himself and explained that she could have wine served in a teacup from a concealed bottle. She sensed from the way he referred to the Prohibition ritual that he didn't care much for drink. He seemed pleased when she declined.

While they waited, she explained that she ate such bland food because of an ulcer scare during the filming of *Sadie Thompson* and her enthusiasm for a little-known doctor in Pasadena who had taught her there were not thousand of physical disorders, but only one—toxemia. People poisoned themselves by eating the wrong foods. Joe said he, too, suffered occasional stomach problems, but when she offered to put him in touch with her Dr. Henry Bieler, he said he already had the best doctor in Boston working on his case.

"This is for you," he said, handing her a small bound book across the table. He watched her surprise when she saw her name in gold on the covers. The book was:

The Story of the Films
As Told
by Leaders of the Industry to
the Students of the Graduate School
of Business Administration
George F. Baker Foundation
Harvard University
Edited by
Joseph P. Kennedy
President, FBO Pictures Corporation.

She guessed that the book, published by A. W. Shaw in Chicago and New York, was what the aide had delivered in the hotel lobby, bringing it directly from the engraver. A bit bewildered, she thanked Joe and asked if he had written it.

"Part of it. The first essay. Remember I told you I organized a sympo-sium on films at Harvard? This is the printed version of the speeches."

He showed her the page listing the speakers. She knew most of them: Zukor, Lasky, De Mille, Kent, Marcus Loew, Milton Sills. She imitated Zukor's Hungarian accent. Joe laughed. She said the idea of Milton Sills as lecturer also exercised her imagination. Milton had been her leading man in *The Great Moment,* and she remembered him as the shyest person in the world, unable to open his mouth unless he had scripted lines to say. Sills, Joe told her, had indeed read his speech at Harvard, but very effectively.

She asked why Joe hadn't had a woman speaker, that no one knew film financing better than Charlotte Pickford. Recalling the lunch joke about Mary Pickford's mother checking box-office receipts in 20,000 theaters every night, he was about to laugh but Gloria suddenly remembered that Mrs. Pickford was terribly ill. "I shouldn't be joking about her," she said.

Joe immediately became serious. She felt he took a heavily sentimental view of the family, because his tone changed each time he mentioned children or parents. He was sorry to hear about Mrs. Pickford, he said. "I should have asked you to speak," he went on. "You act, you produce, and you make films abroad. The French government presented you with an award, didn't they? Did you have to speak then?"

"Hardly," she smiled. She had been in front of the camera during the filming three years ago of *Madame Sans Gêne* at the Fontainebleau castle, drenching wet in a Napoleonic-era washerwoman's garb and a terrible red wig and carrying a laundry basket when Henri, her husband, came over to tell her the gentlemen from the Académie Française were there to present her with the Palms. What palms? A special award for meritorious foreign-ers. The dignitaries in top hats, cutaways, and striped trousers made the presentation and Leonce Perret, her director, kissed her on both cheeks. "I wanted to sink into the ground, but Henri told me what to say, so I lived through it."

Energetically, Joe said he was all for awards. The government or the press should give a prize for the best motion picture and the best perform-ance every year. She didn't particularly like choosing one actor over an-other. But he was thinking of the commercial benefits. "The real problem is, people don't realize the potential of pictures. Properly advertised, they open limitless markets."

Listening to him say the United States produced over eighty percent of the films distributed in the world, as compared with only twenty percent of the world's wheat, she watched his excited blue eyes behind the glasses and told herself he had the most ambitious view of films she had ever encountered. He was clever, too. As head of a small B-picture producing and distributing company, he had shrewdly offered Lasky, Zukor, Fox,

Loew, and the others the one thing that they had never dreamed of—Ivy League attention.

He didn't mention the discreet meetings he was having with Radio Corporation of America's David Sarnoff. *The Jazz Singer* played to packed houses in a few cities, but the industry was holding its breath. Switching to sound would mean wiring studios and theaters at a cost no one even wanted to estimate yet. But if "talking pictures" were the future, Sarnoff had decided that RCA couldn't afford not to join the battle with American Telegraph and Telephone and its Western Electric sound system. Instead, Joe talked about the opportunities the movies offered. Something new and different was happening to motion pictures, and that was the fusion of production and distribution. He was the son of a politician and the son-in-law of a politician, and he was intrigued by the manipulation of people and events. The screen offered that.

"Take Boston," he said animatedly. "The Cabots and the Lodges won't be caught at the pictures or let their children go. And that's why their servants know more about what's going on in the world than they do. The working class gets smarter every day, thanks to radio and pictures. It's the snooty Back Bay bankers who are missing the boat."

Driving back to Manhattan, he said he was interested in financing her next film, but that he was much more interested in personally handling all the business aspects of it. He was sure they could make millions together. Nobody who was smart could lose money in pictures.

She liked what she heard. The man next to her was all calculations, yet nothing seemed planned in what he said. As far as he could tell, he said, everybody in Hollywood thought small and looked no further than his or her next picture. United Artists was not much better than Paramount now, in spite of its promising beginnings. Joe Schenck was not ambitious, not really. Like all the other Hollywood types, he worried only about keeping exhibitors happy and the theaters full. They all wanted their yachts and their race horses and their girls, but their dreams stopped there. The challenge was to make a fortune in pictures and also to exploit the movies' economic and political potential.

She liked the perspective he conjured up, his authority, his enthusiasm. Two years ago she had not only turned down Lasky's million-plus-a-year offer, she had gone a million-plus into debt. Any illusion that life as one of the United Artists would mean board meetings over coffee on the terrace of Pickfair and help in a jiffy should she ever need it had dissolved as she found herself confronting lawyers, accountants, bankers, and Schenck, who expected her to stay on schedule, remain within budget, and turn a profit. She had persuaded Wall Street bankers to finance Gloria Swanson Productions Inc., to the tune of $1.2 million, taking as consideration her box-office

record and the million-dollar insurance policy Schenck had made her take
out. She was paying herself $10,000 a month in living expenses and was
carrying a board of directors; offices in New York and Hollywood; Rene
Hubert, her personal fashion designer; Lance Heath, her personal press
agent; a production manager; four secretaries; and a household staff of
eleven. She had managed to sell the forty-acre farm in Croton-on-Hudson,
but she was carrying the twenty-four-room Beverly Hills home and the
$100,000 penthouse in Manhattan until somebody bought it. If she was
staying at the Savoy Plaza, it was because not staffing the apartment was
one way of lowering her overhead until money from *Sadie Thompson*
started coming in.

She had played it safe with her first independent venture. *The Love of
Sunya* opened with a sequence set in ancient Egypt that enabled her to wear
the series of appropriately exotic costumes her fans expected. But *Sadie* was
the best thing she had done. It was a picture fired with new skills, vigor,
and imagination. She couldn't wait to see it open. And she would have a
delightful revenge to throw in the face of Mr. Kennedy here, as well as the
rest of the righteous moguls, if the Hays office held up the release much
longer. After acquiring the rights to both the original short story and the
stage play from the author's agent last summer, she had written to
Maugham personally to ask if he might be interested in writing the further
adventures of Sadie Thompson. She had finally heard from him:

Dear Miss Swanson,

Thank you for your letter of June 20th. I had made arrangements
with the Fox Film. Co., to write a sequel to "Rain" and I had devised
a story in which I was proposing to take Sadie Thompson to Australia and show what became of her, but when I informed the Fox
people that negotiations had been concluded for the sale of the film
rights of "Rain," they preferred not to go on with the matter. So if
you would like me to do a picture for you on these lines I am not
only at liberty to do it, but should be very glad to. I think I have
abundant material to make a scenario full of colour and action. The
price I had arranged with the Fox Film Co., was $25,000.

Yours very sincerely,
W. Somerset Maugham.

The last thing she wanted to do now was to made a *Sadie Thompson
II.* But the letter showed the hypocrisy of at least one of the signers of the
collective telegram that the studio heads and top distributors had sent to
sabotage her picture. While she had bought the rights to the blasphemous

and frightfully expensive stage play, Fox had tried to get the author to come up with a sequel under another title. The game but not the name.

As the limousine sped back across Queens on Northern Boulevard, she found herself listening to Kennedy saying that for some time he had wanted to produce an important picture, that to him her planned *Rockabye* didn't sound important, that if he became involved he would insist on an important story as well as an important director. She remembered De Mille telling her how studios feared putting too many eggs in one basket, how star talent and star director were the combination they feared most. She had wanted to stay with De Mille, to develop with him, but Lasky had vetoed it. She was a star, De Mille was a star; together they were a threat. So Sam Wood had become her director. The former De Mille assistant was more interested in his off-hour real-estate dealing than the little cocktails of mediocrity, distilled in a tall can of corn, which they were making. She said, "That's precisely what all the people you got to speak at Harvard would advise you *not* to do if you want to make money."

"Well, they're wrong," he said. "You told me at lunch your work in *Sadie Thompson* is your best so far because the story is the best you've ever had. If that's true, why would you consider anything but the next logical step—a great story and a great director? Isn't that what you turned down a million dollars to be able to do, Gloria?"

In his enthusiasm he called her by her first name. Just as confidently, she started calling him Joe. "I think we should make a picture together," she said.

She would remember him shout, "Wonderful," laugh, and clap his hands smartly like a college boy. For the rest of the trip back to the Savoy Plaza they talked business. He asked questions about her agreement with Schenck and UA.

He wasn't sure she was totally candid about her various obligations and agreements, and suggested she give him permission to go through her files and papers. She told him she had a New York office on Fifth Avenue. Before leaving for California on Saturday, she would call her secretary and tell her Joseph P. Kennedy had permission to look through all relevant papers. In cases where important documents were in Hollywood, the secretary would be told to get copies for him.

At the hotel, he escorted her to the elevator. She gave him her private number in Beverly Hills and told him he could call her after he had a chance to look through her New York files.

Going upstairs, she mentally thanked Bob Kane for having put her in touch with his hybrid banker-film executive. After *Sunya* and *Sadie* she knew she needed someone with business acumen and political savvy, qualities in which she and Henri were sadly lacking. As she would put it in her autobiography, "I had no doubt in my mind that I had stumbled on the right business partner to straighten out my career."

He would never write his memoirs, but as events would show—and a host of Kennedy biographers would underline—this second meeting in one day with a woman who had done it all, and done it first, left him eager to pursue what he felt was a bracing challenge. His ambitions and his smarts had brought him connections and money. Straightening out the affairs of this movie queen, whose business agility he was clever enough not to underestimate, offered him new insights into the tangle of the enormous rewards and obligations of movie fame, and into the tumultuous life of a woman whose temperamental sympathies probably were fleeting but for now were flatteringly concentrated on him.

She could never be just a lovely ornament for a rich man's collection of costly symbols. To be associated with her in an ardent screen epic of some kind, a forceful, influential big movie, could make him a producer commanding the same heights as her stardom.

Joe

He was his mother's boy. Whatever his saloonkeeper-turned-ward-politician father may have been in the hierarchy of Irish Boston, his mother fiercely wanted "my Joe" to be somebody in a way her husband was not. She shipped the boy across the bay to a Protestant prep school frequented by the sons of old-line Yankees from the West Side, Beacon Hill, and Back Bay. Yet, however ambivalent Mary Hickey Kennedy may have been about Patrick Joseph ("P.J." to his bar customers) Kennedy's career, politics *was* the central reality of their lives, and Joe, a pugnacious kid with protruding teeth, sandy hair, and a quick temper, grew up in an endless round of musicales and marriages, wakes and ward meetings. P. J. was not good at posturing and he disliked making speeches. He was good at working out compromises, mediating disputes, and controlling patronage. Although Joe later tried to make his accomplishments ever greater by implying that he had known poverty as a boy, his father's intertwined business of liquor and politics made for a comfortable living and enough of a surplus for investments in a local coal company and in Columbia Trust, Boston's only Irish-controlled bank.

Like so many sons of immigrants, P.J. had started working on the docks, but unlike most, he didn't drink away his pay. A man of brawny physique, blue eyes, rosy complexion, and thick red hair, he had bought a working-class tavern on Haymarket Square with money put aside by his widowed mother and loans from his married sisters. He possessed the two most important qualifications for a wise saloonkeeper: He rarely sampled his own wares and he was a good listener. What he heard from the other side of the bar was East End news, gossip, hopes and fears, troubles and tragedies. It was the time of the first barroom associations. Using family friendships and neighborhood prejudices, the Boston Irish began moving into the local Democratic Party in order to serve their needs for jobs, and for protection against landlords and employers. In New York the "machine" was called Tammany; in Boston it was a network of political clubs spread throughout the city wards, each with a "boss" bound to his people by a web of mutual loyalty and self-interest, brokering power for himself and his constituents. At twenty-six, P.J. had opened his own liquor import business, P. J. Kennedy and Company, Importers, at 81 Border Street. He supplied some of Boston's best hotels and restaurants with Haig & Haig scotch. In 1887 he was elected to the Massachusetts Senate.

The same year, he pleased his mother by courting Mary Augusta Hickey, a blue-eyed, imposing girl (she was larger than P.J. himself) who was the daughter of another barkeep and the sister of a doctor, a police captain, and the mayor of Brockton. The Boston Irish considered the Kennedys below the Hickeys, but P.J., who cut a handsome figure with his handlebar mustache, did not. His liquor business and his pub were flourishing, and even if his bailiwick was the social, economic, and political back-water of East Boston's Ward 2, he diligently tended to his constituents' affairs. After a Thanksgiving Eve wedding at the Sacred Heart Church, P.J. and Mary—he called her Mame—moved into a modest apartment at 151 Meridian Street, one of East Boston's main thoroughfares. It was here that Mary gave birth to a son the following September 6. Had P.J. had his way, the boy would have been named Patrick Joseph. But Mary decided she wanted no "little P.J. running around the house," and the boy was christened Joseph Patrick. To the family she said that by inverting Patrick and Joseph the names sounded "less Irish."

The baby was the first grandson for P.J.'s ailing mother. Bridget Murphy had been a twenty-seven-year-old colleen from county Wexford in 1849 when she met Patrick Kennedy, also from Wexford, in the steerage of the *Washington Irving,* which had carried them and some two hundred others from Ireland's potato famine to America in forty days. Bridget lost her Patrick to cholera nine years after their arrival and brought up P.J. and three daughters on her own. Her stationery and notions shop was on Border

Street, and as soon as the girls were old enough to tend to customers, she had taken the ferry across to Boston twice a week to work as a hairdresser at Jordan Marsh, the big department store. She was now sixty-seven and suffered from arteriosclerosis and heart trouble. Two and a half months after her grandson's birth, she suffered a cerebral hemorrhage and died.

When Joe was four, P.J. and Mary had a daughter, Loretta, and six years later, a second girl, Margaret. The family moved to a new house on Webster Street. From the front porch, they had a view of the Boston skyline; the backyard sloped toward the harbor and the ferry slips (there were no tunnels to Boston then, and East Boston was in reality a series of forlorn islands with shipyards and crooked tenement streets climbing toward one center, Maverick Square).

Loretta and Margaret adored their brother. Margaret, who was so attractive and lively she would be called the Kennedys' "It Girl" in the 1920s, would remember thinking her big brother Joe was a prince. "I'd be thrilled even if he asked me to put something away for him—anything, just as long as he noticed me." Loretta would remember her brother's authority in the family, even as a child, and to newspapermen in search of a revealing anecdote would tell of the Christmas when she had undergone a crisis of belief. When she came downstairs Christmas morning, she realized the dollhouse waiting for her in front of the fireplace could not have come down the chimney. When she asked her father, he shrugged and looked away. But Joe had an answer. Santa, he told his sister, had a magic wand which he used to make objects larger and smaller at will.

P.J. became a man of influence in East Boston. Since taverns were the political caucus rooms and campaign headquarters, he ran the places where most political business were conducted. He loaned money, put up bail, gave advice, and provided the beer, wine, and spirits for weddings and wakes. Successively he was appointed a Boston election commissioner (there were three others)—a post that gave him a $5,000-a-year stipend—wire commissioner, and acting fire commissioner.

His bitterest enemy was Martin Lomasney, a stubby Irish immigrant's son who had become the city's first great political boss. Known as the "Mahatma," Lomasney met immigrants at the docks and herded them to his headquarters. In return for helping them get settled, he asked only that the newcomers register as Democrats and vote as he told them. With their vote he got patronage and clout. When *McClure Magazine*'s brilliant investigative journalist Lincoln Steffens came to Boston to expose the Mahatma, he found Lomasney far from defensive. "Who do you think you're kidding?" Lomasney asked. "You get paid for muckraking and I get paid for creating what you call the muck." In 1898 P.J. had the audacity to take on the Mahatma himself by moving the Democratic state nominating convention away from Lomasney's ward to his own bailiwick. Playing by the rules of the day, P.J. had his troops set up blockades around the convention site. They kept rivals out until the Mahatma disguised his delegates as a funeral procession and smuggled them through Kennedy's lines in a hearse.

In recognition of his ability to "deliver" East Boston, P.J. became one of the four backroom politicians who ran the city. Together with soon-to-be mayor John F. Fitzgerald from the North End, "Smiling Jim" Donovan of the South End, and Joseph Corbett of Charlestown, P.J. met every week in a private room of the old Quincy House hotel. Called the Strategy Board for having outflanked Lomasney, the quartet always began its sessions at noon sharp with a sumptuous lunch provided by the hotel. By the end of the meal, Boston might have a new tax collector or police commissioner.

Joe's earliest recollection of politics came one day when two of his father's retainers burst in with the news that each had cast 128 votes. Mary didn't like the constant flow of flunkies and supplicants to 165 Webster Street. "Tell them we're eating," she would say when knocks sounded on the door. But P.J. would get up, carefully wipe his mustache, and go and see them. Often he would stick his head back in as he was putting on his coat and hat, and say, "You'll have to go on without me." The Kennedys had a cook and a parlor maid, and Mary made sure there was a large bowl of clam chowder and crackers for his late-night returns.

P.J.'s sisters had married solid working-class men—one a teamster, the other a school janitor, the third a clerk—and it is doubtful whether they were invited to the big Sunday get-togethers that became a tradition on Webster Street. As several Kennedy biographers would note, P.J.'s sisters and their husbands were an entire social stratum beneath Mary's folks. Joe would remember his mother's family coming over—James Hickey, who was a police captain in East Boston; Charles Hickey, the Brockton mayor and funeral director; and Dr. John Hickey, one of the first Irishmen to graduate from Harvard Medical School. Joe especially remembered Uncle Jim in his police uniform ablaze with ribbons and decorations.

In the stratified second-generation Irish society, the Kennedys were below the Fitzgeralds, Boston's first Irish family since John Fitzgerald became mayor in 1905. Known as Fitzie, Honey Fitz, and Little Napoleon, Fitzgerald was not Boston's first Irish mayor—Hugh O'Brien had been elected mayor the year Joe was born—but he was the most colorful. Loud and pugnacious, something of a philanderer, Honey Fitz was a histrionic politician who could weep at will at a stranger's wake. It was said he was the only man who could sing "Sweet Adeline"—his political theme song—cold sober and get away with it. A heavy-browed, short, slight but athletic man, he was a gate-crasher by nature, and his assault on blue-blooded Yankee institutions had made him a legend in his youth. He had the ability to talk about anything persuasively, and with swarms of facts seemingly produced from thin air. Someone put this knack to verse in a Boston newspaper: "Honey Fitz can talk you blind/On any subject you can find."

Like P.J., Fitzgerald had married above his station, into the "lace-curtain Irish" Hannon family. With the elegant, devout Mary Josephine ("Josie") Hannon, he had five children—three daughters and two sons. His favorite was his eldest daughter, Rose, born in 1890. From her earliest years, Rose showed above-average intelligence, and her father took her on long walks through their historic North End and told her incidents of early American history.

Serving alongside P.J. in the State Senate in 1892, Fitzgerald had gone on to a term in the U.S. House of Representatives (the first Catholic to be elected to Congress). But the commute to Washington took seventeen hours on the train, and the only place that really mattered to him was Boston. Having become moderately wealthy after leaving Congress through publishing a Boston newspaper, *The Republic,* he made his move. Making up to thirty speeches a day and mobilizing his "dearos"—coined after his affectionate reference to his "dear old North End" and, by extension, meaning all Irish Americans—he clinched the mayoral race. On election night he made his way to the Ward 2 headquarters to make his peace with P.J., who had opposed him in favor of another candidate. "Now that the fight is over, Pat, let's get together," he told Kennedy. Although he had just won, Honey Fitz couldn't resist plunging into the crowd. P.J. watched and shook his head in wonder. "He knows them all. I don't know half of them, even though they're in my district."

The Fitzgeralds and the Kennedys socialized on occasion in the summer. Old Orchard Beach on the Maine coast ninety miles north of Boston was a popular resort for the city's Catholics. Families picnicked and visited while their children played. Photographs of Victorian rectitude would survive of the mingled families: Honey Fitz, in summer white and sailor's cap, with wife and five children; Mary and some of the Hickeys; P.J., rotund and bespectacled now; and Joe, a spindly-looking ten-year-old.

What dominated young Joe's life was not politics, but his mother. There were to be no later signs that he suffered fierce Oedipal pains growing up cuddled by a young mother who was—and felt herself to be—above her husband, socially and intellectually. Mary wanted her son "to be somebody" and possessively monopolized his time, quizzed him about schoolwork, and reminded him that Uncle John had been to Harvard. It was her stern stare of disapproval—"the Hickey look," as the rest of the family called it—that spurred him and his sisters on.

Although proud of P.J.'s climb in the community, she felt that politics was faintly disreputable. She also sensed that Boston's Protestant elite might cede City Hall, but by retreating to their Back Bay brownstones, they were drawing social demarcation lines with new sharp edges. It was she who established Joe's ambivalence toward his ethnicity, an ambivalence that would make him both surround himself with Boston Irish underlings and make sure his own children never grew up Boston Irish.

From first to fifth grade, Joe went to local parochial schools and came home every noon to have lunch with his mother and sisters. "He missed me," Mary would happily reminisce when he had become a young tycoon. "He wanted to hurry home and see me again."

The boys he went to school with at East Boston's Xaverian School and, later, the Assumption School were tough, poor kids who were never to leave the home turf. Joe earned his first pennies selling newspapers, working in a haberdasher's store, lighting gaslights in the homes of Orthodox Jews on religious holidays, and doing odd jobs in his father's sundry businesses. One of his earliest ventures was to take a few homing pigeons of his own to Boston Commons in order to lure Commons pigeons back to East Boston, where he would sell the birds for roasting. He organized the Assumption School's baseball team, rented a ballpark, sold tickets, and ended up with a modest profit for the season. When he heard that the Larkin Soap Company was sponsoring a contest, he got his friends to canvass the neighborhood, and he won first prize—an oak bookcase on which he stacked the works of Horatio Alger that Loretta remembered him avidly reading. When he was twelve, Mary arranged a job for him delivering hats to Boston Brahmin ladies across the bay. The job entailed not only delivering the classy millinery shop's hats to grand houses, but waiting to see if they fit. "If you are asked your name," Mary instructed him, "answer 'Joseph.' " No need to dwell on the heritage. After the millinery job, he branched out on his own. He hawked newspapers at the ferry building close to the spot where his grandfather and grandmother had stepped off the *Washington Irving,* and one summer sold candy aboard a harbor excursion boat.

Mary believed that while Catholic schools like those her husband and she had attended might be safe, they tended to isolate students and stunt their ambitions, and sometime in 1901 she made the decision to send her son across the bay to the famed Boston Latin School.

At thirteen, Joe was a tall, wiry, and freckled kid with blond hair and an open, expressive face. He smiled and laughed easily and had a big, infectious grin. He would never match the scholarship of the school's distinguished alumni, who included Cotton Mather, Benjamin Franklin, John Hancock, John Quincy Adams, Ralph Waldo Emerson, Henry Adams, and George Santayana, but he was aggressive and well liked. Sports was his forte. He became colonel of the drill team that won the citywide competition, a good enough baseball player to win the Mayor's Cup—

presented by Fitzie himself—for having the highest batting average in the city. He played on the football, basketball, and tennis teams, and would remember Boston Latin for making "us all feel that if we could stick it out we were made of just a little bit better stuff than the fellows our age who were attending what we always thought were easier schools."

His grades were average to poor, and he had to repeat an entire year. But he was not at Boston Latin only to excel in academics and athletics. He was there to meet the sons of proper families and to have his horizons expanded. Boston's crusty William Cardinal O'Connell tried to persuade parents in his flock to send their young men to Boston University or Holy Cross, both run by the Jesuits. When Joe was fourteen, however, both he and his mother decided he would be going to Harvard.

By the time he was seventeen, he was the teenage sweetheart of Honey Fitz's favorite daughter. They had met at Orchard Beach when Joe was seven and Rose five, and had renewed their acquaintance eight years later. When Rose was sixteen, Joe invited her to the first dance of the 1906 season. It was an afternoon dance and Rose would be home before dark, but her father said no. Joe invited someone else, but told the girl she was his second choice. When Rose heard this, she thought it was admirable of him to be so honest. The following spring, when Rose graduated from Dorchester High School, there was another afternoon dance. Rose was almost seventeen, and after pondering the question for a while Honey Fitz let her go. She promptly invited Joe.

In the summer of 1908 Fitzgerald took his family to Europe. Rose and Agnes, Rose's sister two years her junior, loved the hectic schedule that took them through Ireland, England, Belgium, France, Switzerland, and Holland. Everywhere they went, hizzoner made comparisons, almost always to the advantage of Boston, although he did praise the clean streets in Germany.

Did he and his wife merely want to make sure their daughters were as well "finished" as any Beacon Hill heiress, or did they think a separation would cool Rose's ardor for P.J.'s son? At the end of the summer, the parents decided Rose and Agnes would spend a year at the Blumenthal convent school in Holland. The school, near the German-Belgian border, was a boarding school where classes were conducted in French and German. Separation of church and state had closed teaching convents in France, and, since Bismarck, teaching orders of nuns had been outlawed in Germany, meaning that the Fitzgerald girls spent a year with the daughters of some of Europe's most aristocratic—and reactionary—Catholic families. The Blumenthal took it for granted that its charges, when married, would devote their lives to *Kinder, Kirche, und Küche.* It further assumed that as wives of gentlemen and officers they would leave the cooking to the staff, so the *Küche* part was limited to lessons in how to run a household and how to instruct and supervise servants. What Rose would remember with fondness of her year in Maastricht were the music lessons.

Joe and Rose wrote to each other. When Rose and Agnes came home, they begged not to be sent back to Europe for another year. Their mother had missed them terribly because their father was rarely home, and Mother prevailed.

Even after he went to Harvard, however, Joe Kennedy was not good enough for Rose. The Fitzgeralds were rising to dizzying heights of Irish society. In the mayoralty contest of 1910 the beleaguered Yankees had rallied around formidable James Jackson Storrow, a millionaire investment banker. In response the Irish bosses had shelved their quarrels and united behind Honey Fitz and carried him to victory. The year Rose and Agnes spent in Europe was meant to further enhance the family's social climb.

Joe was a young man in a hurry at Harvard, a wisecracking, profane, and to many, overly pushy freshman. He shrugged off slurs against his background, looking for openings and putting the onus on others by making them show prejudice in rejecting him. He was good in sports but mediocre in his studies. During the summers he demonstrated a knack for making a fast buck. With his classmate Joe Donovan he ran a sightseeing tour to historic Lexington. Joe put $300 into a bus and, with Donovan at the wheel, gave a guided tour over a megaphone of Boston's landmarks. The tourist business netted the two Joes $5,000 during their college years. Decades later, Washington columnist Drew Pearson would tell of young Joe being in with Honey Fitz on an extortion scheme against the Colonial Auto-Sightseeing Company, which suddenly found its city license fee increased by $1,000 a year, payable in monthly installments. The nattily dressed Harvard man who picked up the check every month was none other than Joe Kennedy.

When Joe was asked to list his profession for the 1932 reunion of his Harvard class, he would reply, somewhat facetiously, "Capitalist." Making money was what he was good at, even though he did so poorly in a course in banking and finance that he had to drop it after one semester. He was never above being the toady to important people, and he selected roommates who were All-American football players. From a sports standpoint, Harvard was leagues above Boston Latin, and Joe could not rely on his baseball prowess to enhance his prestige on campus. He made the freshman baseball team, but not the varsity in his sophomore or junior year. Although he failed to make one of the good "final" clubs like Porcellian, A.D., or Fly, he was chosen for Hasty Pudding, an accomplishment for anyone whose father was a saloonkeeper and whose grandparents were of the famine Irish.

He insisted on living in Harvard Yard during his final year, but on weekends took schoolmates to his parents' new seaside home in Winthrop. The college friends spent Sundays walking along the beach in their blue trousers and blazers and feasting on Mary's baked ham and baked beans. After dinner in the parlor, there was the ritual of trying to stump Mary at spelling. Joe would have prepared his chums, challenging them to look up impossible words in the dictionary in advance. Sometimes they came up with a scientific or technical term she didn't understand, but she usually managed to spell it. "No one can stump my mother," Joe would beam.

If he didn't become chums with any of the Adamses, Saltonstalls, Lawrences, Lowells, Cabots, or Lodges, he did become a friend of Guy Currier, whose business it was to know everybody and who would become a rich and influential Yankee lawyer, formidable Massachusetts legislature lobbyist, and investor in Joe's film ventures. Another classmate was the future humorist Robert Benchley.

Joe graduated in 1912 and thought banking promised an infinite variety of possibilities for making oneself rich. Unlike some of his classmates who began as tellers or junior executives in prestigious institutions, Joe had his father use his influence to get him a job as a state bank examiner. Joe was paid only $125 a month, but over the next year and a half, he traveled all over eastern Massachusetts examining bank ledgers, learning how financial institutions made money, and how they were connected to other businesses. The traveling made it a little more difficult to see Rose, but she was impressed by his new seriousness. Looking at bank books, he told her, taught him more about finance than all his Harvard economics courses.

He invested $1,000 in a one-third interest in Old Colony Realty, a new company that, as John H. Davis would write in *The Kennedys: Dynasty and Disaster, 1848–1984*, "capitalized on the misfortunes of others, particularly poor people. It took over defaulted mortgages on modest two- and three-family tenements, repaired and maintained the houses, then quickly resold them." The investment paid for Joe's first trip abroad with Harvard friends, Joseph Merrill and John Hannon.

The trio sailed aboard a new German liner. Anxious not to appear unknowing, Joe had learned the ropes of ocean travel from friends and acquaintances and had his pockets filled with letters of introduction. The first day out, he learned that the ship's imperial suite was empty and cajoled the purser into letting the three friends have it for only a nominal supplement above their first-class tickets. Merrill and Hannon didn't especially care how they got to Europe, but Joe convinced them to sail to Europe like kings. His ulterior motive was that the suite allowed him to entertain Samuel Rea, president of the Pennsylvania Railroad, and his daughter Ruth, knowing that word would get back to Boston and raise his stock with the Fitzgeralds. The ploy almost backfired because Rose became so angry she turned his picture face down on her dresser.

The whirlwind tour included Germany, France, and Britain but omitted the ancestral Ireland. The Harvard men found use for Joe's introductory letters, but in Paris ran into friends from Yale who introduced them to the rue de Lappe (the "wickedest street in the world"), explained just what the newspapers advertised as "Suzy Masseuse" and "les poses vivantes," and one night at the Folies Bergères introduced them to the leading dancer, Nelli Devi. Joining forces, the college boys later escorted Devi to the Dead Rat, a Left Bank nightclub and haunt of celebrities. When the owner begged her to dance, she agreed on condition that other notables would also entertain. John Arthur Johnson, the world's first black heavyweight boxing champion and a fugitive from American justice because his wife, Lucille, was white, followed Devi into the spotlight and took a turn at the bass cello.

As the party picked up, waiters passed out small celluloid balls and the guests happily pelted each other. Joe thought Jack Johnson offered a tempting target and bounced a ball off the prizefighter's head. A powerful, graceful figure, Johnson turned, stared, then broke into a grin. Joe went over and introduced himself. Jack Johnson was from Galveston, Texas, and he had toured as a music hall attraction in London, Berlin, Budapest, and St. Petersburg, His wife was from Minneapolis, and a federal judge in Chicago had sentenced him to jail term under the Mann Act. While his lawyer appealed, Jack and Lucille had made for the Canadian border and, from Montreal, sailed to Europe. A little later, while Joe's friends watched enviously, he was gliding across the dance floor with Lucille. When he returned to his table, he casually showed the champion's card, inscribed: "To Joe Kennedy, a fine fellow."

Joe's chance to put his financial savvy to work for himself came in the fall of 1913 when "downtown" interests wanted to take over Columbia Trust. Boston banking was undergoing a series of mergers and consolidations, and the First National Bank's offer to the Columbia Trust stockholders was not ungenerous. Most board members were ready to accept the buy-out, but P.J., who with other prosperous East Boston merchants had founded Columbia Trust a decade earlier, saw the takeover as a threat to the Irish community. He wanted to preserve Columbia Trust as an independent neighborhood institution, but had neither enough money to buy out the others nor enough stock to block the merger. Instead, he turned to his son.

Columbia Trust had remained small. Its capital was $200,000; its assets $37,000. Joe went into action, gathering proxies, borrowing money to buy additional stock. When this wasn't enough, he called on his Harvard roommate Bob Fisher, a football star well supplied with tickets to big games who had been able to accommodate an old grad, Eugene V. Thayer, president of the Merchants National Bank. Joe visited Thayer, who was more than willing to block First National Bank. Junk bonds had not yet been invented, but the fiduciary paper that Kennedy *père et fils* issued must have been close to latter-day leverage bonds. P.J. and Joe went into the hole to the tune of $45,000—much of it borrowed from Thayer—which was more than the net worth of Columbia Trust. At the first board meeting after the victory over First National, Joe astonished the Columbia directors by saying he wanted to be president. With his father's backing, Joe was voted president. He loved the press attention that followed. When a local reporter asked what the new banker wanted in life, Joe's reply came without hesitation: "I want to be a millionaire by the age of thirty-five."

Styling himself—with only slight exaggeration, historians would ascertain—the country's youngest bank president, the twenty-five-year-old banker was suddenly good enough for Rose. Soon, the society columns of the *Post* reported Rose Fitzgerald's engagement to Joseph Patrick Kennedy.

Young Kennedy's ascension came at the time the fortunes of the ebullient mayor were beginning to slip. Honey Fitz decided to run for a third term in 1914 but was opposed by a politician as crafty as himself, James M. Curley, who had succeeded Fitzgerald as congressman.

The Strategy Board thought it was time for change but reluctantly backed Honey Fitz. Then, as Joe and Rose picked their wedding date, the campaign got rough. Curley delivered a letter to Josie Fitzgerald telling her that unless her husband withdrew from the race the family's reputation would be exposed to the revelation of Honey Fitz's relationship with twenty-three-year-old Elizabeth "Toodles" Ryan, a cigarette girl at the Ferncroft Inn, a scandal that had been one of Boston's poorest kept secrets. While Josie—and Rose, who was the same age as Toodles—confronted Fitzie, Curley gave a first lecture, "Graft in Ancient Times and Modern," that embarrassed the incumbent by calling attention to widespread nepotism in City Hall. When Curley announced that the title of his second lecture would be "Great Lovers from Cleopatra to Toodles," Honey Fitz bowed out of the race.

Two months after the guns of August signaled war in Europe, Joe and friends were present at the wedding in the cardinal's private chapel. Rose's sister Agnes was the maid of honor; Joe Donovan, the best man. O'Connell was a crusty prelate of the old school and kin to Joe's and Rose's friends. Joe O'Connell, who was one of Joe Kennedy's oldest chums, and his sister Mary, one of Rose's close friends, were the cardinal's nephew and niece.

The wedding party was sumptuous but small. Everybody agreed the newlyweds were a handsome couple: the mayor's daughter, a lovely dark-haired girl with agate eyes and a fine-featured face that ended in a strong chin; the groom, a tall, slender twenty-six-year-old with piercing blue eyes, a long lean face, and a winning smile.

Joe and Rose moved into a modest frame house on Beale Street in the predominantly Protestant suburb of Brookline. Most of their young married friends lived in rented apartments, but banker Kennedy would have none of that and borrowed $2,000 from his father-in-law for the downpayment on the house. Their first acquisition was a Model T Ford which, on their first outing, Joe managed to drive into a ditch.

Rose bore Joe a son. There was much speculation as to whether the first-born would be named after Honey Fitz—who had stayed in politics and ran for the U.S. Senate in 1916 only to lose to Henry Cabot Lodge, Sr., by 33,000 votes—or the baby's father. There was a divergence of newspaper opinion. Some journalists held that the important fact was that the ten-pound baby was the former mayor's first grandchild. Some reporters featured the fact that the infant's father was the "youngest bank president in the world." Society-page writers minimized the paternal lines and acclaimed the birth of a son to the founder and president of the Ace of Clubs, Rose Fitzgerald Kennedy. Joe made sure his first son was christened Joseph Patrick, Jr. The boy was vigorously photographed for a year—in his crib, in the arms of his distinguished grandfathers, and on the sands of Palm Beach, Florida, where the young couple spent a fortnight in 1916.

Another son, John Fitzgerald, was born in 1917. Two daughters were also born while Rose and Joe still lived on Beale Street.

War helped Joe toward his millionaire goal. The United States' entrance into the European conflict in 1917 meant a quick buildup of its sea power. Guy Currier, Joe's Harvard classmate, had become a lobbyist for Bethlehem Steel, and when he learned that an assistant manager was needed at Bethlehem's Fore River shipyard in Quincy, Massachusetts, he set Joe up for an appointment with Bethlehem's formidable Charles Schwab. The chairman found the young Columbia Trust president to be positive, irreverent, optimistic, salty, and outspoken, and offered him the job.

Joe accepted, turned over Columbia Trust to his father, and at $20,000 a year plus bonuses set to work. It was a big job. Joe had 22,000 workers under him. He worked as hard as anyone, going home just long enough to sleep. He also discovered Edward B. Derr and C. J. (Pat) Scollard at the yard, a pair of young men with the same capacity for hard work who over the years would join him in a series of business ventures.

Fore River broke all production records, building and launching thirty-six destroyers in just over two years. Schwab, however, had difficulties getting paid for a ship delivered to the Argentine navy in 1915. The thirty-three-year-old assistant navy secretary, Franklin D. Roosevelt, had interceded on behalf of a friendly Latin American power, and Argentina had ordered more ships.

Now, in 1917, several of these warships were not paid for, and Schwab refused to release them. Secretary Roosevelt asked for arbitration, and Schwab sent his assistant manager at Fore River to Washington with instructions to hang tough. It was a confrontation both would remember.

Roosevelt was all patrician charm and reassurances. The State Department would collect the money for Bethlehem, he said.

"Sorry, Mr. Secretary," Joe replied, "but Mr. Schwab refuses to let the ships go until they are paid for."

"Absurd."

"Not at all absurd, sir. Positively no ship will be delivered until it is paid for."

Roosevelt walked Kennedy to the door, an arm on his shoulder. It had been good to meet him; he hoped Joe would look in whenever he was in Washington, but this was wartime, and if the ships were not delivered at once, a fleet of tugboats would be sent to Fore River to get them. Joe protested. Franklin smiled. Joe was sure he was dealing with another rich man's son who never had to work for a living and had nothing else to do but dabble in politics. In fact, when Joe reported to Schwab, he called the assistant navy secretary "a smiling four-flusher." Schwab decided to call "this youngster's bluff," and the battleships stayed in their berths.

Soon, however, four navy tugboats were puffing up the Fore River, with an escort of armed marines. The warships were towed into the harbor, where waiting Argentine crews boarded them. Joe, according to Roosevelt biographer Ted Morgan, was mortified. The smiling four-flusher had gotten the best of him. Roosevelt came to Fore River and the two had other meetings. Privately, Joe admitted that meeting with Roosevelt left him so frustrated he sometimes broke down and cried.

A man who would have more immediate influence on Joe was Galen Stone of the investment house of Hayden, Stone and Company and chairman of the Atlantic, Gulf and West Indies Steamship Line. A portly, balding man with a twinkling eye and carefully trimmed white mustache, Stone was a rural Yankee from Leominster, Massachusetts, who had come to Boston as a young man to enter journalism. He had entered a broker's office and met an energetic young Bostonian, Charles Hayden. The partnership had been a success, balancing Stone's quiet meticulousness with Hayden's nervous dynamics as the house financed copper mines, sugar refining, shipping, and railroads. Both had become millionaires, Stone making his headquarters in Boston and Hayden operating from New York. Joe was anxious to convince Stone that Fore River should build his ships. Stone didn't give the Fore River assistant manager the order but, like Schwab, was impressed by the young man's poise and energy.

Peace slashed navy procurement and caused Joe to look for opportunities elsewhere. He remembered Galen Stone and made an appointment, but when he showed up for the meeting he was told Stone had had to cancel and was, in fact, on his way to the station to catch a train to New York. Undeterred, Joe ran downstairs, hailed a cab to South Station, boarded the train, found Stone, and cornered him for three hours on the way to New York. Impressed a second time, Stone had his firm check Joe's references and, two weeks later, gave him a job as stock department manager. The salary was $10,000 a year, half what the Fore River job had paid, but Galen Stone was exactly the man Joe wanted to be—independent. Under Galen's tutelage, Joe learned to use inside information to maximize returns and minimize risks.

Besides parenthood, Joe and Rose shared the social whirl of the upwardly mobile. Rose introduced him to classical music, Joe took her to the much-admired Professor Charles Copeland's—"Copely" to a generation of English Department graduates—"readings" of the classics and to football games at Harvard Stadium. Together they stood in line to be introduced to the Prince of Wales during his stopover on his American tour. Meeting the "dancing, drinking, tumbling, kissing, walking, talking—but not marrying" heir to the British throne was the highlight of the 1919 season.

P.J. lost his first election, and Joe and Rose had their third child, Rosemary. Mayor Curley (prototype of the demagogic civic leader in Edwin O'Connor's *The Last Hurrah*) had moved quickly to centralize power and destroy the old ward system, and while Honey Fitz ran for the House of Representatives again in an election that was disputed and saw him removed when voter fraud was uncovered, P.J. retired to Winthrop as an elder statesman.

In one respect Fitzgerald's loss was his son-in-law's gain. Eddie Moore had been Fitzie's secretary and confidential assistant during the years in City Hall. Slightly older than Joe and Rose, Mary and Eddie Moore, who had no children of their own, would become trusted friends of the family over the years—Mary as Rose's confidante and unfailing support, Eddie as Joe's trusted, efficient personal assistant.

Prohibition became law in 1920, and during the thirteen years of the noble experiment, Joe made money bootlegging, starting by taking his father's business underground. Harvard classmates would tell Richard Whalen, Joe's biographer, that Kennedy supplied all the liquor for his class's various reunions, and years later a number of mafia bosses would testify to doing business with Joe. Former Luciano crime family boss Frank

Costello would tell author Peter Maas he had a bitter falling out with Kennedy before the repeal of Prohibition in 1933. "I helped Joe Kennedy get rich," Costello told Maas, a quote that Cosa Nostra leader Joseph Bonanno repeated in his 1983 autobiography, *A Man of Honor.* Sam Giancana, boss of the Chicago syndicate, would call Joe "one of the biggest crooks who ever lived," while New York gangster Meyer Lansky would tell how some of his "East Side boys" had once tried to hijack a shipment of whiskey that Kennedy and others had financed, only to be stopped by the Boston Irish guards of a small truck convoy.

If Eddie Moore was Joe's shadow, stand-in, and all-around aide-de-camp, Ted O'Leary, a heavy-set, pink-faced former bouncer, took care of the liquor business. Together with Derr, the pigeon-toed wizard with figures who had first worked for Joe at Fore River, and Charles (Pat) Sullivan, they formed the Joe Kennedy inner circle and were called the four horsemen.

Stock manipulation, not bootlegging, brought Joe in contact with his first real big money. The stock market in the 1920s was a primeval forest, and Joe's first experience in the market was a disaster. On a tip, he bought a stock at 160, only to see it promptly drop to 80. The lesson made him coin the adage: "If you have enough inside information and unlimited credit, you are sure to go broke."

Inside information, nevertheless, was what made him rich. Not long after Joe joined Hayden, Stone and Company, Galen told him he had quietly sold Pond Creek Coal to Henry Ford, who planned to fit the acquisition into his growing automobile empire. Never afraid to go out on a limb, Joe borrowed all the money he could and bought 15,000 Pond Creek shares at $16 a share. When news of Ford's buyout hit the papers, Joe sold out at $45, making $435,000 in profits which, after repayment of his $225,000 loan, netted him $210,000.

The way to make money in this free-for-all market was to create pools and spreads, forms of trading that, with some measure of irony, Joe would outlaw when President Roosevelt made him chairman of the newly created Securities and Exchange Commission in 1932.

As a Wall Street "plunger" in the early 1920s, Joe specialized in setting up pools with such partners as Harry Sinclair and Bernard ("Sell'em Ben") Smith. The tactic consisted of inflating cheap stocks through rumors and erratic but well-publicized buying and selling until the action attracted unwary outsiders. When the price of such a "churned" stock hit the pool operators' aimed-for-price, they dumped it, took their profits, and left the suckers they had attracted high and dry.

The first pool Joe managed at Hayden, Stone churned the Todd Shipyards stock to a feverish value, and when the Wall Street habitués began buying, he and his fellow pool members dumped Todd, making huge profits and leaving thousands of investors losing their shirts. Joe's reputation soon had Walter Howey, a top Hearst newspaper executive, calling on him to help stabilize the stock of the Yellow Cab Company, in which Howey had a large interest. Joe called in John Hertz, the president of Yellow Cab, and outlined a program to support the stock, saying he would need five million dollars for the operation. Hertz agreed to raise the money.

Joe went to New York where, suffering from one of his recurring attacks of ulcers, he checked into the Waldorf-Astoria and did the rest on the phone. After he learned that the Yellow Cab stock was being driven down by a brokerage firm, he started putting in anonymous buy orders through agents all over the country. His action was able to halt the decline of the stock so quickly that he didn't have to dip into the five million dollars he had asked Hertz to raise to support the operation.

Wall Street considered Kennedy something of a mystery. He never appeared on the market, only operated through others. "He moved in the intense, secretive circle of operators in the wildest stock market in history, with routine plots and pools, inside information and wild guesses," *Fortune* magazine would recall in 1957.

It was a tricky market. The portly Galen Stone suffered sharp reverses. His income in 1919 had been so huge that his tax bill was $1.5 million; in 1920, his losses were so huge that he had no taxable income. The once supreme optimist Schwab believed peace had brought about an economic slowdown, and he advised against stock investments. But Kennedy was smelling the rising breeze of Wall Street. Farmers were suffering, but Boston was doing well in shipbuilding, textiles, and shoe manufacturing. Even more exciting were the new industries: automobiles, radio, telephone, electric refrigerators, phonographs. Women were taking up smoking, and cigarette production was doubling.

When asked what her husband did, Rose airily answered, "Business." Kathleen had arrived in 1920, and Eunice, named after Rose's sister, followed in 1921, the first child born in the twelve-room house Joe bought on Naples Road in the more fashionable part of Brookline. On Sundays, Joe would pile the five children into his Ford sedan and drive out to visit his parents, sometimes leaving Rose behind for a rare moment of rest. Seeing them all troop into her kitchen, Mary would shake her head: "Good Lord, Joe, one of these days you'll need a bus!" After lunch on days when the weather was good, Joe would walk with his father on the beach, gesturing, explaining. On the way home Joe would sometimes drive by the old Meridian Street house where he had been born and park and sit for a minute of silence.

Mary was diagnosed as suffering from inoperable stomach cancer in 1923. She didn't want to die in a hospital, and P.J. took her to the seaside at Sagamore, on the Cape Cod Bay. Joe and Rose came down, bringing Joe Jr., John—whom everyone called Jack—Rosemary, Kathleen, and two-year-old Eunice for a last family visit. In early summer, Joe's mother was readmitted to the hospital. After she died, P.J. took his two daughters to Europe. Eventually he moved in with Margaret and her husband.

Joe's sandy hair was thinning, and although still athletic, he was beginning to fill out. His big grin retained its boyishness, but the children were learning to fear "Daddy's look." Physical punishment was never his style. Instead, he had a way of putting his glasses down and giving the nine-year-old Joe Jr. or the seven-year-old John an icy blue stare that stripped them to the soul. Rosemary was going on six, and it was becoming apparent that she was retarded. She was slow in everything, and there were things she seemed unable to learn. Both four-year-old Kathleen and three-year-old Eunice were delightful toddlers. Eunice, her mother noticed, was attentive and helpful to Rosemary. Kathleen, whose family name was Kick, was close to Jack.

Joe was deeply involved in the Yellow Cab stock rescue and was holed up in the Waldorf-Astoria in New York with a ticker tape and a battery of phones when Rose bore him another daughter, Patricia, in 1924. The girl was a month old before he got back to Boston and saw her for the first time.

As the tribe increased, so did the fortune. The Yellow Cab deal made Joe a millionaire a few months after his thirty-fifth birthday. He became an expert at market maneuvers that others considered shady and even illicit. He was blunt and profane. Rumors of illegal dealings and even ties to the criminal world added a piquant touch to his reputation and made him seem all the more romantic, Gatsbyesque.

He was no rival to such sharpies as Jess Livermore and William C. Danforth, both products of Boston brokerage houses. But when he played golf with Danforth he kept his ears and eyes open for tips and indiscretions. Livermore had emerged from the Panic of 1907 with short-selling profits of three million dollars, and from hidden offices near Wall Street equipped with a standard-sized quotation board, thirty telephones, and statisticians, he sometimes racked up million-dollar profits on a single deal. Joe made friends easily, but confided in few people himself. In the phrase of one fascinated observer, Joe was "an angle shooter who liked to move around the table." The billiard metaphor would stick, as friends, speculators, and eventually journalists would describe his career as consisting of adroitly executed carom shots. Like a pool hall hustler, his financial acumen relied on shooting the angles rather than trying to hit anything straight on, constantly shifting his own position. While he might join other lone wolves in buying blocks of an inactive stock, creating the appearance of a boom until less sophisticated investors bid up the action, he was never responsible to anyone other than himself. Get in and get out fast was his operational motto, expressed in his often-quoted corollary: "Only a fool holds out for the top dollar."

He was often away from home for long periods, living with Eddie Moore and other cronies in a hotel somewhere, involved in unspecified deals. He admired Galen Stone for his independence, and after Stone gave up his partnership and retired at the end of 1922, he decided to strike out on his own. He stayed at Hayden, Stone and Company's 87 Milk Street address, but moved into a separate office. The name on the office door was simple: Joseph P. Kennedy, Banker.

He remembered in detail who had knocked him on the way up. One who took it on the chin was his father-in-law. Fitzie would keep running for office (the last time in 1942 when he was seventy-nine and lost the Democratic primary for the U.S. Senate), but would never again be elected. The former mayor sold his home in Dorchester and moved into a suite in the Bellevue Hotel, spending time at the zoo and at Red Sox baseball games, and becoming a character around Boston. When he went visiting in Brookline, he would peer in the screened back porch to see if "Big Joe" were home before knocking. Joe teased Rose about the time when he had not been good enough to marry her. "Were you lying when you said your father didn't like me?" he asked. "I met him today, and he told me what a helluva fellow I am."

Ascending Star

In 1924, Hollywood movies were made on sets built on stages and back lots. Newfangled rear projection and process-screen photography even enabled characters to sit or stand in front of a screen and appear to be anywhere in the world. To go overseas to make a picture was unheard of. Except for the brightest star in the firmament.

With the possible exception of Mary Pickford, who never managed the transition from the girlish image that had made her "America's sweetheart" to full screen womanhood, Gloria Swanson was the most popular female celebrity in the movie-crazed mid-1920s. When, in September 1924, she sailed to Europe to make *Madame Sans Gêne,* she was twenty-five, had starred in thirty movies—six in a row with De Mille—and her leading men had included the great heartthrobs from Wallace Reid to Rudolph Valentino.

Zukor and Lasky were thrilled with the fanfare that attended Gloria's dockside departure in New York, the press party that took up two railway cars on her Cherbourg-to-Paris boat train, and the mob scene that accompanied her limousine's progress from the Gare St. Lazare to the Hotel

Crillon on the Place de la Concorde. The first big Franco-American coproduction was a success foretold.

Adolphe Osso, the energetic Famous Players–Lasky chief in Europe, immediately realized that La Swanson could not get around Paris anonymously, that the first order of things was to find a translator-escort for her. René Hubert, a young Swiss graduate of the Paris Ecole des Beaux Arts who would design Gloria's wardrobe, and André Daven, the *Aurore* film critic whose enthusiastic reporting had softened establishment opposition to an American playing a role so utterly and significantly French, said they knew exactly the person she needed.

A planned meeting with director Leonce Perret—and his wife—added to the urgency of finding a socially adept translator. Perret was a dark, svelte man of forty-five who had made movies since 1908 and was known for his use of backlighting and other dramatic effects, even in natural settings. A former actor, he had worked for Pathé in Hollywood during the war, shooting mannered comedies and patriotic propaganda, and since his return to France had directed a pair of romantic costume films. Madame Perret was a former actress, a tiny, plump, and corseted person who had seen better days and was quick to let Gloria know she had once been the mistress of a nobleman. "She insisted on acting as translator between us," Gloria would remember, "but her contribution consisted mainly of henpecking him and flattering me."

The next morning, however, Hubert and Daven showed up with an elegant young aristocrat, handsome and reserved, with slicked-back hair, pencil-thin mustache, and winning blue eyes. His name was James Henri Le Bailly de la Falaise, Marquis de la Coudraye. He spoke English well enough to be witty in it. "Americans," he said, "generally call me 'Hank.' "

She wanted to know more. His great-grandfather had died on the guillotine during the French Revolution. His father, a soldier and an instructor at the St. Cyr Military Academy (France's West Point), had married the daughter of Richard Hennessy, head of the cognac distillers, meaning Henri was of Irish ancestry on his mother's side. The French ancestral home was a manor in St. Florent des Bois on the Vendée river in a lost corner of Brittany. His means of existence was obscure. He would, however, be available, full time, for the two months *Madame Sans Gêne* was being filmed. She hired him.

Immediately, he sat down, dialed the hotel operator, and began straightening out dozens of aggravating details. "Before I knew it, he had become indispensable," she would recall. "He picked me up and drove me to the studio in Joinville when we were shooting there, he knew how to dismiss the press politely when I was tired, and he delighted in showing me the Paris tourists never see. He chummed with the best of Paris society. His friend

Bob turned out to be a baron, and his friend Paul was a count. Henri knew the quickest way through bureaucratic channels was often to send flowers to this minister's wife or a small gift to that one's mistress, and he could overcome the toughest obstacles with charm and grace, leaving everybody involved feeling he or she had performed the one act that made everything else fall into place."

It was the right year to be an American in Paris. The Revue Nègre was knocking Parisians out with waves of energy and noise that engulfed audiences from the floodlights. Fred and Adele Astaire were showing them how to dance, while the onrushing literati set sat at the Dôme debating how lost their generation was. The making of *Madame Sans Gêne* created excitement among the younger set of expatriates, and Gloria was as anxious as any of them to prove that not every Yank, as Stephen Longstreet put it, was a goddamn Babbitt, Bible-belt boob, or mere wowser. Gloria found the atmosphere exciting and enchanting and said she wanted to live forever in this font of art, flowers, and fashion. When they weren't filming, it was Sherry's or the Tienda Oyster Bar for lunch, a midnight supper at Le Perroquet in the rue de Clichy, Harry's Bar around the corner from the Ritz for after-hour music, or a last drink with friends at Jimmy's. Her name opened doors, and there was fun at Jean Cocteau's little gatherings where opium was smoked and Forrest Halsey, Gloria's gay screenwriter, met interesting young men. While Hubert created gorgeous clothes for the film, Gloria quickly adapted the Coco Chanel silhouette off-screen. Scarves tied stiffly, in airplane bows like propellers, were the thing, *Vogue* decreed.

Victorien Sardou's 1893 comedy—*Madame Sans Gêne* was to be his one lasting success*—was based on the true story of Catherine Hubscher, an illiterate Alsatian laundress who married François Lefebvre, a miller's son who entered the French guards at eighteen. The storming of the Bastille favored François's military career, as it did that of another young colonel, Napoleon Bonaparte. Lefebvre's command of the ragged armies that defeated the Austrians at Fleurus in 1794 was his finest hour, and when Napoleon crowned himself emperor, he made Lefebvre a marshal and gave him the title Duke of Danzig. The Lefebvres cut quite a figure at court, Catherine earning the nickname "Madame Sans Gêne" for her sharp tongue and overfamiliarity.

Perret cast Charles de Rochefort, who had acted both in America and France, as Napoleon, and the grande dame of French cinema, Suzanne Bianchetti, as Napoleon's second wife, Marie-Louise. Warwick Ward, an English actor, played the Austrian diplomat—and Marie-Louise's lover—

*The Perret screen version was the third of six film adaptations. The latest one, made in 1961, starred Sophia Loren.

Adam Neipperg. Gloria had only praise for Perret's direction and for the Empire wardrobe Hubert created for her, including an ermine mantle that had Paramount's accounting department in a fit. Scenes of Catherine's early life as a laundress were filmed in the drafty Joinville studio, but thanks to Henri's diplomacy and the financial weight of this transatlantic coproduction, both interiors and exteriors of the chateaus at Compiègne and Fontainebleau were filmed. Bianchetti awoke in the bed where a succession of French queens had slept, and Madame Sans Gêne's presentation to Napoleon was filmed in the Salle Henri II in Fontainebleau. At each of the major locations, officials greeted the film company, and, each time, Henri primed Gloria with all the proper responses and right gestures. *"Vous n'avez qu'à demander au Marquis de la Falaise de la Coudraye,"* was the mouthful Gloria learned. It meant that all anyone had to do was ask the marquis, and the sentence allowed her to spend a lovely autumn in France without confronting the pricklier side of the Gallic psyche.

During a short hiatus between exterior shots and studio filming in Joinville, Osso asked Gloria to attend, with a few other members of the cast, a Paramount festival of her movies in Brussels. She had never visited Belgium and said yes to a tour that would include appearances at the U.S. embassy, an orphanage, and a war veterans' hospital. In Brussels, the line of limousines snaked past bunting-draped cinemas showing Gloria Swanson pictures. Henri was with her in the first automobile and between the kisses she blew to the crowd, he asked her how long her life had been like this.

"Too long," she said with a truthfulness that surprised her. "I was nineteen when I made my first real big picture." She began to tell the story of her life, backward. To her amazement, Henri compared his own experiences to hers. The year she had made *Don't Change Your Husband* for De Mille he had received the Croix de Guerre for bravery in battle. While Albert Parker and she had made *Wife or Country* at Triangle, Henri had been at a field hospital in Flanders. When she had made slapstick two-reelers for Essanay, he had been in the trenches. Sixteen when the war broke out, he had to wait one year before his mother gave him permission to join up. As the son of an officer, he was selected for the cavalry. One of the first dead he saw at the front was his cousin Raymond Hennessy. Wounded at the Somme, Henri volunteered for duty in a commando unit and slogged through 1917 in Flanders and northern Italy. On furlough in Paris in 1918 he fell in love with Alice Cocea, the Romanian star of a popular operetta.

Gloria could imagine him at twenty, in uniform at the Opéra Comique. On his next furlough, he found the beautiful Alice in the arms of a rich older man and tried to commit suicide. He took his revenge on his next leave by courting Alice's costar.

He was embarrassed by his own candor. When they passed a poster showing Gloria and Rudolph Valentino in an ardent embrace, she asked if he had seen *Beyond the Rocks.* No, he hadn't. In fact, he admitted, he had never seen any of her pictures. He had only seen three movies in his life, all while he had been in the army.

"Is that true?" she asked.

"Perfectly. I wouldn't lie to you."

"Why not?"

Their eyes met. In a lighter tone, he said, "Because you're my boss, *ma patronne.*"

The war veterans knew her pictures. They had movie nights at the hospital. Gloria couldn't help noticing how Henri was very much the soldier, the comrade among the sick and mutilated men. When the two of them began to talk again on the last night of the Brussels visit, she wanted to know more about his war experiences. He described the occasional agreed-upon truces, during which Germans and French stopped shooting, crawled out of their trenches, and swam together in the same river, before going back to murdering each other again. "That's what war movies should be about," he mused, "about the folly of war experience. Not about spies and patriotism."

They were in a nightclub with the rest of the Paramount party. Henri asked Gloria to dance. Later, they all drifted back to their hotel and sat at the bar. One by one, the others said good night and went up to their rooms. Henri paid the bar tab without a word, then seemed on the verge of saying something, but checked himself. When he finally spoke, he said, "I am sorry I have nothing to offer you, Gloria."

"Such as?" she whispered.

"Money. I have none. I'm sorry."

They sat a while longer, then took the art deco elevator to her suite.

December 1924, Gloria would write in her autobiography, "was the happiest month of my life." Henri was one year older than she; he had no faults that she could find; he was not in pictures, he didn't drink, and he didn't drag a string of failed marriages behind him. Falling in love while filming the remaining interiors out of public view at Joinville was sweet irony for her. *Madame Sans Gêne* had started as a rebellion against the studio system, as her revenge for Paramount's betrayal when her second husband had sued her for divorce and blackmailed her.

She had met Herbert Somborn after *Why Change Your Wife?* had made her and Bebe Daniels De Mille's new sensations in 1920. Wrapped and unwrapped in a million dollars' worth of lace lingerie, Swanson and Daniels fought like tigresses over a hapless Tom Meighan in this personal and autobiographical social comedy (perversely, C.B. had told Jeanie Macpherson to write scenes reflecting her loathing of Julie Faye). *Why Change Your Wife?* advised against divorce, in long and exhorting titles, but showed that a wife shouldn't put too much of a leash on her husband.

On a spring furlough, Joe Swanson came for a visit, and Gloria took him and Bea La Plante to dinner at the Alexandria Hotel in downtown Los Angeles, the place to be seen if one was anybody in the picture business. Gloria had arranged for the Alexandria to send a car for them. When they entered the dining room, the maître d' smartly sprang into action. "Your table is ready, Captain Swanson."

Because her father was uncomfortable with any attention and afraid he might embarrass his daughter if any film people came to the table, she was determined not to speak to anyone. They had hardly ordered, however, before a waiter arrived with a card that read, Equity Pictures Corporation; Herbert K. Somborn, President.

Gloria felt terribly guilty for having turned Bea into her answering service, private secretary, and general drudge, so when Bea picked up the card and guessed Herbert K. Somborn was from New York, where, in her opinion, all really important people in films were from, Gloria decided to let the man come over. "He might get you a part in something, Bea."

Somborn turned out to be an undistinguished New Yorker of forty with a round face, blue eyes, and large arched nose. He announced that he had just been on the telephone with Clara Kimball Young and had told her Miss Swanson was here. "She insisted I tell you how much she enjoyed you in *Don't Change Your Husband.*" He smiled.

A regal beauty, famous for her yearning eyes and her portrayal of Anne Boleyn in *Cardinal Wolsey* in 1912, Clara Kimball Young was a household name even Captain Swanson knew. Addressing Gloria, Somborn said, "Miss Young told me if I didn't bring you out for dinner at her home one evening soon, she would never speak to me again. I couldn't afford that, which is why I took the liberty of sending over my card."

Captain Swanson invited the president of Equity Pictures to join them for a drink. Gloria tried to interest Somborn in Bea, telling him her friend had been in several films with Sessue Hayakawa. He listened with polite interest. Equity Pictures, he explained, had no studio. It was a distribution company, distributing Clara Kimball Young's films. He was in California to arrange the release of her newest, *Eyes of Youth*. The director was Al Parker. Gloria mentioned she had worked with Parker at Triangle but said nothing about Wally punching the director in the nose. The costar was a young Italian dancer named Rudolph Valentino. Nobody seemed to have heard of him, but everybody associated with *Eyes of Youth* thought he was very good. "We hope to use him again in a new picture called *Silk Husbands, Calico Wives.* Wonderful title, isn't it?"

Finishing his drink, Somborn stood up and asked Gloria what he should tell Miss Young.

"Tell her I'd be honored," she answered. "But Sunday is my only day off."

He was sure that would be fine.

Later, Gloria danced with her father. She kidded him, saying everybody was wondering who the officer she was dating was. He smiled and asked who Somborn was. She had no idea.

"Is he important?"

"I guess so. Why?"

"I was just wondering if he lived with Clara Kimball Young, that's all."

Gloria laughed. "One week out here and you've started gossiping. You'll be believing everything they say about *me* next."

"They don't say anything bad, do they?"

"They just say I'm going to marry a millionaire. Would you like that?"

"I don't know. It's hard to imagine that much money. How much was that other fellow worth?"

"Herbert Somborn? I have no idea."

"No, I mean that fellow Addie married. Burns."

"Oh, Daddy."

Gloria's millionaire suitor was Craney Gartz. She didn't present him to her father for fear that even if she could persuade Craney to stay off the subjects of "free love" and Bolshevism, his superiority would intimidate Dad. But two nights after she drove her father to Fort MacArthur, she was having dinner with Craney at the Pasadena Country Club, where more people recognized him than her. Their cat-and-mouse pursuit of each other was blowing as hot and cold as before. Gloria's success made Craney realize that in her devotion to her work and to De Mille he had formidable rivals. She resisted his bantering suggestions that they live together. He insisted he loved her. She said she loved him, too. Instead of trying to take her to bed, she told him, he should perhaps ask her to marry him.

"Would you?" he'd ask.

"I don't know. Would you ask?"

"I don't know. You know I hate the whole idea. Everybody I know is miserable because they're bound into marriage."

Gloria was convinced he was afraid she wanted to marry him for his money. He was sure she wanted matrimonial respectability so she could pick up her film career should things not work out between them.

Their sparring never got any further. She recognized they both feared each other's lack of trust. After a roller-coaster evening with Craney, a dinner date with Herbert Somborn was an oasis of calm. Herbert never raised his voice, was considerate, and invited Bea along to a private screening of *Eyes of Youth.* He seemed to know everything about Gloria, including her short marriage to Wally Beery.

Their first dinner with Clara Kimball Young had been an eye-opener for Gloria. Not only was their hostess a gracious, amusing woman, and her candle-lit dinner for four exquisite; she, Herbert, and Harry Garson, the general manager of Equity Pictures, talked about movies on a level Gloria had never heard before. Clara's story paralleled Gloria's insofar as marriage was concerned. James Young and Clara Kimball, soon to be his bride, had come from a Salt Lake City stock company to appear in Vitagraph pictures, and before long both were making $1,000 a week. As with Gloria and Wally, problems had started when Young's ascent didn't match his wife's. Clara's breakthrough picture had been *My Official Wife* in 1914, in which Leon Trotsky had been an extra. Success had brought her offers from Vitagraph's rivals, and she had accepted a contract from World Films, managed by the ambitious Lewis Selznick, who had made her a star in *Trilby, Camille,* and *The Common Law,* sophisticated pictures dealing with feminine martyrdom. Her women admirers were legion, and here she was talking distribution deals, stock issues, mortgages, injunctions, and powers of attorney. The names of Selznick and Patrick Powers came up several times. When Herbert mentioned that Powers saw motion pictures as a smarter form of advertising than newspapers, magazines, and billboards because movies could *show* cars, clothes, curling irons, whatever, the hostess turned toward Gloria and said "He's absolutely right. Don't you think so, Miss Swanson?"

Harry Garson was a silver-haired former owner of the Broadway Strand Theater in Detroit. He was to direct Clara in her next picture. While taking Gloria home, Herbert explained to her that Clara would soon be free. Her husband was finally suing her for divorce.

Gloria went out five times with Somborn, enjoying his company and thoughtful attention. When, on their sixth date, he surprised her with a jade necklace, she realized this man who was almost double her own age was seriously courting her.

Craney barged into her dressing room a few days after Herbert had proposed to her. Brandishing a copy of the *Los Angeles Times,* he began furiously to read a society item saying Gloria Swanson was about to marry Herbert Somborn, "a wealthy Pasadenan." The reporter had mixed up her two suitors—Craney was the wealthy man from Pasadena—but when Craney angrily asked her to tell him it wasn't true, she said Herbert Somborn had asked her to marry him but that she had not decided whether to accept.

"You can't marry him," Craney yelled. "He's a *Jew!*"

Gloria wasn't a good enough actress, she would remember, to pretend she knew. She wasn't sure she had any prejudices against Jews—the picture business was certainly full of them. Adolph Zukor was a Hungarian Jew; Carl Laemmle, a German Jew; Louis B. Mayer and Samuel Goldwyn (né Goldfisch) had been born in Russia and Poland, respectively; and the Warner brothers were the first-generation American children of Polish-Jewish immigrants. That had never bothered Gloria. What she couldn't figure out was whether Craney's outburst was a new facet of his snobbery or of his jealousy.

They had a stormy face-off during which he outlined a financial arrangement—if she lived with him, he would make her his heir should anything happen to him on his planned trip to the new Soviet Union—and she told him the only thing he wasn't offering was what she wanted most—marriage. She almost willed him to drag her off to bed, where they could resolve their argument, but at the crucial moment he didn't make the right move. On the rebound, she promised Herbert she would marry him in a month's time, when her divorce became final. She realized that she hardly knew this rather plain Jewish bachelor who was old enough to be her father, but also that she felt safe with him.

To celebrate, Herbert took her to the glitziest nightclub in town. He ordered champagne, by name and year, making him the most cultivated man she had ever met beside De Mille. Before they had a second sip, a friend of Herbert's came to the table, bantered for a moment with Herbert, and invited Gloria to dance. A man in his late twenties with granny glasses and curly, sandy-colored hair, he was astonished when, on the dance floor, she said she didn't know who he was.

"Marshall Neilan," he introduced himself. "Everybody calls me Mickey."

Totally forgotton by posterity, the meteoric Neilan was, in the late 1910s and early 1920s, the Hollywood wonder boy and highest-paid director of an unbroken string of box-office hits. He squandered the millions he made with an abandon that was often spectacular, sometimes arrogant, and always ruinous. An orphan with a Charles Dickens childhood, he had become Griffith's chauffeur. Griffith urged the tall, handsome, and gifted Mickey to try the movies and helped him get an acting job at the Kalem Studios in Santa Monica. Allan Dwan hired him next and taught him to write scripts. By 1914 Mickey had charmed Kalem officials into letting him direct in their new Glendale studio; he was all of twenty-two. Mary Pickford made him her leading man before he directed her in her greatest hit, *Rebecca of Sunnybrook Farm;* in *Stella Maris,* a brilliant production in which she played both a pathetic Cockney girl and a rich paralytic; and in her hilarious

Daddy Long Legs. He lived in a beautiful home—he started the fad of having Oriental houseboys as servants—and entertained lavishly, often hauling friends and cronies to Tijuana, Mexico, or Catalina Island. He always knew where the best party was, and everybody from Zasu Pitts to William Randolph Hearst adored him.

As he danced, he told Gloria he would be her future husband. She had just agreed to marry Herbert, she said, laughing. He said that was all right. He was still married himself. "You and I are both probably going to be married a number of times. I just want my name on your list." Before she could think of a snappy answer, they were back at the table. "She's wonderful, Herbert," he said, and walked smartly away.

The dashing Mickey had directed Clara Kimball Young for Harry Garson a year earlier, Herbert told her. A propaganda film called *The Unpardonable Sin,* the picture also featured Blanche Sweet and Wally Beery as a brutal Prussian officer. Financial difficulties had delayed production, and by the time *The Unpardonable Sin* was finished the war was over. Exhibitors felt audiences were tired of war pictures. The woman Mickey was married to was the beautiful Gertrude Bambrick, the costar in *The Billionaire.* The two had eloped and married in Hoboken, New Jersey, with Dorothy Gish as the bridesmaid.

Before starting her fifth picture with De Mille, Gloria had the Christmas–New Year's season off. In December 1919 she married Herbert in a civil ceremony held in a suite at the Alexandria Hotel. In her memoirs Gloria would claim that if the presiding judge and witnesses were Herbert's friends, it was because she knew her parents would be miserable in each other's presence and she felt awkward having only Bea. In reality, her friends, and possibly Addie and her father as well, found Herbert undistinguished. "He looked like a shoe salesman," Lasky, Jr., would remember. "I don't know what she saw in him." The general speculation at the studio was that she must have married him for his money.

When the next morning's newspapers all announced the newlyweds were in San Francisco, Gloria and Herbert decided to stay right where they were. They notified the hotel that they would keep the suite until further notice, hung a DO NOT DISTURB sign on the door, and spent the next two weeks seeing virtually nobody except hotel personnel.

"It was heaven," she would remember. "Neither of us had had a real vacation in years. I was never bored for a minute, and Herbert turned out to be the most generous and considerate man in the world. On Christmas morning we sat propped up in bed opening stacks of gifts and sipping champagne. On New Year's Eve we went downstairs at midnight and danced until 3." In January she went back to work for De Mille—*Something to Think About,* another Jeanie Macpherson concoction, was about two men who fought for Gloria's affection—and Herbert went to New York.

For Gloria, the marriage became a cram course in economics and contract law. Persistent long-distance phone calls during the Alexandria suite honeymoon had forced Herbert to admit he was, momentarily, in some difficulty. For different reasons, Selznick and Powers had turned against Equity Pictures. Selznick, who was worth sixty million dollars, lived in a seventeen-room Park Avenue apartment, and made fifty films a year, was in a new scrap with his rivals. To make sure they rented all their movies, regardless of quality, film companies resorted to "block booking." In order to get pictures with big box-office stars, theater owners had to accept a block of less profitable movies. Now, Selznick was breaking away from the practice and offering the new Clara Kimball Young features separately at considerably higher rentals. That made everybody else's less salable celluloid suffer, and Selznick's relations with his rivals were at a low point. Exhibitors didn't want to be caught in any high-power crossfire and simply refused to book *Eyes of Youth.*

Herbert didn't agree with Selznick's tactic. Although the legal bills would be enormous, he planned to sue. What made matters worse was that Powers was withholding funds for *The Forbidden Woman,* the new Clara Kimball Young picture, because Harry Garson was over budget.

Herbert's patience in explaining the intricacies of block booking made Gloria order the hotel chauffeur to drive her to the Harper Avenue house to pick up her own contracts.

There were two of them. One had expired with the making of *Don't Change Your Husband,* but with an option clause giving Famous Players–Lasky the right to continue the use of her services. The second, her current contract, also had an option allowing Paramount to renew it until 1922 with only a very small increase in her $200-a-week salary.

Herbert read everything in concentrated silence. When he was through he spat out the names of Zukor and Lasky. "We got to get you out of the hands of these European Jews!"

She was stunned. Under Herbert's grilling, she admitted she had not had a lawyer look over the contracts. But De Mille's lawyer had. She became defensive about De Mille, saying that she trusted him completely, that she would sign anything he asked her to sign. Herbert explained that Equity Pictures paid Clara Kimball Young $25,000 plus a share of the profits for each film, even though her pictures made much less money than Gloria Swanson's movies.

"But they're not *my* pictures," Gloria cried. "They're Mr. De Mille's pictures."

"Then why are theater owners all over the country putting your name up on the marquee?" Herbert rifled through a Los Angeles newspaper and found the ad for *Male and Female*. Gloria Swanson's name was on top, above Tommy Meighan's, ahead of Cecil B. De Mille's. "They have sewed you up for no money at all! And there's no limit on the number of pictures you have to make for them. They're telling you they're doing you a favor letting you be in De Mille's pictures for $200 a week!"

In her case, he explained, block booking meant that if theater owners wanted four Swanson pictures a year, they'd have to take twenty-five or thirty other pictures, sight unseen. Everybody was cashing in on her.

She should be working with Mickey Neilan, Herbert said. In fact, if she were free, Pat Powers would surely bankroll such a powerful star-director combination. Before Herbert left for Chicago and New York, he had a lawyer express his legal opinion on her contracts. They were unenforceable in a court of law, the lawyer said in a written opinion, because the option clauses were binding on Gloria but not on the Famous Players–Lasky company. She was still in the company's thrall for the rest of the year, "but were Miss Swanson to leave their employ after January 1, 1921, the company would never be able to get an injunction against her." Herbert was elated. That gave them a year to look for a perfect combination of story material and director to come up with an independent production as classy as anything Clara Kimball Young could produce.

Gloria finished shooting early one afternoon after Herbert's inconclusive business trip east and was lying down for a nap when the hotel manager phoned to say their bill was overdue. She was sure it had slipped her husband's mind, she answered. The manager had already mentioned the bill twice to Mr. Somborn. In fact, he said, if the more than $3,000 they owed wasn't paid by the end of the week, the Alexandria would have to cut off their credit. Mortified, Gloria confronted Herbert when he came in. Equity Pictures, he admitted, was in difficulties, temporarily. Now that she brought up the question, he would need a few thousand dollars to tide him over. The next day she had him find a modest apartment, took out all the money she had in the bank, and paid the Alexandria so they could leave without a scandal.

Like couples in one of the melodramas Macpherson wrote, De Mille directed, and Gloria starred in, the Somborns confronted their mutual delusions in a modest apartment on Yucca and Wilcox Streets on the northern edge of Hollywood as Gloria discovered she was pregnant.

Each had thought the other rich. In marrying the president of Equity Pictures, Gloria had thought she had married security if not wealth. Herbert was by no means destitute, but his worth was on paper. He had counted on his young actress wife to bring in at least a large salary to see him through temporary volatility while he consolidated his operations. He was proud and happy when she told him she was expecting a baby in October and probably wouldn't be able to work after De Mille wrapped *Something to Think About.* He also realized the unborn child could be used in the contractual fight with the studio.

The trick worked—beyond their wildest expectations. But it set them on a collision course over who was in charge of her career. Gloria made an appointment with Lasky and, primed by Herbert, announced that she was expecting a baby, that motherhood was more important to her than making another picture, that, in fact, she probably wouldn't be able to start working again until January, and that her husband's lawyer believed her contract would by then be null and void. Lasky peered at her over his rimless pince-nez, glowered when she mentioned her husband and his lawyer, cajoled her by saying she was a star, and tried to scare her into submission by saying her box-office power would slump if she stayed off the screen for a year.

Although she didn't work for the rest of her pregnancy, Lasky kept her on salary. She was huge in her seventh month, so unbecoming, she thought, that she decided not to attend the funeral of her stepfather, Matthew Burns. A new contract was worked out. Starting January 1, 1921, she would make five pictures a year for two years for which Famous Players–Lasky would pay her $2,500 a week. After that the studio could renew for three more years paying her $5,000 a week. To protect its investment, the company would choose her directors and story material. De Mille, she was told, had agreed to get his assistant, Sam Wood, to direct her. In reality, the Philadelphia-born Wood was already the specialist in directing pictures tailored for stars whose careers had been largely shaped by De Mille.

The birth was difficult. Gloria wanted to have the baby at home, and the wife of Marshall Neilan's assistant director acted as midwife until, twenty hours into labor, Gloria gave in to Herbert's pleas to let him call a doctor. It was a girl.

Born October 6, 1920, Gloria Somborn's first visitor was C.B. himself, bringing a string of pearls for the week-old baby. When the new mother thanked him, De Mille said he had a favor to ask. Before starting her new contract, would she make one last picture for him? "Oh, Mr. De Mille, you know I'd rather do that than anything."

Herbert was furious. Lasky and De Mille were not going to get another film out of her for next to nothing. Gloria, in turn, got angry. She owed everything to De Mille. If Mr. De Mille wanted another picture out of her for next to nothing, he was going to get it.

The picture was *The Affairs of Anatol,* a toned-down Jeanie Macpherson adaptation of Arthur Schnitzler's amoral 1893 play *Anatol.* What made *The Affairs of Anatol* De Mille's most sophisticated and dazzling silent comedy was Paul Iribe's set decorations. Lasky had discovered the French designer and forced De Mille to use him. Despite long wranglings during the film, De Mille embraced Iribe in gratitude when he saw the finished film. Like a series of Beardsley illustrations to Oscar Wilde, the art nouveau ambiance created by the suave and elegant designer was so intoxicating that art critics discussed *The Affairs of Anatol* in serious journals.

Wallace Reid, a blue-eyed, chestnut-haired, six-foot charmpot who was fast becoming the newest matinee idol and made $2,000 a week, played the title-role philanderer, a man entangled in successive love affairs, witty in his melancholic disillusion and fascinated with his own erotic addiction. Macpherson and C.B. changed the story to include a loving wife to whom Anatol returns when his mistress cheats on him with an elegant elder roué and who is there in the fade-out. When De Mille told Gloria she could have any part, she chose the role of the wife. Bebe Daniels played "the wickedest woman in New York."

A walk-on was created for a fifty-six-year-old Englishwoman who was to have a tonic influence on Gloria and help her set higher goals for herself.

Lasky's scouting trip to England in 1920 to find distinguished authors to write "famous plays for famous players" had not lured too many literary lights, although Famous Players–Lasky publicity mentioned H. G. Wells, Arnold Bennett, and Edward Knoblock as would-be screenwriters. One belles lettres lioness who had answered Lasky's summons (and $10,000-per-picture contract) was Elinor Glyn, a widowed author of sinful books, a gossip, and an intimidating presence. Boarding the *Mauretania* to New York that autumn, she noted in her diary, "It was a considerable adventure for me, a lone widow no longer young, to venture forth into this strange, utterly different world of Western America, and to attempt to master the intricacies of a new and highly technical craft, but it was just such an adventure as I have always loved." Lasky met the *Mauretania* with a chauffeured limousine, but the authoress had only one wish—to walk up Fifth Avenue. "But Miss Glyn," the vice president of Famous Players–Lasky said, "I want to drive you to your hotel." "No, Mr. Lasky, let's walk up Fifth Avenue. This is my first trip to New York." Madame Glyn, as she styled herself, had flaming red hair, tiny eyes, false eyelashes, a haughty chin, and smelled like a cathedral of incense. For her arrival in New York she was wearing a leopardskin coat and a very short skirt. Gallantly, the dapper Lasky, with his pince-nez, spats, and cane, walked the lady up the avenue pretending to notice neither the gestures that accompanied her exclamations nor the natives' stares.

Glyn's biggest best-seller had been written before 1914 and reflected a prewar world of blue-blooded aristocracy, but *Three Weeks* still thrilled

Americans with its descriptions of luxury and depravity, including mad passion consummated on a tigerskin. Her suite at the Hollywood Hotel looked like an Oriental tent, with divans, scarlet drapes, purple pillows, Buddhas, and tarot cards. She intimidated movie hostesses, and from the moment of her arrival gave interviews on the ever-popular subject: What's Wrong with Hollywood? Two women went everywhere with her. One was her secretary and personal maid, the other the creator of the wardrobe Madame Glyn dreamed up herself. Her sister was Lady Duff Gordon, the owner of the London fashion house Lucile (her brother-in-law's notoriety stemmed from his slipping into one of his wife's nightdresses in order to answer the "women and children first to the lifeboats" command during the sinking of the *Titanic*). Elinor said her role was not to follow fashion but to set it on its ear.

The first time Madame Glyn cast her eyes on the star of *The Affairs of Anatol,* she pronounced Gloria to be extraordinarily Egyptian. "You're such a tiny, dainty little thing. Your proportions are Egyptian; anyone can see that when you turn your head. You have lived there in another time. Definitely Egyptian." To mark her approval of the new mother and to help raise her fashion consciousness, Madame Glyn lent her Ann Morgan, the ravishing young English dressmaker she had brought to America with her.

Lasky decided the authoress would write the next Swanson picture. In the meantime, *The Affairs of Anatol* was physically trying for Gloria. The difficult childbirth had left her with gynecological aftereffects. One day her doctor would ask her to agree to be hospitalized for corrective surgery; on the next visit he insisted she merely take time off to rest and heal. Nursing little Gloria added to the long studio hours. Herbert's concern for her health, combined with his irritation at her making this picture at all, strained their relationship.

Run-ins with Macpherson added to Gloria's annoyance. The screen-writer made a point of attending Gloria's costume fittings and made remarks about Gloria's breast-feeding and her "plumpness." C.B. had to soothe his star.

Before Sam Wood got to shoot one foot of *The Great Moment* in the spring of 1921, the Elinor Glyn story was a presold sensation. Her tale of a titled Englishwoman falling in love with an American engineer featured a scene where the heroine is bitten on her breast by a rattlesnake and the hero, to save her life, is obliged to suck out the poison. The publicity department had a field day, reporting that fearful theater owners wanted the snakebite moved to the wrist, but that Madame Glyn was holding out for the bosom, or at least an unmistakably nearby area of Gloria Swanson's anatomy. That area eventually turned out to be the shoulder.

Milton Sills—a handsome leading man who, as Gloria had done with Bea La Plante, took his friend Rudy Valentino to the studio commissary every day in the hope someone important would hire the Italian—played the engineer. The costume department broke all records creating an evening dress for Gloria that ended in a four-foot train composed entirely of pearls and ermine tails.

Herbert's affairs were not improving. He continued to have business lunches and to sound important on the telephone. Gloria picked up the tab. For their daughter's sake, she tried to get him on his feet. He persuaded her to move from the apartment to the newly opened Ambassador Hotel on Wilshire Boulevard. When she saw the first month's bill, she moved from there to one of the Beverly Hills Hotel's bungalows. Not yet the home of the stars, Beverly Hills had orange groves and foothills and canyons of the scrawny Santa Monica Mountains and, Gloria decided, healthy air for the baby. In May, they moved. An indelicate remark about the vaginal baths she was taking strained their relationship further. If she was taking douches, she snapped, it was because the surgery had been postponed a second time. And the reason for *that* was that she had returned to work to support the three of them.

The Great Moment was a hit, but the next two quickies Lasky put her in—*Under the Lash,* a drab rural story set among South African Boers, and *Don't Tell Everything,* little more than leftover footage from *The Affairs of Anatol*—were the first Swanson features that failed to make money.

Lasky quickly found out why. He called Gloria and told her the reason was that women stayed away, and the reasons they stayed away was that she had worn dull, gray, buttoned-up housedresses. "We won't let that happen again," he said. "Starting right now, with *Her Husband's Trademark,* anything you want in the way of fancy clothes, you can have. Never look drab again, because the public won't stand for it. In fact, I've already spoken to Elinor Glyn about your next picture. I told her to come up with an elaborate costume drama."

Before Madame Glyn started writing *Beyond the Rocks,* the story of a poor but aristocratic English girl who is married to an elderly millionaire only to meet the love of her life on her honeymoon, Gloria had packed the baby and a full-time nurse and moved to a little inn in the Silver Lake area, leaving the Beverly Hills Hotel bungalow to Herbert. When she called the hotel for messages a few days later, she was told her husband had left. Herbert sent her a sad, short letter saying he had left for what he hoped was the best for all three. He loved his little daughter. He intended to stay in California and hoped Gloria would not create difficulties when it came to visitation rights.

By leaving Wallace Beery three years earlier, Gloria had forfeited the right to a speedy divorce. This time she had committed the same mistake, but she now had Herbert's letter saying he had left her and their child. Desertion would be her legal grounds for divorce.

Mickey Neilan swept her off her feet that summer with his madcap, brilliant, vivacious insouciance and his claim that there were only some 290 days before he was free to marry her. "After Herbert, how could I not love him?" she would ask. "After one afternoon with him, how could I not forget Craney Gartz and every other handsome man who had ever tempted me? As Mickey waltzed me into my first real love affair, it never occurred to me to utter a syllable of protest."

While waiting for his divorce to become final, Mickey lived like a young lord at the Los Angeles Athletic Club next to Charlie Chaplin, who was trying to escape the sensational charges surrounding his divorce from the teenage Mildred Harris. Mickey's romance with Gloria was particularly torrid and came after his affair with Peggy Hopkins Joyce, a former Ziegfeld Follies girl who distracted him so much from his long and confused *Stranger's Banquet* that cast and crew had had to wait two weeks after the starting date before Neilan showed up. The term "gold digger" had been coined in honor of Peggy around 1920. Born Margaret Upton in Virginia, the big blonde had arrived in Chicago in 1914, changed her name to Hopkins, and landed her first millionaire husband, Stanley Joyce. Divorced with a million-dollar settlement, she had, in quick succession, netted four more millionaire husbands. Dressed in stylish mourning outfits, because Henri Letellier, a famous Parisian publisher and man-about-town, had just taken his life on her account, she had cruised into Hollywood with a three-million-dollar bankroll, bent on a movie career. After Mickey's infatuation with her had cooled, he introduced her to Chaplin, who used the story of her relationship with Letellier as a basis for *A Woman of Paris.*

Mickey's friends were a tony crowd. He worked and played hard, often with Antonio Moreno, a Latin-lover actor soon to star in another Elinor Glyn concoction, and James Kirkwood and William Desmond Taylor, a pair of actors-turned-directors who, like Mickey, had started out with Griffith, and their actress friends Colleen Moore, Mabel Normand, and Mary Miles Minter. Colleen was a fast-rising new face, Mabel was currently Sam Goldwyn's $1,500-a-week leading lady, while Minter was Lasky's newest Mary Pickford imitation. Kirkwood and Minter were former lovers, and their deep dark secret was an abortion Mary's mother had force her teenage meal-ticket daughter to have.

When they didn't sail to Catalina Island on Sundays or go for spins to Lake Arrowhead—Mickey was born in San Bernardino—or Palm Springs in their fabulous roadsters, they tagged along to parties with Elinor. They sipped bootleg cocktails, one-stepped and Charlestoned in nightclubs, and listened to jazz (Mickey boogie-woogied on the piano with the best of them) at Nat Goodwyn's on the Santa Monica Pier. They could also be found at the Sunset Inn on Ocean Avenue where Fatty Arbuckle—now a $7,000-a-week Paramount star heading his own unit and separated from Minta Durfee—and Buster Keaton entertained everybody on Saturday nights. The men wore dinner jackets and the women dressed in clothes that emphasized slimness—flexible, tubular slimness, like a section of a boa constrictor. For Gloria, it was fun to be twenty-two and in love with the dashing Mickey Neilan.

Over the Labor Day weekend, Arbuckle threw a party in San Francisco's St. Francis Hotel. Virginia Rappe, a bit player whom Keaton would later describe as being "about as virtuous as most of the other untalented young women knocking around Hollywood for years," had one orange blossom too many, fell ill, and began tearing off her clothes—a habit of hers when she had had too many cocktails. Partygoers would disagree on what happened next. Friendly testimony would allege that Arbuckle, in the presence of the other women, viewed the prostrate Virginia on his bed, tested to see if she was faking by holding a piece of ice against her thigh, then helped carry the nude body to a bathtub to try and revive her while somebody called the house physician. Less friendly witnesses would tell of screams from behind the locked door, of Fatty emerging, his pajamas dripping under a dry bathrobe, and the girl on the bed moaning, "I'm dying. He broke me inside. I'm dying." Four days later she was dead.

Coming on the heels of Mary Pickford's Nevada "quickie divorce" from Owen Moore and her marriage, a month later, to Douglas Fairbanks; Charlie Chaplin's nude carrying-ons on Catalina with Peggy Joyce; and the California State Board of Pharmacy revelation that over five hundred prominent film personalities were listed on its rolls as drug addicts, the Arbuckle scandal inflamed public opinion. The press, ever mindful of the healthy effect of scandal on circulation, whipped up the sex-orgy-with-murder investigation until the popular image of Hollywood was one of Gomorrah with modern plumbing.

Gloria felt the full fury of the storm a week later when she told Lasky she wanted a divorce. "No, you don't," he snapped, his pince-nez twinkling. Apprised on the one hand of the incredible salaries paid to stars like her, and on the other hand of the riotous living of a few, the public was ready to tar the entire industry with a brush of resentment that bordered on vindictiveness. In her case, Lasky continued, she would be divorcing for the second time and that less than a year after having a baby. Did she think Herbert Somborn would give her a quiet divorce when he had everything to gain by making a stink? If the newspaper hysteria proved anything, it was that people got a greater thrill out of seeing stars fall than watching them shine.

Gloria wondered whether Lasky knew about her and Mickey. There was an edge of warning in his voice when he said that in the public's mind she stood for "love, passion, glamour, the whole sophisticated atmosphere of Cecil B. De Mille and Elinor Glyn." The public could turn in one minute.

Carrying on with Mickey was playing with a loaded gun, but it didn't stop them. If only they could get away from the Hollywood fishbowl. When Elinor broke the supposed secret that Gloria's costar in the new film would be Rudy Valentino, Mickey had an idea. Gloria listened carefully to Mickey's game plan, and when Lasky called her to tell her Sam Wood would direct her new picture, with Valentino as her costar—indeed that Elinor was writing the script with Valentino in mind—Gloria coolly asked if her contract allowed the studio to costar anyone with her. When Lasky admitted it didn't, she asked if her contract said anything about her going abroad and the studio paying for her vacation. Lasky smiled. She agreed to have Valentino as her costar, and the studio agreed to send her on a nice trip to Europe after the filming. If there was one place a pair of lovers could be themselves, it was Paris. Mickey would join her.

Hollywood fought the cesspool-of-iniquity image by talking "clean." Director King Vidor, who carried on an affair with Colleen Moore, was the first to sign a "Creed and Pledge," promising not to make pictures containing "anything unclean in thought and nature." Famous Players–Lasky touted "Clean entertainment" and promised that "crime, vulgarity, obscenity, dances, profanity, nudity, national feelings, religion and repellent subjects such as hangings and surgical operations" would henceforth be treated "within the careful limits of good taste." Without being consulted, Gloria was thrown into the counteroffensive. Press releases quoted her as saying she had no sympathy with free love. Newspapers immediately dug up the fact that, since May, Gloria Swanson had been living apart from her husband.

An attack came from an unexpected corner. The family of the late Matthew Burns filed suit against Addie, charging that she had conned her second husband into leaving his estate to her. Sleazy press reports intimated that Addie had used her then seventeen-year-old daughter as a "baby vamp" to lure Burns. Gloria told her mother to fight the suit and went on the offensive herself. The charges were preposterous, she told reporters; she had been a married woman herself at the time of her mother's marriage. She was gratified when the studio backed her with respected character witnesses. The legal action against Addie was dismissed in court.

During the fall and winter, Arbuckle faced trial for manslaughter in which the evidence against him was considered so unspeakable that much of it was passed around silently in typewritten notes. At his first court appearance, the head of the Women's Vigilante Committee of San Francisco was so aroused by the sight of women applauding the famous comedian's entrance that she cried, "Women of America, do your duty," and with the members of her committee covered Fatty with spit. Two trials resulted in hung juries and a third trial acquitted him, but his screen career was finished.

Gloria and Mickey were together on the night in February 1922 when the murder of their friend Bill Taylor brought the notion of Hollywood as Sodom to a new low. "MABEL NORMAND QUIZZED IN SCREEN CHIEF'S MURDER," the *Los Angeles Evening Express* headline screamed the next day. Mabel was indeed the last person to have seen the director alive in his Alvarado Street bungalow, and as the details became known, the murder case sold more newspapers than the outbreak of World War I. When the police arrived at the murder scene, they found Paramount executives burning papers in the fireplace, and in the bedroom they found love letters and undergarments belonging to the underage Mary Miles Minter.

Mickey spent the day in an emergency meeting at Paramount. When Gloria met him at the studio commissary at the end of the day, he said he had to talk to Mary Minter. Together they picked up the young actress and drove to Mickey's place. Mary seemed all right. She made scrambled eggs for the three of them and shared a bottle of champagne. Forty-five years later, when King Vidor interviewed Gloria for a film he planned to do on the Taylor murder,* she would claim Mickey had sent her home because he had some "heavy talking" to do with Mary, and that he came over to her place later. When he showed up in the morning, in time to shower and shave before heading for the studio, he kept silent about the night's talk. "When everything started coming out in the papers," Gloria said, "I knew better than to ask." In reality, she knew plenty. She knew Mabel was a cocaine addict seeking help and rehabilitation in a friendship with Taylor. She thought that the neurotic Mary Minter's infatuation with the fifty-five-year-old director was unrequited, that Mary's love letters and panties— bandied about by police as evidence—had been planted by the studio to cover Taylor's homosexuality. She knew that Charlotte Shelby, Mary's

---

*Officially unsolved after sixty years, the Taylor murder was the object of an intense investigation by King Vidor, ostensibly for a film he and his 1920s paramour Colleen Moore would produce. After Vidor's death in 1983, Sidney Kirkpatrick, his biographer, published Vidor's research and solution to the murder mystery: Believing her daughter was having an affair with Taylor and therefore slipping from her control, Mary's mother shot and killed the director on February 2, 1922, and for years paid off successive Los Angeles district attorneys.

ruthless stage mother, had threatened to kill Kirkwood when she discovered he had made her then fifteen-year-old daughter pregnant.

Shooting *Beyond the Rocks* was a distraction from headlines that grew ever more lurid. Taylor was discovered to have had an earlier life in New York under the name Tanner; he had been scheduled to testify the next day on behalf of his black manservant, who had been accused of soliciting young boys.

Getting to know Valentino was a pleasure for Gloria. He, too, was caught in a miserable marriage. His wife was the dancer Jean Acker. He was an excellent horseman, and on Sunday mornings he and Gloria rode together in the Hollywood hills. He told her that he needed to be in love with a strong woman and that he believed in occult powers. They talked about *Eyes of Youth,* the picture he had made with Clara Kimball Young two years earlier, and Gloria learned how precarious Herbert's finances had been from the beginning. Rudy felt sorry for Clara. She had been Lewis Selznick's mistress for years. The reason Selznick had pulled the financial rug from under Equity Pictures was that Clara had fallen in love with Harry Garson. It was Garson who had persuaded Clara to produce her own pictures. Now she was reduced to selling her jewelry. The studios wouldn't touch her.

Valentino had just finished *The Four Horsemen of the Apocalypse* for Metro, and he was well aware that casting him was thought to jeopardize an already risky venture. Vincente Blasco-Ibanez's anti-German novel was also antiwar, and only screenwriter June Mathis had believed the picture might appeal to the new mood of exhausted cynicism about wars to make the world safe for democracy. Under Rex Ingram's direction, Rudy explained, *Horsemen* became a film that introduced audiences to a glamorous international moneyed aristocracy shuttling between Buenos Aires and Paris, between dives and *thés dansants.*

Stupendous success came to Rudy the first week in March when *The Four Horsemen* opened in New York. Within days he was second only to Doug Fairbanks. Before MGM realized the gold mine he was becoming, Lasky signed him for the *The Sheik,* to follow right after *Beyond the Rocks.*

Elinor Glyn wrote *Beyond the Rocks* in the form of historical flashbacks so Swanson and Valentino could be seen in romantic periods of European history. A tango sequence was also added so that Rudy could lead an enraptured Gloria into Latin ecstasy. The wardrobe department made her a shimmering gold-beaded and embroidered lace evening gown designed to outshine the robe and shawl that Helena Domingues wore when she tangoed with Valentino in *Horsemen.* Madame Glyn insisted on supervising all the details, and got down on a leopardskin to show Gloria how to play the love scene she had written for her. Relief from Glyn's sometimes bizarre and erratic demands came when Sam Wood moved the cast and crew to Catalina Island for the shipwreck scenes and Elinor announced they would have to shoot the exteriors without her. They all enjoyed filming Gloria tipping over in a rowboat "beyond the rocks" and Rudy rescuing her and carrying her, unconscious and dripping, through the surf. The nights at the hotel were relaxed. In retrospect, the short week on Catalina would remain a happy, innocent interlude for both Gloria and Rudy.

The roar of disapproval over the Arbuckle and Taylor scandals gave churchmen, clubwomen, schoolteachers, and editorial writers the chance to inveigh against the new Sodom, and pushed politicians to vote for stricter censorship laws. The reformers demanded regulations governing the treatment of sex, the depiction of crime, and the use of weapons, drugs, and liquor on the screen. They organized successful boycotts against pictures starring offending players—although never charged with anything, both Mabel Normand and Mary Miles Minter were finished—and threatened reprisals against the entire industry.

But the shocks didn't let up. Valentino impetuously married Winifred Shaughnessy de Wolf (who preferred to call herself Natasha Rambova) in Mexico without waiting the full year required by California law for his interlocutory divorce from Jean Acker; he was jailed for bigamy by an ambitious district attorney who saw to it that reporters had the story before Rudy's lawyers and friends did. While Paramount managed to suppress the fact that both Acker and Rambova were lesbians—and that both had been introduced to Rudy by the exotic and equally lesbian actress Alla Nazimova, whose Bohemian soirees at her famous Sunset Boulevard estate, The Garden of Allah, were notorious—the studio was less lucky when its all-time, all-American Wallace Reid died a drug addict. If that wasn't enough, his widow, Dorothy Davenport, charged that, in order to maintain the grueling shooting schedule Famous Players–Lasky demanded of its stars, the studio had supplied him with morphine and that toward the end of *Clarence* they had propped him up before the camera in order to finish the picture. De Mille had visited Reid in a padded cell in a private sanatorium and came away shocked at seeing the strapping actor reduced to a gray skeleton weighing just over a hundred pounds.

In self-defense, Zukor, Lasky, and twelve other studio chiefs came together, hired Will Hays, and created the formidably titled Association of Motion Picture Producers and Distributors of America—better known for the next three decades as the Hays office.

A Presbyterian elder and Indiana politician who had risen high in the ranks of the Republican Party and served as postmaster general in the Harding administration, Hays was a little man with great ears. Given absolute authority to police the morals of the industry (and a $100,000-a-year salary), the new "czar" acted swiftly. He began a public-relations campaign to induce the press to report Hollywood news fairly, and made it clear to everybody in the business that personal lives would have to withstand public scrutiny. He gave covert assistance to Davenport so that she could produce and star in *Human Wreckage,* an antidrug film that she promoted as a warning to the nation's youth in memory of her late husband.

The studios inserted "morals clauses" permitting contract cancellations if players were so much as accused of immorality, while those whose behavior was beyond the pale were blacklisted. The Doom Book soon included 117 names deemed "unsafe" because of their no longer private lives. To put a stop to the influx of eager young actresses lured west by "scouts" from shady talent schools, Hays established a central casting agency through which extras could find employment at the studios and where applications were screened. To further shelter the Goldilocks, Bess Lasky and several other matrons organized the Hollywood Studio Club, where "decent" girls could find inexpensive lodging, board, and protection, often from the good ladies' own producer husbands.

A thornier issue for Hays, trickier than anything his fellow czars in baseball and horse racing had to deal with, more difficult than storming around the country to put out censorship fires, was what to forbid. How do you protect the public by removing from the screen what people pay to see? Snipping films to the varying requirements of different censorship boards brought constant headaches. No two censors seemed to agree on what would most corrupt an audience, and the definition of vice varied not only from state to state but from country to country. In Indiana a screen kiss was considered deeply offensive. In Ohio you couldn't show female undergarments fluttering on a clotheslines. The answer was a code—a codification of existing state and municipal censorship regulations that would allow producers to get their movies shown in a maximum of territories with a minimum of costly changes.

A morals clause was forced on Gloria after she had spent a carefree month with Mickey in Paris, far from prying eyes. With her salary now $5,000 a week, the risk of ruinous exposure was too much to bear. So was Neilan's alcoholism. Back in California, Mickey loaned her $18,000 for the downpayment on the twenty-four-room house King Gilette had built for his sister in Beverly Hills. The property at 904 Crescent Drive was on the corner of Sunset Boulevard across from the Beverly Hills Hotel and featured a majestic indoor staircase and a private elevator. Next, Gloria adopted a four-and-a-half-month-old baby boy from a San Francisco orphanage.

The adoption idea had come when, slightly hurt in a fall on the park-sized lawn on Crescent Drive, two-year-old Gloria had run sobbing to her nurse instead of her mother. Then and there Gloria promised herself she would spend more time with her daughter and give the child a greater sense of family. Little was known about the baby boy she adopted except that his father was Irish. Variously nicknamed Brother and Buddy, little Joseph had violet-blue eyes and looked a lot like Lois Wilson. The resemblance was so striking that Gloria teasingly asked her friend if she hadn't spent a weekend in San Francisco with an Irishman a year earlier. Little Joe's face lit up each time he saw Lois.

Little Gloria was two and a half and Brother was about to celebrate his first birthday in March 1923 when Herbert sprang his bomb. The legal papers served on Gloria alleged adultery with fourteen men, ranging from De Mille, Lasky, Wood, Zukor, Mickey, and Famous Players–Lasky's three K's—Robert Kane, Sidney Kent, and Samuel Katz—to people she didn't even know. Herbert also demanded a $150,000 settlement, claiming it was he who had obtained the contract that, over three years, was worth more than one million dollars to her.

Livid, she got Herbert on the phone and told him he knew it was all a pack of lies.

"Not all of it," he answered, "and it will take you six months to disprove the rest. What will happen to your career in the meantime?"

She hung up.

To Paramount, Herbert and his attorney, Milton Cohen, sent word that unless $150,000 became part of a divorce settlement, news would break of the affair Gloria Swanson and director Marshall Neilan had conducted in Europe and at a hotel in downtown Los Angeles. Lasky was in New York with Zukor, and De Mille took charge. A frantic flurry of telegrams was exchanged between De Mille and the bosses in New York. Notes scribbled by De Mille, his biographer Charles Higham would reveal, indicated a meeting at his Los Feliz residence between him, Gloria, Herbert, and others. In her memoirs Gloria described a meeting at De Mille's house without mentioning her husband's presence. When she was alone with De Mille, she wrote, he said that, no matter how angry she was, the divorce would have to be settled secretly or her career would be ruined. She was ready to fight, she objected.

A year earlier she could have had a divorce, alleging desertion. But Lasky had been so terrified of scandal that he had persuaded her to wait, she said. It was all the studio's fault. De Mille said he agreed. He was sure Lasky, too, agreed. Wouldn't she at least think it over for a day or two? He put an arm around her shoulder and led her toward the entrance. A Western Union boy was standing at the front door when De Mille opened it. The boy handed him a telegram. The director excused himself, read the wire, and without a word, handed it to Gloria. Over Will Hays's signature she read that the Swanson matter would have to be settled out of court, since it jeopardized not only her career but the entire industry.

She drove home in a state of rage, despair, and embarrassment that made it difficult for her to concentrate on the road. When she reached Crescent Drive she saw her father sitting on the lawn with little Gloria and Brother. She had forgotten about his weekend visit. With tears in her eyes she ran up to him. The most awful thing had happened, she told him. "I'm being blackmailed and I don't know what to do."

After the nanny had taken the children inside and Gloria had explained, her father, too, suggested caution. A sensational divorce trial in which she would stand accused of adultery with a dozen men might result in Herbert's being awarded custody of Gloria and might move the adoption authorities to try and take back little Joe. After a while she agreed that the best thing she could do for the children, for the people she cared for, was to compromise. When De Mille called later in the evening, again urging out-of-court settlement and expressing the belief Paramount would help cover the legal costs, she gave in. "Tell Mr. Lasky I'll settle," she sighed. "But tell Mr. Lasky's lawyer to haggle with Herbert."

When the divorce papers were presented to her, she was tempted to sign it all without seeing her own humiliation spelled out in black and white. She steeled herself, however, and began to read. Paramount was indeed picking up the attorneys' fees, but she gagged when she came to the face-saving provisions that awarded Herbert $70,000 because he had "assisted in procuring" her much-improved contract. He was paid $35,000 in cash and another $35,000 in installments, deducted from her salary at the rate of $500 a week. There was more. To keep her job, she had to sign a morals clause waiver. Should she in the future "be charged with adulterous conduct or immoral relations with men other than her husband, and such charges or any of them be published in the public press," her contract would be null and void. Angry and embarrassed, she signed and went back to work.

Two months later she was in the middle of filming *Bluebeard's Eighth Wife*, a Sam Wood adaptation of Alfred Savoir's farce, when Lasky asked her to attend an industry banquet. She hated such affairs, but since she had said no so many times decided to go. When she arrived and was escorted to the dais, she discovered she was seated next to Will Hays. A small man even next to the diminuitive Gloria, the new director of the industry's morals tried to talk to her, but except for an icy hello saw only her famous profile as she studiously spent the evening addressing the man on her right. When Hays finally asked what he had done to deserve her cold shoulder, she faced him down and said, "Only one thing. You sent a telegram to Mr. De Mille."

"What telegram?"

"The telegram that concerned me and my divorce."

He insisted he had never sent any such telegram. She was adamant. She had seen it. "Mr. De Mille showed it to me. You said if I contested my husband's suit for divorce, it would endanger the entire motion picture industry."

The little man stood solemnly and gave her his word he had never sent such a telegram. "Then I apologize for my behavior, Mr. Hays."

When she got home she called Mickey, but he was too drunk to listen. Lasky was capable of anything, she realized, but De Mille was her idol, the one man in the industry by whom she judged others. Had he known the telegram was fake? She spent a sleepless night going over the whole affair. Convinced De Mille had betrayed her, she nevertheless didn't feel up to facing the ugly scene her confronting him would entail. Instead, she walked in full costume and makeup to Lasky's office the next morning, past his secretary, and found him sitting with a visitor.

"Gloria," Lasky smiled, "What a marvelous dress. What picture is that for?"

"The picture is *Bluebeard's Eighth Wife,* but that isn't what I'm here for."

After Lasky diplomatically asked if anything was the matter, she burst out that she had talked to Hays the night before about a certain telegram. "I could have you put in jail," she shouted.

Lasky asked his visitor to wait outside. Gloria felt triumphant; the guest had heard the most important part of what she had to say. She had a witness. When they were alone, Lasky said he understood her feelings. He had done it for her own good. De Mille had told him she was planning to fight Somborn in court. That would have meant the ruin of a great career.

She turned around and walked toward the door. "I just wanted to hear you admit it. That's enough for one day," she said and left. In reality, she didn't know what to do. Leave Famous Players–Lasky? Sue the studio? She remembered how Clara Kimball Young had broken with the studio system and how Lewis Selznick had finished her, Herbert, and whomever else had worked with her.

Once more Mickey Neilan came up with an idea that, if it didn't quite add up to sweet revenge, at least allowed her to exploit her predicament. Since Lasky was unlikely to refuse her anything right now, why not ask him for a chance to make better pictures, to work with a top director? Sam Wood was something of a lightweight, on most days more interested in his real-estate deals than the scene they were shooting. *Bluebeard* was Gloria's tenth with Wood since *The Great Moment* and, she felt, each was worse than the one before. The only thing that changed was the number and length of the dresses she wore and the faces of her leading men. When she suggested to Mickey that she demand *him* as her director—that surely would upset Lasky and Zukor—their schedules proved to be a too solid obstacle. He was in the middle of a picture and had signed to do *Dorothy Vernon of Haddon Hall,* Mary Pickford's next picture, after that. Lasky wouldn't pay Gloria $5,000 to wait for *any* director to become available.

Instead, Mickey suggested the man who had started him out in the business, Allan Dwan. Of course, Allan didn't work in Hollywood. He hated the place. Zukor was Dwan's biggest fan, and Allan had persuaded the senior Paramount partner to build him a small studio in Astoria, Queens, and to let him direct as much as possible in New York and as little as possible in California.

The best thing Gloria could do for her career, Mickey said, was to try and work with Dwan, to find a pretext for going to New York and meeting him. "When all is said and done," Mickey said, "Hollywood is nothing but sunshine, and eventually that fries everybody's brains. Just look around." She didn't quite know what to tell Lasky. The studio was paying her to make pictures in Hollywood, not to traipse off to New York in search of an inspired director. Mickey called Dwan and reported back to Gloria. Allan had just talked Zukor into buying *Zaza,* Leslie Carter's Broadway play. This comedy about a French maid falling in love with a distinguished but very married gentleman was just right for her.

Gloria went to see Lasky. It was their first meeting since she had told him she could have him put in jail, and he was nervous. Since little Gloria's birth, she told him, she had needed minor surgery. She had made arrangements as soon as *Bluebeard's Eighth Wife* was finished to have it done in New York. To her surprise, Lasky quickly agreed to let her have two weeks in New York before her next picture.

Allan Dwan was a chubby, balding, thirty-eight-year-old Canadian who had worked with everybody. He was the director everybody hired to apply brains to idiot projects—a no-nonsense problem-solver, tinkerer, fixer, and doer whose involvements in a project were never overwhelming nor ever anonymous.

His film career had begun five hundred miles from his native Toronto, when his work as an electrical engineer specializing in lighting had brought him to the Essanay studios. After a year he left with several others to form the American Film Company, then worked as a script editor in Chicago, and later was head of a production unit in Arizona. In addition to the 217 one- and two-reelers he had directed between 1911 and 1913, Dwan, since then, had made over fifty features. He was Doug Fairbank's favorite director—they had just made *Robin Hood,* a picture that set new standards for splendor and wit in the swashbuckle genre—which meant he knew Wally Beery, Gloria realized. Dwan had also directed two pictures with Clara Kimball Young after the actress had left Lewis Selznick to become an independent producer, which meant Dwan knew Herbert as well.

Gloria had dinner with him on her first night in New York, and before they started the first course she decided Mickey had been right again: Dwan was a delight.

Zaza, he explained, was a brash, realistic little comedy. To play the distinguished gentleman Zaza falls in love with only to discover he is a husband and a father, Dwan had cast H. B. Warner, who knew the author, Leslie Carter, herself an actress. What would be different for Gloria was that she would play a brash, tough girl, which meant her wardrobe would be sassy and unladylike. He had a couple of young designers doing the costumes and had found a mansion on Long Island that looked like a French chateau, as well as an apartment on Park Avenue for Gloria for the duration of the filming.

"I can't wait to start," she said.

Dwan persuaded Zukor and, via long-distance phone, Lasky, to let their biggest star try this one realistic picture. He promised he would speed up production so that Gloria's whole East Coast trip would take no longer than the preproduction and shooting of a Swanson picture in Hollywood. They wouldn't be sorry, he added. Lasky thought the whole thing smelled of collusion, if not sedition, but when Zukor said yes, he had to agree also.

The Long Island Studio on Thirty-sixth Street and Thirty-fifth Avenue near Astoria's huge Steinway piano factory was full of free spirits, defectors, and refugees all trying to get away from Hollywood. *Zaza* turned out to be the fastest, easiest, and most enjoyable experience for Gloria in forty-one pictures, but it was only a warm-up for a sparkling trio of movies she and Dwan did together. Lasky schemed to get Gloria back to Hollywood, but working with Allan was such a bracing experience that she was ready to try anything to get to stay in New York.

If Dwan rebelled against the studio straitjacket, he was no misunderstood genius taking out his anger on the material. Like the aging Picasso, who would turn flotsam objects he picked up on beaches into art, Dwan worked with what he found. His flair for blocking a scene, his framing and camera movements, and his ability to extract performances from low-voltage actors had a way of transforming the most hackneyed drivel into often exciting screen fare. He prepared everything with such care that the first take was often the best and, Gloria would remember, he had the confidence to know it. "Allan used a script like a blueprint. The best things in the picture we made up as we went along. We were always stretching, always trying to improve the scene up to the last minute before we shot it."

Forrest Halsey was another pleasant surprise. A screenwriter by day and bon vivant by night, this Southern gentlemen was the first homosexual Gloria had known who was not the least embarrassed about his sexual inclination. In Hollywood, homosexuals were targets of blackmail and thieving rogues, some hounded to suicide because they lacked the protection of the law. When a group from the studio went out, Forrest usually had a young male friend in tow. Most important to Gloria, he had a keen literary judgment and over the next two years would steer her in increasingly challenging directions.

It was out of the question for Gloria to live alone in New York. For the duration of *Zaza,* Lasky hired Jane West, a Boston society girl in open rebellion against her family, as Gloria's chaperon. Allan, Forrest, and Gloria soon realized that Jane was also the studio's mole, the in-house spy positioned to report on any plots director, writer, and star might try to hatch. The trio wasted little time wooing the aristocratic Jane over to their side. Although counterespionage was distasteful to her, within weeks she was reporting back to *them.* When they learned that Lasky didn't have the next Swanson picture in the pipeline yet, Forrest immediately began to look for a script that would keep Gloria in New York.

What Halsey found was *The Humming Bird,* the story of a gamine Parisian pickpocket who, when the newspaperman she loves is assigned to the front during the war, puts on men's clothes, enlists the thieves and cutthroats of Montmartre, and goes off to the trenches to save her sweetheart. Again, it became Allan's job to work on Zukor and Lasky. They agreed to let Swanson do one more in New York. Audaciously, Gloria cut her hair short. This was 1923. Gabrielle "Coco" Chanel was putting women into sweaters and pleated skirts ten inches off the ground, but under cloche hats, women's locks still reached below their ears. Playing a girl playing a man in *The Humming Bird,* Gloria also reasoned, put her in line to play Peter Pan. Zukor and Lasky were in the process of acquiring the rights to J. M. Barrie's children's drama. Marilyn Miller was currently playing Peter Pan on Broadway, and a long succession of actresses, from Maude Adams to Eva Le Gallienne, had played the boy hero. What egged Gloria on was that *Photoplay* had launched a campaign to give the *Peter Pan* title role to May McAvoy, one of Zukor's Realart stars, whom Carl Sandburg called a "star-eyed goddess."

In October, when they were midway through shooting *The Humming Bird,* Joseph Swanson died at Fort MacArthur in Los Angeles. The cause of death, the army reported, was an acute heart attack. He was fifty-two. He had expressed the desire to be buried in Chicago, and if it was agreeable to his only daughter, the army would arrange a military funeral there.

With Jane West, Gloria rushed to Chicago. The press pestered her, but relatives she hadn't seen in years joined her at the cemetery to listen to the volley of guns and the bugle call. She realized her father was the most complicated figure in her life. She had adored him until she was fifteen, and during the past nine years had felt a mixture of love and pity for him. She thought she had tried to replace him by marrying twice, and if her relationship with him had been incomplete, all relationships were to some extent imperfect. She was sorry for him for never having been able to love anyone but Addie, who did not come to the funeral, and consoled herself by realizing that her father had been happy whenever they had seen each other. She was also happy he had gotten to know little Joseph.

Zukor and Lasky were no fools. By the time *The Humming Bird* was in the can, they recognized that Dwan and Swanson were a winning team. They had no objections to another picture right away. Gloria brought her daughter and little Joseph to New York. Because she didn't want them to grow up in Manhattan, she found a house for sale in Croton-on-Hudson, forty miles north of the city, and bought the estate. For her Manhattan living, she rented a string of three suites at the Gladstone Hotel.

Like other studio executives, Sidney Kent itched to play with the Hays taboos. Going through the Production Code, he discovered a subparagraph under the ban on white slavery that forbade manhandling a woman on the screen. Why didn't Allan and Gloria call their next picture *Manhandled?* All they'd have to do was to find a story mischievous enough to live up to the title yet innocuous enough in its resolution not to offend the guardians of codified morality.

Dwan got a studio writer, Frank Tuttle, to do some research, and soon enough they had a *Saturday Evening Post* story about a department store salesgirl who leaves her inventor boyfriend for a fling in high society only to return to him when she realizes that upper-crust morals don't live up to the smart clothes. Allan, Jane, and Gloria worked long evenings with Tuttle on the details of the story without quite getting it right. Gloria suggested a week in Florida. Allan was all for showing his new girlfriend a good time at studio expense. He got Zukor to say yes to the ostensible location-scouting. Miami, however, proved as drearily rainy as New York, and soon they were off to Havana. The trip turned dramatic when a former president of Cuba and a Spanish grandee convinced themselves they were enamored of Gloria and Jane and tried to carry them off to a yacht in Havana harbor. Only Gloria's icy cool saved the situation. The incident became the clincher in the *Manhandled* plot. Suppose the salesgirl, on a cruise to Havana, gets abducted—manhandled—by the richest, most distinguished man in

Havana? Allan's girlfriend thought such a plot twist too unbelievable, and they went back to the inventor boyfriend.

With the less-than-dynamic Tom Moore as the boyfriend, *Manhandled* was a raucous social comedy, notable for the early scenes of Swanson as a Gimbels sales girl being mobbed by shoppers in search of bargains. For Paramount it was a worldwide critical and box-office success, the biggest Swanson hit since *Male and Female.*

Manhandled would remain Dwan's favorite, a picture that had "an ingratiating charm." As for Swanson, he would say "she was always just perfect, a pleasure on and off, and everywhere. She was a wonderful worker to start with, and very jolly—a clown if there ever was one. A little bit of a woman, yet she was the prize clotheshorse of her day. Astonishing. She was quite short, but perfectly put together, I guess."

Le Roy Pierpont Ward and Gloria became fast friends. Called Sport by everybody, Ward in turn called most of New York society by first name. Speakeasy doors flew open at his approach, Follies girls waved to him from the stage, and out-of-towners were nobodies until they had been the butt of one of his elaborate jokes.

Sport introduced Gloria to the *Vogue* crowd—owner Condé Nast, editor Frank Crowninshield, and photographer Edward Steichen—who did a gorgeous avant-garde layout of her. The day Steichen spent with her was long and difficult, with many changes of clothes and lighting effects. At the end, he took a piece of black lace and hung it in front of her face. "She recognized the idea at once," he would write in *A Life in Photography.* "Her eyes dilated, and her look was that of a leopardess lurking behind leafy shrubbery, watching her prey."

She met Irving Berlin the composer, James Hilton the novelist, and James Walker the mayor. The mayor was the most fun. Walker wrote lyrics for Tin Pan Alley, never started work before noon, kept showgirls on the side, though he was married, and took seven vacations during his first two years in office. A group of six or eight would convene in Gloria's Gladstone suite in black tie and evening dress for a drink, followed by theater and dinner, and in the early morning, jazz and dancing in Harlem. Gloria saw Jeanne Eagles in *Rain,* Walter Huston in *Desire Under the Elms,* and John Barrymore in *Hamlet.* On February 12, 1924, she was at the Aeolian Hall to hear George Gershwin's first performance of *Rhapsody in Blue.* At the Metropolitan Opera, she heard the divas she had once wanted to be.

If she didn't want to go back to Los Angeles, the reason was also Pola Negri, a Polish seductress who came via Berlin on the coattails of Ernst Lubitsch and was publicized as La Swanson's new rival. With his perpetual cigar, ponderous shoulders, and twinkling Berlin Jewish eyes, the short, thickset Lubitsch was a genial director. Full of anecdotes, bons mots, gossip, tall yarns, and interjections, and with a sensual guile and sharp insights, he commanded a natural obedience. There had been no Hays office in avant-garde Berlin, and the population of the devastated postwar capital suffering hunger riots and revolutionary outbreaks had enjoyed the half-dozen movies about scorned queens, slave girls, whores with hearts of gold, and whores with no hearts at all that Lubitsch had directed and Negri had starred in. Their biggest hits were *Madame Dubarry,* the story of the *midinette* who became the mistress of Louis XV and ended on the guillotine, and *Passion,* a very earthy rendition of the Carmen story. First National had paid $30,000 for the American rights to *Passion,* a picture that soon cleared one million dollars. While Mary Pickford hired Lubitsch to guide her through *Rosita,* a picture designed to vault the now twenty-nine-year-old actress from her "America's sweetheart" girlishness to full screen womanhood, Lasky signed up Negri and started looking for a *Passion* sequel.

Pola had come to America aboard the *Majestic* and became friends with fellow-passenger Mabel Normand, who coached her on how to become a greater star than Swanson. "Always say no," Mabel counseled. Since Negri and Swanson had roughly the same screen image, the studio publicity department invented wholly fictitious jealousies. Supposedly, Pola demanded a bungalow as big as Gloria's and Gloria was notoriously envious of Pola's pretensions to nobility—she having been married twice, by her own account, once to a Baron Popper and once to a Count Dombski. (Evil tongues said Negri's real name was Schwartz.)

Dwan came up with *A Society Scandal.* Based on a play called *A Laughing Lady,* in which Ethel Barrymore had starred on Broadway, the story involved a society woman, her husband, his possessive mother, who sows the seeds of divorce in her son's mind, and a handsome attorney. Allan convinced Gloria that she could top herself if she had not one but two strong leading men to play off. Rod LaRocque and Ricardo Cortez, both Valentino types, were cast.

Allan started the filming with a Swanson-LaRocque love scene. After a day of pretending, the two stars had an impassioned affair that ended—as abruptly as it had started—when LaRocque became jealous of Sport, Crowninshield, Steichen, and the rest of her tony friends. "Rod had nothing to worry about, he was a match for the best of them in almost every department," she would remember. "But his jealousy was painful to see. It was torture for him to share any part of me with my dearest friends. We tried to talk it out, but he simply couldn't understand that I liked to have lots of people around me, and that the people I enjoyed most were invariably men—the brighter, the better."

Dwan and Swanson made a fifth picture in Astoria. Based on a story by detective writer Mary Roberts Rinehart, *Her Love Story* was a romantic costume drama about a Balkan queen who is forced into a political royal marriage when she is already married to a guardsman. Once more Lasky insisted on an extravagant wardrobe.

By 1924, as *Vogue* would put it a few year later, all the people of the reckless twenties had arrived, and the party that would end only with the Crash in 1929 was in full swing. A hundred million people around the world went to the movies every week, watching De Mille's *Ten Commandments,* Borzage's *Secrets,* and Douglas Fairbanks in *The Thief of Bagdad.* Everybody loved Felix the Cat, Mickey Mouse, the slapstick acrobatics of prim, shortsighted Harold Lloyd, and the surreal world of poker-faced Buster Keaton. Four years earlier, the vamp had been the screen's sexual prop prototype, but she and her ilk were giving way to a more sophisticated type, a woman no less predatory in her amorous tendencies but not necessarily evil in her primal nature. Gloria portrayed this new, independent woman, albeit a little hokily, in some of the worst clotheshorse melodramas. She was the bad-but-good lady who could fall for illicit love yet manage to retain a place in respectable society.

At the pinnacle of stardom, however, Gloria was angry with Lasky for not allowing her to escape the couture romances that made her famous and Paramount rich. Halsey told her to show more initiative, to be more aggressive. If she wanted to play Peter Pan—and he was convinced she would be marvelous in the part—she should go to England and talk to J. M. Barrie. If she could persuade the elderly author, known for his whimsy and sentimentality, that she was his choice, Zukor and Lasky would relent. She should remind Barrie that more people had seen her in *Male and Female* than would see *The Admirable Crichton* in a hundred years, and that she had just played a tomboy pickpocket in *The Humming Bird.* And if she went to Europe, Halsey had a second idea. Why not cross the channel and see if she could secure the rights to *Madame Sans Gêne?* One night Forrest read the Sardou play to her. She agreed that Catherine Hubscher was a great woman's role.

The more they talked, the more she psyched herself up for a confrontation. Lasky, however, yielded without a fight. Without mentioning her literary pursuits, she told him she needed a short European vacation. He agreed on condition she let Adolphe Osso, Famous Players–Lasky's European chief, arrange for interviews to promote her last three films in London and Paris.

With Jane, Gloria sailed for Europe in June 1924. At London's Claridge's, Gloria spent two days giving interviews. Before she could contact Barrie, the British press reported that a young American actress named

Betty Bronson had been the author's personal choice to play Peter Pan in the upcoming Paramount film. The girl was an elfish seventeen-year-old who was to show her lovely legs in the Peter Pan costume and do little else in her short career.

In Paris, Gloria and Jane stayed at the Plaza Athenée and let Osso orchestrate the continental Swanson campaign. André Daven was a pleasant surprise. Besides his fluent English, he knew all her films and directors and said perceptive things about her career. Osso ruled out *Madame Sans Gêne* the moment Gloria mentioned it, even if she planned to ask Zukor and Lasky to make the film in France. National sensibilities would be offended if an American played the famous washerwoman. "You don't know the French," he said. "I do." Daven's judgment was less categorical. The journalist was sure the French establishment would be thrilled if she brought capital to Paris to employ French talent. He would sound out a number of people in government and the arts. "If the French don't like the idea," he told Gloria over lunch, "they will not be shy about letting us know."

What helped sway the powers that were in Paris, New York, and Hollywood was Daven's elegant newspaper piece, an object lesson, Gloria thought, in diplomacy and salesmanship. Famous Players–Lasky came out smelling like roses, and Zukor and Lasky like potential ambassadors of hands-across-the-sea goodwill. André received letters from directors, actors, designers, and politicians, all saying it was a brilliant idea.

Lasky had only one condition: that Gloria spend six weeks in Astoria shooting a picture with Allan Dwan first. She wired back that she would be delighted, and while Osso started preproduction on a picture he had said couldn't be done, Gloria and Jane went on a toy-buying spree for the children and booked passage to New York aboard the *Leviathan*.

The ocean crossing opened new professional and private vistas for Gloria. After she and violinist Jascha Heifetz played a practical joke on Douglas Fairbanks and Mary Pickford, barging into their stateroom one morning dressed as stewardess and steward and pretending not to understand Doug and Mary's broken French entreaties to leave, the celebrities spent a short week together talking business and friends. Doug and Mary were jealous when she told them about *Madame Sans Gêne*. Doug said he was envious of her perhaps being able to shoot in actual palaces, and recalled how he and Dwan had spent a fortune building a castle set for *Robin Hood*. Later he asked her when her Paramount contract expired. When she said in a little more than a year, he told her Chaplin, Griffith, Mary, and he had discussed inviting her to join the United Artists. If she could do what she had just done in Paris all by herself, he grinned, she certainly didn't need Lasky anymore.

Gloria was flattered but not quite ready. Thinking, no doubt, of Clara Kimball Young's downfall in trying to go it alone, and too keyed up about *Madame Sans Gêne,* she merely stored in the back of her mind Fairbanks's list of advantages: As a member of the United Artists she could choose her own material and directors and arrange her own schedule.

Gloria and Mary were seated together in deckchairs when their conversation turned to Mickey Neilan. Mary was at first evasive, then admitted that, like *Rosita* with Lubitsch, *Dorothy Vernon of Haddon Hall* with Mickey had been a disappointment. The Tudor drama had been gorgeously mounted but, she intimated, Mickey was no longer the director he used to be. Gloria suspected his drinking. The more they talked about him, the more she wanted to see him again.

Seaborne reverie about the man she called "my wild Irish love" was cut short by the quick six weeks on *Wages of Virtue* with Dwan in New York, the return to France, filming *Madame Sans Gêne,* and falling in love with Henri. In her memoirs, Gloria would write that she had fleeting thoughts of Mickey the night in Brussels when she and Henri became lovers, of deciding then and there that Mickey was not for her.

CHAPTER · 6

Go for It!

A fool there was, and he paid his coin
To a dark-haired dame from the Ten-der-loin.
He took her out to a West Coast town,
Dressed her up in a form-fit gown,
Filled her eyes with Bel-la Don-na,
and said, "Now kid, forget your hon-na,
for henceforth, you're a scarlet scamp,
a re-gu-lar, red-lipped, black-souled vamp.
She signed his con-tract, for she was weak
He made her fa-mous within a week;
And when I tell you his pro-fits within a week
And when I tell you his pro-fits,
You'll agree that, perhaps he wasn't a fool.

—"THE VAMPIRE"

If anyone inspired Joe Kennedy to shoot a fastball at the movie industry in 1924, it was that other Boston banker Patrick A. Powers, a real born-in-Ireland, rags-to-riches financier who had started life in the New World as a Boston policeman.

Joe had known Pat Powers, nineteen years his senior, since his days as bank examiner, and the man had never ceased to surprise him. Powers had entered business as an Edison phonograph salesman and was known to his business associates for the poker-faced fashion in which he conducted million-dollar deals. To the rhetorical question: How does a cop become a banker? the answer going around Hollywood (and possibly disseminated by Pat himself) was that he was the kind of policeman who, when he caught a butcher with his hand on the scale while weighing meat, wouldn't arrest the man. Instead, he just didn't bother paying for meat when he ordered it from the butcher after that.

In 1912 Powers had joined other freebooters in a rebellion against the

Edison-Biograph chokehold on the nickelodeon business. A full-blown monopoly of the kind Theodore Roosevelt's "trustbusters" were trying to outlaw, the Edison-Biograph combine was made up of the largest companies, and through a pooling of patents, it controlled the licensing of both cameras and projectors—the cameras were licensed solely to its member producers; the projectors, to those theater men who agreed to purchase Edison-Biograph movies only.

Carl Laemmle, an impulsive and cheerful little haberdasher, had joined the laconic Powers. Legend has it that when Laemmle, Powers, and three others sat down in Manhattan at their first director's meeting to come up with a name for their new independent company, Laemmle glanced out of the window and caught sight of a passing truck advertising Universal Pipe Fittings. A less reverent version of the birth of Universal Pictures has it that the vehicle Laemmle spotted was a Universal garbage truck.

Powers was a loner. He sold out to Laemmle and for the next decade was in and out of film investments with a variety of partners. Known as a "bonus shark," he loaned production money at steep interest rates or became a participant in the profits. One partner was Lewis Selznick, the former jewelry dealer from Kiev who had persuaded his sons they were heirs to a kingdom, but who had lately lost his fortune. When he hadn't been able to pay a debt of a mere $3,000, Selznick's enemies had forced him into bankruptcy. His sons, Myron and David, vowed vengeance.

Clara Kimball Young adored Powers and believed him to be the most wonderful, clever man in the world. He had lost money, however, by becoming a major stockholder in Equity Pictures. A year later he had invested $120,000 in one movie—*The Miracle Man* with Lon Chaney—and made three million dollars.

Now in his mid-fifties, Pat had become infatuated with the icy blond charms of Peggy Hopkins Joyce. Since she had distracted Mickey Neilan and told Chaplin of her gold-digging days while skinny-dipping with him on Catalina Island, Peggy had added MGM's frail wunderkind, Irving Thalberg, to her list of conquests. Pat wanted Erich von Stroheim to write and direct a film starring his Peggy. Pat was courting the stormy, individualistic Stroheim because in *The Merry Widow,* MGM's current hit, the director had managed the feat of turning Mae Murray, another ex-Follies hoofer, into a star.

Reflating the careers of former chorus girls was not among Joe Kennedy's ambitions in 1924. He had bigger fish to fry. With Galen Stone and his Harvard classmate Guy Currier, Joe had bought a modest chain of New England movie houses. The idea dated back to his days as president of Columbia Trust. After examining a local exhibitor's books, he had looked at a business associate in amazement and exclaimed, "We must get into the picture business. This is a new industry, and a gold mine. In fact, it looks like another telephone company."

In addition to the thirty-one-house Maine–New Hampshire Theaters, Joe also acquired the territorial franchise for Universal Pictures. Still, he and his partners had a hard time spreading into the greater Boston area. Standing in the way of such expansion were the big Loew's and Paramount chains. It was not until 1923 that they bought their first movie house in Massachusetts, in the town of Stoneham north of Boston. To feed the theaters more than Universal products, Joe bought New England rights to a number of British films and built up contacts among film people in London.

Kennedy's prospects in the movie business were given a major leg up by Will Hays, who came to Boston in 1924 to help stamp out censorship fires in this election year and, more discreetly, to recruit "clean" business personalities for the film industry.

In the name of free speech, Hays rallied citizens' committees against censorship proponents and tried to persuade lawmakers of both parties that to rush through movie censorship legislation would be ill advised. Joe met the czar in Galen Stone's office. What was supposed to be a short chat about money and politics turned instead into an economic analysis of the film industry that lasted all afternoon. What the picture business lacked most, the three men agreed in the end, was substance. An independent like Samuel Goldwyn had enough studio space and equipment to shoot eleven pictures at the same time. He paid his stars as much as $15,000 a week, but his operation was so leveraged that he was at the mercy of bonus sharks. Only a few banks, most notably Amadeus Peter (A. P.) Giannini's Bank of America, were willing to issue lines of credit to film companies. What the industry needed, Hays told Stone when he was ready to leave, was people like Joe here, "a man who, in his business ideals and concepts as in the fine character of his home life, would bring to the industry much that it has lacked in the past." Joe knew how to charm.

When it came to politics, Joe had learned on P.J.'s knee the value of a liquid ideology. Candidates and voters in Massachusetts got a taste of his cynicism in the 1924 election. While working sincerely to defeat a film-censorship proposition that had made it onto the Massachusetts ballot, he concocted a Machiavellian scheme to scare disaffected working-class and Catholic voters into continuing to back the Democratic ticket.

Though a Democrat by birth, Joe was less than enamored with the party. Irritated both by his father-in-law's "Fitzblarney" (Honey Fitz had run for governor in 1922 and lost by over 60,000 votes) and by the parochial schisms that divided Democrats, Joe was unenthusiastic about his party's standard-bearer—Wall Street lawyer John W. Davis, who had won the 1924 Democratic presidential nomination after a bitter convention contest that lasted a mind-numbing 103 ballots. Nonetheless, Joe was not about to bolt to the Republicans and Calvin Coolidge.

The problem was: how to galvanize support for a Democratic ticket that he himself found less than impressive? The answer came in the form of the Progressive Party.

Under the Progressive banner, rebels from both Democratic and Republican ranks had gathered in Milwaukee that summer of 1924 to nominate a third-party presidential candidate—Senator Robert La Follette of Wisconsin. The Progressive platform hammered away at Davis's Wall Street connections, opposed internationalism, and called for government control of natural resources, public ownership of railways, and lower taxes.

La Follette's vice-presidential running mate, Senator Burton K. Wheeler of Montana, was of particular interest to Kennedy. A Massachusetts native who had gone west to practice law in the copper fields of Montana, he was lustily campaigning on Cape Cod when Eddie Moore approached him to say his boss wanted to meet him.

"We discussed the political situation," Wheeler would remember of his visit with Joe Kennedy, "and I outlined the philosophy by which La Follette and I intended to save the world." A week later Wheeler and his family were invited to dinner with Joe and Rose at Galen Stone's house. To the candidate's surprise, the two speculators listened sympathetically to his pitch. "We can't take much more of Cal Coolidge," Joe said, and he offered to contribute a thousand dollars, his limousine, and his driver to the La Follette-Wheeler campaign.

"So here was the Progressive candidate for vice president, who was regarded by some as a radical and had been accused by one labor leader of being financed by Russian Communists, campaigning in a Rolls furnished by a rising investment banker," Wheeler would marvel years later.

Meanwhile, Joe worked hard to defeat the censorship referendum, introducing Will Hays to influential newspaper editors and lobbying opinion-makers. Censorship bills had been introduced in thirty-six states, but the Massachusetts vote would be the first real test of how the public felt about film censorship.

As election day approached, Wheeler found that Kennedy's Rolls-Royce was no longer available and that Kennedy's money was drying up. When he asked why, Joe didn't mince words. His support for the Progressive ticket had been a maneuver to scare wavering Democrats into voting for the Democratic ticket by making it seem as if the Progressives had a real chance of winning. "We told [the voters] that a Progressive party victory would close the mills and factories," Joe had the effrontery to explain to Wheeler. "And in South Boston we told the Irish that the La Follette program would destroy their church."

As it turned out, Kennedy's efforts were in vain. On election day it was Coolidge who triumphed. But Joe still had cause to celebrate. In Massachusetts, voters defeated state movie censorship by a two-to-one margin.

Winning, as a way of life, was what Joe believed in. "Go for it!" was the lesson he instilled in his children. Coming in second was never good enough. Goaded by an ambition to be accepted in an ever wider world, he pushed himself relentlessly as a stock manipulator, whiskey importer, and theater owner. To make money was to acquire power and social acceptance. He mixed with all kinds of people and was equally at ease with hard-eyed stock plungers like Jess Levermore, William Danforth, and "Sell 'em" Smith, with Wall Street patricians like Jeremiah Milbank, with bantering newspapermen and press lords like William Randolph Hearst and Colonel Robert E. McCormick. But there were still prejudices. To be called a Boston Irishman galled him. "I was born here," he said. "My children were born here. What the hell do I have to do to be an American?"

A particularly smarting snub came in 1925 when Joe tired of summering in predominantly Catholic Nantucket and decided to storm the more fashionable Yankee bastion of Cohasset. He and Rose rented a summer place there and had themselves driven around in the plum-colored Rolls-Royce—only to find themselves and their children ostracized by the rest of the summer residents. Rose was snubbed by the Cohasset matrons and Joe was blackballed when he applied for membership in the country club. Years later the memory of that summer still rankled. "Those narrow-minded, bigoted sons of bitches barred me because I was an Irish Catholic and son of a barkeep."

As a result, he sent Eddie Moore to New York to look for a place, preferably in the Westchester County suburbs, where he could settle his family and turn *his* back on Boston.

In the meantime he took a closer look at the picture business, which was currently riding a tide of prosperity. He saw what others didn't: that the wildcatting days were over and that the industry was being concentrated in the hands of a few big companies, each of which maintained film factories in Hollywood and showed their finished productions in company-owned chains of cinemas in the United States and Canada and, increasingly, overseas. True to his instincts, he saw an opportunity for someone coming in from the sidelines.

Before Joe began lining up his finances, he briefly became an assistant to Jesse Lasky. The junior partner of the formidable Zukor-Lasky combine,

Lasky liked to hire bright young men, and had already groomed Walter Wanger, an elegant San Franciscan with international connections, and Gilbert Miller, a British theatrical producer active in Paris who brought Maurice Chevalier to Paramount and made Lasky use more stage plays as source material. In Kennedy, Lasky saw a valuable connection to money, to banking and financing.

Jesse Lasky, Jr., would remember his parents inviting Joe Kennedy to dinner at their apartment at 910 Fifth Avenue. "My father was very good about telling me who was coming to dinner so that I would make a sensible intelligent appearance. Even though I was only sixteen, I was writing poetry and I was always brought in for conversations because it was good for me to speak with adults and to know who everybody was. My father said, 'Mr. Kennedy is coming to dinner. He's a Harvard man and he's joining my staff as a personal assistant, to get experience in the film business. And you'll like him.' "

Young Lasky, who would spend fifteen years as one of De Mille's screenwriters, thought the dinner guest was very nice because Kennedy did the wonderful grown-up thing of inquiring about Jesse's school, what he like best in school, where he intended to go to college, and whether he had considered Harvard. "He had a great personal fascination which hit you immediately," Lasky, Jr., would remember, "a little like Franklin D. Roosevelt or Neil McCarthy, De Mille's great lawyer. Kennedy was great fun, very loquacious, very dapper. And when I sat down and listened to my father familiarizing him with the setup of Famous Players–Lasky, I realized Kennedy knew how to ask the right questions. They talked about the structure of the company, about Zukor as the chairman of the board, Sidney Kent, Walter Wanger, and B. P. Schulberg, who had taken over the day-to-day administration of the studio from my father. I think my father felt Kennedy would be very useful as a contact with eastern banking. Here was a chance to install someone in the company who knew money."

Judging by the events of the next half-dozen years, Kennedy profited more from these dinner conversations than Lasky. In 1936 Lasky would lose a financial power struggle to Sam Katz and would lose Zukor's vote of confidence in a boardroom confrontation. (There was a chilling premonition at Lasky's luncheon with Zukor before the crucial board meeting: When Lasky reached for a cigar to offer Zukor, his breast pocket was empty.)

In 1926, however, Lasky readily explained to his new "assistant" that low-budget westerns, action pictures, and stunt thrillers were the bread-and-butter of the picture industry. In small towns, the films had a life-expectancy of half a week, sometimes less. More interesting from a financial point of view were two other classifications: "Rialto specials," films that ran as long as the public wanted them, and the several annual "roadshow" pictures that lent prestige and goodwill to the industry. It was Lasky's theory that you could both pay dividends to your stockholders and advance the art of filmmaking by a judicious mix of the various genres.

The place to start, Joe decided, was in bread-and-butter pictures. Galen Stone was very much the retired millionaire, always good for a couple of hundred grand in an attractive deal, but an adroit angle shot at even a modest bread-and-butter film company might demand higher stakes. Joe turned to Guy Currier, whose ascent had been as spectacular as his own, and, with his old college chum and some of his clients, put a package together.

The suave, darkly handsome Currier had moved from law and politics to high finance, becoming what New Haven Railroad president C. S. Messen called "the shrewdest lobbyist on Beacon Hill." Currier was one of the so-called Big Four who stage-managed the Massachusetts legislature, controlling the men who controlled the votes. Almost never in the public eye and rarely seen in the corridors and cloakrooms of the Capitol, he operated by telephone from his Hancock Street law office. He gave intimate dinners in private rooms at his club, and maintained his silken grip with carefully calculated introductions of aspiring lawmakers and well-timed contributions to election campaigns. Women admired Currier and fondly recalled his impulsive gifts. He had married Marie Burroughs, a Shakespearean actress, and the Curriers were increasingly spending their winters in Florence, Italy, surrounding themselves with people who united finance, politics, and the arts.

One of Currier's clients was Frederick Prince, a Yankee Democrat twice elected mayor of Boston before Fitzgerald and the Irish tide engulfed City Hall. Almost by accident, Prince had become the owner of forty-four railroads. A short, powerful man, he had clashed with J. P. Morgan in the railroad wars, and lived in baronial splendor on a thousand-acre North Shore estate. Eighty polo ponies filled Freddy Prince's stables, and the best players rode on the teams he fielded. He had a zest for new ideas and, before the war, had sent a promoter to czarist Russia with the idea of setting up a mail-order business. Taking a flyer on the picture business looked to be both fun and profitable. At Currier's request, he agreed to come in on the deal.

When Joe moved, his first action took him and his lawyer, Bartholomew Brickley, in a direction geographically opposite to Hollywood—to London. Joe's goal was to persuade two British firms, Lloyd's and Graham's Trading Company, to let him buy control of a small Hollywood production company known as FBO which owed them three million dollars and was losing more money every week.

Originally a subsidiary of H. F. Robertson's vaudeville empire, FBO had begun life as the Robertson-Cole Company, founded in 1918, the same year such established firms as Edison, Selig, Mutual, and Essanay had been forced out of business. Robertson and Rufus S. Cole built a studio on land purchased from the Hollywood Cemetery at 780 Gower Street, near Melrose Avenue, the heart of Hollywood's "Gower Gulch," where low-budget companies specializing in cowboy movies were concentrated, and plunged into a feature-a-week production. Its stars were Bessie Barriscale, a dark-eyed redhead who alternately played sweet maidens and sultry vamps, and such leading men as Sessue Hayakawa, Richard Talmadge, and William Desmond. Its biggest box-office attractions, however, were western stars Bob Custer and the popular Fred Thomson, who earned $15,000 a week and had his famous gray stallion trucked to location in a custom-built Packard van.

In 1919 Robertson-Cole had snapped up the Triangle Studio, including its sprawling Santa Monica ranch, for one dollar, but the company had not fared well in the turbulent postwar boom in theater construction and studio expansion. Through a series of mergers, in which Pat Powers had a hand, it had become the Film Booking Office of America Inc. (FBO). The name had been the idea of merging partner Hyman Berman, a former Universal film booker and salesman who had the reputation of being one of the sharpest promoters in the business. A dedicated budget-cutter and penny-pincher, Berman had run FBO on a shoestring and put a mean-minded Frenchman named Emile Offerman in charge of the studio. A twenty-four year-old former Sennett gag-writer named Darryl Zanuck toiled for a while at FBO and would remember a great many lowly paid deadbeats on the payroll, most of them relatives of the Berman family, or cousins and nephews of other shareholders, few of them with any knowledge of filmmaking.

Zanuck wrote two-reelers for a series called *The Telephone Girl,* taking a cut in salary in return for screen credits. The title role was played by Alberta Vaughn, an actress who had the roundest eyes in the movies and always looked as if she had been startled out of her wits—which was what she was supposed to be over the shocking things she heard at the switchboard. The series proved so successful that Zanuck was lured to Universal and asked to take over a two-reel boxing series.

On behalf of Stone, Currier, Prince, and himself, Joe offered Lloyd's and Graham's one million dollars for FBO. But the British bankers were elusive. As Brickley would later tell the story, Joe and he were having breakfast one morning, wondering what to do next, when Joe read in the newspaper that Prince Edward was in Paris on a brief vacation.

"Let's go to Paris and see the Prince of Wales!" Joe said.

"Why?" the lawyer asked.

"Leave that to me."

They rushed across the channel, went to Edward's favorite restaurant, and bribed the maître d' to seat them next to the future king. At the appropriate moment, Joe introduced himself. "You might not remember me; Boston 1919." When the prince asked what Joe was doing in Paris, Joe told him he was just having fun before heading back to London to finish some banking business. "Anything I can do for you?" Edward inquired. Joe answered no in such a way as to make it clear there was something. The next morning a letter of introduction arrived by messenger at Kennedy and Brickley's hotel.

The royal commendation was not enough. Joe had tackled his biggest transaction thus far, and it involved seemingly endless transatlantic stumbling blocks. When he and his lawyer sailed home, Joe was suffering an ulcer attack that would worry his father. "I'm afraid he's bitten off more than he can chew," P.J. told one of his son's friends.

Fortunately for Joe, movies weren't the only business in which a fellow with a nimble sense of odds and timing could make some real money. Florida real estate was another.

The Florida Boom of 1924–26 could only have happened in America, and only in the 1920s. The city of Miami was one frenzied real-estate exchange. Two thousand real-estate offices and 25,000 agents were marketing house lots and talking binders and options, water frontage and hundred-thousand-dollar profits—with such frenzy that to prevent traffic congestion, the city fathers passed an ordinance forbidding the sale of property in the street or even the showing of maps.

Joe and Rose had spent the previous winter in Florida, and the land boom suited Joe's talent and temperament perfectly. His interest focused on the classy Palm Beach area. Addison Mitzner, the "society architect," was transforming Palm Beach into a pseudo-Spanish playground for the wealthy. Everybody was making money on land. Prices went climbing, and those who came to scoff often stayed to speculate. Joe was sure the boom wouldn't last. He stayed away until the hurricane season of 1925 ended the land rush. Then, by long-distance telephone, he began picking up small bargains amid the debris.

In February 1926 Joe and three other Harvard alumni were ready to go to Florida to play some golf and see if the real-estate slump could be organized to their advantage. The four men had rendezvoused at the Harvard Club on New York's Forty-fourth Street and had only fifteen minutes to catch the Havana Limited for Palm Beach. Porters were piling luggage and golf bags aboard taxis for the ride to Penn Station when a page boy dashed out, shouting, "Phone call for Mr. Kennedy. They say it's important."

Joe stopped the cab and went back into the club. A few minutes later he came out again. "Sorry, but you fellows will have to go to Florida without me. Seems I've bought myself a motion picture company."

The first-person singular was an exaggeration. To clinch the deal, Currier had invested $125,000, and Freddy Prince had lined up Louis E. Kirstein, head of Filene's Department Store, and "Buck" Dumaine of Amoskeag Mills.

Joe's irrepressible father-in-law leaked the news back in Boston, inflated the purchase price to ten million dollars, and managed to insinuate himself into the center of the story so that the *Boston Post* headline the next day read, "FITZGERALD A FILM MAGNATE."

Independence

My candle burns at both ends;
it will not last the night;
but ah, my foes, and oh, my friends
it gives a lovely light.

—EDNA ST. VINCENT MILLAY

If the winter of 1924–25 was the happiest time in Gloria's life, it was also the most dramatic. She was young, rich, and until Josephine Baker arrived and danced on the Casino de Paris stage in nothing but a frill of bananas, the toast of the town.

Henri talked the Marquise de Brantes, a friend of a friend who was leaving for the Côte d'Azur season, into loaning him her private mansion and staff, and Gloria had Addie bring the children over. The two new words you simply had to know, Gloria discovered, were chic and surrealism. So many new influences were coursing through the arts and fashion. Chanel—whose friends included Pablo Picasso, Jean Cocteau, and Igor Stravinsky—and the new Elsa Schiaparelli—whose friends were the surrealists—competed to raise women's skirts, drop waistlines, and impose flamboyant simplicity. Kees van Dongen and Vertes illustrated the new fashions with striking magazine covers. Sonia Delaunay, the Russian-born painter, worked with Jacques Heims to produce patchwork color coats that embodied the jazz age, and the Gillette company placed the first ads in ladies' magazines for razors to shave the armpits.

To mark the completion of *Madame Sans Gêne,* Gloria bought gifts for every member of the cast and crew. In the Marquise de Brantes's mansion on the place des Etats Unis, she threw a costume party at which guests danced to the music of three bands. When Henri became alarmed at the rate she was spending money, she told him not to worry. Starting January 1 she would be making $7,000 a week. He was stunned.

Back in Hollywood, meanwhile, Jesse Lasky decided the next Swanson picture would be *The Coast of Folly,* and that Allan Dwan would direct it. *Coast of Folly* would be the first movie in which Swanson would play two parts—an Elinor Glyn–type society tigress and the lady's modern, athletic daughter, who was about to ruin her young life. *Madame Sans Gêne* would premiere in New York in early spring 1925, and Zukor and Lasky planned full-blown gala openings, with their star in attendance, in major cities across the United States. Gloria wanted to stay in Paris until after New Year's, and she suggested that Dwan come over to discuss the new script and meet René Hubert, whom she wanted to bring back to America with her and launch as her personal costume designer.

News of Gloria Swanson's sumptuous wrap party reached American gossip columns, together with rumors that the screen idol had gone totally French—indeed, that as soon as her divorce became final in January, she would marry a French millionaire and quit the movies. Zukor told Allan to catch the first boat to Europe and bring Gloria to her senses before she made some awful mistake. In the middle of preparations for an elaborate joke to be played on the onrushing Dwan, a charade in which Gloria would pretend to be going off the deep end, she discovered she was pregnant.

Her first thought was of the morals clause in her contract with Lasky. She couldn't marry Henri immediately because there was still another month to go before her California divorce became final. After that, a very premature baby would provoke press speculation or worse. Even if Lasky chose not to invoke the morals clause, her violation of it meant he could dictate terms that might lower her earnings and force her to compromise on material and directors. She could also have Henri's child, but alas, Henri was no millionaire. She sensed she might lose him in the exchange, because they had both gone past the stage where they could live in a garret. Abortion was inevitable.

She decided she couldn't tell Henri; to burden him with the demands of her career would be unfair. The only French person she could trust to find a doctor to perform an abortion and to keep it secret, she decided, was André Daven. One afternoon when Henri was out she asked the journalist to the house, showed him her contract, and explained her dilemma. When she said she saw no other solution but an abortion, he agreed. "You and Henri are both young," he said. "You have all the time in the world to have another child." The words stung. When she was seventeen a nurse had told her the same thing. She had judged Wallace Beery harshly then, had never really forgiven him, and now she was ready to do the same thing.

André arranged the abortion while Henri arranged a civil wedding. At first, the *maire* of the sixteenth arrondissement would not accept newspaper accounts of her divorce. When no official papers arrived from her California lawyer after two weeks, she assumed they were lost. Finally, Henri persuaded the municipal authorities to waive the legal obstacles on condition that a representative of the U.S. embassy be present to vouch for her. Henri rushed home to tell Gloria they had permission to be married on January 28, 1925. Gloria paled. André had arranged the abortion for the day after.

She decided to go through with both.

To avoid pandemonium or a full Paramount production number, they decided that, with the exception of a handful of people they wanted present in the town hall, they wouldn't tell anyone—not even Addie. The friends and witnesses included Daven and Hubert, Henri's brother Alain, Leonce Perret and his wife, plus a Hewlett Johnson from the U.S. embassy. Henri said *oui;* Gloria, yes; and Mme. Perret cried. When Gloria called her mother to tell her the news, Addie was furious. Gloria had made a terrible mistake, she said, marrying a penniless Frenchman, whatever his name.

They had rented a suite at the Plaza Athenée for the wedding night and had invited a few more friends to a reception. To make sure the facts were correct the next morning when Lasky and everybody would read about it, Basil Woon, the Hearst papers' Paris correspondent, was among the guests. Little Gloria knew what it meant to have a father; the experience was new for Brother. He said he liked having a dad. Addie wouldn't talk to her new son-in-law, and the next day made arrangements to sail back to America alone.

Before Gloria and Henri fell asleep that night, she whispered she would be out most of the next day with Daven to approve press releases and editing arrangements for *Madame Sans Gêne*. Woon had left a copy of his wire story—"Gloria Swanson is now a full-fledged marquise," it began. The next morning there were mountains of telegrams, but she rushed past them downstairs. André was waiting. They drove to a doctor's office in an elegant apartment building without talking.

The doctor spoke a few words in halting English before she succumbed to the ether. When she came to, André was there. He had phoned Henri and told him they would see him at the hotel in the afternoon. Gloria was surprised she could walk. André took her for a long drive. When she felt recovered, he took her back to the Plaza Athenée.

The suite was in chaos, with boxes and flower baskets lining even the corridor. With difficulty, Gloria got everybody to leave. André was told to take Henri to lunch, Jane West was instructed to have the hotel switchboard hold all calls, and Hubert was instructed to take Addie to the boat train. When she was alone, Gloria flopped down and buried her head in the pillows.

By nightfall she was drenched in fever. Henri called a doctor, who had her hospitalized. Each time she woke up, Henri was there. She told him the truth; he told her she had tetanus. He didn't say that such infections were often fatal and characterized by violent spasms and rigidity of many or all the voluntary muscles. Nurses tried to make her stand up; her feet folded under her. Finally, she had her first meal sitting in a wheelchair. Everybody applauded when she began moving her toes.

"What happened to my hair?" was her first question after regaining consciousness. The nurses had cut it off so they could wrap her head in towels at the height of the fever attacks. When Henri took her for a first short drive, he pointed to the café across from the hospital where for two weeks reporters had kept a death watch, tried to bribe hospital personnel for news, and took turns using the one telephone. Every newspaper in Europe and America had carried daily bulletins on her recovery.

Jane sailed to New York with little Gloria and Buddy in mid-February, and the newlyweds went to Nice, Monte Carlo, and other Riviera resorts for a short vacation. There were minor irritants, such as Gloria's being fined by a New York court for failing to appear as corespondent in a divorce case. Janet Beecher Hoffman was suing her wealthy psychiatrist husband and, to gain custody of their child, claimed her husband had been Gloria's lover. The psychiatrist had indeed been a friend of hers during her Sunday salon days in Manhattan, but it was not the first time she had been named in divorce proceedings because a wife had discovered a picture of her in a husband's wallet. She had ignored the subpoena and, as a result, was fined $250 for contempt of court.

Before Gloria and Henri were ready to leave for New York, they went to the movies to see Lois Wilson in *La Caravane de l' Ouest,* as James Cruze's epic western, *The Covered Wagon,* was called in French. Gloria thought Lois was fabulous. A starring role couldn't have come to a nicer person. In late March, when they embarked on the *Paris* at Cherbourg, they found that Ignace Paderewski, the Polish composer, pianist, patriot, and statesman, was also a first-class passenger.

The return to America was a triumph. Gloria's marriage to a nobleman and her long battle with death had provided Famous Players–Lasky/Paramount with millions of dollars' worth of free publicity, and Zukor and Lasky pulled out all the stops. Adoring crowds nearly smothered the far from recovered movie star, but it was out of the question for Gloria to lie low. The night of the April 17 premiere at the Rivoli Theater police rerouted traffic on Broadway. As the line of limousines crawled up to the theater, a moving wedge of policemen stood guard while Henri got out. When the crowd saw Gloria, a mass of people surged forward. The police advised Gloria and Henri to leave by a side entrance as soon as the picture started.

After the premiere, Paramount threw a dinner at the Park Lane, where

Allene Talmey, the columnist, caught Gloria at her apotheosis. "After the usual publicity spasms of superlatives, the daughter of Capt. Joseph Swanson, and the former wife of actor Wallace Beery and businessman Herbert Somborn stood up in front of those paunchy, bald-headed men who remembered a hard-faced Sennett bathing girl and a spit-curled De Mille vamp. They saw a formal, cool woman, the Marquise de la Falaise de la Coudraye, magnificent in her recreation of Gloria Swanson."

Gloria couldn't wait to board the private railway car Zukor and Lasky had provided for the trip to California and the West Coast premiere. Instead of a leisurely trip through a spring landscape, the cross-country trip became an unending whistle stop. "We wanna see your haircut," hundreds of girls lining the track squealed. "We wanna see the prince." Gloria had lost twenty pounds and felt half dead. The conductor promised she would be able to rest up after Chicago. Paramount had other ideas, of course, and milked the transcontinental trip for all it was worth, winding it up with a party for studio salesmen that, Lasky would write in *I Blow My Own Horn* in 1957, "has never been eclipsed in my Hollywood experience of elaborate functions."

Madame Sans Gêne inaugurated Sid Grauman's million-dollar theater in downtown Los Angeles. Police formed a phalanx around Gloria, Henri, and Addie as thousands struggled for a glimpse of the star. The picture had already started when usherettes escorted them to their seats, but the darkened theater burst into light. Gloria saw Mickey Neilan with Doug Fairbanks and Mary Pickford. From the balcony people pelted her with orchids and gardenias. She blew kisses. Henri was seated between Constance De Mille and Addie; Gloria between C.B. and Mack Sennett, who was drying his eyes. A few minutes after the lights dimmed again, ushers crawled forward to tell Gloria police couldn't handle the crowd. They were bringing the car around to the alley and wanted her and her party to leave immediately through the orchestra pit.

With Addie and Henri, Gloria sneaked out through the back. Police escorted them to Crescent Drive for their first quiet moment in weeks.

Gloria's illness in Paris, her recovery, and her return combined to send her popularity soaring. After some hesitation while they made sure Henri's pedigree was genuine, the movie colony adopted her affable marquis. The moment Gloria and Henri accepted Mary Pickford and Douglas Fairbanks's invitation to dine at Pickfair, social invitations began to flood in; acquaintances, near-acquaintances, and perfect strangers wanted to size up "Hank."

"The Marquis is of medium height, athletic build and blond, not at all the tall, dark and haughty figure of the traditional nobility," wrote editor James Quirk of *Photoplay*. "I am inclined to think the Irish in him is predominant, for he wins you at once with the frank, easy smile and easy manner. That laugh of his is natural and infectious, and more than once I have seen him laugh Gloria out of her troubles when she was sorely beset by a multitude of worries and harried by a score of people intent on talking business with her."

Elinor Glyn approved of Henri. So did Marion Davies and William Randolph Hearst. Bess and Jesse Lasky were taken by his charm and hand kissing, and made sure he met Jean de Limur, a Frenchman of similar ilk who was technical director for Chaplin and De Mille. A few people thought Henri was a lightweight, almost a gigolo, but in the charmed circle he discussed Napoleonic history with Chaplin and the Great War with De Mille, and he greeted Sir Henry Wood when he arrived as a guest conductor at the new Hollywood Bowl.

"Oh the parties we used to have!" Gloria would recall years later. "In those days the public wanted us to live like kings and queens. So we did—and why not? We were in love with life. We were making more money than we ever dreamed existed and there was no reason to believe it would ever stop." Marion Davies threw a costume ball to which Mary Pickford came as Lillian Gish in *La Bohème,* Douglas Fairbanks was Don Q from *Son of Zorro,* Chaplin was Napoleon, Madame Glyn was Catherine of Russia, and Marshall Neilan and Allan Dwan came disguised as the bearded Smith Brothers of coughdrop fame. The marquis and marquise de la Falaise came as themselves.

It took $10,000 a month to pay Gloria's living expenses at the Crescent Drive mansion and the country estate near Croton-on-Hudson that Henri hadn't even seen yet. Their permanent staff included four secretaries, a full-time press agent, several business managers, and a full staff of household servants on both coasts. As the nation's leading fashion queen, Gloria ran up a yearly clothes bill that included $35,000 for fur coats and other wraps, $50,000 for gowns, $9,000 for stockings, $5,000 for shoes, $10,000 for lingerie, $5,000 for headdresses, $5,000 for purses, and a $6,000 cloud of perfume. Just before leaving for France to make *Madame Sans Gêne,* she had bought the top floor of the Park Chambers Hotel at Sixth Avenue and Fifty-eighth Street and commissioned her friend Sport Ward to redecorate it. Sport had converted what had been a large set of servants' and utilities quarters into a splendid penthouse and now was writing to Gloria that her new Manhattan pied-à-terre was ready whenever she was.

Still, her accommodations were modest compared to the hundred-room Ocean House that William Randolph Hearst was building for Marion Davies on the Santa Monica beach or Harold Lloyd's forty-room Greenacres. Gloria may have had a golden bathtub in her black marble bathroom, but Pola Negri boasted a Roman bath in her living room; Barbara

LaMarr, an enormous sunken bath with gold fixtures; Tom Mix, a rainbow-colored fountain in his dining room; and John Gilbert, Cossack servants and a private balalaika orchestra. If Gloria had herself driven down Sunset Boulevard in a leopard-upholstered Lancia, Rudy Valentino drove a custom-built Voisin touring car with a coiled-cobra radiator cap, Clara Bow drove a red Kissel convertible with chow dogs to match, while Mae Murray could be seen in either a canary-yellow Pierce-Arrow or a more formal white Rolls with liveried chauffeur.

Gloria and Henri attended La Murray's 1926 wedding to Russian Prince David Mdivani, the handsome brother of the gorgeous twenty-year-old Princess Roosadana Mdivani, who was the toast of avant-garde Paris. Whether Murray had become a real princess by virtue of her marriage was a question that agitated the film colony. The status of the Mdivanis in their native Georgia had never been well defined. Their Moslem grandfather's "chateau" was little more than a heap of ruins in Adzharistan, but the last tsar had indeed made Alexei Mdivani, David and Roosadana's father, the governor of Batumi. The Bolshevik Revolution and a costly mistake by their mother were blamed for Prince David's need to marry a rich movie star. On the family's dash to the Turkish border in 1917, Madame Mdivani had inadvertently taken a trunk containing her petticoats instead of the trunk containing the family jewels.

The pursuit of European titles by Negri, Swanson, and Murray created something of a backlash. Gloria saw the danger signals when she found herself being referred to as "la Marquise de la Etcetera" or "the Marquise of Gloria." In response, she stopped using her crown-embossed stationery and began referring to her husband simply as Henri. Still, even before Mae Murray married her prince, the press questioned the legitimacy of Henri's title.

Deeply offended, Gloria had him hold his own press conference in October 1925. "To have the title of marquis has not caused me vanity," he told the assembled press, "but since the point has been raised, here are the facts: I have authenticated birth and marriage certificates of all my ancestors since 1271, when a member of my family addressed a memorial to the king complaining that his castle had been ruined in the late wars. The document is now in the Rouen record office—a sort of thirteenth-century tax complaint.

"My title actually is Marquis de la Coudraye, conferred in 1707 on my fifth great-grandfather, then named Baron de la Falaise, by Queen Casimira of Poland, at the time he was ambassador to Rome. This title is confirmed by several documents signed by Louis XV, especially one dated Versailles, November 22, 1766, countersigned by the king's secretary. This was the grant of the governorship of Fontenay le Comte, in the Vendée, to Marquis de la Coudraye, and in case of his death to his son, Count de la Coudraye."

A genealogy that stretched back nearly six hundred years impressed the reporters, and after *The New York Times* had its Paris correspondent check several records, the queries stopped.

To Gloria's relief, her children took to Henri. Little Gloria was four and half; Brother, a three-year-old toddler just beginning to talk. They clung to Henri who, to Gloria, seemed to possess all the right paternal instincts.

With the gentle Alec B. Francis as her leading man, she started filming *The Coast of Folly* in the spring of 1926. Once again she found working with Allan Dwan a pleasure. In this Forrest Halsey adaptation of Coningsby Dawson's sentimental novel, she was playing both a mother and her daughter. Nadine Gathaway is a woman who abandons her home and child for the pleasures of a frivolous life on the French Riviera; then, years later, she meets her daughter and tries to prevent the young girl from making the same mistakes. San Diego and Coronado substituted for the Côte d'Azur. To play the jaded Nadine, Gloria let herself be inspired by both her mother and Elinor Glyn. She made the daughter a vigorous, athletic flapper and thought the difference between the two amazing. Critics were less overwhelmed; they found Swanson as the older woman very bad, and said her portrayal of the daughter was merely a series of baby stares. *The Coast of Folly* was released in late August to less than enthusiastic reviews. *Variety,* for one, wondered whether Paramount hadn't decided that Swanson's salary and her wardrobe budget were so high that it could afford to skimp on the rest of the production.

More disturbing to Gloria personally that summer was Lasky's handling of *Madame Sans Gêne.* To allow theaters to squeeze in five showings a day, Paramount cut thirty minutes from the film, thereby reducing the historical romance to a series of barely related scenes of Gloria in fabulous costumes. In Paris, Leonce Perret could not get assurances from Adolphe Osso that the French release would not be similarly truncated, and in desperation the director wrote a string of letters to Henri urging the de la Falaises to take up the matter with Lasky himself.

Gloria tried to use her husband as a foil in her sparring with Lasky. With her contract coming up for renewal, gossip columnists and trade papers speculated that she would join United Artists. Griffith had left UA and was working at Paramount as a hired hand, but Gloria had not forgotten her long conversation with Doug Fairbanks on the voyage back from Europe the year before, and she listened willingly to UA's Maurie Cleary, a short, lively executive authorized by Fairbanks, Pickford, and Chaplin to invite her to join.

Essentially a distribution company for movies the partners made themselves, United Artists wanted her to invest in the partnership in return for the chance to produce her own pictures. She could make one or two films a year, choose her own stories, be her own boss, and be the equal of the founding artists. Doug was the most active of the trio, and UA was actively seeking to enlarge the partnership, possibly to include Rudolph Valentino and Sam Goldwyn. To remain viable, the company had recently added a tough, aggressive executive who knew the business inside and out—Joseph Schenck. Cleary told Gloria that if her pictures made money, which they had almost all done, she could expect to earn more than she did working for Lasky.

Cleary's comings and goings at *The Coast of Folly* set did not escape the notice of Lasky, who was receiving frantic phone calls, first from Sid Kent, and then from Zukor, to sign her up again at any price. Finally, he showed up on the set and asked to have a word with her in private.

"Is this about business, Mr. Lasky?" she asked.

"Yes," he answered, "it won't be long."

"Well, I'd prefer to discuss any business at home in front of my husband. Can you come there tomorrow at three?"

Lasky's glance turned icy behind the pince-nez. She was seeing Cleary on the Paramount set but didn't have five minutes for him. "Of course, Gloria," he said, "I'll be there."

Lasky arrived at the appointed hour flanked by two lawyers and an accountant. Gloria had rehearsed the scene with Henri and prompted him to get involved in the discussion as much as he could. When the butler showed the Paramount foursome into the library, Henri was seated behind the desk; Gloria was in a comfortable chair to his right. It was her hour of sweet revenge—for the morals clause, for the fabricated telegram from Will Hays instructing the studio to settle her divorce, for the abortion in Paris that had nearly cost her life. As she listened to Lasky's flattering summing-up of her seven years with Paramount, she knew she held all the trump cards. First and foremost, she had a firm, enthusiastic offer to join UA.

Before Lasky could get to her contract, she and Henri brought up the matter of *Madame Sans Gêne.* The cut-down version released in the United States was raising concerns in France, Henri explained. Perret had approached Adolphe Osso, but the Paramount chief for Europe had been evasive. What exactly were the French going to see at the upcoming December premiere? A film version of Sardou's famous play or a series of scenes with Gloria in fabulous costumes? "Mr. Perret requests that Paramount send my wife and me personally to Paris to tell the French that they will see the complete Sardou play on the screen."

Lasky nodded enthusiastically. If *Madame Sans Gêne* had been short-

ened in the U.S. release, it was because Americans got restless in the
historical parts. "I would be delighted to have you and Gloria go to Paris
as studio representatives before the premiere and tell your countrymen we
won't cut a frame over there. You could function as our official, salaried,
international appointees to handle the matter. Would that be agreeable
to you?"

"Perfectly," said Henri.

Gloria was appalled. Lasky had retired her husband from the field in
a minute by accommodating him. Henri had accepted the job offer not
realizing that Lasky would get back a hundred times what it would cost him
to have Henri and Gloria promote the film in France.

Turning to Gloria, Lasky told her Paramount was ready to double her
salary.

"Fourteen thousand a week? Why, Mr. Lasky, for two months all the
columnists have been naming a higher rumored figure than that." She
smiled.

"Has anyone else offered you more?"

After she told him United Artists was offering her complete artistic
freedom, Lasky upped his offer to $18,000 a week. Gloria asked the accoun-
tant if $18,000 a week added up to a million a year.

"Not quite," Lasky answered for him.

In his autobiography, Lasky would remember finally offering her $300,-
000 a picture for three pictures a year plus fifty percent of the profits, her
pick of directors, a voice in her stories, and her own wardrobe designer.
"When she still showed no glimmer of interest, I returned to my office
disheartened. Calling Zukor, I admitted my failure. He listened to the terms
I had promised and, after conferring with Kent, authorized me to raise the
ante to a million dollars a year, and half the profits."

Gloria and Allan were both anxious to get back to New York—she had
yet to show Henri the Croton-on-Hudson estate—and together they picked
a wistful story of a smalltown waitress who dreams of becoming a famous
actress and winds up on a showboat on the Ohio River. Lasky okayed *Stage
Struck* for late summer production and location shooting in Martinsville,
West Virginia.

Samuel Goldwyn joined United Artists. In June, Gloria had Cleary
explain to her and Henri exactly what her joining UA would mean. She
would be expected to purchase $100,000 worth of preferred stock in the
partnership, and as a partner, she would profit from all the films the company distributed, including Chaplin's long-awaited *Gold Rush*. A separate
affiliate called Art Finance Company lent money to the member artists to
bankroll their films. Once she had made a film, her only obligation would
be to pay back her Art Finance loan with interest. Although a UA stock-

holder, she would be under no obligation to sell all or any of her pictures to UA for distribution. She could sell her films to any distributor.

Turning to Henri, Cleary said, "You are interested in producing, I presume?"

"Oh yes, I am," Henri answered.

Gloria promised an answer within three weeks. After Cleary left, she asked Henri if he really wanted to get into the business. Yes, but only if she wanted him to. She was twenty-six and, if she dared take the jump, she would be her own boss. She would get off the four-pictures-a-year treadmill. On the other hand, she would no longer have anyone else to blame when things went wrong.

Lasky increased his offer to $22,000 a week, or $1.2 million a year. She asked Dwan what he would do. "Take it, probably," her director answered. When he asked what *she* wanted to do, she said she felt like she did the night in San Pedro harbor when she had dived off a pier for Jack Conway rather than confess she couldn't swim.

Since that day in 1915 when she had taken the streetcar to Mack Sennett's studio on Glendale Boulevard, she had been under contract to somebody. Keystone, Triangle, De Mille, and Famous Players–Lasky had told her which film she would make next, and who else would be in it, and who would produce and direct it. She had rebelled on occasion, but the studios had justified the contracts on the grounds that they invested time and money in developing her career and, whatever she thought, both she and her employers had benefited from the security of a long-term contract.

Life without a studio contract was an unnatural existence. It was something few actors, directors, or anyone else considered valuable to the industry would dare.

On June 15 Gloria signed to join United Artists. Two weeks later she left for West Virginia without talking to Lasky. *Stage Struck* would be her last film for Paramount. It was also different. She hadn't played a broad comedy in years. *The Gold Rush* opened in New York to a roar of applause, and she thought of it—and Chaplin—as the example to follow. Chaplin took his time but came up with masterpieces. If only she could do half as well.

In the meantime, she had to face life without a $7,000-a-week paycheck.

If Gloria Swanson expected that becoming one of the United Artists meant sipping tea at Pickfair with Doug, Mary, and Charlie, Joseph Schenck soon disabused her.

Schenck was a plain, oafish-looking man with a congenital cast in one of his eyes who insisted his surname was pronounced "Skenk." When Gloria first met him she thought he looked like a secondhand furniture salesman. Others thought of him as one of the smartest executives in pictures, and women usually adored him because he had loads of charm and possessed a rich sense of humor. Like Jack Warner and Carl Laemmle, he was a daring gambler who would get $50,000 on the turn of a card and not twitch a hair when he lost. He was a smooth operator with an aura of power.

With his brother Nicholas, Schenck had come to America from a Russian *shtetl* at the age of twelve and had risen from drugstore clerk to drugstore owner to controlling partner of the Palisades Amusement Park in Fort Lee, New Jersey. The brothers had become aides to Marcus Loew, and in 1917 had gone their separate ways—Nick to become Loew's heir-apparent, Joe to produce Fatty Arbuckle slapsticks and two-reelers starring his wife and sister-in-law, Norma and Constance Talmadge (a third Talmadge sister, Natalie, was married to Buster Keaton). Joe and Norma were the first mogul-star couple. They had been the first of the Hollywood pilgrim couples to build on the Santa Monica beach and now had Hearst, Bess and Jesse Lasky, and Margaret and Louis B. Mayer as neighbors. They were unorthodox hosts. As the Mayers' daughter Irene observed, Joe casually invited the great and the raffish, Norma asked whomever she pleased, and neither cared about the mix.

It was Doug Fairbanks who had convinced Schenck to become the administrative head of UA. The last seven pictures of Griffith's had lost money, due in part to the pioneer filmmaker's proud and senseless practice of keeping a studio on line year-round although he made only one picture a year. Schenck had a powerful impulse to take Griffith into his protective custody to save him from his own impracticalities. To keep United Artists humming, however, Schenck had brought Norma and his sister-in-law into the partnership. After Goldwyn and Swanson, he wanted John Barrymore, Rudy Valentino, and Buster Keaton to follow.

In Schenck, Gloria found a worthy adversary and teacher. Before Art Finance could bankroll her first picture, he explained, it needed collateral to borrow money from Bank of America, meaning she would have to take out a million dollars' worth of life insurance to protect the investment. She should be careful in choosing the doctor who would examine her, he warned. Physicians were often on the take, ready to diagnose an ailment she would have to pay them to conceal. He also suggested that, although the United Artists' lot on the corner of Hollywood Boulevard and Formosa Avenue was small and unstructured, she make her debut as an independent producer-star there because of the available backup of talent. But Gloria couldn't wait to move into her new Manhattan penthouse. She would make her first UA picture in New York, she announced.

Incorporating Gloria Swanson Productions Inc. was a frustratingly slow process. The insurance company wouldn't take her word for her age, and Grandma Bertha had to travel to New York to vouch for her. Since

Henri was not a citizen, Addie became a reluctant officer of the company. Nothing was simple. Cost calculations, distribution deals, options, loan negotiations, rental of space at the Cosmopolitan Studio that Hearst had built in Harlem so Marion Davies could make pictures in the East occupied May and June—all that, and no income, left her humbled, confused, and anything but adventurous. As a Paramount star, she had had a huge organization at her disposal. As an independent, she felt she was not only incurring Paramount's enmity but that of the other studios as well. She was setting a dangerous precedent. Other stars might want to follow her example.

She lived on a scale that not even top producers could afford. Frank Crowninshield, now editor of *Town and Country,* introduced her to José Maria Sert, the Spanish artist whose murals were all the rage and who was Roosadana Mdivani's lover. Gloria hired him to design the doors for her penthouse, at $1,000 apiece. She couldn't find stories or directors to suit her. She couldn't hire the players she wanted. Worst, she had to fight the paralyzing impression that failure was a foregone conclusion—that, between her extravagance and her independence, she was destined to mess up. Finally, after listening to advice and suggestions from scores of people, she picked a 1917 play, *Eyes of Youth,* as the vehicle for her independent debut.

Written by Charles Guernon and Max Marcin, *Eyes of Youth* had made a Broadway star of Marjerie Rambeau in 1918. It was the play that Clara Kimball Young and Valentino had made for Equity Pictures, which Herbert Somborn had screened for Gloria and Bea La Plante on their second date. Clara Young was supposed to have been washed up back then, but the role in *Eyes of Youth* had brought her back with a bang. The story was a series of variations on a theme. In a prologue, a Roman maiden flings herself into a flaming abyss rather than submit to an Egyptian brute. In a modern-day continuation, the maiden is a young woman uncertain about which suitor in her life she should choose. The Egyptian reappears, and in order to atone for his two-thousand-year-old crime, allows the heroine to see three of her possible futures in a crystal ball and to pick the man who will make her happy.

In July, Gloria hired Earle Browne to write a fresh screenplay and looked for a top director—only to discover that all the good ones were under contract. She settled on Albert Parker, her old friend from her Triangle days, who had directed her in two pictures and, behind the Beverly Hills Hotel, had taken a black eye from Wallace Beery. More important, Parker had directed Young and Valentino in *Eyes of Youth,* which meant he knew the material and would want to top himself. He had just completed *The Black Pirate,* the latest and most acrobatic of Douglas Fairbanks's swashbucklers, and his lawyer was insisting on a two-picture, $100,000

contract. Gloria balked, but remembered Mary Pickford's formula for success as an independent—find the best people, pay them well, and keep them
under contract.

Parker was signed.

Henri left for Europe in August amid reports that Gloria and he were
getting a divorce. He was sailing for France because his immigration permit
had expired and had to be renewed in the country of issue, he explained to
New York reporters who confronted him with the divorce rumors that
allegedly originated with the couple's "most intimate woman friend on the
Pacific Coast." "We are as happy as the birds of May, and why the public
should wish us to be unhappy is more that I can understand," the marquis
told the press. He would be back in four weeks to attend a prize fight
between Jack Dempsey and Gene Tunney in Chicago.

Gloria was totally absorbed by her film. The script Browne delivered
was promising. In one of the reincarnations, she would play an opera singer
living in sin with a dirty old impresario who makes her the toast of Paris.
To play the poor but honest swain with whom she decides to settle down
in the fade-out, she and Parker chose John Boles, a Southern gentleman
Gloria discovered in a Broadway musical. Boles's enthusiasm at the idea of
making a movie, she thought after meeting him backstage, would compensate for his lack of film experience. To play her brother, she and Parker
chose Raymond Hackett. They also cast André de Segurola, a former opera
star, and Pauline Garon, an actress De Mille had once ordered to study
Gloria's acting. Parker recommended an English actor named Hugh Miller
for one part; Gloria chose Ian Keith for another, and together they gave
Flobelle Fairbanks, a niece of Doug and Mary, her first movie role. Gloria
told René Hubert she was counting on him to design a wardrobe for her
that would turn the world of fashion on its head.

Sam L. Rothafel, a flamboyant New York impresario, was building the
ultimate movie palace, a 6,214-seat house on Seventh Avenue and Fiftieth
Street. The Roxy would open in seven months, and Rothafel, who liked to
be called Mr. Roxy, wanted to inaugurate his new theater with the world
premiere of the upcoming Swanson picture. It will be the biggest opening
night in movie history, he promised Gloria. She said yes, appeared on the
construction site, and with flashbulbs popping, signed her name on the
gold-leaf dome. So far so good, she told herself. She had borrowed $200,000,
promised a picture for March 1927, and had yet to shoot one foot of film.

United Artists was not a charitable institution. Griffith was back after
failing at Paramount, no longer a producer, but now a hired hand working
for his former partners and trying to come up with a remake of his 1914
success, *Battle of the Sexes.* As Gloria prepared to start shooting, UA's
other new prospective actor-producer, Rudolph Valentino, died. Valen-

tino's death on August 23 provoked mass hysteria. Rambova had divorced him, revealing the marriage had never been consummated, and Pola Negri rushed to his bier, accompanied by a nurse and a publicity man, claiming she was the only woman Rudy had ever loved. Thirty thousand women gathered at Campbell's Funeral home at Broadway and Sixty-sixth Street in New York when it was announced that his body would lie in state there. Rioting ensued, windows were smashed, and in an attempt to control the hordes of grieving women, mounted policemen were mobilized en masse. What angered Gloria was the medical negligence that had precipitated his death at age thirty-one. A month earlier, his Hollywood physician had examined Rudy and pronounced him in perfect health, and up to the very end, the New York doctors who kept him sedated issued reports of his improving health.

Henri returned from France in time for the start of shooting at the Cosmopolitan studio that Hearst had built for his winsome Marion Davies and for the Dempsey-Tunney fight. Billed as the match of the century, the gate reached an incredible $2.6 million as 45,000 people crammed into the Chicago amphitheater and forty million others followed the match on radio. So huge was the arena that two-thirds of the audience in the outermost seats didn't know who had won when the fight was over (ten people dropped dead of heart failure at their radios when Tunney was announced the winner).

The action on the set of *Eyes of Youth* was barely less uproarious. The crystal-ball plot required trick photography and special effects that cameraman Dudley Murphy was not up to. Within a week, they were behind schedule. For Parker, the problem was working with an unfamiliar crew. Boles and young Fairbanks had never been in front of a camera before. Gloria was swept up in the maelstrom of anguish. She panicked at the thought that her first independent production would be laughed off the screen as both dramatically and technically inept, and whipped cast and crew into sixteen- and eighteen-hour work days that resulted in more delays, second-rate effects, and new cost overruns.

Yet there was something exhilarating, Gloria discovered, about being in over one's head, about being in charge of lighting experts in the last throes of nervous collapse.

Her savior turned out to be a Russian refugee working on vertical-takeoff aircraft. George de Bothezat knew nothing about movies, but he was an engineer, and Gloria was desperate. He came up with unconventional solutions to the special effects problems, allowing Parker to concentrate on the acting. Gloria borrowed more money, and by early December the picture was in the can.

After spending a quiet Christmas and New Year's with Henri and the children in Croton, Gloria, Albert, and Henri began working on the editing,

Henri concentrating on the French titles. In February they screened a rough-cut for friends who had a million suggestions for changes that Gloria knew there was no time to make. Nobody liked the title. Gloria wanted to call the picture *The Secret of Life,* but everybody told her it sounded like a biology text. A list of possible titles was submitted to the Roxy's formidable boss. Rothafel picked *The Love of Sunya.*

There were things that could have been better, but they had met the deadline. Gloria felt she had learned a lot; she would know how to avoid the same mistakes the next time. She had worked harder and longer than ever before, with more responsibility than she ever thought she could handle, and she'd loved it.

Making It

A hog, it was said, could travel across the United States without switching trains; a person could not. The fastest way from New York to southern California was through Chicago, and it took four days. In the spring and fall, the journey could be a restful time-out, but in the summer, in those days before air conditioning, it was hell. If one didn't want one's clothes blackened by soot, it was seldom safe to open the windows. In winter, it was often too stifling in the cars close to the locomotive, too cold in the rear coaches.

For his first trip west in January 1926, Joe Kennedy had booked "drawing rooms" on both legs of the 2,985-mile journey—the New York Central's 20th Century Limited to Chicago, and the Santa Fe's no less famous Super Chief from Chicago to the coast.

Future chroniclers of the Kennedy family saga would have much fun with the founding father's Hollywood years. The story was Balzacian, all about passion and lucre. Most biographers would treat it all as a lark, a period of truancy to be told in racy prose and colorful anecdotes. They would describe Joe as both star-crossed rube and wily cardsharp. They would emphasize the essential amateurishness of his thrust into an industry that was in the middle of a vulnerable transition. They would describe his formidable cadre of right-hand men, accountants, and advisers as baby-sitters, valets, or the Irish mafia of the day, all, like their boss, more lucky than savvy. Joe found in Hollywood a speculator's paradise without substance and system that offered him an endless variety of situations capable of being organized to his advantage. He had no feeling for the artistic, no sense of social responsibility. His game was the trashy product that always appeals to the masses.

The true story was, as it so often is, both more complicated and more intriguing.

The new president and chairman of the board of Film Booking Office, Inc., was greeted by studio representatives, and from Union Station was whisked up Beverly Boulevard and then along Melrose Avenue to 780 Gower Street. Going through the books at FBO's corporate headquarters at 1560 Broadway in New York, Joe had already discovered that the company's health was perhaps more robust than its British creditors had suspected. What had killed the investment for Lloyd's and Graham's Trading and forced them to sell their seven-million-dollar holding for a fraction of its worth was the ruinous eighteen percent interest they had had to pay for short-term working capital. Kennedy, Galen Stone, Guy Currier, and Frederick Prince knew that in the current bull market—stock prices had more than doubled in the last five years—there was nothing easier than raising cash. Joe simply created Cinema Credit Corporation as an affiliate of FBO; Freddie Prince bought a hefty bundle of Cinema Credit preferred stock and then arranged a loan of half a million dollars through the Chicago Union Stockyards, one of his companies. A line of credit from four banks gave FBO enough working capital to finance a year's movie production at nominal interest rates. Joe put himself on the payroll at $2,000 a week.

Besides his banker's grasp of finance, Kennedy brought with him his blunt and profane vitality, his sardonic blue stare that could reflect mock surprise at anything new, his ability to internalize in seconds relevant data about new people, and his wisecracking self-confidence. He looked like a man who could also make money for others, and people flocked to him, sensing exciting possibilities. Alexander Korda, formerly of Budapest, Vienna, and Berlin (and a future British movie mogul himself), was a newcomer who hated the perpetual California sun. To direct a screen test of Barbara Stanwyck, he had dressed himself in suit and homburg. He would remember greeting his new boss with a bow and, to show his cosmopolitanism, sprinkling his broken English with literary allusions. Joe, however, turned to an assistant and remarked, "Who does that guy think he is, some kind of fucking baron or something?"

The reaction of the town's moguls to the new boss of bread-and-butter

Gower Gulch was a tad less earthy, but no less eloquent. "A banker!"
Marcus Loew exclaimed in a line Joe would often repeat with delight. "I
thought this business was only for furriers." Others prophesied that the
Wall Streeter would "last quick" and leave his roll behind. That he might
have come into the film business to actually run a production company
occurred to no one. But then again, many both inside and outside the
fast-changing, cutthroat movie game weren't sure it was a business at all.

For his part, the abrasive Boston banker had no high regard for the
studio monarchs. He called them "a bunch of pants pressers." Carl Laemmle, the formidable if erratic boss of Universal Pictures, had fired himself
from a clothing store and stumbled into the nickelodeon business. William
Fox had made the leap from clothes sponging. Adolph Zukor had loaned
money to an arcade operator and, to protect his investment, had taken over
the business. Samuel Goldwyn had graduated from glove salesman to part-
time associate of his former saxophonist brother-in-law Jesse Lasky. The
brothers Warner had worked in their father's shoe store until twelve-year-
old Jack got a job singing in a nickelodeon.

It was, of course, the moviemen's experience that bankers first made
suggestions, later imposed restrictions, and finally gave orders. Back in
1919, Zukor had been the first to go hat in hand to Kuhn, Loeb and
Company to have the investment firm underwrite a stock issue. The need
to raise capital to finance exploding and ever more expensive production
kept even the pacesetters like Famous Players–Lasky, Metro-Goldwyn-
Mayer, and First National dependent on a few sources of big money.

Joe was convinced the studio system was wasteful and inefficient. Inflated budgets and salaries were compounded by imperial ambitions as
studios needlessly built and bought cinemas, thereby making themselves
property-rich, cash-starved takeover targets. He discovered that his surname stood for order and punch, if not stifled competition. Jeremiah J.
("Fighting") Kennedy was no relation, but the man who had worked his
way up through railroad construction and mining camps to become the iron
boss of the old Edison-Biograph trust, the first to put a fist of discipline to
the chaotic nickelodeon wildcatting in 1907.

Joe was ruthless during his first months at FBO. To run the corporate
end in New York, he brought in his horsemen and Pat Scollard, his friend
since the Fore River shipyard days. None of them knew much about moviemaking, but all knew a great deal about the Kennedy way of doing business.
At Gower Street, he hired a seasoned production chief, William Le Baron.

At forty-two, Le Baron was a scholarly and kindly New Yorker who
had been in the film business for a decade. His talent for theatricals had first
asserted itself in 1906, when he wrote the book of an undergraduate show
at New York University. Jesse Lasky, then an ambitious young vaudeville

producer, had caught the show and impulsively hired him. Le Baron had a flair for musicals, and by 1918 was associated with the great theatrical producer Charles B. Dillingham and had brought forth *Apple Blossoms, Her Regiment,* and other plays. The following year he embarked on a movie career as a scenarist, eventually directing the Marion Davies vehicle *When Knighthood was in Flower* and *Little Old New York* for Cosmopolitan Productions in New York. In 1924 Le Baron moved to Paramount, where Lasky put him in charge of the Long Island studio in Astoria. His latest assignment had been an unhappy one—overseeing the second picture the declining Griffith was making for Paramount. *That Royle Girl* had been planned as a modestly budgeted programmer, but Griffith's misgivings had put pressure on Lasky to have the director live up to his contract.

Le Baron's job wasn't to humiliate the most important figure in the American cinema, merely to make sure he delivered the pictures in his charge on time and on budget. *That Royle Girl,* starring Carol Depster, Griffith's young mistress, was not a commercial disaster, but it added nothing to Griffith's prestige.

While Joe cut salaries and budgets, Le Baron cranked up the FBO production schedule to one movie a week. The output was all "program pictures," low-budget westerns, action pictures, and stunt thrillers. Ralph Ince was directing *Bigger than Barnum's* when Joe walked on the set. A performer was swinging on a high trapeze. Three times Joe watched the acrobat swing, leap, miss, and fall ignominiously into the safety net below.

It was more than the bottom-line banker could endure. "Why," he asked Ince, "don't you get somebody who can do the stunt?"

"I can," the director replied, "if you insist. But you see, it would spoil the story, which calls for a flop. I've been two days getting this fellow to miss."

The anecdote was told in the September 1927 issue of *Photoplay* to illustrate the hopes Joe incarnated. "Kennedy has come in afresh, without any of the twenty-year-long tangle of feuds and foibles and superstitions and habits of the motion picture clique and clans to hamper him," wrote the monthly magazine's influential Terry Ramsaye. "He carries the authority of preproven success. He knows figures and bookkeeping and millions do not make him dizzy."

Since *Bigger Than Barnum's* was the first movie FBO completed after Joe became president, he arranged for a preview in Boston and added a new title card to the opening credit crawl: "Joseph P. Kennedy Presents . . ."

Joe enjoyed Hollywood. He rented a big mansion with a swimming pool and tennis court on Beverly Hills' Rodeo Drive. Rose and the children never came to California. Instead, he made frequent trips east, usually with one or several of the horsemen so he could spend the cross-country train

ride doing business. He was back east in the spring when the family moved
to New York.

Eddie Moore had found a house for lease in Riverdale, on the Hudson
River just above Manhattan, and Joe okayed the choice while they looked
for a place to buy. With so many children—another son, Robert, whom
everybody called Bobby, had been born just before they left Brookline—
house hunting had become increasingly difficult. One real-estate agent involved in the search complained, "Mr. Kennedy can't use a residence; he
wants a hotel!"

The move from Boston was carried out in style. Joe put the family and
household staff into a private railway car for the trip south. Almost immediately, a permanent home was found in Bronxville, a select, largely Protestant community in Westchester County known for its restrictive covenants.
Situated seventeen miles north of New York City, the twenty-room red
brick colonial had been built for Anheuser Busch and came with five heavily
wooded acres and cottages for the gardener and chauffeur. When the
Kennedys took possession, family biographers would relate, they arrived in
a convoy of limousines that disgorged children, nurses, governesses, and a
heavy-jawed Irishman who functioned as Joe's handyman.

Joe spent most of the next three years in Hollywood. Like her mother,
who had learned to cope during John Fitzgerald's prolonged absences, Rose
learned to be a single parent for months on end. Bronxville was less parochial than Brookline, and Rose kept trying for acceptance. "Since it was
Joe's duty as the head of the household to do whatever he must to support
the family," she would later write, "it was my responsibility to take charge
of the day-to-day activities."

Now eleven and nine respectively, Joe Jr. and Jack took the school bus
to Riverdale, where they had adjusted well. Kathleen and Eunice were sent
to a Catholic school in Connecticut, while two-year-old Patricia and one-
year-old Bobby were still with their nurses. Eight-year-old Rosemary,
meanwhile, was so retarded that she never learned to use a knife and fork
and her meat had to be cut up before it was served to her. Rose and Joe
were so ashamed of having such a hopelessly incompetent child that for
years they never told anyone of her condition. A sweet, shy girl who looked
a bit like her mother, Rosemary could not stand commotion or violence and
was, from her earliest years, a spectator in the family sports.

While Rose saw to the children's catechism, Joe enforced a different
kind of discipline when he was home. Even when they were young he
treated his children, in a sense, as equals, respecting each as a unique
individual and trying to bring out whatever that individuality was. "Except
to adjust his vocabulary to theirs," Rose would write in her autobiography,
Times to Remember, "he never 'talked down' to them, never patronized

them from the lofty holier and wiser attitude that I have seen some parents take. He said what was on his mind and in his heart. There was a marvelous combination of sternness and warmth, severity and great good humor, the greatest of expectations along with the knowledge of human frailties and a very deep sense of justice."

Joe drilled his own competitive code of life into his children. They were expected to arrive at meals five minutes ahead of time, and if one was late, he or she got hell. When Joe spoke to a child, he expected an intelligent answer back, no small talk or wisecracks. Rose wanted the children to have at least a few years of Catholic schooling, but Joe disagreed. A child could learn morals and faith at home. Joe wanted his children—especially his boys—to be able to deal with people of all faiths or none, and he wanted them to meet all men on their merits. As a result, only the girls spent some years in parochial schools.

Joe never talked about his business at home. The strictest taboo forbade discussing money at the dinner table. In Joe's view, there was no need for such talk. There was enough money, and that was all that mattered. Still, as a matter of discipline, Rose kept the children's weekly allowance below a dollar. Jack chafed under such character-building restrictions and addressed solemn appeals to his father to have his allowance raised from forty to sixty cents.

Rose was never clear which companies her husband was connected with; Joe made so many moves that it would have been hard for anyone to follow his activities, even if he had been more open about financial matters. Eunice would later say, "My father built his financial empire with a secretary and a telephone," but she would also admit he was not around much during her formative years. Joe Jr. and Jack were allowed to express an opinion about Harold "Red" Grange, a football star under contract for a series of FBO college pictures. A sensation with the University of Illinois during the 1925–26 season, Grange shocked a country not yet used to athletes becoming business properties. The crowds that had adopted him as an amateur had turned away when he began sharing the gate receipts of the Chicago Bears. Inclined to let Grange go, Joe asked his sons if they would like to see a Red Grange movie. "Yes, we would," they shouted.

FBO's moment of notoriety came in 1923 with *Human Wreckage,* the exposé of the evils of drugs made by Wallace Reid's widow, Dorothy Davenport. The company produced and distributed it as a film "of vital national interest," and sent Davenport on a cross-country tour. Encouraged by its box-office success, FBO produced Davenport's next two moral warnings: *Broken Law,* about the horrors of juvenile delinquency, and *The Red Kimono,* an antiprostitution melodrama. Most of the company's pictures, however, were as forgettable as they were cheap to make. *A Poor Girl's*

Romance, Rose of the Tenements, The Dude Cowboy, The Flame of the Argentine, and *Red Hot Hooves* were among the titles that graced its catalogue.

Joe caught on quickly. Red Grange was paid on a per diem basis, meaning he was only paid on days when he was working. The reason: Kennedy decreed no picture could cost more than $30,000. Grange starred in *One Minute to Play* and, ably directed by Sam Wood, it was a big moneymaker.

The immensely popular Fred Thomson was one of the few early FBO figures who were spared the ax. Even the economy-minded Kennedy was impressed by the western star whose pictures had the widest distribution of any actor.

Thomson owed his career to Frances Marion. He had earned a Ph.D. from Princeton University with the intention of becoming a college teacher, but while serving in the army during the Great War, he had met and had been stirred by the beautiful movie scenarist turned war correspondent for the *San Francisco Examiner.* She allowed him to pursue her until she caught him. Married in 1919, they spent a year honeymooning in Europe. While in Ireland, they both fell in love with a stallion, which they bought and named Silver King. Seeing what a handsome pair her man and Silver King made, Frances exclaimed, "Fred, you were born to be a western star." Back in Hollywood, however, Fred first played Mary Pickford's leading man in *The Love Light.* Frances, who had written many of Pickford's scripts, was allowed to direct this one, the only time Mary was directed by a woman. Next, Frances wrote a western, and Fred's career was off at a gallop. Frances, meanwhile, had become Irving Thalberg's favorite screenwriter.

Joe realized moviemaking was subjective, and almost wished he was in a more concrete line of business. To an interviewer he said that a steel company making rails knew it was "making something that is so long and so heavy and of such a quality, but when you make a foot of film, it is subject to the judgment of millions of people, each with his own standards of measurements."

An avid movie fan himself, Joe nevertheless walked out after watching only five minutes of FBO's biggest hit, the top-grossing *The Gorilla Hunt.* The company's B pictures may not have made it to New York often, but they did a roaring business in Iowa and Kansas. Peter Collier and David Horowitz would write in *The Kennedys: An American Drama* that "while other producers fought to get their works on Broadway, he was content to have a monopoly on Main Street." Nothing could be further from the truth. Joe wanted to crack urban markets and the big box-office receipts, and on one of his trips to New York went to see Mr. Roxy himself.

"Try a Fred Thomson picture," Joe urged Sam Rothafel.

Rothafel demurred. His audience, he said, wanted "flesh and the devil," and plenty of both, not horseflesh.

"It won't cost you anything," Joe coaxed.

He won his point. When *The Sunset Legion,* a Fred Thomson western, was booked into the Roxy, it proved to be a hit. With disdain and some exaggeration, Joe claimed Rothafel didn't know his own audience.

Other sagebrush heroes at FBO included Tom Tyler, a champion weight lifter and strongman with a relaxed acting style; Bob Steele, a bantam youngster who came across as a true cowboy; and at the top of the roster, the king of westerns, Tom Mix, who signed with FBO after leaving Fox. Joe also signed up nineteen-year-old Jean Morgan on one of his trips east and put her in pictures with Ranger, FBO's popular dog star. Among the directors lured to the Gower Street studio was George Brackett Seitz, a cultivated crossover from Pathé who had been responsible for numerous segments of the *Perils of Pauline* series. His big one for "Joseph P. Kennedy Presents" was *The Great Mail Robbery,* billed as a "slashing melodrama of the roaring rails and Uncle Sam's Marines."

FBO began to make money.

Joe could not have picked a better time to make his debut as a movie mogul. The years 1926–27 were one of the most prosperous periods in Hollywood history; almost every one of the 740 films made each year was a box-office success. Movie-going had become a worldwide obsession. There were now over 50,000 movie theaters around the world, more than a third of them in the United States and Canada. Annual receipts in North America alone came to more than $120 million.

With Pat Powers, Joe plotted to fold the ailing Producers Distribution Corporation into Associated Exhibitors with the view of merging the fused entity with FBO to make an even bigger company. Joe was on the financial periphery of Pat's efforts to launch Peggy Hopkins Joyce. Riding high on the success of his uninhibited and lavishly rich version of *The Merry Widow,* Erich von Stroheim declined to take part in the furthering of Peggy's screen career. Instead, Mickey Neilan undertook the mission. The result was *The Skyrocket,* a thinly disguised retelling of Neilan's torrid affair with Gloria Swanson.

Mickey had incurred the wrath of Louis B. Mayer while directing his former wife Blanche Sweet in *Tess of the d'Urbervilles.* Not only did he walk out on one of Mayer's lengthy, sentimental addresses to MGM personnel, he also told *Photoplay* a wounding Mayer joke ("An empty taxi drove up to the studio and Louis B. Mayer got out"). The studio chief had taken his revenge by ordering a happy ending added to the Thomas Hardy classic.

Mickey had roundly abused Mayer but, shielded by Irving Thalberg, had stayed to complete two more films called for under his MGM contract.

Free, Mickey had bought the Edendale studio from bankrupt Harry Garson and Clara Kimball Young for $300,000, refurbished it, and with financing from Powers started a movie about Hollywood. *The Skyrocket* was the story of Sharon Kimm, an extra girl who breaks into pictures only to become a snooty star who flops. With the weight of bankruptcy on her shoulders, she tumbles into the arms of her childhood sweetheart and, in the fade-out, is ready to begin all over again. Though Peggy played the part of Sharon Kimm, Gloria Swanson was generally identified as the prototype, and many saw Neilan himself in Dvorak, the star-maker director with a thirst for power and women, played by Earle Williams. Critics found Peggy beautiful but thought her characterization lacking in expression and personality. Powers released *The Skyrocket* through the undercapitalized Associated Exhibitors. Lack of sales and promotional staff kept the film from making any real money. For Mickey, however, *The Skyrocket* was a success; it allowed him to negotiate a releasing contract with Paramount and to turn out two hit films for Zukor and Lasky.

Ensconced at FBO, Joe Kennedy renewed his acquaintanceship with Will Hays. By 1926 "the dictatorship of virtue" was a success and the Prebyterian elder was at the height of his power. With only two exceptions—Louisiana and Connecticut—his office had managed to block state censorship bills everywhere. The Hays office was now revising its list of *don'ts* and *be carefuls.* The idea was to codify a series of prior judgments and standards so that motion picture companies would be able to figure out, before any camera rolled, if a story would pass scrutiny. For their part, the studios agreed to submit to Hays's office outlines of any material they were considering for production, along with explanations of how they proposed to handle tricky details. By 1927 the first version of what was to be variously called the Production Code, the "Formula," and the Hays Code detailed eleven *don'ts* and a number of *be carefuls.* Absolutely forbidden were pointed profanity, licentious or suggestive nudity ("in fact or in silhouette"), drug trafficking, inference of sexual perversion, white slavery, miscegenation (defined as "sexual relationships between the white and black races"), sex hygiene and venereal diseases, scenes of actual childbirth, children's sex organs, the ridicule of clergy, and "the willful offense of any nation, race or creed." Among the *be carefuls,* producers were advised to be wary of depicting "the sale of women, or of a woman selling her virtue, rape or attempted rape, first night scenes, man and woman in bed together, deliberate seduction of girls, and excessive or lustful kissing, particularly when one character or the other is a 'heavy.' "

Of course, most producers regarded sex and violence as box-office insurance, and the Code was often more honored in the breach than in the
observance. Revised in 1930, 1934, and 1956, it would survive until the Age
of Aquarius, finally expiring for good in 1967.

In 1927 sixty million people went to the movies every week in 21,000
theaters in the United States and Canada (there were 37,000 cinemas in the
rest of the world). In Hollywood, where the weekly payroll totaled two
million dollars, real-estate values were climbing, better houses were being
built, and restaurants, hotels, and department stores were booming. To
counterbalance the haphazard, intuitive, shirtsleeve approach of the founding entrepreneurs, Hays tried to endow the industry with an atmosphere of
substance and Americanism. Joe Kennedy was exactly the kind of man the
czar had in mind—someone substantial, a banker who had already made
money elsewhere, and an American (in the sense that he was not an immigrant from central or eastern Europe). Kennedy was a man still in his
thirties who oozed confidence, whimsy, and money, and he was refreshingly
unlike the early movie moguls—even though he, too, owed his rise to
shrewdness and fast footwork.

Joe in turn pledged to Hays, and to his Boston-born general counsel
Charles Pettijohn, that FBO would make nothing but clean pictures. That
didn't prevent him from raiding the Hays office for executive talent. Arthur
Houghton joined FBO principally for his contacts and his knack for business intelligence. Through Houghton, Joe knew who was making the hot
deals, who was on the way out, who was sleeping with whom. Later, Harry
Eddington joined the Kennedy staff to become Joe's permanent West Coast
representative.

If Eddie Moore remained Joe's senior aide, secretary, valet, and confidant, Charles E. Sullivan became the titular head of FBO's Hollywood
operation. Nicknamed Pat or Charley, Sullivan knew little about filmmaking, but he was a wizard with figures. E. B. Derr, Joe's other mathematical
genius, and Ted O'Leary, the fourth horseman, traveled with the boss and
fleshed out those dreary, five-day coast-to-coast train trips with work discussions in Joe's compartment. Derr, who would break with Joe and stay
in Hollywood to become an MGM executive, was a small, pleasant man
with a wife and daughter in Boston. The pink-faced O'Leary, the heaviest
of the four, took care of Kennedy's liquor business. He could always be
reached at the New York Athletic Club at Fifty-ninth street and Sixth
Avenue.

However much Joe despised the pants pressers, he also wanted to impress them. In the spring of 1927 he persuaded his alma mater to put up
money for a series of lectures by tycoons on the hitherto academically

neglected film industry. Thirteen movie personalities, half of whom had never finished high school, wound up giving a series of addresses at the Harvard Business School.

Paramount fielded the choicest team. In addition to Zukor and Lasky, Sidney Kent was there with Samuel Katz, the dwarflike president of Publix Theaters, Paramount's glittering six-hundred-cinema chain. MGM was represented by Marcus Loew, Warner Brothers by Harry Warner, and Universal by Laemmle's oldest associate, Robert Cochrane. The raffish William Fox, ever ready to imitate competitors and to beat them to market, represented himself. Joe searched hard for a passably "highbrow" actor and came up with Milton Sills, a former De Mille player, current First National Pictures star, and a graduate of the University of Chicago. To represent filmdom's financial interests, Joe invited Attilio Giannini, a former surgeon and member of the powerful Bank of America dynasty. Other lecturers included Will Hays, Earle Hammons of Educational Pictures (sure to appeal to the university for his efforts in promoting nontheatrical films), and Joe himself. Several of the speakers were suing each other—Katz and Kent, for example—and had to be assured that process servers would be kept out of Baker Memorial Library. Loew almost choked with emotion when he faced the lectern. "I cannot begin to tell you how it impresses me, coming to a great college such as this to deliver a lecture, when I have never even seen the inside of one before."

In his own speech, Joe called for a consolidation of the film business. "Vertical integration" of production, distribution, and exhibition was not only desirable, it was inevitable. Acting as moderator, he told the students that their questions after each lecture would "lead in the long run to a mighty searching of consciences, in which our industry and every other must justify itself as a ministry to human needs. In the last analysis every merchant and every manufacturer is a public servant, and all our works are, or should be, public utilities, even though we operate under a private charter."

The affair drew capacity crowds of students and resulted in sixty job applications from Harvard men. Arthur Poole was a young man who joined the FBO staff to become a controller of many Kennedy ventures. Joe made sure his own name would appear in print alongside those of filmdom's pioneers, rulers, and policymakers by having the lectures edited and printed. He had leather-bound copies of *The Story of the Films* sent to each lecturer. "This is in essence the first important academic recognition of the existence of the films," Terry Ramsaye wrote glowingly in the September issue of *Photoplay*.

For five frenzied months Joe pursued "vertical integration" on his own. His target was the corporate tangle that was backing C. B. De Mille and his underfinanced and overbudget *King of Kings,* rumored to be the greatest picture the world had ever seen.

Too many bruising fights with Zukor over autonomy and the power to hire stars had made De Mille quit Famous Players–Lasky. With a hefty investment of his own and his wife's savings, plus a number of Wall Street backers, De Mille managed to buy the sixty-acre Ince Studio in Culver City for a bargain $500,000 a few weeks after founder Thomas Ince had died. In March 1925 De Mille led his intimate crew of Jeanie Macpherson, Julie Faye, Mitchell Leisen, Paul Iribe, and his personal cameraman Peverell Marley, plus two hundred stars, feature players, directors, and technicians, in a mass defection from Paramount to the reopened and rededicated new studio. The Cecil B. De Mille Pictures Corporation would make forty pictures a year and the master showman would direct one big film a year himself. His principal backer was Jeremiah Milbank, a deeply religious banker who had made a fortune in railways and who was taken by De Mille's idea of making a picture of the life of Christ.

The first two films De Mille made at the Culver City studio were disasters, and he felt too distraught to attempt *King of Kings,* which he had promised Milbank was the main purpose of creating the new studio. Instead, he merged with several small studios and placed the combined operation under the management of William Sistrom, a professional administrator. The merger brought De Mille the huge Keith Albee chain as an outlet for his studio's productions (Keith Albee had seven hundred theaters in the U. S. and Canada, compared to Loew's two hundred cinemas), but it also brought in Edward A. Albee and his right-hand man John J. Murdock.

The aging Albee was the most hated man in show business, a hard-bitten veteran of vaudeville who had started as a circus barker and, as a ruler of variety bookings, thought nothing of tapping the phone of his associates or of planting stool pigeons backstage to report the grumblings of his performers. He was said to have ruined vaudeville by flogging the genre to death with schedules that called for five shows a day. Murdock was a Scottish immigrant, a small, intense man with white hair and a white mustache who was famous for keeping in touch once a month with every Keith Albee house in North America by telephone and for having settled one San Francisco stagehands' strike by long-distance phone. A pioneer Chicago showman, Murdock had amassed a twenty-million-dollar fortune as Albee's faithful general manager.

Murdock was not impressed by De Mille's staggering forty-one-pictures a year schedule for 1926–27. From his office above the Keith Albee flagship Palace Theater on Broadway, Murdock asked De Mille and Sistrom probing questions on the phone.

Inspired or not, De Mille no longer dared delay acceding to Milbank's wish to see the Christ story filmed, even if Murdock was opposed to a religious movie. In the summer of 1926 De Mille thrust his family Bible into Macpherson's hands and told her to come up with the script of her life. She suggested she write a counterbalancing modern story into the script, but he ordered her to follow the New Testament to the letter. After casting the gentle and fragile H. B. Warner as Jesus, Dorothy Cumming as the Virgin Mary, after offering the part of Mary Magdalene to Gertrude Lawrence, Seena Owen, and Gloria Swanson and finally signing Jacqueline Logan, after firing Iribe for creating biblical sets that De Mille thought too plain and too severe, *King of Kings* started shooting in October.

De Mille filmed through the fall and winter as relations with Albee and Murdock deteriorated. *King of Kings* threatened to destroy the De Mille company as costs soared toward two million dollars. Murdock became convinced that without the restraining force of Zukor and Lasky, De Mille was a man out of control. He persuaded Milbank that the only way to save them all was to merge with cash-rich Pathé Pictures.

Charles Pathé had sold his American holdings at the end of the Great War. In 1923 the company that had given the world Harold Lloyd, Hal Roach, the Our Gang serials, and *Nanook of the North,* had been purchased by Merrill Lynch. Currently it was owned by Blair and Company, another Wall Street house. De Mille resisted the merger, cabling Murdock and Milbank that Pathé stood for cheap pictures, but his own name stood for class. He sent Neil McCarthy, his brilliant attorney, to New York to defend his interests. Meanwhile, filming continued with Milbank singlehandedly keeping the payroll going.

From New York, McCarthy reported back that Joe Kennedy, the boss of the bread-and-butter FBO operation, was associated with Blair and Company and also knew Lehman Brothers, the bankers for Keith Albee. There was a distinct possibility that these forces would combine and force a takeover. Through the Hollywood grapevine, De Mille heard that Kennedy had very mixed feelings about De Mille's administration of the Cecil B. De Mille Pictures Corporation.

The situation worsened. The banks were demanding $1.6 million immediately, and another $1.5 million worth of notes would mature in eight months. Milbank insisted that Cecil B. De Mille Pictures merge with Pathé, which would then issue debentures and lend it five million dollars, with the distribution of all De Mille films being given to Pathé in order to secure one million dollars. In desperation, De Mille asked his lawyer to see if Zukor and Lasky, anyone, would buy him out.

The merger took place in March 1927. It brought together the Keith Albee circuit, the Orpheum chain of West Coast theaters, Pathé, and the

Gloria at 18—a Mack Sennett bathing beauty.
(Academy of Motion Picture Arts and Sciences)

With Mack Swain and the
Mack Sennett bathing beauties in a
1917 comedy. Gloria hated
Sennett's "vulgarity," and provoked him
into tearing up her contract.

(Academy of Motion Picture Arts and Sciences)

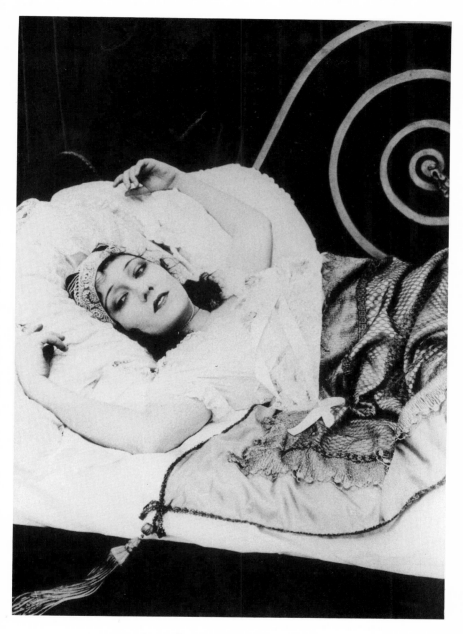

Gloria as the snobbish Lady Mary in
Male and Female, Cecil B. De Mille's 1919 adaptation of
James Barrie's minor classic, "The Admirable Crichton."

(Private Collection of Axel Madsen)

Gloria with De Mille and her co-stars in
Paramount's 1921 *The Affairs of Anatol.* From left:
Bebe Daniels, Agnes Ayres, Gloria, De Mille, Wanda Hawley.

(Marc Wanamaker/Bison Archives)

Gloria with Elinor Glyn, the flamboyant English novelist
who created the notion of "It" and declared
Clara Bow the "It Girl." Upon meeting Gloria for the first
time in 1921, Glyn pronounced her "definitely Egyptian."

(Paramount Pictures)

Valentino
monstrates
nan love and
ess. His article
his preference

With Glori
Swanson
"Beyond th
Rocks"

and Love

Gloria with Rudolph Valentino in a 1922
publicity still from *Beyond the Rocks,* one of several
pictures Elinor Glyn wrote for her.
Both trapped at the time in loveless marriages,
Swanson and Valentino became good friends.

(Private Collection of Axel Madsen)

Gloria and her husband of two months, Henri, the Marquis de
la Falaise de la Coudraye, being welcomed to America by
Jesse Lasky and Adolph Zukor in March 1925. FROM LEFT:
Lasky, Henri, Gloria, Zukor.

(Paramount Pictures)

The Marquis and his Marquise in Los Angeles, 1925.
(Private Collection of Axel Madsen)

The FBO studios at 780 Gower Street, Los Angeles, in 1926, the year Joe Kennedy took over.

(Marc Wanamaker/Bison Archives)

The 1926 FBO sales convention banquet. Joe is the bespectacled man at the center of the table. E. B. Derr is seated immediately to his right.

(Marc Wanamaker/Bison Archives)

Gloria with Raymond Hackett in
The Love of Sunya (1926), her first
independent production. There was something exhilarating,
she discovered, about being in over one's head.

(Academy of Motion Picture Arts and Sciences)

Joe with Jesse Lasky on the steps of
Harvard University's Baker Memorial Library.
Lasky was one of a half-dozen movie moguls Joe brought
to his alma mater for a 1927 symposium on the film business.

(Marc Wanamaker/Bison Archives)

As the innocent convent girl Kitty Kelly,
Gloria is charmed by Walter Byron's Prince Wolfram
in the never-completed 1928 debacle, *Queen Kelly.*

(Academy of Motion Picture Arts and Sciences)

In another scene from *Queen Kelly*—
this one reflecting Erich von Stroheim's lavish taste—
the wicked Queen Helena (Seena Owen) drives
poor Kitty from her opulent palace.

(Academy of Motion Picture Arts and Sciences)

As Somerset Maugham's classic
fallen woman, Gloria tempts Lionel Barrymore
in her 1928 hit, *Sadie Thompson.*

(Raoul Walsh Archives)

Rivals on holiday.
Joe and Henri on the beach at Biarritz, 1928.
(Private Collection of Axel Madsen)

The Kennedy clan in London in 1937,
just after Joe was appointed Ambassador to the
Court of St. James's. FROM LEFT: Teddy, Jean,
Bobby, Patricia, Eunice, Kathleen, Rosemary,
John (the future president), Rose, and Joe.

(Keystone)

The new ambassador. Joe deliberately shocked
British newsmen by planting his feet
on his desk. "You can't expect me to develop into
a statesman overnight," he told them.

(Keystone)

Henri and his new wife, Emmita, celebrating
New Year's 1942 in New York with Gloria and Sport Ward.
"Henri's the only gentleman I ever knew,"
Gloria told the new Marquise.

(Private Collection of Emmita de la Falaise)

De Mille studio. Albee was president of what was now named Keith Albee Orpheum, and although the fifty-six-year-old Murdock on occasion had to pay mulish respect to Albee, it was his show.

De Mille quarreled bitterly with Murdock. The Easter release of *King of Kings,* however, was a sensation, and muted Murdock's hostility. De Mille then created more publicity for himself by announcing that his next picture would be about a girl in a reform school who utterly rejects God, a film that would show such horrors of juvenile detention as solitary confinement, semistarvation, and flogging, which was still lawful in fifteen states. After lengthy planning, Joe approached old Albee with an offer to buy 200,000 shares of Keith Albee Orpheum for $4.2 million.

The impetus was "talking pictures."

Sound recording has a history as long as motion pictures. Legend has it that when Thomas Edison returned from a visit to the Paris Exposition in 1889, his assistant W. K. L. Dickson ushered him into the darkened attic of his new photographic building and projected a strip of film that showed Dickson raising his hat, smiling, and saying, "Welcome home again."

A German professor recorded sound waves on film in 1901, a Frenchman patented an optical sound track five years later. In 1919 two Englishmen perfected the French sound-on-film method, but for lack of funds folded their operation. Two years later Germany's Tobis-Klangfilm discovered the basic means of transcribing varying impulses of sound waves into varying impulses of electricity that could be photographed on a strip of celluloid. The system became the basis for Photophone, the procedure that Lee De Forest, the inventor of the radio tube, introduced in 1921.

Backed by Radio Corporation of America (RCA) and its principal stockholders—General Electric and Westinghouse Electric—Photophone was by no means the only American system. American Telegraph and Telephone had engineers at its Western Electric subsidiary experimenting with synchronous sound on disks for motion pictures, and by 1925 was offering its system to film companies.

The only taker had been Warner Brothers. In the face of another internecine war that had seen the Warners frozen out of several cinema circuits by a powerful combination of Paramount and First National interests, the brothers Harry, Jack, Sam, and Albert decided they had nothing to lose. They signed an agreement with Western Electric to develop Vitaphone, as they called their system. Intended for music and effects, and using wax disk recordings synchronized with film, Vitaphone would enable the music of a first-run cinema to reach the tiniest movie house. In a test program featuring a series of musical items, the sole concession to the spoken word was an introduction by Will Hays.

The topic came up at the Joe Kennedy-generated Harvard lectures in

March. One student asked Marcus Loew what Vitaphone would do to pictures in foreign countries. Would actors be speaking English? The MGM chairman responded to his questioner: "All I can say to you is that it is a mighty good thing some of the actors do not speak." William Fox and Harry Warner were a little more enthusiastic. To a student's question, Fox said he thought the future of the "so-called talking film" would be limited to the realm of education. "We have an instrument called the Movietone," he added, "but Mr. Warner seems to be so set on his Vitaphone that I would rather leave that subject to him." Warner said Thomas Edison had just pronounced talking pictures a failure. "It is not so comfortable to have your life's wealth invested in a thing which such a great authority as Edison says cannot succeed."

In August, the premiere of Warner's first Vitaphone feature proved Edison right. *Don Juan,* starring John Barrymore and directed by Alan Crossland, was silent except for orchestral music and certain sound effects. Moviegoers in the few big city theaters wired for Vitaphone were less than overwhelmed. Accustomed to a fair-sized orchestra beneath the screen, audiences saw no reason for transferring the music to tinny speakers besides and behind the screen, especially since squeaks and howls accompanied the new process.

Still, the Warners decided to go ahead with a second Vitaphone feature, a sentimental Jewish story from a stage play by Sam Raphaelson, on its specially refurbished and soundproofed stage on Sunset Boulevard. Again directed by Crossland, *The Jazz Singer* was not a talking picture, nor had it been planned as one. Al Jolson was merely to sing three or four songs that could be edited out for the vast majority of movie houses not wired for Vitaphone. Encouraged by Crossland, the irrepressible Jolson turned from the piano during one scene and improvised some chatter with Eugenie Besserer, who was playing his mother. "I'll take you up to the Bronx, where you'll meet your friends the Goldbergs, the Freibergs, and all the other bergs." Another ad-lib was the immortal line, "You ain't heard nothing yet!" Sam Warner managed to persuade his brothers to leave the ad-libbing in, and it was this talk that made the picture a sensation when it premiered at the Warner Theater on Broadway and Fifty-second Street in New York on October 6.

Joe was in California, but he told his New York staff to go and see *The Jazz Singer.* They reported back that it was certainly a novelty but that it probably wouldn't do too well in the hundred-odd cinemas wired for sound outside New York. Within days Joe was involved in the deal of his life with David Sarnoff.

Three years younger than Joe, Sarnoff was a living legend and the most powerful man at RCA, although the presidency kept eluding him. As a twenty-one-year-old Marconi wireless operator in 1912, Sarnoff had picked up faint Morse signals: "S. S. Titanic ran into iceberg. Sinking fast." He alerted other ships in the area and informed the press. While President William Taft ordered all other American transmitters to stay silent, young Sarnoff stuck to his keys for seventy-two hours, relaying news of survivors to next-of-kin. A member of an immigrant family of poor Russian Jews, his role as the sole link with the disaster scene off Newfoundland won him world fame. Within a few years he was commercial manager of American Marconi, and as the company grew, so did he. In 1916 he urged his bosses to manufacture "radio music boxes," but the idea was rejected as too harebrained. Early in 1920, by which time the company had become Radio Corporation of America, Sarnoff mentioned the idea again. The bosses still thought the future of wireless radio was in transmitting telegrams, and they were too involved in international diplomacy over frequency allocations to consider Sarnoff's idea much more than a digression. By 1922, however, radio sets had become a national craze and RCA was selling more than 600,000 "music boxes" a year.

By the time Sarnoff used Boston department-store tycoon Louis Kirstein to make overtures to Kennedy and FBO, he had behind him a bruising series of explorations, deadlocks, confrontations, retreats, and new beginnings in the war to establish network broadcasting. He had spent the mid-1920s fighting off AT&T's "toll stations"—that is, programming and commercial messages carried to local stations through long-distance telephone lines. Now he saw his old enemy reaching into motion pictures, and he decided RCA could not afford to stay out of the battle.

Joe rushed to New York.

What he heard when he huddled with Sarnoff at the Grand Central Oyster Bar in midtown Manhattan sounded more than promising. Despite the big-city success of *The Jazz Singer,* theater owners were reluctant to jump on the talkie bandwagon. Installing sound cost as much as $20,000 per cinema. Many theaters still featured vaudeville as part of the program; this presented the technical problem of where to install the amplifying horns, since the area behind the screen was needed for the stage presentations. Joe had already realized that if sound should prove to be irresistible, exhibitors would face huge expenditures, and the studios even bigger outlays to upgrade their production lines, from soundproofing stages to retraining technicians and on-screen talent in the new technology. What the film industry needed was people who knew how to raise colossal sums on Wall Street.

Sarnoff, however, talked movies, not financing. As he and Joe were speaking, RCA engineers were in Hollywood to lay a sound track under aerial combat sequences in *Wings.* Paramount had sunk millions into this

war epic, which was largely filmed at an army base in Texas and directed
by William Wellman, himself a combat pilot in the Lafayette Escadrille.
Although Wellman had Lasky and Zukor's support, Sam Katz was calling
Wings a lunacy and waiting to see Lasky stumble if the picture flopped.
Adding the rat-a-tat-tat of spitting machine guns and the whine of diving
flying machines could only enhance the picture's box-office chances, especially since RCA's engineers thought they could make the effects more
lifelike than Jolson's scratchy Vitaphone voice.

That didn't mean RCA underestimated Vitaphone, Sarnoff added.
Rather, it was the system to beat. But Paramount, MGM, Fox, and United
Artists were naturally reluctant to pay royalties to their rival, Warner
Brothers. In fact, William Fox had made overtures to Sarnoff, suggesting
they join forces. But why should RCA share the spoils with Fox? Sarnoff
was setting RCA on a breakneck course to improve Photophone. Very soon,
RCA's sound system would be technically superior to Fox's German-
derived Movietone. It suddenly dawned on Joe why Sarnoff was talking to
him. To create a market for Photophone in Hollywood, RCA needed a film
company. Sarnoff didn't want to go half-and-half with one of the big boys,
but was seeking a minority stake in a modest film factory.

Between succulent mouthfuls of Long Island bluepoints, the two of
them made a deal. RCA bought a stock interest in Film Booking Office of
America for $400,000. The arrangement gave Sarnoff a toehold in Holly-
wood and it gave Kennedy a sound system. What the combined RCA-FBO
still didn't have, of course, was an outlet of theaters for the sound pictures
they planned to make.

A week after Sarnoff and Kennedy shook hands on the deal in the
Oyster Bar, rumors that Joe was allying himself with powerful radio and
electrical interests wafted up Broadway from Wall Street to Murdock's
office above the Palace Theater. The acute Scot wondered whether
he should go after Sarnoff and Kennedy or whether they would come
after Keith Albee Orpheum, a crown jewel in anyone's quest for sound
supremacy.

Sadie

"There was a young lady from Guam
who peddled her charms, charm by charm,
Inspired I suppose
by the classical prose
of W. Somerset Maugham.

—OGDEN NASH

William Somerset Maugham didn't meet Sadie Thompson in Guam, but 3,300 miles to the east, in Honolulu.

Always a tourist with a taste for the spicier folklore, the forty-two-year-old author had just published *Of Human Bondage* and could finally afford an exotic journey. Together with Gerald Haxton, his twenty-four-year-old American lover, "Willie" was spending a leisurely three weeks in Hawaii in November 1916, seeing the sights, including the Iwilei redlight district. Prostitution fascinated the bisexual writer—he had met Gerald while his own wife, Syrie, was pregnant with their daughter the year before—and the two men watched the shacks the whores rented to dispense their charms for a dollar a throw. One night they saw a seventy-five-foot-long line of marines from Pearl Harbor snaking toward one popular hut. The men jingled silver dollars in their pockets to remind the woman inside that they were waiting under the stars.

As a novelist, dramatist, and short-story writer, Maugham worked beautiful, sensual women of loose morals and cheerful disposition into his skillful prose, using the opportunity for cynical or sardonic observations on society. In Honolulu he was vividly interested in a newspaper campaign to clean up and close down Iwilei, a campaign that one night resulted in a police raid and the arrest of 108 prostitutes and fifteen pimps. Gerald befriended the judge before whom whores and pimps appeared, and he and

Willie sat in the courtroom as the women were brought in and put on a year's probation.

The two travelers' next South Pacific ports of call were Tahiti and Pago Pago on American Samoa. They embarked in early December on a steamer whose ultimate destination was Sydney and discovered that the only other passengers were a Reverend and Mrs. J. J. Mulqueen, and a Miss Thompson. A flashy blonde, plump and, in Maugham's words, "coarsely pretty," Miss Thompson was one of the ladies from Iwilei, en route to a barmaid's job in Apia in Western Samoa. During the 2,278-mile journey from Honolulu to Pago Pago, she played her gramophone and partied in her cabin for the entire trip. The Mulqueens, with whom Maugham once strolled the deck, complained to the steward. Mulqueen was a medical missionary, and he and his wife were returning to their mission on the Gilbert Islands. The wife spoke with horror of the depravity of the natives and told Maugham that when they first got there they could not find one "good girl" in any of the villages. Maugham wondered what would happen if Miss Thompson and the missionary came into sexual conflict.

A health quarantine in Pago Pago prevented Miss Thompson from leaving for Apia, the Mulqueens for the Gilbert Islands, and Haxton and Maugham for Sydney. Instead, they were all thrown together under the tin roof of Pago Pago's only lodging house. Miss Thompson took a Samoan lover. Lying and listening to the tropical rains coming off Rainmaker Mountain, Maugham also had to listen to the rusty bedsprings next door.

Out of his distaste for the enforced immobility, perpetual rain, and the "horrid disturbance" next door came Maugham's classic story of repressed sexuality. His first notes read: "A prostitute flying from Honolulu after a raid lands at Pago Pago. There lands also a missionary and his wife. Also the narrator. All are obliged to stay there owing to an outbreak of measles. The missionary, finding out her profession, persecutes her. He reduces her to misery, shame, and repentance. He induces the governor to order her return to Honolulu. One morning he is found with his throat cut by his own hand. She is once more radiant and self-possessed. She looks at men scornfully, exclaims, 'Dirty pigs!' "

From these lines Maugham wrote "Rain," or "Miss Thompson," as the story was first called. Published in 1920 in the collection of short stories entitled *The Trembling of a Leaf,* the tale of the South Seas harlot (Maugham never bothered to change her name) and the Reverend Davidson who falls prey to her vitality while trying to reform her would eventually earn its author one million dollars in royalties.

The first movie sale was to Jesse Lasky and was made the year of its publication. With Haxton, Maugham visited Los Angeles and spent one evening with Chaplin, Mary Pickford, and Douglas Fairbanks, telling them the story of Sadie Thompson before selling an option to Lasky for $15,000. The story's dramatization was written by John Colton, an author Maugham met in Los Angeles. Colton, the story goes, lived in the same hotel as Maugham and Haxton, and one night knocked on Maugham's door, asking if he had anything he could read. Maugham gave Colton the galleys of "Miss Thompson." The next morning, an excited Colton said he wanted to make a play out of it.

Written by Colton and Clemence Randolph, *Rain* opened on Broadway on November 7, 1922, with Jeanne Eagles playing Sadie in a costume she had picked up on Seventh Avenue for six dollars. For four years Eagles electrified playgoers. She was an actress of irresistible freshness and strangely corrupt beauty who would come to an end in 1929, a drug addict barely able to finish her last film. The stage version invented a Sergeant O'Hara, a happy-go-lucky marine with whom Sadie sails into the sunset at the end.

Gloria had seen *Rain* twice, and like every actress with a brain and a figure, as she put it, wanted to play Sadie. The movie rights to the short story "Miss Thompson" and the play *Rain* had been sold jointly in 1923 for $150,000, a record for a literary property. Then came the Fatty Arbuckle scandal and Will Hays. "Ridicule of the clergy" was the tenth *don't* on the Production Code.

After their return from the March 1927 opening of *The Love of Sunya* at the Roxy, Gloria and Henri had been among the guests attending a lawn party celebrating the completion of *East of Suez* and its star, Pola Negri. Jesse Lasky had rented an absent oil millionaire's Beverly Hills mansion, and on a studio-built dance floor next to the swimming pool *le tout Hollywood* danced under Japanese lanterns. Raoul Walsh, the director of *East of Suez,* circulated among the guests and spotted Gloria sitting with Harold Lloyd and Alice Terry. He thought Gloria looked more radiant than ever.

"Nobody but a louse would desert a beautiful lady," he grinned sliding down besides her.

They had met at Mack Sennett's ten years earlier. Like Mickey Neilan, Raoul was a one-time Griffith actor (playing John Wilkes Booth in *Birth of a Nation*) who had discovered his talent was behind the camera. Of an Irish father and a Spanish mother, the thirty-four-year-old Walsh was a rugged, tough-talking director with a weather-beaten quality about him, as if he had been lashed by the desert wind. He was currently under contract to William Fox and riding high on the acclaim of *What Price Glory?*

"Where's your husband?" he asked.

Gloria laughed, put a hand on his, and told him flattery would get him everywhere. She looked at the dancers and spotted Henri trying to teach Marie Dressler to do the black-bottom. Raoul thought her eyes were wistful as she watched her husband and Dressler. In his autobiography, *The Story of a Director,* Walsh would put a curious quote in Gloria's mouth: " 'My playboy.' It was almost a whisper. 'I think he must have had himself born as a dirty trick on his mother.' " Then others broke in to congratulate him on *East of Suez* and the conversation became general.

Nothing in Swanson's memoirs prepares us to believe that two years after she risked an abortion in Paris to marry Henri she would think of him as destiny's dirty trick on his own mother. In retrospect, she would depict Henri as having a reserved and trusting nature, a man she had wished more assertive, more of a match for the financiers, lawyers, and accountants whom independent filmmaking had brought into her life. She would describe him as an essentially noble character, ill suited for the crasser power play of American show business. But also as a man who at crucial moments in their marriage, when she wanted him to speak up, was unable to face the consequences of such boldness and instead held his tongue. Like the exasperating Craney Gartz, the marquis never quite made the right move, but she would never make the comparison herself, never wonder why she fell in love with such men.

Raoul and Gloria got up to dance, he thinking she suspected his feelings. He was recently divorced, and more interested in playing the field than finding a second wife, as he would note in his memoirs. Their dancing was physical and, he thought, full of thinly controlled urges. "In a strange sort of way, I was glad when the next number began that I could dance with Alice Terry," he would write. "With her no dissembling was necessary."

Two weeks later, Walsh got a call from Schenck. Guess who was sitting in Schenck's office and telling him she wanted Raoul to direct her next picture?

If anyone was responsible for Gloria's overtures to Raoul, it was Henri. No great moviegoer, Henri had never been as taken with a film as he had been with *What Price Glory?* The screen adaptation of Maxwell Anderson's and Laurence Stallings's 1924 play appealed directly to the disabused war veteran in Henri. Centered on the rivalry of a captain and a sergeant for the favors of a French girl, the play had caused a sensation with its frank presentation of the profanity and brutality of soldiers and the wearying ugliness of war. Henri had seen the film three times and told Gloria he considered it a masterpiece.

If Raoul was invited for breakfast at Crescent Drive the next morning, it was not because Gloria had a crush on him, but because she wanted to quickly redeem herself after *The Love of Sunya.* The premiere at the Roxy had been a triumph, but the reviews were mixed, many insisting she had out-Swansoned herself as a clotheshorse, others complaining that it was a draggy affair. As coffee was being served, the praise that both Henri and Gloria heaped on *What Price Glory?* was so extravagant that Walsh blushed. What Gloria wanted to know was how he had managed to film situations that were clearly proscribed by the Hays code. Raoul grinned. He had assumed audiences would forgive fighting men for acting like men at war because there was no other way they *could* act.

Gloria told him she was, quite frankly, looking for a challenging script and an exciting director. She was aware that he was under contract to Fox, but if Schenck could arrange a loan-out, would Raoul be interested in directing her, and did he have any suggestions for a story?

"You mean like *What Price Glory?*" he asked.

"Not necessarily, but something solid and real like that. I don't want to spend the rest of my life making fancy-dress pictures."

"Well, there's always *Rain.*"

They kept coming back to *Rain* as they sat in the sun-speckled garden and kicked around ideas. Henri was initiated into the Production Code subtleties and the tendency of all producers to walk right up to the *don't* line, while suggesting in their advertising that they had crossed it.

Before Walsh came for tea the next afternoon, he had read both the original "Miss Thompson" and *Rain.* Sifted to its essentials, the story of the tawdry, persecuted Sadie and the deluded Reverend Davidson was an indictment of missionary pretentions, if not of Christian hypocrisy. Davidson was a man for whom holiness as well as sin was a misery from which he could only escape by punishing others. By inventing Sergeant O'Hara, the stage version had a more powerful ending than the short story. By having Sadie leave the mire and rain of Pago Pago and sail off to Australia with her marine, you came away with a feeling that tattered human love could be as healing as divine purification.

Over the next weeks Gloria, Henri, and Raoul spent afternoons on the Crescent Drive terrace figuring it all out. As a producer, Gloria had never signed the Motion Picture Producers and Distributors pledge to abide by the Hays code. She suspected that because she was a woman no one had bothered to even inquire whether she was interested. That was one ace in the hole. They could see another fudge. Suppose they adapted "Miss Thompson," the short story, instead of *Rain.* The sticker was, of course, the tenth *don't,* forbidding "the ridicule of the clergy." But there again, suppose they made the Reverend Davidson into plain Mr. Davidson, a misguided, overzealous reformer? Okay, but would Somerset Maugham go for it? Would he consider that cheapening of his material? As for prostitution, the *be careful* section of the Code merely cautioned that special care should be exercised in treating "the sale of women, or of a woman selling her virtue." "Who's to say if we treat Sadie's profession with taste?" Gloria asked.

Before Gloria Swanson Productions entered any delicate and secret negotiations with Maugham's literary agent, the agents for playwrights Colton and Randolph, and Sam Harris, the Broadway producer of *Rain,* met with Gloria's lawyer. Milton Cohen had come into her life as Herbert's attorney. After the galling terms and final divorce, Cohen had called to apologize for his tactics and volunteer to serve as her lawyer. He had been invaluable to her since, and now suggested Will Hays should be sounded out first.

Together with a number of business associates, the diminuitive czar was invited to lunch at Crescent Drive. When the guests began drifting onto the terrace for coffee, Gloria detained Hays, saying she had a quick question for him. She had produced only one picture so far and had not yet been asked to join the Motion Picture Producers Association. Still, to be sure she wouldn't be transgressing against the Production Code, she wanted to know what he thought of a marvelous story she had found, a story that would make a beautiful film, except for one impediment: the male lead was a missionary. It was, of course, entirely possible to turn the missionary into a reformer, that is, a man not of the cloth, but—and here was the hitch—the author might not sell her the rights if she denatured the story. Her question, therefore, was this: Could she use Mr. Hays's name in trying to persuade the author?

"Of course, Miss Swanson," he smiled. "What's the author's name?"

"Somerset Maugham, the Englishman. He's supposed to be very strict when it comes to altering his stories."

"And what is the name of the story?"

"It's called 'Miss Thompson.' Have you read it?"

"No, I don't believe I have."

"You should. It's a classic. I suppose you're not much concerned with magazine stories, though, are you?"

"Not really. But I recognize Maugham's name. And you're right. Some of his works are classics."

"So I may use your name, Mr. Hays, when I tell him I must make Reverend Davidson just plain Mister Davidson?"

"Of course you may. And good luck."

Schenck was impressed. And apprehensive. Every studio was lusting after *Rain,* everybody would be furious to find out Gloria had outsmarted the entire industry and obtained Hays's permission. Suppose he reneged. To preempt all comers, they agreed Gloria Swanson Productions should buy both the original short story and the Broadway play—the latter hopefully below the $100,000 asking price, since they wouldn't be using it. Schenck found a Los Angeles playbroker who agreed to go to New York, never to reveal whom he was negotiating for, and, in all communications, to refer to *Rain* only as the Maugham-Colton-Randolph play or in code.

Gloria and Raoul were too excited to wait for a confirming telegram before starting on the script. Raoul was full of ideas. They couldn't use the play, but he could jog audiences' memories by shooting a torrential downpour for the opening sequence. "Please make me a good whore, won't you?" Gloria laughed one afternoon. "Let's write in a few more love scenes, hot ones that will bring the viewers out of their seats." When the agent wired that GS Productions was "NOW THE OWNER OF THE TWO MOLEHILLS OF NEBRASKA WHICH COST YOU SIXTY THOUSAND" and Schenck had a legal expert on copyright confirm that the literary property was indeed legally Gloria's, the roof caved in.

Attorneys for Maugham, Colton, and Randolph charged the broker with misrepresentation and threatened to sue Swanson and Schenck. Worse, on June 10, fifteen studio heads and theater circuit chiefs sent Schenck a collective telegram protesting "the making of *Rain* either under the name of 'Sadie Thompson' or any other name or the making of this story even with variations and changes." The thrust of their objection was that if this one slipped through, the carefully developed Production Code would be shown to be no more substantial than the emperor's new clothes. The signers ranged from Raoul's boss William Fox, Marcus Loew, Zukor, and Universal's second-in-command Robert Cochrane, to Keith Albee Orpheum chief John Murdock and newcomer Joe Kennedy. Within twenty-four hours, Hays added his own voice. The Motion Picture Producers Association had decided to ban *Rain* a year ago, and "the agreement was that if it was made by anyone outside, it would not be exhibited by the members of the Association." In other words, if she and United Artists went ahead and spent their own money to shoot the Sadie Thompson story, no movie house would show it.

Gloria was ready to fight back. First of all, why wasn't the ultimatum addressed to her? *She* was producing the picture, she told Schenck; *she* had talked Will Hays into saying it was all right. "So why are they sending their telegrams and letters to you, Mr. Schenck? I'll tell you why. Because I'm a woman. They refuse to recognize me as a producer. They expect you to handle me like a silly, temperamental star."

Realizing she could not avoid putting Hays on the spot for letting her believe she had his permission in the first place, she appealed to her critics. In telegrams to all fifteen Motion Picture Producers Association heads, she related how she had told Hays of her intention to produce Somerset

Maugham's "Sadie Thompson" and how he had given her to understand that there would be no objections if she did not use church or clergy. Since then she had invested over $200,000 in the project, and being in no condition to sacrifice that amount, she was asking them to be sufficiently generous and broadminded to withdraw their protest. The film could be made, she said, "in such a manner that there will not be the slightest objection to it by any censor board or any religious body. As far as the story itself is concerned, it is a great lesson in tolerance. Please do not think I am using the latter word in conclusion to point out to you the necessity of you being tolerant."

The most powerful of the fifteen broke ranks and apologized to her. In a telegram and follow-up letter, Marcus Loew said that if Hays had given his consent, even though in error, the MGM chairman would do his utmost to make sure the association agreed. Loew's sympathy was particularly welcome as both Gloria and Raoul wanted Metro's contract star Lionel Barrymore to play Alfred Hamilton, as the distanced-from-Reverend Davidson but still sanctimonious protagonist was now called.

When after ten days no word had come from the Motion Picture Producers Association either protesting or acquiescing to Gloria Swanson Productions' plans to shoot *Sadie Thompson,* preparations went into high gear. The American Express Company offered to transport the cast and crew to Samoa, an idea sure to generate reams of publicity—and, American Express hoped, interest in South Seas travel. It was now midsummer, however, and the old standby for Hollywood exotica, Catalina Island, would have to do. William Cameron Menzies, who had done a masterly job for Walsh creating the sets on *The Thief of Bagdad,* was chosen to design *Sadie Thompson,* and in a cove near Avalon Harbor he built a Pago Pago set. A duplicate of the hotel front and interiors were built at the United Artists studio. The biggest challenge for Menzies, who ten years later would design the sets for *Gone With The Wind,* was to make his exteriors waterproof. They would be drenched daily with artificial thundershowers.

Schenck got Fox and MGM to loan out Walsh and Barrymore on short, one-picture contracts, and he convinced the less than enthusiastic Sam Goldwyn to loan them his top cameraman, George Barnes. Blanche Friderici was hired to repeat her Broadway role in *Rain* as Barrymore's prissy wife. Charles Lane became Maugham's alter-ego narrator, and Jim Marcus, Walsh's assistant for the past eight years, was chosen to play the paunchy trader, Joe Horn. Douglas Fairbanks, Jr., showed up in a marine uniform, wanting to play Sergeant O'Hara, but at seventeen he was too young to carry the lusty Sadie off to a new life in Australia. To Raoul's annoyance, Gloria turned down all the actors he proposed for the part. Finally Schenck had to enlighten the director.

"Don't you get it? She wants *you* to play O'Hara."

For a moment Walsh wondered what Henri would say. Then he shrugged off his scruples, telling himself Gloria Swanson obviously knew what she wanted. Casually, he mentioned to her that he wouldn't mind playing the marine sergeant.

Gloria beamed. "You'll make a fine O'Hara, Raoul."

In the middle of the casting, Gloria began having stomach pains. She tried to ignore them, but when they persisted, she became convinced she had ulcers, the disease of producers. Henri and Gloria's friend Lois Wilson begged her to see a doctor. "After winning the battle to obtain *Sadie* and after borrowing a fortune to produce it, all I could think of was that I would collapse on the set the first day with a bleeding ulcer and have to hire Norma Talmadge or Dolores Del Rio to replace me," she told journalists a year later.

She finally consulted a doctor in Pasadena named Henry G. Bieler, a tiny man who believed a person was what he ate. After filling three pages of a legal pad with a list of everything she had eaten the night before, he prescribed a series of enemas. Henri protested that she was making herself ill, not well, but a week later when she returned to Dr. Bieler's office, she felt better. He believed that there were not thousands of physical disorders, but only one—toxemia—that humans poison themselves and one another, that pain is a divine signal telling us to stop poisoning ourselves. Gloria would remain his devoted patient for the next forty-eight years and become a health-food advocate herself, espousing proper diet and natural foods, and campaigning against additives, overindulgence in sugar, and the harmful effects on food of polluted air, soil, and water.

Filming started in June on Catalina Island. Walsh was afraid the tightly written script wouldn't be long enough and added opening scenes in which Trader Joe Horn is told the ship from Honolulu is arriving. One week into shooting, Goldwyn recalled Barnes to film a picture starring Gilda Gray. Frantic calls went to the mainland for a replacement. Schenck was out of town, but Douglas Fairbanks promised to see what he could do. In the meantime, one hundred people sat waiting for the producer and director to come up with a solution. The assistant cameraman was tried and found not to be able to handle a major picture by himself. Walsh got Robert Kurrle, the only available cinematographer at Fox, but he, too, proved inadequate. Mary Pickford loaned them the industry's best-known cameraman, Charles Rosher. His sharp, clear images, however, didn't blend with the shadowy, impressionistic style of Barnes. In the meantime, both Barrymore's and Walsh's loan-out contracts were ticking toward expiration.

When Gloria phoned Schenck only to be told it was about time she learned to make do, she exploded. On an impulse, she called MGM and asked for Marcus Loew. He was ill, she was told. She sent him a detailed telegram. For a second time he came to her rescue, ordering the studio to give her anyone she wanted. Oliver Marsh saved the film, although parts of it had to be reshot.

As the lecherous reformer, Barrymore gave an arresting performance. He adopted a hunched posture, always walking with his legs slightly bent as if he were forever toiling up a stony hill. A few weeks from his fiftieth birthday, his angular face made him look ascetic and, Walsh would remember, appear on camera like an inquisitor hunting heretics. The director thought that Gloria displayed a kind of feral grace in her depiction of a waterfront fancy girl, that her lack of self-consciousness turned her into a believable floozy. Raoul wasn't sure he could compete with his two stars when he directed himself as the handsome O'Hara. "Remember that you are O'Hara, the battle-tested marine," Gloria told him. "You are in love with me, and I am beginning to fall for you."

The delays and frustrations galvanized cast and crew. Though Henri tried to adapt to the location mentality, Gloria had little time for him, and Raoul thought Falaise (as he called him) got in everyone's way. When the director noticed that Henri seemed to have disappeared, Gloria told him her husband had gone fishing, or that he was out hunting. "Her offhand manner when making these announcements made me suspect that she did not care if he had gone to hell," Walsh would write. However, there is no evidence that the relationship of the love-smitten director and the trying-to-keep-it-all-together star-producer went beyond a setside flirtation.

During the filming, Barrymore had to leave the location and rush to the San Francisco bedside of his beloved uncle John Drew. The death of the seventy-three-year-old trouper on July 9 broke the last link to the stage tradition of Lionel and John Barrymore's parents' and grandparents' generation. When Lionel came back, they shot the climactic scene. Here, Hamilton strides to Sadie's door, abruptly stops, clasps his hand, and bows his head before grasping the handle and opening the door. Walsh cut to a downpour here, as a challenge to the Hays office. It was left intact. Not so, however, the next morning's resolution in which beach boys discover the reformer's body in the surf and alert the lodging house. The narrator comes running, finds and holds up the razor with which Hamilton had ended his life. The Hays office objected that the suicide's death instrument could not be *shown,* only mentioned in a title. The scene was reshot.

When they got back to the studio to shoot interiors, Gloria clashed with Schenck. She was over budget, he told her. What did she plan to do?

"Borrow more," she answered. "This picture is going to be dynamite. I know it."

Schenck mentioned that *The Love of Sunya* had also been over budget and hadn't exactly been dynamite.

"Look," she snapped, "two years ago you were all begging me to join United Artists, telling me I couldn't fail. Now you seem to be saying I can't succeed. I know I'm over budget, but I also know *Sadie Thompson* is the best thing I've ever done. Ask Raoul Walsh. Ask Lionel Barrymore. When Irving Thalberg reshoots a third of a picture, you call him a genius. When Sam Goldwyn does it, you say he's maintaining his reputation. But when I do it, you treat me like a silly female who can't balance her checkbook after a shopping spree."

She knew Schenck would advance the money to finish the picture, but she felt he wanted her to grovel for it. Instead, she called her production manager and a Guarantee Trust executive who was on the Gloria Swanson Productions board and told them to sell her forty-acre country home in Croton-on-Hudson, her New York City penthouse, and a property she owned in Malibu.

Gloria pushed for a Christmas release, but the Hays office caused delays. The censors hired lip readers to scrutinize the first roughcut. They could not object to Raoul's diluvian downpour under the opening titles, but they asked that the world "rain" be deleted or changed in title cards. In mid-October, Gloria finally heard from Somerset Maugham. Thanking her for her letter of June 10, the author told of Fox Films' interest in a differently-named sequel that would tell what happened to Sadie in Australia.

The bastards, she thought. William Fox had headed the list of the high and mighty trying to shame her out of doing *Sadie Thompson.* She showed Maugham's letter to Hays and would have sent a copy to her only supporter, Marcus Loew. However, the fifty-seven-year-old MGM chairman had died a month earlier.

There was no Hays office in Europe. UA distribution executives thought *Sadie*'s prospects overseas would be so-so; everybody else felt it had great potential. With each delay making Gloria Swanson Productions' finances more precarious—the accountants weren't sure *Sunya* would ever pay for itself—Gloria and Henri decided he should go to Europe to investigate the situation and get *Sunya* into European distribution as soon as possible.

Henri left a week before *Sadie Thompson* was previewed in San Bernardino, sixty miles east of Los Angeles. In true sneak preview tradition, the audience got to see the unannounced film for free as a second feature in exchange for jotting down one-sentence opinions afterward. If the cards were "good," Gloria would take them with her to New York to show UA distribution; if they were bad, she would try to figure out another way of selling the picture. Thalberg had brought previewing to ritualistic and ruthless perfection. MGM pictures were previewed, returned for doctoring, and previewed again until audiences in outlying Los Angeles and San Francisco areas laughed or cried at the right places, or at least didn't walk out in the middle.

The first card was not encouraging. "Acting was wonderful but as a church member think religion should be left out of pictures," it read. Gloria knew it didn't matter whether you called the moralist Reverend Davidson or Mr. Hamilton; the public wasn't fooled. Then, racing through the rest of the cards, Gloria realized she had a hit. All she needed was tie-over money until Sadie began paying off. She remembered Bob Kane had expressed interest in her Malibu property and called him to say it was for sale.

"Why?" the executive asked.

"Surely you've heard I ran into debt making *Sadie Thompson*. I'm not worried. This picture is going to be a great success. In the meantime I need cash."

While she rushed to New York—and, at Bob Kane's suggestion, agreed to see Joe Kennedy—Raoul was invited to a party by Doug Fairbanks and Mary Pickford. The guest of honor was Somerset Maugham. The author was pleased with the previews and praised Gloria's interpretation. "Just as I imagined her," he said graciously. "I thought Barrymore's performance a showstopper, and you acted a splendid sergeant," he told Walsh, reserving his only negative comments for the Hays office.

United Artists wanted to open the picture in San Francisco, with Gloria in attendance, in January 1928. She was eager to see it premiere. Not counting the *Love of Sunya* disappointment, there had been no new Gloria Swanson picture since *The Coast of Folly*. Her future seemed so intricately linked to the fate of *Sadie* that it was not only on her mind on her second date with Joe Kennedy, but after her return to Los Angeles a week later, the subject of their first transcontinental phone conversation. With her permission, Joe told her on the phone that he and his staff had gone through the files in her New York office and, quite frankly, what they had discovered was a mess. There were tax liabilities she hadn't mentioned to him. And everybody, he said with indignation, was taking her for a ride.

Merger talks would take him to California in a couple of weeks, he said. In the meantime she should not breathe a word to anybody. When he asked about the *Sadie Thompson* release date and she told him Hays office delays meant some time in the New Year, he said that might be just as well. "By then I should have your company back on the tracks again with a whole new set of books. Don't worry about a thing, Gloria."

Joe and his horsemen arrived for a short visit in early December, Joe installing himself in a rented Rodeo Drive mansion. Rodeo Drive was three blocks west of Crescent Drive, past Canon and Beverly. He and Gloria were practically neighbors, they discovered when he called, and she invited him and his men to dinner on his first free evening.

It was her first introduction to the horsemen. Her New York secretary had told her that when the quartet showed up to go through the books they looked like a cadre of gangsters. Gloria thought they looked more like four working-class Irishmen who had risen to responsibility under an Irish boss whom they obviously admired. "Whether it was to please him or me I couldn't tell, but within a quarter of an hour they were behaving with me like Snow White's dwarfs," she would remember. "I couldn't mention the word 'butler' before one of them had rung the bell to summon him; and every time I reached for a cigarette I all but went up in flames as two or more of them struck matches to light it."

She thought the slender, older Eddie Moore was obviously the boss's chief brain and auxiliary memory, the one who kept track of everything. Charles Sullivan looked like a New York cop. He was the silent one who never seemed able to express himself until a pile of papers with digits were in front of him. E. B. Derr spoke of his daughter, who was the same age as Little Gloria. Ted O'Leary looked like a bouncer.

She introduced everybody to her children. Little Gloria and Buddy coaxed the captive group of guests to play a game with them, and the four horsemen got down on the floor and really played. The children had such a good time that, before Gloria knew it, she and Joe were on the floor playing, too. When she started to get up, she wrenched her knee and let out a sharp cry of pain. One of the horsemen quietly took the children upstairs to their governess. Another phoned a doctor to meet them at the nearest hospital. A third went to the kitchen to tell the cook to hold the dinner. The fourth picked her up and carried her to the car outside. Joe went with them to the hospital to give orders. Within an hour, Gloria's knee had been x-rayed and bandaged and they were all back on Crescent Drive sitting down to dinner. The incident was minor, but Gloria was impressed by the horsemen's way of dealing with emergencies.

Nothing seemed to deter the quintet because they knew how to anticipate difficulties or how to avoid them. They had ready responses to most of her questions, and when they didn't know something, they knew how and where to find the answers. After dinner they got down to business. First there were the back taxes the Commissioner of Internal Revenue said she owed, totaling $102,743. Since 1921 she had deducted extraordinary expenses for clothing, trips, and entertainment. Her contract with Famous Players–Lasky had indeed called for her to appear in public whenever possible, "in attractive and fashionable costumes," but the studio had paid for the apparel. And the commissioner had ruled that all amounts spent on clothes represented personal rather than professional expenses and as such were not deductible. Then there were her employees. She was paying salaries and retainers totaling $900 a week to staff personnel, who ranged from P. A. Bedard, her production manager, to Ann Morgan, her dressmaker, not to mention Milton Cohen and Irving Wakoff, her lawyer and her accountant, who were both on permanent retainer. Derr suggested that cutting out Bedard and Wakoff alone would diminish her weekly personnel expenses by a third. Eliminating Morgan, who had come into Gloria's life from Elinor Glyn six years ago, would save another $125 a week.

To cover Gloria's short-term debts, Joe would arrange a special $20,000 loan for her from East Boston's Columbia Trust Company. To make sure the money actually went to pay off tradespeople, Eddie Moore would hold the Columbia Trust check until Gloria's New York secretary was ready to send out payments to the creditors. It was humiliating not to be trusted with $20,000, but as the evening wore on and Joe and his men drew an increasingly stark picture of her financial situation, she nevertheless felt a growing sense of comfort. She was in competent hands, and as they told her, everything was negotiable.

The first thing was to dissolve Gloria Swanson Productions and form a new corporate entity. She objected that forming the company had been difficult enough—she had even had to have her mother cosign—but they told her the new incorporation could be done in Delaware in a month. If she would sign a power of attorney, Deer could handle everything. While he, Moore, and Sullivan would run the corporate Gloria Swanson as it should be run, she and Joe could devote themselves to planning her next picture.

The proposal was flattering and reflected her deepest wish to bounce back financially. "You're offering me all I've wanted for two years," she told Joe, "freedom from business worries." Still, she said, she would have to talk to her husband. Henri would be coming home for Christmas in ten days.

Joe was touching her where she was most vulnerable, her inability to control her finances. She was a woman, he learned through the grapevine, who hired and fired, shot scenes that were never used, ordered sets and countermanded them, paid for subtitles and threw them away, announced she could not be bothered by details and then insisted on licking each fan-mail stamp. He would have her on *his* terms.

In the waning weeks of 1927 he was concentrating on the possibilities that his alliance with David Sarnoff offered. Every corporate maneuver seemed to promise boundless wealth for him, and the next time he met Gloria he couldn't help telling her about it. He talked so much, in fact, that she asked how he could possibly find time for her and her problems.

"You know what they say?" He grinned. "If you want something done, get a busy man to do it." He had an army of employees, all on trial, as it were, all anxious to prove themselves. By putting them through their paces, he could give them any number of extra things to do and be certain they would scramble to do them right.

Neither Kennedy nor Sarnoff could foresee the roadblocks and detours that lay ahead. Stock prices rose on each move they made, but there were moments when Joe wondered whether he was teamed up with the loser in the talking pictures battle. AT&T's Western Electric system was, with Fox's help, gaining acceptance. MGM, Paramount, United Artists, Universal, and First National (soon to be taken over by Warner Brothers) were understood to favor the Western Electric system, and Fox was said to be building a record number of new theaters. To be sure he possessed impeccable inside information, Joe urged Guy Currier to buy into the enemy and, if possible, get on the board of Western Electric.

To Joe, it looked as if the way to play it was to raise his hand by getting control of the Keith Albee Orpheum stake. He wasn't much interested in the wobbly conglomerate's moviemaking—De Mille was about to start *The Godless Girl,* starring Lina Basquette, George Duryea, and Marie Prevost—but the combined Keith Albee and Orpheum chains plus the Pathé Exchange added up to the biggest aggregate of screens as yet uncommitted to a sound system. Not that anyone was entirely convinced "talkies" had a future. De Mille was going to shoot *The Godless Girl* as a silent. And why not? *King of Kings* was winning universal acclaim. As De Mille and Milbank reinvested their profits in new prints, the religious epic played to worldwide audiences that would eventually total a third of humanity.

Joe's circling of the Keith Albee prey led him to Elisha Walker, a Wall Street acquaintance who over the next few years would have an important impact on the Kennedy ascent. Walker was a native New Yorker, nine years older than Joe, who in ten years on Wall Street had become president of the blue-ribbon banking firm of Blair and Company. As the banker for Sinclair Consolidated Oil, Walker had gained a national reputation as the architect of some of the biggest oil deals of the decade. Since

Blair and Company had held the controlling interest in Pathé—and at the critical point in November had accepted the complicated merger with Keith Albee and De Mille interests—Walker had earned Milbank's eternal gratitude.

Walker liked what Joe had done with FBO and was optimistic about the possible merger of Joe's bread-and-butter studio with mighty RCA. He put Joe in touch with Lehman Brothers, the bankers for Keith Albee Orpheum.

A few days after Gloria had entertained Joe and his horsemen, Eddie Moore called to make an appointment for his boss. Mr. Kennedy wanted her to meet him and Mr. von Stroheim.

Mr. von Stroheim

Erich von Stroheim believed in fortune tellers. When his career as one of the screen's originals was over, and no studio would let him direct anything, his favorite clairvoyant in Santa Monica told him to accept an acting job in France. The film was nothing much, but it led him to Denise Vernac, the woman who would share the rest of his life with him, to director Jean Renoir, and to *La Grande Illusion.*

There is no record of what Stroheim's psychic told him before he met Gloria Swanson and Joe Kennedy in December 1927. Appropriately perhaps for someone whose colorful, stormy, and tragic life would be summed up in "legends," there were to be at least two versions of *where* they met. In her memoirs Gloria would remember Joe Kennedy bringing Stroheim to Crescent Drive and the three of them sipping coffee on her patio. Thomas Quinn Curtiss, one of Stroheim's several biographers, would place the meeting on Catalina Island, the Sunday playground for tony film people. It was after an invigorating swim and a lunch, Curtis would put it, that the trio got down to "yessing" each other.

All three wanted a success, but each came with his or her own unstated

needs, fears, and aspirations. The trick, as so often in show-business prelimi-
naries, was to make ambitions coincide.

Gloria was looking for a follow-up to *Sadie Thompson,* the film she was
sure was a winner but which United Artists so doubted that the studio
wanted to open it in San Francisco rather than on Broadway. As her UA
partners made her understand, she couldn't afford *not* to have another
project in the works.

If she had learned anything from *The Love of Sunya* and *Sadie,* it was
that it took just as much out of her to make an "easy" movie as it did to
produce a brilliant, creative film. She was determined to come up with
something provocative. Gloria would be twenty-nine in March, and she was
feeling the hot breath of rising stars like Greta Garbo on her neck. Elinor
Glyn had pronounced Clara Bow, her new protégée, the "it girl" supreme,
and told Gloria that *It,* starring Bow and directed by Clarence Badger, was
the picture of 1927. As much as she indulged in pooh-poohing Hollywood
pretentions, it was seven years since she had worked with Cecil B. De Mille,
and there was nothing quite like making a film with a forceful director. In
The Merry Widow, Stroheim had made a star of perennial flapper Mae
Murray, while Gibson Gowland and Zasu Pitts had never equaled their
performances in *Greed.*

Joe wanted to show he could create a prestige success. Corporate raiding
kept the adrenalin and money flowing, but he had few illusions about the
artistic worth of the FBO output. When an ingratiating reporter had mentioned that "Joseph P. Kennedy Presents . . ." had made some good films,
Joe had brought the newsman up short by asking, "Which ones?"

If Joe was the biggest "yesser" of the three, it was because he saw his
chance to impress the pants pressers by bringing the box-office queen together with the eccentric "Von" to produce a winner. Difficult people
didn't scare him. He knew Patrick Powers had been out of his depth
bankrolling Stroheim's last film, but Joe wasn't risking his money renting
FBO studio space to Gloria Productions. Deep down he knew he wasn't
good at gauging public taste, but he also knew talent was something you
could buy. He showed himself to be eager because exploratory talks had
a way of unraveling unless they were firmed up with commitments to
proceed to the next step. If he were to be Gloria Swanson's business
partner, they would have to decide on a property and get a script in
development.

Mr. von Stroheim—nobody called him Erich—had been through monstrous fights with studio potentates who would eat the likes of Joseph P.
Kennedy for breakfast. He had been fired off *The Merry Go Round* and
dismissed from *The Merry Widow,* only to be hired back. *Greed* had been

hacked to a fraction of its intended length. He had no high regard for actresses—Louis B. Mayer had punched him in the nose for calling Mae Murray a whore—and he had yet to submit to the indignity of having his leading lady double as coproducer. Unlike Pat Powers and Peggy Hopkins Joyce, Swanson and Kennedy were obviously not lovers—not yet anyway. What they were, however, was a loathsome combination of movie star and smart-ass newcomer. Unfortunately, because the novel *An American Tragedy* had been banned in Boston, Will Hays had refused to sanction the filming of the Theodore Dreiser classic, which both Dreiser and Lasky wanted von Stroheim to direct. So Stroheim, too, had to swallow. He knew there weren't many money men willing to take a chance on him. Not that humility had ever gotten anyone anywhere in this town.

Stroheim, who had just celebrated his forty-second birthday, was gracious and charming, aloof and conceited. He called Gloria "Madame la Marquise" and often referred to her in the third person: *if Madame were to do this. . . .* Gloria wished Henri, with his titled poise, had been there to counterbalance the Austrian's spooning superiority.

Stroheim told her how much he had admired *Madame Sans Gêne*. The taste in costuming had been flawless, and he could only admire her for having obtained permission to film on the actual historic locations. We all know there is nothing worse than having to shoot in plaster palaces!

Gloria created a bond of commiseration when she said she was happy Mr. von Stroheim had seen the uncut version of *Madame Sans Gêne,* because Paramount had butchered the American release. Alas, the director sighed, Paramount was in the process of doing the same to his *Wedding March.* Gloria thought he was a touch condescending toward Kennedy when Joe admitted he had not seen *Madame Sans Gêne.* Joe, however, let it all wash off, and when Stroheim wasn't watching him, winked to Gloria as if to say, *Isn't this guy something!*

Of all the directors who managed, one way or another, to get into mortal combat with the Hollywood establishment, Stroheim would remain, with Orson Welles, the most notorious.

In the final years of the silent era, Stroheim was *the* Continental influence on themes, manners, and—to the extent the Hays office allowed—the implied wickedness of European morality. His *Foolish Wives* ran for almost a year on Broadway, and *The Merry Widow* was one of the most profitable pictures of the 1920s. As an actor in the films he both wrote and directed, he played the hand-kissing, heel-clicking cad who used and abused women. As the director, he was a creator obsessed with the *size* of his ideas. This

Viennese Jew, who masked his origins behind Teutonic arrogance and a fake "von," needed total control to fully express himself, and as a consequence, his career was littered with a series of unfinished, mutilated, and never-started movies.

An imposter extraordinaire, he convinced hundreds of millions of moviegoers that all Austrian aristocrats reflected his image, that a German officer could only be incarnated as the lascivious, cruel, elegant, repellent, and seductive Erich von Stroheim. Audiences, he knew, loved pomp and passion, stately behavior and volcanic emotions, and they were familiar with the thrilling depravity of Paris, the desperation of Monte Carlo's casinos, the infidelities of prewar Vienna. The romance of Ruritania, after all, preceded even Elinor Glyn's savant creations of luxury and disolution, but Stroheim's visions of decadence had a detailed, apparently firsthand intimacy that carried new conviction. Aware of all perversions, he managed to insinuate pathological refinements that eluded the more simple-minded censors.

Research by French *cinéphiles* in the 1960s would reveal Stroheim to be his own fabulation. The so-called Erich Hans Carl Maria Stroheim von Mordenwall was actually born Erich Oswald Stroheim, son of Johanna and Benno Stroheim, milliners on Lindengasse in Vienna's Jewish ghetto. The self-described cavalry officer and intimate of Emperor Franz Josef was a deserter. The incarnation of Continental chic was an immigrant who earned a precarious living as a dishwasher and trackwalker before making his Hollywood debut as a stuntman and sometime wardrobe assistant.

Stroheim's ferocious eroticism had little of De Mille's titillating calculation. Through derision and provocation, he rejected social conventions, cataloging in his films the darker side of the human soul. Impotence and frigidity, disguised as madness and physical impairment, invariably occupy center stage. Women are always subordinate to men; whether rich or poor, his heroines are condemned to be Cinderellas, while the males strut in peacock uniforms. Rape is the normal form of sexual encounter, especially on wedding nights. A libertine, usually played by Stroheim himself, gallantly turns his back while a woman undresses but, with the help of a pocket mirror, peeks over his shoulder. Women are beautiful, sincere, and touching so as to embellish the rake's progress, their sole purpose being to excite the cad and eventually suffer his most churlish demands.

What kept audiences spellbound was the extremism of his subject matter. In a medium as yet devoid of speech and dialogue, Stroheim knew how to portray unspeakable ambition and extravagant desire, unavowable obsessions and grandiose emotions. Left with shards only, posterity will have a hard time assessing and understanding the man who is perhaps the screen's most tragic figure. Stroheim's films were mutilated by distributors; *The Devil's Passkey* was lost entirely, and it was only as fragments that others survived.

Stroheim had arrived in New York in the steerage of the *Friedrich-Wilhelm* in 1909. After a tour and a short marriage in Oakland, California, he turned up in Hollywood in 1914. He worked as an extra in Triangle quickies for Jack Conway until, in *Old Heidelberg,* John Emerson promoted him from Prussian-officer extra to assistant director because he knew how German officers saluted. D. W. Griffith later made him technical adviser on the military wardrobe for *Intolerance.* War pictures were a bonanza for him, and to millions he soon became "the man you love to hate," the very image of the hideous Hun. Stroheim married Griffith's decorator, May Jones, who bore him a son, but the marriage ended in divorce in 1919.

Peace ended the hideous Hun career. One evening Stroheim accosted Carl Laemmle at the studio gate, hoping to interest the Universal Pictures boss in a scenario he had written. Laemmle was on his way home, but invited the Austrian along. At midnight the two men were still talking, switching from English to German and back. The result was a typical Laemmle gamble. On condition that the film wouldn't cost more than $25,000, he assigned Stroheim to direct, design, and star in *Blind Husbands.* The tale of an American couple vacationing in the Alps, with Stroheim playing a would-be seducer of the wife, heralded a major new talent. His handling of actors, his camera angles, and his cutting all derived from Griffith, but the intensity of the storytelling was new.

For comic relief in *Blind Husbands,* he invented a pair of honeymooning newlyweds whose spooning and kissing contrasted with the strained state of the American couple's marriage. A handsome Belgian girl, Valerie Germonprez, played the young bride. Stroheim fell in love with Valerie, and on Saturday evenings the two of them were often found at the Alexandria Hotel and other fashionable places where movie people dined and danced. His Heinous Hun image at first scared off her family. But they relented when they got to know him better, and Valerie became the third Mrs. Stroheim. (Her brother Louis became his longtime assistant.)

Blind Husbands became Universal's prestige hit of 1919. It was followed by *The Devil's Passkey,* a melodrama set in the world of high fashion. Starring the Australian Mae Busch, it told of a playwright who turns a gossip item about a notorious liaison into a play, only to discover that the rumored adulteress is his own wife.

His next film, *Foolish Wives,* revealed the true Stroheim. In his first two movies, story and cast had been acceptably normal; now plot and characters became monstrous. Made in 1921, *Foolish Wives* was a crazy epic of wealth, crime, and degeneracy, starring Stroheim, Mae Busch, and Maude George as three swindlers posing as Russian aristocrats in postwar Monaco trying to palm off counterfeit money and blackmailing the American ambassador's wife. Stroheim spent almost a year shooting the picture in a plaster Monaco of opulent luxury hotels and a full-size replica of the Casino erected at Point Lobos, California. The finished film was five and a half hours long. Universal installed a luminous sign on Forty-fourth Street and Broadway in New York proclaiming *Foolish Wives* to be the first picture ever to cost a million dollars, only to slash its running time by two-thirds. Still, it was an enormous financial success, Universal's biggest to date, and Stroheim was kept on in all his tyrannical glory.

Irving Thalberg, the rising boy wonder at the studio, decided to cut Stroheim down to size when the director began *Merry Go Round*. The twenty-three-year-old Thalberg was outraged to discover that Stroheim ordered silk underdrawers with the monogram of the Austrian Imperial Guard for the guardsmen even though they would never appear on the screen in anything less than full uniform. (Stroheim: "The public, of course, will not see the underwear, but the actors *must* know they are wearing authentic undergarments!") When Thalberg heard that Stroheim had spent three days teaching extras how to salute for a shot that would last a few seconds, he halted production, fired Stroheim, and turned over the direction to Rupert Julian, a director whose only other claim to fame was the first film version of *Phantom of the Opera*.

For reasons wrapped in obscurity, Samuel Goldwyn hired Stroheim at a higher salary than he had at Universal and gave him carte blanche to film Frank Norris's 1899 novel *McTeague,* the story of a huge and physically gross San Francisco dentist and the miserly wife he finally murders. Stroheim wanted to film the tale as written, page by page. The director took his company to San Francisco, bought a lodging house to use as his principal set, and had the outside walls torn off so he could shoot by natural light.

While Stroheim filmed in San Francisco and in Death Valley, Goldwyn sold out to the Metro and Mayer companies. The finished film was nine and a half hours long, but Stroheim reduced it to four hours' running time before he presented it to his new boss, Louis B. Mayer. Unfortunately, Mayer had just brought in Thalberg, Stroheim's nemesis at Universal, to be second in command at the new studio to be known as MGM. Once more Thalberg took away Stroheim's picture. This time, after having Rex Ingram reduce it to three and a half hours, Thalberg cut it himself to just under two hours and titled it *Greed.*

Stroheim did have one man on his side: William Randolph Hearst, whose Cosmopolitan film unit was now under the MGM banner. When Hearst saw the film at a preview he was enormously impressed. (He was a San Franciscan, and Frank Norris had been a Hearst foreign correspondent before he turned novelist.) Hearst called *Greed* the greatest motion picture he had ever seen and arranged its world premiere in his New York theater, the Cosmopolitan. Audiences, however, actively hated it. Posterity would classify it among the screen's few masterpieces.

Mae Murray, the former Czech nightclub dancer who had so besotted Marcus Loew that he allowed her to dictate her own choice of material, wanted to make *The Merry Widow*. Thalberg, who hated her, had the diabolical idea of having Stroheim direct her. Stroheim accepted, and even agreed to costar John Gilbert although the actor couldn't dance. The shooting was tumultuous. Though Murray insisted on her own cameraman and her choice of camera angles, "Von" nonetheless managed to turn the Franz Lehar operetta into a characteristically depraved Ruritanian hallucination. To begin with, he divided the male lead into Cain and Abel cousins, one a deceitful seducer, the other an addled incarnation of vices, and had them compete for Murray's attentions. Gilbert played the seducer, Prince Danilo, while Roy d'Arcy, who had played a foppish schemer in a musical comedy Valerie and Erich Von Stroheim had attended, was cast as Crown Prince Mirko. Next, the director transformed the court of Monteblanco into a snake pit of cripples and degenerates. Finally, he made the richest man in the central European principality, who dies on his wedding night and makes Murray the merriest of windows, a foot fetishist.

"That madman is making a filthy picture," Murray complained to Thalberg. "All this business of a dirty old man kissing girls' feet and drooling over a closet of women's shoes! It's repulsive."

Stroheim, in turn, complained that Murray ignored his instructions and on more than one occasion called him a "dirty Hun." She railed that he neglected to take close-ups of her, and when she played her love scenes with Gilbert, the director turned his back and commented, "Let me know when it's over."

Open warfare on the set continued for twelve weeks. Stroheim worked his actors day and night. The studio was forced to engage two shifts of crews, and even then, the director worked into the morning hours. To get him to stop, the production manager one night cut off the electricity to the set.

To cap things off, Stroheim filmed an orgy so lewd—complete with voyeurs, Nubian servants sporting padlocked chastity belts, and a female orchestra wearing nothing but face masks—that the entire scene had to be cut.

What remained made millions for MGM. *The Merry Widow* even appealed to intellectuals, who appreciated the sly sarcasm and the sharp irony beneath the popular formula story. Wrote the influential Richard Watts, Jr., in the New York *Herald Tribune,* Stroheim "is, in my opinion, the most important figure in motion pictures, not excepting Chaplin and Emil Jannings."

Soon after *The Merry Widow* was finished, Stroheim agreed to have lunch at the Ambassador with Pat Powers and the canny Irishman's new protégée, Peggy Hopkins Joyce. Powers wanted to launch the former Ziegfeld beauty as a film star. Stroheim, however, was still smarting from his experience with Mae Murray and was in no mood to start another ex-Broadway hoofer's screen career. Instead, he hypnotized Powers with a project of his own, a double feature to be called *The Wedding March* and *The Honeymoon* that he would write, direct, and star in himself, and that would make tons of money for whoever financed it. As he explained to Pat and Peggy, the appeal of his project was that it could be shown in two parts, to be screened with an hour's intermission. "To convince myself that I was right in my assertion that filmgoers would prefer to see one long film, even in two parts, than to sit through a 'double feature,' one of which was a cheap 'B' picture, a slapstick comedy or a medley of assorted cartoons," he would remember, "I sent one thousand printed postcards through the agency that handled my fan mail asking for the opinion of my fans who had previously written to me asking for photographs and complimenting me on my previous work. Over eight hundred answered that they would love to see a picture that would correspond to the original book or play from which it had been taken, and that they did not care how long the picture would run."

The setting for the two-part project was Vienna 1914, where ruined and enfeebled aristocrats marry rich commoners' daughters and don resplendent parade uniforms one last time before the guns of August sweep them and the Austro-Hungarian empire away. Powers loved the story, called the second part "pure velvet," and said he'd get back to Stroheim.

Powers took the project to Jesse Lasky, who was so impressed with the normally laconic Irishman's enthusiasm that he took a share in the venture and arranged for the film's release through Paramount. It was, of course, well known that Stroheim was hard to handle, Lasky warned. He advised extreme caution and, with Powers, imposed a collaborator. Harry Carr, a level-headed newspaperman and a friend of Stroheim's, would work on the script with the director and have veto power over the finished scenario.

Together, Stroheim and Carr rented a huge seaside villa in La Jolla, near San Diego. Carr was impressed with Von's self-discipline. With the surf and gorgeous sunshine beckoning at the doorstep, the director stayed at his desk all day. Creakings and scurryings in unoccupied bedrooms convinced the superstitious Stroheim that the house was haunted. He insisted the lights burn all night throughout the house to drive the ghosts away.

The way Stroheim created characters impressed Carr. Like Zola, Stroheim believed that characters were the end products of heredity and environment. The writer's role was to imagine the circumstances, most often social factors, that would produce a particular personality. Stroheim sketched out entire family trees for the people he invented. For example, when it came to describing a rich man's crippled daughter, for whom he had the frail, wistful Zasu Pitts in mind, he began talking about her dead mother.

"But the mother won't appear in the film," Carr objected.

"No, but how do you know the real truth about any girl unless you know something about her mother?"

Carr came away believing Stroheim was convinced that his characters had a real existence and were living human beings, and he wholeheartedly approved the final script submitted to Powers and Lasky.

Shooting started at the MGM lot in June 1926. Stroheim played Prince Mikki; Maude George, his impoverished mother; Zasu Pitts, a greedy pharmacist's infirm daughter, whom his mother forces him to marry; and Fay Wray, the poor young girl whose love Mikki doesn't have the courage to return. Stroheim quickly exhausted Powers's original budget. For a love scene in an orchard, the director had thousands of artificial apple blossoms made. He was said to have lost one day's studio filming because one out of a dozen chimneys in an establishing shot of the Vienna skyline didn't smoke.

Powers sold the two-part movie to Lasky while filming was still in progress. Stroheim's rough-cut totaled nine and a half hours, and he had to sacrifice entire sequences to bring the two parts down to the stipulated running time of less than five hours. Lasky, however, had no intention of releasing any double program. Instead, *The Wedding March* would be released as one picture, then recut to become explanatory footage for a totally new picture called *The Honeymoon.* While Stroheim met with Gloria and Joe, Josef von Sternberg, the future discoverer of Marlene Dietrich and director of *The Blue Angel,* was performing the re-edit.

As they talked, Stroheim praised Gloria's acting and, getting to the point, declared it was his fondest wish to make a film with her. To that end, he had, in fact, at Mr. Kennedy's suggestion, created a story he thought would allow her to display her talent to its fullest potential.

The heroine Stroheim conjured up was named Patricia ("Kitty") Kelly.

The orphaned daughter of an Irish painter, Kitty is an innocent convent girl when we first meet her, spirited and full of fun. An aunt in far-off Dar es Salaam in German East Africa is paying for Kitty's convent upbringing in Kronberg, the capital of Hesse-Nassau, one of the Duedez, or twelve petty states, of Wilhelmine Germany.

The ruler of Hesse-Nassau is Queen Helena, a mentally unbalanced monarch who spends her time taunting her rogue cousin and fiancé, the dashing young Crown Prince Wolfram. On an outing one day with his cavalry, Wolfram meets Kitty, out walking with her fellow convent girls and nuns. It is love at first sight.

That night a spectacular banquet is given by Queen Helena, who makes a surprise announcement that her wedding to Wolfram will take place the next day. The prince decides to take advantage of his last night of freedom to see the convent girl. With an aide, he scales the convent wall and starts a fire. In the resulting confusion, the nuns and their charges run into the night. Kitty, who swoons in the excitement, is swept up into the arms of Wolfram and carried in her nightie back to his private palace quarters for a midnight supper. As they declare their love and Wolfram takes her to his bedroom, the queen bursts in, sees the remains of the supper, enters the bedroom, and discovers the couple. In fury, she drives Kitty, who is wearing Wolfram's officer's coat over her nightie, from the castle and has Wolfram thrown in the tower.

Kitty attempts suicide by jumping from a bridge. She is rescued and taken to a convent hospital. Eventually she travels to Dar es Salaam, where her very sick aunt demands her presence. The aunt owns a dubious hotel frequented by planters and sailors. Before the aunt dies, she draws up a will that leaves the hotel to her niece on condition that Kitty marry a filthy rich old planter, Jan Vooyheid, who is paralyzed from the waist down. Kitty does, and becomes the reluctant ruler of her own depraved domain. Then Wolfram is set free. He transfers to a colonial regiment, finds Kitty, and after a thrilling chase through African swampland that leaves old Vooyheid dead, marries her. Back in Hesse-Nassau, Queen Helena is assassinated. Wolfram is called to the throne but will accept only if Kitty becomes his queen.

Stroheim called the story "The Swamp." He had shot the ending of *Greed* on location in the California desert and planned to do similar justice to this picture by filming the chase in authentic swamps. Indeed, he said in conclusion, he planned to make the telling of the story richly cinematic from beginning to end.

The Swamp was not the most exciting title Gloria could think of, and she wasn't sure what to think of a picture in which her entire wardrobe for the first half would consist of a novice's uniform and a nightgown. But Joe was enthusiastic. It sounded very powerful to him.

Sensing Gloria's reservations, Stroheim said he was willing to drop everything and go to work on a script. Joe interjected that he had to go back east and was impatient to choose a property before he went. When he asked Gloria what she was thinking, she almost said she was wondering whether she wasn't a little too old to play a convent girl, although the story also offered her a chance to portray mature scenes of dramatic conflict. If she finally smiled and, after a poignant pause, said she thought Mr. von Stroheim should begin on a script at once, she would write in her memoirs that it was "because something told me this was the film that would change my life."

They stood and shook hands. After the director left, Gloria asked Joe if he knew Stroheim had a reputation for being undisciplined, spendthrift, and a temperamental perfectionist. Joe said he did. "I also know he's our man," he added. "I can handle him."

Setting her finances straight was uppermost in Gloria's mind during the next weeks as letters from Henri made it clear he could not perform economic miracles with *Sunya*. United Artists now planned a San Francisco launch of *Sadie Thompson* right after New Year's. Joe invited Gloria to dinner at Rodeo Drive.

She was greeted by an Irish maid, caught a glimpse of a butler, and heard mention of a gardener and cook, but despite the homey furnishings, the place felt very much like a clubhouse. Eddie Moore was there, and when the three of them sat down together to eat, it was obvious that dinners were business sessions in this house. Joe was upbeat. He smothered her with attention and repeated several times how proud he was of having landed Stroheim. His enthusiasm began to rub off on Gloria. What she needed, she told herself, was someone with Joe's aggressive enthusiasm and business acumen.

Turning to her affairs, he said the first thing was to set up her new company. Pat Sullivan would handle all the legal aspects through FBO's New York office. In the meantime, she should not tell her employees or advisers anything. When she asked why, Eddie said, "Because if they find out they're going to get kicked off the gravy train, they'll try to set up obstacles and cause delays." Joe agreed. "We've got to sneak up on them while they're asleep, or else we'll be sitting in meetings for a year."

Leaving E. B. Derr in charge of California affairs, Joe, Eddie, and the other two horsemen returned east for Christmas and New Year's with their families. Joe called Gloria almost every day, talking, laughing, and working to insinuate himself into the center of her life. Henri returned from France in early December. He would soon meet the financier—Gloria imitated Joe's Boston accent for Henri—who would no doubt be the answer to their problems. And Henri would meet the Teutonic aristocrat, the director of *Greed* and *The Merry Widow,* who was now writing her next picture. But first they would have a wonderful Christmas with little Gloria and Brother.

Gaily wrapped parcels covered the foot of the Christmas tree. There was a big gift for little Gloria from her father. One surprise that had greeted Gloria on her return from France with Henri was Herbert Somborn's success as a restaurateur. With money from her settlement, he had opened the Brown Derby across from the Ambassador Hotel on Wilshire Boulevard and turned it into a fashionable hangout for movie people. Once settled in California again, Gloria had made arrangements for Herbert to see his daughter on a regular basis. The real gossip about the Brown Derby—the exterior was built to resemble a two-story bowler hat—came from Lois Wilson, who advised Henri never to go there because it was the favorite lunch place of Wallace Beery. The idea of Gloria's three husbands sitting down to lunch together was just too much.

Derr came to the house several times to have Gloria sign papers. The new company would be called Gloria Productions Inc. and would be incorporated in Delaware. When she asked why, Derr said, "Because Pat Sullivan knows people there. Pat says that never has a corporation been formed faster than this one. He told me to tell you that."

Gloria and Henri made a New Year's toast to a very promising 1928. The money mess was being solved, the Stroheim picture would be an opulent showcase of her talent. And before that there was *Sadie.* The premiere was only weeks away, and Gloria knew that in the innocent-at-heart tramp she had a winner.

As soon as the holidays were over, the funny voice was on the telephone from Boston. Joe wanted Gloria and Henri to meet him in Palm Beach in two weeks. That was exactly when UA wanted her in San Francisco for the *Sadie* opening. Joe insisted. There were lots of things to discuss—her new corporation, the Stroheim film, and perhaps an important place for Henri in the corporate scheme of things. During their three years of marriage, Henri's responsibilities had been nebulous. The idea of seeing her husband add substance to his appeal as an aristocrat and man-about-town was very alluring to Gloria. She agreed they would come to Florida. Eddie Moore would book the tickets for them, Joe said. In the meantime she shouldn't tell anyone about the trip. She informed the UA publicity department that she would not be able to attend the San Francisco opening.

On January 5, *The New York Times* reported acquisition by the Radio Corporation of America of a substantial interest in FBO Pictures. The move was described as opening to motion pictures the resources of radio by giving movies the use of all the patents and technical knowhow of RCA, General Electric, and Westinghouse Electric. "A complete revolution of present-day entertainment may easily develop as the result of the close affiliation between the important leaders of motion pictures and the powerful engineering organization of the radio group," Sarnoff and Kennedy's joint statement said.

A few hours before Gloria and Henri's January 14 departure for Palm Beach, Derr came to the house with the last papers to sign and a telegram from Sullivan announcing the creation of Gloria Productions Inc. Gloria was chairman of the board, Derr was president, and Joe's old friend from Fore River, C. J. Scollard, was vice president and treasurer.

The business world intruded into their trip across the South. When the train stopped in Yuma, Arizona, the conductor brought Gloria a telegram. She assumed it was from Joe or E.B., since nobody else knew she and Henri were on their way to Florida. She tore open the telegram and asked the conductor to wait in case she had a reply. The wire was from Milton Cohen. "A REAL FRIEND SHOULD NEVER BE DESTROYED STOP REGRET YOUR ATTITUDE EXCEEDINGLY STOP WISH ALWAYS TO BE YOUR FRIEND BUT NEVER YOUR LAWYER PLEASE ARRANGE IMMEDIATELY FOR OTHER COUNSEL. MILTON."

Gloria gasped. Milton had been her lawyer for the last five years. Was it what Eddie Moore had warned? The people getting kicked off the gravy train were getting nasty. The conductor was waiting, but she couldn't think of an answer. She had been dismissed. She sent a telegram to E.B. quoting the lawyer's wire and asking whether she should cut her throat.

Eddie Moore and Ted O'Leary were on the platform, dressed in tropical suits and white shoes, as the train pulled into Palm Beach early Sunday morning. Gloria called out the open window, and Henri jumped off one end of the car to introduce himself.

Joe came charging through the narrow corridor toward her. He pushed her back into her compartment and kissed her.

"I missed you," he said without embarrassment before he began rubbing off her lipstick. "And I wanted you to know."

She felt herself shaking. She had missed him, too, she said.

He jumped down on the platform and cheerfully introduced himself to Henri, standing with Moore and O'Leary. Next, Joe ordered porters to load all the luggage into two shiny, long automobiles. He had booked Gloria and Henri into the Poinciana Hotel, he announced. He told Eddie and Ted to ride with Henri in one car, and helped Gloria into the other car.

On the way to the hotel, Gloria avoided Joe's eyes. There had been more than a new business associate's enthusiasm in his greeting on the train. Casually, she asked if he knew Milton Cohen had resigned in a telegram delivered to her in Yuma. He knew, he said. "Let's say it saved E.B. from firing him, along with your business manager and quite a few others. Pat Sullivan is coming down tonight. He'll tell you what a bunch of worthless passengers you were carrying. Anyway, things are going to be different from now on."

This Sporting Life

"And during the winter seasons,
all the right people betook themselves to
the gilded apathy of Palm Beach."

—ANITA LOOS

The manager of the Royal Poinciana Hotel greeted the celebrated actress with a corsage of orchids. Gloria hated orchids, but she could tell by the expression on Joe's face that the manager was following instructions. A bell captain and a parade of bellboys led the marquise, the marquis, Joe, and the horsemen to a suite that looked like a flower shop.

"Everybody in Palm Beach is lining up to meet you," Joe beamed with a grand gesture as they entered the suite, which faced magnificent gardens and the ocean. "Eddie typed up a whole schedule for your stay. Give it to her, Eddie. And Ted, show Gloria Mrs. Stotesbury's flowers."

Gloria would remember O'Leary dutifully moving from bouquet to bouquet before stopping at a large vase of yellow roses.

"And Gloria," Joe continued, "just look at all these calling cards and invitations. Here, Marquis, look at this one, right on top."

Henri took the envelope. Mrs. Stotesbury had arranged, with Mr. Kennedy's concurrence, a party in their honor. "People will be arriving from all up and down the eastern seaboard for it," Joe added, flopping down in a chair.

"That's right," Eddie said in his driest vein of humor, "anybody who doesn't get an invitation has just one week to commit suicide or leave town."

Joe laughed and banged his hand on his thigh.

The 1926 hurricane, which had tossed big steam yachts upon the avenues of Miami, ripped roofs off thousands of cottages and villas, and left behind some four hundred dead, had slowed the evolution into an American Riviera of the sixty-odd miles of coastline from Palm Beach south to Miami.

Still, sprawling mansions were lining Palm Beach's Ocean Avenue. Marjorie Merriweather Post's 118-room Mar a Largo was the newest addition, although El Mirasol, the winter home of Edward T. and Lucretia Stotesbury—Ned and Eva to the winter colony's in-crowd—was still the biggest.

Stotesbury, of the Philadelphia & Reading Railroad fortune, with an annual income of seven million dollars, was a slightly ridiculous septuagenarian who cavorted through an endless series of social functions organized by his sixty-three-year-old wife, who liked to say she had taught her husband "how to play." The Stotesburys' parties, planned with the help of seventy-five servants, were among the most sought-after affairs on the Palm Beach social calendar.

Joe got up and announced that Eddie, Ted, and he were going to Mass. Was Henri coming? Was he Catholic? He was, Henri answered cheerfully, but he'd stay with Gloria, unpack, and have some breakfast. Joe seemed to want to say something, but didn't. Before leaving he merely insisted they all have lunch later.

They spent a lovely afternoon and decided to postpone business until Pat Sullivan arrived from New York. When he did, they deferred business until the next day, dressed for dinner, and were Joe's guests at one of the big new hotels—five men and a movie star with an orchid corsage she didn't like.

Gloria would recall the following days as a mix of business, teas, receptions, and dinner parties. All of Palm Beach, it seemed, wanted to entertain the Marquis and Marquise de la Falaise. After three years, these affairs were beginning to bore Henri and Gloria, but Joe Kennedy beamed as if he were P. T. Barnum presenting Lavinia and Tom Thumb or a pair of unicorns. She observed Joe as perhaps only a woman would, and saw an endearing, boyish pride, the saloonkeeper's son enjoying the Palm Beach glitter because he could pay for Palm Beach. "About his background and his religion he made no apologies," she would recall, "and I admired him tremendously for that; after all, I hadn't been a star or a marquise so long I couldn't remember exactly how much a ride on the trolley cost." Joe was the *nouveau riche* who knew he was nouveau. His vividness, originality, and flair surfaced in the challenge of appearing a seasoned man of the world.

They were quite a crew arriving at the palatial playgrounds. There was the movie queen, dressed to the teeth but ready for practical jokes; followed by her handsome, world-weary nobleman; followed by the take-charge Kennedy; followed by the forever uncomplaining Eddie, the pink-faced and beefy Ted, and the silent Pat. Moore, O'Leary, and Sullivan squirmed in the tuxedos their boss made them wear, and they stuck out like sore thumbs at the parties he had them all attend—soirées given by Ray Goetz, impresario of Cole Porter; Herbert and Minnie Weston, pets of Park Avenue society; Princess Anita Lobkowitz; and, with his front teeth missing, the Pennsylvania novelist Joseph Hergesheimer, who commuted between nests of Palm Beach snobs and Bess and Jesse Lasky's beach house in Santa Monica.

"And how are you, you?" Ted asked Gloria one night on the dance floor. He, Pat, and Eddie were becoming friendlier, addressing her as "you," rather than as Marquise or Miss Swanson.

She winked back. "And you, *you?*"

The horsemen sprang to life when it was time for business, when they were called to the telephone, or had to call Joe to the phone for long-distance. To them, what was important was what was happening in snowy New York.

Together with Elisha Walker and the brokers at Lehman Brothers, Joe and his people were working out a grand strategy, a stock swap that would give them control of the Keith Albee Orpheum circuit. Less than a month after Joe had diluted his shares of FBO by selling a minority stake to David Sarnoff, a second Kennedy stake in FBO was being sold. The money from it was to be invested in Keith Albee Orpheum, which owned a controlling interest in the ill-matched Pathé–De Mille Pictures. The idea was to sell the whole caboodle, perhaps with the help of the foxy John J. Murdock, to Sarnoff or another electric group interested in getting into talking pictures with an already integrated film plant–theater chain operation.

Rumors had it that Murdock was ready to ally himself with Kennedy, but whether the canny Scot opposed or joined the raiding party, the situation was shaping up for a colossal merger. Wall Street thought it heard one shoe drop when, in February, the Walker-Lehman associates had Joe appointed special adviser to Pathé–De Mille Pictures. C.B. remembered his gracious host at Harvard and welcomed Kennedy as a potential ally against Murdock. Joe could hardly contain his pleasure at De Mille's reaction. The appointment came with a $2,000-a-week salary. Combined with the $2,000 a week he was drawing at FBO, Joe could certainly afford to impress the Gold Coast gentry.

When they got to Gloria's business, Sullivan was the first to speak. Only Lance Heath, Gloria's chief of publicity, had been spared the ax. Without resorting to notes, Pat rattled off a list of specific reasons for dismissing everyone else. Henceforth, E.B. would take care of Gloria Productions' business affairs with a smaller, hand-picked staff. Henri sat in silence as the details of the corporate housecleaning were outlined. Gloria felt a burden lifted from her shoulders. When she was asked if she approved, she said yes.

Next, Joe addressed the la Falaises' finances. His solution was bold.

Gloria should sell all rights to *The Love of Sunya* and *Sadie Thompson* to Joe Schenck immediately. That would wipe out her debt to Art Finance, Schenck's finance company, which had bankrolled most of the productions, and more important, would eliminate her steep interest payments. The sale would also provide her with some liquid capital and make the problem of distributing *Sadie* to Bible Belt theaters Schenck's headache.

Gloria's intuition told her *Sadie* would be a hit. Joe answered her objections by predicting the picture would open to great reviews in New York, then die because theater owners in the hinterlands were leery.

"You and Raoul Walsh might have taken the dirty words out and turned Davidson's clerical collar around," Joe continued, "but religious groups, from Catholics to Baptists, are still going to find it pretty hot stuff. The thing to do is to unload the film to Schenck the day after the New York opening."

"E.B. had a social charity lined up for the premiere," Pat added on cue.

"Because arranging for *Sadie's* distribution will be a monumental undertaking," Joe continued. He turned directly to Gloria. "Why not invest that energy in the new picture, which Stroheim told me yesterday is going to be a masterpiece?"

"I think *Sadie* is something of a masterpiece," Gloria answered. She felt manipulated, but wondered if she shouldn't trust Joe's superior business sense.

"Even though *Sadie* has passed the Production Code," Joe said, "the Hays office will never *recommend* it."

Turning to Henri, he asked, "Have you seen it?"

With some embarrassment, Henri confessed he had not.

Gloria had never been so keenly aware of her own business worth, of movies not as graven images of mystery and allure, but as products for the entertainment industry. The mistakes she had made in her year and a half as an independent producer-star were the reasons she was here, the reasons she felt cornered. Joe had shown her the view from the top, Zukor's and Lasky's view of movies as commodities that produce both money and a need for money. In his dealings with her, Joe had made no mistakes.

Reluctantly, she told him to do what he thought best.

"I'll have E.B. start on it tomorrow," Joe said. "After the premiere Joe Schenck will owe you money for a change instead of you owing him." Next he offered Henri a marvelous position as European director of Pathé studios.

In retrospect, Gloria would remember the tact with which Joe made the offer that could make her husband distinctly his own man and, if Henri was clever, rich as well. In her autobiography, her smile of gratitude to Joe when the two men came to a quick verbal agreement immediately precedes her account of how the next day she and Joe tumbled into bed. Her indebtedness to Joe no doubt softened, in her own eyes, the adultery that, since the kiss on the train, she knew was inevitable. In a reversal of the story of the biblical David, who sent Uriah into the most dangerous part of the battle so he could possess Bathsheba, Joe was ready to heap gold on the man he wanted to cuckold.

Kennedy biographers would wax saucily on how Joe eliminated, with some permanence, the coveted movie queen's husband, but neither Gloria nor the Kennedy memorialists could explain how Joe was able to offer Henri a Pathé directorship in January when he himself didn't become a Pathé adviser until February. Gloria was, of course, writing for posterity, and by having Joe's generosity and Henri's opportunism precede her surrender, she softened her image. If she acknowledged what seems to be the case—that the Paris job offer was an afterthought, an idea the lovers came up with a month later—an unattractive coarseness might have crept into her self-portrait.

Henri would leave no memoirs of his own, and we can only speculate on whether it all passed over his head or whether he knew he was defeated and went for the proffered brass ring. There is even the possibility, as subsequent events will suggest, that however much he was the impoverished aristocrat forced to play along with a blustery parvenu rival, he might have been the first to sense he was on a sinking ship and that his wife's impending adultery set him free, morally, to concentrate on enriching himself.

Joe's infatuation was hard to ignore. Others saw how he was dazzled and drawn by Gloria's presence, how his own success—Palm Beach, Gloria, the lot—all made him live beyond the rules, how she exerted an attraction that went beyond physical beauty.

It happened, in any case, the next afternoon.

Once business was settled, they all told each other they were there to enjoy the nation's newest winter resort. Eddie asked Henri if he would like to try an afternoon of deep-sea fishing. Henri said he would be delighted. At breakfast the next morning Eddie announced he had chartered a boat and hired a photographer to be on the dock at sunset to take pictures of them and their trophies. They'd all leave right after lunch.

Joe begged off. He had business calls to make. Ted asked Gloria if she was coming. No, she trusted nothing smaller than an ocean liner and, in any case, would prefer to go shopping for her children.

Worth Avenue consisted of three blocks of unique and pricey shops, interspersed with charming vest-pocket "vias," accessible through short, fashionable alleys leading into courtyards embellished in Mediterranean style with fountains, wrought iron, and greenery.

Returning from her shopping, Gloria slipped into a kimono, and while the maid brought in some dresses that had been ironed, handled a threatening orchid crisis. The hotel florist phoned to tell her that because of Mrs. Stotesbury's party there was a shortage of orchids, that Mr. Kennedy had ordered him to find out what color dress she would be wearing so the appropriate orchids could be reserved for her corsage. Nodding to the maid to indicate there was nothing more she needed, Gloria explained on the phone that she didn't like orchids.

She was vaguely aware of the maid leaving as she told the florist she would be perfectly happy if he would save her two or three carnations. No wire, no tinfoil, no pins, no ribbons—just plain carnations.

She hung up and saw Joe in the doorway, standing in his white flannels, argyle sweater, and two-toned shoes. He had obviously overheard her conversation with the florist. "Well," she winced, "now you know."

He wasn't listening. He stood there and stared at her. Then he closed the door behind him, and before either of them could speak, was kissing her. "With one hand he held the back of my head," she would write, "with the other he stroked my body and pulled at my kimono. He kept insisting in a drawn-out moan, 'No longer, no longer. Now!' He was like a roped horse, rough, arduous, racing to be free. After a hasty climax he lay beside me, stroking my hair. Apart from his guilty, passionate mutterings, he had still said nothing cogent."

He looked into her eyes with a strange mixture of gravity and timidity. There had been one or two infidelities in his past, quick tumbles, but nothing like her. He excited her more than she had expected. They were good for each other, liked what they saw and felt in each other. He didn't mention Rose, but he knew he wanted more of the woman lying next to him. She, too, knew it would go on, even if they were both married with children and had no domestic feelings for each other.

He was a practicing Catholic; she was married to a man she thought unexceptional yet had no intention of divorcing. She felt her new lover owned her more than her husband. He was married to a wife of demanding views and little sensuality, a wife who didn't want to know about his business. The woman beside him engaged his mind and talent. He had never met, never possessed a woman who was worshiped, envied, and emulated by millions. She knew he was a man she could never control.

They both knew deceits would follow.

Long before the fishermen returned, Joe got up and dressed. Before he left, they grinned softly and agreed, "No more orchids."

They were relieved to have a reason to smile.

Gloria arrived at the Stotesburys' party wearing a dove-gray gown designed by René Hubert and carrying a single red carnation. She was flanked by her husband and Joe, each with a red carnation that she had put in their buttonholes in the lobby of the Poinciana. Eva Stotesbury said everyone was dying to meet them and asked if they would stand beside her in the receiving line.

They graciously consented.

Gloria noticed that many of the women filing past were wearing variegated orchids and that they noticed her single red carnation.

PART 2

Rose

Honey Fitz can talk you blind
on any subject you can find.
Fish and fishing, motorboats,
railroads, streetcars, getting votes,
Proper ways to open clams
How to cure existing shams.

—ANONYMOUS VERSE
in *Boston Herald*

When Rose Kennedy found out about Gloria, she reacted with rage and despair but refused to show her feelings. She had grown up watching her mother cope with a philandering husband, and she was eight months pregnant.

At thirty-eight, she was a short woman with the healthy outdoor tan of someone who likes salt air and sunshine. The closest she ever came to acknowledging her husband's infidelity may have been during a walk with a woman neighbor along the Cape Cod beach. Alice Harrington, a Catholic neighbor in Hyannisport whose daughter played with Eunice, brought up the question of when and where a wife should show iciness toward her husband. Rose seemed not to understand what her friend meant. "Well, you know, everybody does it in marriage. Haven't you shown iciness toward your husband?"

After a pause, Rose said, "Yes, I have. And I made him pay for that iciness. I made him give me everything I wanted. Clothes, jewels, everything. You have to know how to use that iciness." Later, to the wife of Gloria's former boss, Rose stood infidelity on its head. She had closed her bedroom door to her husband, she told Bess Lasky, implying that she had done so before Joe had a chance to stray.

Rose's key to survival was to willingly narrow her field of vision and ignore much of what went on around her. She taught her children a certain emotional repression or detachment, which they would come to resent. Any emotional display was discouraged. By her own example and through frequent admonition, she taught her children to hide their true feeings, fearing that if they showed their emotions too openly it would make them vulnerable to taunts and attacks. Prudish in the extreme, she discouraged pleasurable stirrings and developed an aversion to all sexual innuendo. In her daughters, she was quick to condemn the slightest display of sensuality. There is a measure of irony in the fact that as a parent she would eventually become more remote than Joe.

Jean, the youngest daughter, would complain, "I was shuffled off to boarding school at the age of eight. That's why I'm still trying to get my head screwed on straight." Kathleen would become the only child to emancipate herself from the family, but only after monstrous fights with her mother. John told his friend Bill Walton, "My mother was either at some Paris fashion house or else on her knees in some church. She was never there when we really needed her. . . . My mother never really held me and hugged me. Never." To one of his girlfriends, he mentioned that his mother never stood up to his father. "My mother is a nobody," he said.

John's womanizing would lead him to compare himself to his father and to compete with him. To Clare Boothe Luce, Jack said, "Dad told all the boys to get laid as often as possible."

Late in life, Rose would tell English friends not to be tempted to read Lord Longford's book on the Kennedys because of Joe's "predatory ways toward women."

Rose refused to consider her marriage an unhappy one. She did her best to focus on the good things—the beautiful homes, the achievements of the family, the comfort and security of wealth, the opportunities to travel and meet famous people. When they traveled, Rose and Joe would stay in different hotels—in New York, he at the Waldorf Towers, she at the Plaza; in Paris, he somewhere convenient to a golf course, she near the couturier houses. They would meet for dinner or an evening at the theater and talk about what they had done that day. She attributed the fact that they always got along so well together to their frequent separations and independent existences.

Life without father threw responsibilities on Rose. "You have to remember my father was away a lot of the time," Jack would say. "He was in Hollywood four years. My mother was the glue. She's not as forceful as my father, but she was the glue." Joe's influence on the children increased as they grew older; it was in the early years that Rose was the immediate presence in their lives. A friend detected her all-pervasive influence even in the inflections of their voices. "When Jack spoke, I could hear his mother's voice."

She set the family rules and, like her father, pinned memos on her clothes so she would not forget all the things she had to do. Although a nurse and a governess helped with the smaller ones, she took her meals with the youngsters, read to them by the hour, led shopping and sightseeing excursions, and faithfully heard their nightly prayers and, every Friday night, their catechism lessons. Comforter and confidante, she was also the disciplinarian. Justice was immediate; she never said, "Wait until your father gets home."

Eunice would remember her mother, not her father, being the first one to emphasize the family motto, "Finish first!" "I was twenty-four before I knew I didn't have to win something every day." When Joe was home, Kennedy biographer Ralph Martin would write, Rose was something of a shadow. In a houseful of people, she would quietly retire to her room for privacy. No matter what the weather, she would go out alone for a walk wearing her favorite black coat and old-fashioned kerchief. When she needed surgery, she had it done without telling the family.

She was seventeen when she fell in love with Joe. In her eighties, when Joe had long been dead, she would remember their courtship in Victorian Boston with tenderness. "Mr. Kennedy and I were not supposed to have dates," she would tell her secretary, Barbara Gibson.

She had been her father's beloved first child from birth. With nine boys in his family and no female relatives in the United States and none that he knew of in Ireland, he was overjoyed with having a girl a year after he had married Mary Josephine Hannon in 1889. Already active in politics, John Francis Fitzgerald was soon elected to the Boston Common Council, then to the State Senate, and then to the U.S. House of Representatives. He was one of the youngest men in Congress, the only Democrat from New England, and the only Catholic. Rose had a little sister and a little brother, and spent what she would remember as a wonderful childhood in a big, rambling, and comfortable house in West Concord, a few miles from Acton where her mother's parents lived. Two more children were born during the years the Fitzgeralds lived in Concord.

Honey Fitz and his wife, Josie, were total opposites. He was outgoing and loved being "on stage" and feeling the vibrations emanating from a crowd. She was reserved, bored with small talk, happiest among close friends and members of her family. "I was influenced by her conviction that children need firm discipline," Rose would write in *Times to Remember*. "She, perforce, was the disciplinarian in our house because my father was not there most of the time." Her mother instilled deep religious feelings in

Rose, talked about the fasts and feasts and special seasons of the Church.

Rose was fifteen when Honey Fitz ran for mayor of Boston. She remembered election night when the crowds outside Quincy House were so big he couldn't get inside to attend his own victory party. In the end, some of his admirers realized who he was and hoisted him up on the iron awning. There, to thunderous cheers, he made his victory speech.

The mayor established his family in a large and expensive home in Dorchester, complete with scrollwork porch, mansard turret, and stained glass in the front door portraying what he insisted was the family coat of arms. His slogan, "A bigger, better, busier Boston," carried him to reelection in 1910. His political savvy and relentless campaigning were marvels to his contemporaries. Presidents courted him in the belief he could "deliver" the city in a national election.

Mayor Fitzgerald might have been innovative in public life, but when it came to raising his daughters, he couldn't have been more conservative. Rose might be seventeen, but dating was taboo and "going steady" totally out of the question. To see each other, Joe and Rose had to invent excuses. "Could anyone object if we happened to be at the same place at the same time?" she would write. "Joe was captain-manager of the Latin School tennis team. When I went for a weekend visit with an aunt of mine in Concord, he arranged a match between Concord High School and his team, at Concord. We spent quite a few hours together that day. We also met at informal get-togethers with friends at somebody's house, usually in the afternoon and always, of course, with a responsible adult on the premises. We would push back the parlor furniture, lift the breakable bric-a-brac out of the way, make lemonade or punch and cookies and fudge, and someone would play the piano. We gathered around and we sang and we danced. Joe and I had many mutual friends. If I were invited, he would just drop in."

At first, Honey Fitz encouraged his eldest daughter's lively independence, but then, to avoid exposing her to the personal and political scandals that his brash charm could not permanently disguise, he crushed it by forbidding her to attend secular Wellesley College and insisting she go to one of the Sacred Heart convent schools. When she was eighteen her father tried to interest her in Hugh Nawn, the son of a wealthy contractor and treasurer of the Democratic City Committee. The Nawns lived in Dorchester, not far from the Fitzgeralds, and when the young Harvard man was planning to be in Europe at the same time as the mayor was abroad with his wife, and daughters Rose and Agnes, Honey Fitz made sure the young people's paths crossed. To Rose, however, Hugh was too much the proverbial boy next door.

Rose and Agnes spent a year at the Blumenthal convent school in

Holland but, through their mother's intercession, were spared a second year
there. Rose was now nineteen, but in a last attempt to discourage her
infatuation with P.J.'s son, she was sent to the Sacred Heart convent school
in Manhattanville, New York. At twenty she was a young lady with an
acquired taste for culture, travel, and study abroad, well ahead of other
"high Irish" young women. She was the youngest member of the Boston
Public Library examining committee, which selected reading materials for
children, and she taught Sunday school in her father's old North End
neighborhood. Honey Fitz started using her in his perpetual rounds of
dedications, cornerstone layings, banquets, picnics, parades, wakes, rallies,
grand marches, and ceremonials, which so annoyed his wife because she
never knew what to expect. Rose became his hostess at political events.
When he was campaigning, she would introduce him and play "Sweet
Adeline" on the piano. He loved to travel, and as mayor could always find
a good official reason for a jaunt of some sort, together with a plausible
reason for taking his favorite daughter along.

"I was with him in Chicago for the international meeting of municipal
executives. And in Baltimore for the 1912 Democratic Convention where
Woodrow Wilson was nominated. On some of the trips, Agnes was along.
One winter my father led the Boston Chamber of Commerce to Panama to
ponder the possible effects on Boston of the recently opened Panama Canal.
I was along as hostess-companion-helper." For her coming-out, her father
declared a holiday in her honor and threw a party attended by four hundred
people, including two congressmen, the governor, and the entire city council. "Joe was there," she would recall, "so were a couple of would-be rivals
and a number of other young men and girls, all good friends. After the older
people had left, we went upstairs to a room festooned with ropes of roses,
where we had a sit-down dinner and sang and joked and laughed and
danced."

There were rumors that she would marry the Irish-born millionaire tea
trader and yachtsman, Sir Thomas Lipton, a good friend of her father. The
Fitzgeralds had met the middle-aged bachelor in England, but the rumor
sprang from a Boston visit of Sir Thomas. During a party at the Copley-
Plaza Hotel, Sir Thomas was pressed to declare when he would forsake
bachelorhood. "If you want to know who Lady Lipton is going to be," he
answered, "she is right in this room. Stand up, Rose!" To which Rose, in
the spirit of the jest, answered, "I won't accept you, Sir Thomas. I think
you are altogether too fickle." To which he replied, "Now I know how it
feels to be jilted."

Rose continued to see Joe and to cooperate with his ruses to monopolize
her attention. Occasionally she donned a black veil and went figure skating

with him on one of Boston's neighborhood ponds, her disguise fooling almost no one. At dances she helped fill out her dance cards with fictitious names so that nobody else could reserve a dance.

Charges of corruption and graft swirled around her father's second term, and she was conscious that she was not invited to join any of the fashionable women's clubs of proper Boston, and was not on the visiting lists of the better families. In retaliation against the exclusion of all Irish, she founded the Ace of Clubs, which rapidly became the top Irish women's club.

Joe slipped a flawless, white two-carat diamond on Rose's finger in the spring of 1914. His success at Columbia Trust made it difficult for Honey Fitz to pretend P.J.'s son wasn't good enough for his daughter. Conflict was brewing in Europe, but President Wilson declared America's neutrality, and Rose and her fiancé spent the summer going to the Boston "Pops" concerts and eating ice cream, and on weekend afternoons went to tea dances at one of the good hotels. She loved dancing and Joe knew the newest fads–the two step, the turkey trot, the tango (the latter two considered rather naughty), and a dance called "the boston." She was a happy, serene young woman, secure in society's forms and structures. There was a time for courtship, for discovering love, a time for engagement, marriage, parenthood, each in its own season and marked by traditions and rituals. She talked with Joe about plans for their wedding and honeymoon, where they would live, what kind of furniture they should have, their hopes and dreams about their future together.

The Elizabeth "Toodles" Ryan scandal emancipated Rose in one brutal evening. She stood behind her mother, rigid and even less understanding than Josie, when Honey Fitz came home and was handed the blackmailer's letter. He denied he was having an affair with Toodles, begged his wife and daughter to believe him, to come to their senses. To resign from the re-election campaign now was to commit political suicide.

But Josie was unflinching. For years he had left her to manage the house and bring up the children while he gave himself to his political ambitions. She had accepted it without much complaint, but public humiliation was beyond her. The scene shattered Rose, as it shattered her father. Much later, he would tell Eddie Moore that he literally collapsed that night.

To Rose, her father was a fallen idol, and whatever objections he might still have harbored against Joe Kennedy no longer mattered. On October 7, 1914, she married Joe. Only the immediate families were present at William Cardinal O'Connell's private chapel. Rose would claim that neither she nor Joe had wanted "a public fiesta." Others would wonder if the modest size of the wedding didn't reflect a lingering political shame on the part of the outgoing mayor.

After a three-week honeymoon that took them to the Greenbrier resort in White Sulphur Springs, West Virginia, the newlyweds moved into a small house in Brookline. Rose paid little attention, deliberately, to the scandals surrounding her father. She stayed with her friends—contemporaries in age, experience, and background—continued as president of the Ace of Clubs, and when her already busy husband had time, shared her time with him.

The greatest thing they shared, Rose felt, was parenthood. Joe Jr., Jack, Rosemary, and Kathleen arrived in the space of less than five years. By the time Rose was pregnant with Eunice, Joe's stock speculations allowed them to move to a twelve-room house, with high ceilings and a formal parlor, in the more fashionable, Protestant area of Brookline. Rose, fortunately, didn't have to cope with the growing family single-handedly. In addition to domestic servants, she had a nurse and a governess, and Joe, in his infrequent free moments, willingly pushed a baby carriage.

Domestic help allowed Rose to enjoy her children. Rose believed firmly in raising the first child well and making him the model for the others. Joe Jr. thus early assumed a major role in the upbringing of his brothers and sisters. He was both patient and something of a bully, quick-tempered, sometimes even cruel, the kind of boy who would shove somebody aside so he could catch the ball. He was a good athlete who became his kid brothers' and sisters' hero as he taught them to throw a ball, ride a bicycle, and sail a boat. He often fought with Jack, their younger sisters cowering in terror upstairs as the brothers wrestled on the first floor. The fights usually ended with Jack pinned and humiliated. Their father was aware of these one-sided contests, but did nothing. He said he would not step between the boys so long as they fought together against outsiders.

Long before the much publicized mass gambols on the playing fields of Hyannis—the Fourth of July softball games and the bruising touch-football scrimmages—Joe thrust each child into individual sports, believing swimming and sailing would best develop self-reliance. He firmly planted his conviction in them that how one played the game was not as important as whether one won it. "Even when we were six and seven years old, Dad always entered us in public swimming races," Eunice would recall. "The thing he always kept telling us was that coming in second was just no good. The important thing was to win: don't come in second or third—that doesn't count." By the time they were teenagers, a hierarchy had been confirmed, with Joe Jr., or "Young Joe," as he was also called, the pretender to the throne. His face was Fitzgerald, but in body and soul he was like his father—sturdy and pugnacious, with a quick smile, a biting tongue. Because the parents were so often absent, he saw himself as an example for his siblings. As several family biographers would note, Joe had given Young Joe this feeling of responsibility and had encouraged an almost tribal quality among the children by also making Joe Jr. godfather to the youngest children, Jean and Teddy. It was he who coined the term "Kennedy clan."

The mentally retarded Rosemary was a torment for a family committed to the ethos of winning at all costs. The misfortune was accepted by Rose as something for which God in His infinite wisdom had a reason, although she couldn't fathom what it was. To suggestions that the child be institutionalized, Joe bristled and asked, "What can they do for her that her own family can't do better?" So they took her along on the boat races at Hyannisport.

There was also something wrong with Jack and Eunice, a mysterious ailment that sapped their strength. Often shy, withdrawn, and quiet, Jack was sick in childhood and adolescence, so ill at times that biographers would wonder whether his maladies were not psychosomatic reactions to his elder brother's—and father's—advertised drive and virility.

Jack was born with an unstable back that made him vulnerable to injury and frequent severe pain. Doctors couldn't get a handle on strange episodes of pain and lethargy that the boy periodically suffered. His parents refused to acknowledge any serious problems and instead acted as cheerleaders in the boy's attempts to cope. His mother talked of him as being a boy "whose body could not keep pace with his dreams," and school friends remembered him as frequently pale, with lines around deep, sunken eyes, and a voice that was sharp and high-pitched. In early adulthood, Jack was diagnosed as suffering from Addison's disease, a chronic disturbance of the suprarenal glands. The family would always refuse to admit to Jack's debilitating illness.

Rosemary's retardation made Kathleen in effect the first daughter. From early childhood, Kick—her father gave her the nickname—was a beautiful and enchanting child with alabaster skin like her paternal grandmother and the deep-set agate eyes of her mother's side of the family. She was the liveliest and most vivacious of the girls. There was a defiant streak in her; more than any of her sisters, she was outspoken and blunt, challenging the family system in ways not even Young Joe and Jack dared. Like Jack, Kick learned to get her way with charm. A friend of the family called Joe Jr., Jack, and Kick the charmed triangle within the family—the trio Joe thought would write the story of the next generation. In college she provided dates for her brothers and went out with their classmates.

Competitive, smart, and athletic, Eunice was unable to compete with Kick's charm and drew into a defensive alliance with her mother. Awkwardly in the middle, between the charmed elder trio and the second tier of younger children, Eunice had an unpredictable and volatile sense of humor. She was usually the first to talk and was one of the livelier participants in family conversations. She was good with Rosemary and the young ones, and helped waifs, strays, and anybody else who needed her.

Patricia was born in Brookline while Joe was in New York trying to stabilize the stock of the Yellow Cab Company. It was a month before he returned to Boston and was met by his family at South Station. "Daddy, daddy, we've got another baby!" Eunice yelled. A year and a half later Bobby came along, the seventh baby. Pat and Bobby had a special empathy with each other, trotting around together, she sometimes admonishing him and sometimes scrapping with him, but mainly she was his valiant friend and big sister. Bobby was small, inarticulate, accident-prone, and shy, ten years younger than Young Joe and eight years younger than Jack. Not much was expected of him.

Rose was both defensive and proud of her many children. "I looked on child-rearing not only as a work of love and duty, but as a profession that was fully as interesting and challenging as any honorable profession in the world, and one that demanded the best I could bring to it," she told interviewers. Her mother-in-law had been the first to question the need to reproduce with such prodigality. After Bobby was born, some of Rose's best friends indicated delicately but unmistakably, as she would note in her memoirs, that he should be the last one. "When Jean, our eighth, arrived, the broad hints turned to admonitions." To avoid being regarded as a phenomenon by strangers, she evolved a strategy. If a conversation turned toward family and children, she would quickly ask if the person had children and, if so, what ages they were. That usually allowed her to say she had children of just about the same ages and that at those ages—whether five or fifteen—children were fascinating, and then change the subject.

Trying for acceptance, she assaulted her surroundings through her children. They were out there *doing*. Action, and the accompanying distrust of inner dimensions, became a Kennedy characteristic. Rose's exalted view of motherhood became, in her memoirs, an assertion that she would rather be the mother of a great son or daughter than the author of a great book or the painter of a great masterpiece.

She never did anything because she enjoyed it. Although she liked to travel, she always needed an excuse to do it—for example, she needed to buy clothes in Paris to uphold the standards set for her by her husband.

If being the mother of a great son or daughter was fulfilling, being the wife of a successful man had its own blessings. At the birth of each child, Joe gave Rose an increasingly expensive gift. But when *Fortune* magazine in the 1950s estimated Joe's personal fortune at nearly half a billion dollars, she was utterly stunned. She and Joe had never discussed money. There had almost always been enough of it, and that was all that mattered. Joe always handled all expenditures, and in old age Rose lacked both the full knowledge and real responsibility to make sensible judgments about how much she could spend.

Bringing up nine children was a burden that fell increasingly on Rose, a burden she bore stoically and, in her own way, cheerfully. How much love each child got was a question a number of family observers tried to answer. "Rose made sure they learned and did all the right things, but I don't know how much physical love she gave them," *Look* reporter Laura Bergquist said after spending time with the family. "After Joe, Jack, and Kathleen, I don't think there was that much love left for the other side." Jack complained to his friends that by the time he was a teenager he rarely saw his mother. Ann Kelly, a neighbor in Bronxville, would remember Pat and Eunice always saying, "Dad says this, Dad says that. But if I hadn't finally met him, I never would have known he existed." Mary Pitcairn Keating, who visited Hyannisport while dating Jack, would say of his mother, "Of course, she never saw things or acknowledged things she didn't want to. I had the feeling that the children just totally ignored her. Daddy was it. I mean, I was the one who went out and picked her up when she was coming down to Washington for dinner. . . . When she went to play golf, she'd go by herself. She did everything by herself. I never saw her walking with one of the children on the beach." Kirk Lemoyne ("Lem") Billings, a lifelong friend of the Kennedys, noted that the Kennedy children had no rooms of their own to come home to from boarding school—that when he and Jack arrived at Hyannis for the summer, Jack would ask his mother, "Which room do I have this time?"

The family clannishness had its origins in Rose and Joe's fear that their children would suffer social snubs. The Kennedys never really fitted into predominently Protestant Brookline, yet at the same time they had the upwardly mobile family's aversion to their own ethnic roots. Joe hated to be called Irish or Irish-American, and Rose went out of her way to tell stories of the Pilgrims on Plymouth Rock and to skip Celtic folklore—only one of the seven children who would marry took an Irish spouse. In Bronxville, she and her daughters were considered terribly parvenu by the Irish-Catholic families there, and were ridiculed for their alleged lack of etiquette. The Kennedy children were taught they were a tribe. "If one shut you out, they all did," Alice Roosevelt Longworth would say. "That's what made them so intriguing—they didn't seem to need anyone else. When they were together, they seemed all alike. You had to get them apart to see how different they were."

Young friends of the children quickly became acquainted with the Kennedy clannishness and "rough love." Robert Downes would remember his clothes, his speech, everything being ridiculed. "The razzing would begin the moment you stepped inside the house. Nothing was sacred. It was like getting pecked by a flock of chickens." Jack would grow up hating large families because experience had shown him, he once commented to a writer, that it involved "institutionalized living, children in a cellblock." The tribal ways were particularly annoying to future in-laws, who would feel left out at family gatherings. After marrying Jack and moving to Hyannisport, Jacqueline Bouvier would be dismayed by her husband's insistence on dining with his parents, sisters, and brothers every night. When she became first lady, she would be appalled by her father-in-law's hold on the president.

If Joe believed experience formed character, Rose was certain it was religion. Her belief in the afterlife was unwavering, as was her trust in her church's teachings and tenets. She observed its rituals, respected its demands, and invariably closed letters to members of the Catholic clergy, "Your respectful child." She taught her children a muscular Christianity that abhorred weakness and tolerated no slackers. She didn't think of herself as being particularly religious, but Catholic customs were observed. They went to Mass on Sundays, holidays, and first Fridays. They said grace before meals, and Rose chose a different child each time to offer the prayer.

Rose's Catholicism could be ferocious. When Kick married William Cavendish, the son and heir of the Duke of Devonshire and scion of a long line of Protestant aristocracy, in 1944, Rose checked herself into a Boston hospital so she wouldn't be available for the London wedding. When Cavendish was killed on the Normandy front a month later, Rose kept taking Kick to Mass. When after the war Kick found solace with another Protestant Englishman and the two of them were killed in a plane crash, Rose said it "was God pointing his finger at Kick and saying *no!*"

Rose regularly had Mass said for all of her dear departed. The death Joe could never accept was that of Young Joe. Two weeks before a German ambush killed Cavendish, navy pilot Joe Kennedy, Jr., was ferrying a planeload of explosives toward the Normandy front when he and his copilot were killed in a midair explosion. The news reached Hyannisport on a Sunday afternoon. Rose would remember Joe going out on the porch and telling the children. "He said they must be brave: that's what their brother would want from them. He urged them to go ahead with their plans to race that day and most of them obediently did so. But Jack could not. Instead, for a long time he walked on the beach in front of our house. There were not tears from Joe and me, not then. We sat a while, holding each other close, and wept inwardly, silently. Then Joe said, 'We've got to carry on. We must take care of the living. There is a lot of work to be done."

Joe's journalist friend Arthur Krock thought the death of Young Joe was the severest shock to a father he had ever seen. When Joe saw Franklin

Roosevelt's vice-presidential nominee, Harry Truman, during the 1944 campaign, he asked, "Harry, what are you doing campaigning for that crippled son-of-a-bitch who killed my son Joe?" Much later, Young Joe's death would set in a motion a drama of incarnations, a tragedy of myths carried out as dynastic policy. Each of his sons, in turn, was to enact the dream he had fluffed himself. First Jack became the incarnation, then Bobby. Ultimately Ted took up the burden, by then almost too heavy and too bitter to bear.

In January 1928, Teddy was not yet a gleam in his parents' eyes.

With her firm belief that all her desires must be kept under complete control, Rose's only thought was to repress and silence within herself the reality of Joe's affair with the movie star. Rose didn't rush to Florida to confront, accuse, or demand. Exacting a price was not for now. The withholding of herself in the marital bed was a preposterous weapon for a woman in the final weeks of her pregnancy. Joe was easily flattered, amused, aroused. She knew that.

Rose went to Boston, where in February she gave birth to a daughter. Joe showed up and, as usual, brought a gift. A friend of hers was visiting when Joe turned up at the bedside with three diamond bracelets. Rose put all three on so she could compare, and her friend turned to Joe and gasped, "What can you possibly think of to give her next if she has a ninth baby?"

Joe glared at Rose. "I'll give her a black eye," he laughed.

They named the girl Jean.

Multiple Lives

Readers of the *Kalifornische Staats Zeitung* (California State Newspaper), a monthly popular among German-speaking immigrants, were informed in March 1928 that an Alsatian movie featuring German cavalry was in preparation in Hollywood and that the film's producers were looking for veterans of cavalry regiments. Men with such qualifications were requested to contact Wilhelm von Brincken at the Goldwyn Studios with full particulars. Brincken, who claimed he had been a German spy during the Great War, was a superb horseman himself. He had played a cavalry officer in *The Wedding March* and was now Stroheim's assistant.

While Brincken interviewed former comrades-in-arms, Joe took over Gloria's life. He arranged everything, including Henri's departures. The lovers had two distinct lives: one with each other when Henri was in France, another when the marquis was in town. Joe arranged his own existence so as to be in Hollywood when Henri was not and in the east when Gloria's husband was home.

Gloria and Joe rarely saw each other during the day. As Joe whirled through the hectic spring, overseeing three film companies, being attentive to the chattering stock ticker, and looking for opportunities for new corporate takeovers, his working day was seldom less than fourteen hours. He insisted on keeping all business transactions in Gloria's name confidential. E. B. Derr handled Gloria Productions, and Charles E. Sullivan signed the checks. If Joe was in New York, he would communicate with Gloria through channels, usually Derr, and always refer to her as "the client." A telegram to Derr would say, "HAVE YOUR CLIENT CALL ME AT 6 TODAY, NEW YORK TIME," or "INFORM CLIENT I ARRIVE FRIDAY AT 4."

Whenever Joe was in Hollywood, it was as head of FBO and manager of Pathé, never visibly as the power behind Gloria Productions. Which didn't mean nobody knew. Hedda Hopper certainly was au courant.

This was the golden era of press columns and fan magazines. Stars and executives cringed before the peephole columnists while wooing them with corruptive flattery and self-destructive cooperation. Hopper, her sister columnist Louella Parsons, and a host of lesser gossips employed networks of informants while affecting a stewardship of public morality. Nothing was more provocative than the misdemeanors of the privileged. To see them spanked in print, as Jesse Lasky, Jr., would say, was both edifying and entertaining. In her winking, knowing phrase, Hopper reported that "Miss Swanson found in Joe Kennedy a friend, a patron saint and a bankroll all in one and the same person."

Gloria was very much one of Hollywood's own, an honored player of the movie colony's most popular pastime, party-giving and party-going, but Joe was not. His Catholicism and Boston sense of propriety prevented him from a too ostentatious display of his double existence. Though many in Hollywood would later make the comparison, Gloria and Joe were no Marion Davies–William Randolph Hearst twosome who flaunted their liaison.

For one thing, Gloria and Joe were both married with children. She was no starlet looking for a sugar daddy; he, no elderly tycoon hopelessly in love with a chorus girl. She saw in him someone who was plainly going far, and she fell in love with his business savvy and can-do openness. He was the one man in her life she trusted when it came to money. To him, she was one of the most desirable women, one of the symbols he had grappled with all the way up from East Boston. He fell in love with a woman who was everything Rose was not. Gloria was, first of all, fame—a woman whose public personality spoke to people of golden youth and glitter. To discover that she was also a creature of shadows was part of his lover's ecstasy. She was a woman of her own means, self-confident and elusive, possessed of a dignity that was both paralyzing and magnificent. In their intimacy, she was almost tomboyish—terse and disarming. Fun, too.

Smitten with her from the first meeting at the Savoy Plaza two months earlier—with the idea of her as well as the fact—he was not only giving her advice but smothering her with attention. He loved uncovering the Gloria Swanson millions would never know—the quiet, slightly weary person with soft hair and a dark, husky voice so different from the screen image, the woman who boasted that she had never been kept. None of her homes, he happily discovered, was a place into which friends casually dropped. Her smallest talk and actions translated into movie terms, but she saw a lot of the show-biz display of herself as a gag. At home, the extravagant clothes and the borrowed personalities came off, rouge and lipstick were abandoned.

They made love at his place. Here, he was in control of comings and goings of staff and underlings. On Crescent Drive, her waking hours were a series of disturbances by butler and maids, secretaries and assistants, and her moods ran in channels dammed up by her staff. On Rodeo Drive, order flowed effortlessly from the master.

She loved absurd games, spelling matches—Joe thought he was back with his Harvard friends trying to stump his mother—and practical jokes, which Gloria carried to elaborate extremes. Joe was sexually excited by provocation, playacting, and dalliance, but whatever the time of night their appetites were slaked, he had one of the horsemen drive her home. A new dawn meant tearing up the previous day's assignations, and it was accompanied by a spontaneous desertion of memory on his part. No regret, guilt, or lassitude was retained.

There was one thing that crimped his lover's swagger, one thing that lighted a long fuse in their relationship, and that was *Sadie Thompson*. Contrary to his dire predictions in Palm Beach, the picture was a hit. When it opened in New York on February 3, 1928, *The New York Times'* Morduant Hall called it "a stirring pictorial drama with a shrewd development of the plot and admirable characterizations." Critics had fun revealing how Lionel Barrymore was no longer the man of the cloth of *Rain* but a heartless reformer (*Variety* thought all the titillating rumors of censorship pressures had resulted in so much poison being extracted that the film was actually pretty "fangless"). The biggest accolade came in the February issue of the National Board of Review of Motion Pictures magazine. *Sadie* was a film "far exceeding the average in telling a story of meaning and interest to the mentally adult picturegoer," and the title role was Gloria's best. "Here for the first time one feels she has been given a character and a story worthy of her mettle. The raw, true nature of Sadie emerges an object not only of pity but of essential grace, a human being struggling for a fuller life, and worthy of it."

Joe resented Gloria's portrayal of a whore, of a woman available to any man with enough money. On a deep psychological level he was offended by the atheist premise that human love can be quite as effective as divine love in leading a bruised life toward healing redemption. But even on the level of business, where Joe was supposed to excel, *Sadie*'s success humiliated him. The more money *Sadie* took in, the more the picture became a reminder of his miscalculation and a tribute to Gloria's intuition. Had she not listened to him, it would be she, not Schenck, laughing all the way to the bank.

To regain the high ground, he involved himself compulsively in *their* film. Borrowing sets from other studios—Stroheim's Ruritanian decors for *The Wedding March* were still at Metro—was not good enough. The opulent interiors that Stroheim wanted for a spectacular banquet with hundreds of extras would be built on the FBO lot. In fact, anything Stroheim or Swanson wanted, Joe told production chief Bill Le Baron, should be provided forthwith. No matter that Joe also wanted Le Baron to keep a tight curb on the director's notoriously extravagant ways.

When Stroheim finished the first draft of the screenplay, Joe got the noted playwright Robert Sherwood to read it. Without telling Gloria, Joe ordered a new dressing room, a veritable setside apartment, built for her.

If partying was out of the question for the discreet lovers, catching a movie every night was not. The Rodeo Drive mansion came with a screening room, and after dinner the two of them spent most evenings watching and discussing new movies. The private theater was not wired for sound, and one film they didn't see was *The Jazz Singer.* Warner's was shooting a follow-up called *The Singing Fool,* also starring Jolson.

Gloria was in tune with the general mood in Hollywood in the early months of 1928 when she said she was in no hurry to make a sound picture. She gave Joe good arguments. When she and Henri had reached New York after *Madame Sans Gêne,* Lee De Forest had asked her to do a little talking segment as a stunt for a presentation at the Lambs Club. The inventor had asked Allan Dwan, Tommy Meighan, Henri, and her into a tiny Manhattan studio and had them talk to each other while a camera filmed them and a technician waved a microphone around on a fishing pole. A few days later, they had seen—and heard—the result. "We all sounded terrible; none of us could believe our own voices."

Joe wondered whether sound hadn't improved since.

Not as of a year ago. For the *Sunya* premiere, the Roxy had shown a Vitaphone short with opera singers. They sounded no better than Allan, Tommy, Henri, and Gloria in De Forest's studio. "Believe me, the gala night audience was relieved when the real picture came on," Gloria noted.

Films depended on a form of mime, it was true, but it was a form of acting that had reached sublime sophistication. An accomplished actress could express the most passionate emotions with brooding, heavy-lidded stares, heaving bosom, and anguished clutchings of the throat—her own or someone's else's. Gestures, timing, facial expressions, Gloria said, signified intentions in a universal language. Directors and cameramen achieved the effects they wanted through subtle camerawork. Intertitles were shorter and sparser than ever, usually merely a counterpoint to the visuals instead of a narrative backup.

Joe had an ear closer to the ground. What he knew through David Sarnoff was that despite the tinny sound and the hiss of the recordings, audiences loved the synchronized human voice. Deeply involved with Elisha Walker, Lehman Brothers, and Jeremiah Milbank in a takeover attempt on Keith Albee Orpheum, he was in daily contact with John J. Murdock, who told Joe he was putting pressure on De Mille to make *The Godless Girl* a "part talkie."

In May, as Henri returned from Paris, bringing his brother Alain with him for a visit, Joe and his associates gained control of Keith Albee Orpheum. Raising five million dollars, Kennedy, Walker, Lehman Brothers, and Milbank exercised a stock option that Murdock sold them. At the same time, Joe approached Albee himself and suggested he sell out. Joe offered the vaudeville veteran twenty-one dollars a share at a time when the stock was selling for sixteen dollars. At first, Albee declined, but then, on the advice of those he thought were his friends, he changed his mind and sold. Three months later the stock soared to fifty dollars.

Old Albee was kept on as president, while the post of chairman of the board was created for Kennedy. Albee announced Joe's association with the eight-hundred-theater chain in glowing terms. "Mr. Kennedy has shown in a brief but colorful career in the picture business such constructive and organization genius that we consider him a tremendous asset to our business." Joe continued as head of FBO and in his position with Pathé. Drawing a salary of $6,000 a week as chairman of the FBO and Keith Albee boards, he set to work to engineer a complete consolidation between his conglomerate and RCA.

One of the emergencies Joe had to deal with was a recalcitrant Cecil B. De Mille. After fighting with Murdock, the flamboyant director was not sure he could face yet another series of quarrels with yet another front office moneyman. "When the banks came into the picture, trouble began," he liked to say.

De Mille gave Kennedy a tour of the Culver City studio one spring afternoon. Joe would remember the director taking him through the old Jerusalem set built for *King of Kings,* the main administration building (a replica of George Washington's home, Mount Vernon), the eight big stages, the property department, camera shops, commissary, and scores of editing rooms. De Mille proudly recalled the history of the studio: the days of

William S. Hart and the birth of the western, the days of Triangle when Griffith, Ince, and Mack Sennett worked on the lot.

De Mille and Kennedy danced politely around each other for a month. The director was putting out feelers to Louis B. Mayer about moving himself, his personal staff, and his contract players to MGM. Joe had no high regard for C.B.'s administration of Pathé–De Mille but was inclined to leave him to make his own films within the conglomerate alphabet soup of FBO-KAO.

With Murdock's connivance, Joe consolidated his corporate grip by eliminating Albee's men in the company. Little love was lost on old Albee in the industry, and the trade press reported gleefully how Kennedy's "machinegun squadron," as *Variety* put it on June 27, "turned its attention to agents and bookers this week, executing many of each, with more to follow." Albee himself failed to realize he had sold his authority along with his stock. His awakening came one day during the summer when he entered Joe's New York office with a suggestion.

Joe was brief and blunt. "Didn't you know, Ed? You're washed up. You're through."

Albee, at last, understood. He quit and began plotting his revenge.

Gloria found her husband had changed—for the better. Nobility and the mettle of the war veteran had given him poise and presence; now responsibility gave him identity. The Pathé Frères empire might be a shadow of its former self, but Henri established himself in the interstices of the last remaining links between the Paris headquarters and the spun-off American subsidiary, Pathé News. There were rumors that sixty-five-year-old Charles Pathé was ready to pull out and liquidate the remaining pieces. Henri was sure he would have to spend more time in Paris.

There was a measure of irony in the fact that it was his wife's lover who gave him substance and weight. Did he suspect the affair? "If he had any suspicions about my relationship with Joe," Gloria would say later, "he never voiced them, perhaps out of gratitude for the Pathé job, perhaps out of a cultivated European's good sense to let such affairs run their course, particularly inasmuch as this one could almost certainly never lead to marriage."

The bombing of a Russian café punctuated Henri's short stay and caused his name to graze the gossip columns. Dining with business friends a few tables away from Charlie Chaplin when the small bomb went off, both marquis and star were subpoenaed as material witnesses in what police thought was a case of arson with political overtones. Several columnists mentioned that Henri had not only been with business friends but with a dinner companion who was not his wife. Tactfully, neither he nor Gloria mentioned the gossip, but both seemed relieved when the time came for his return to France.

Lois Wilson was the first of Gloria's friends to know about the affair. The former Alabama schoolteacher was a convert to Catholicism and, in her own estimation, something of a prude. Happily unmarried, she had long resisted three things in her career: taking a bath on screen, drinking, and cutting her hair (even when starring opposite Valentino in *Monsieur Beaucaire* in 1924). In 1926, however, she had done all three for director Herbert Brenon in *The Great Gatsby*.

Her disapproval of her friend's liaison with a married Catholic translated itself into a plot to have Little Brother baptized. Gloria's sense of religion was tolerant and distracted. The daughter of Swedish Lutherans on her father's side and Alsatian Calvinists on her mother's, she had grown up in the kind of interdenominational Protestantism favored at army posts during the first decade of the century. Married in succession to a Baptist from Kansas, a nonpracticing New York Jew, and a lapsed French Catholic, she had been under the influence of Christian Scientists when pregnant with Gloria and, when the adoption of Brother came through, was too bitter over Herbert's blackmail and Paramount's betrayal to think about baptism.

Though Joe rarely spoke of their separate families, he often brought up the fact that Brother was almost six years old and still had not been christened. Genuinely shocked, he joined Lois in prodding Gloria to agree to Brother's baptism. Joe wanted to throw a huge christening party. Gloria agreed to a small gathering that included the four horsemen, E.B.'s daughter Betty, who was little Gloria's age, and some of Beverly Hills's prominent Irish—Winifield Sheehan from Fox and his opera singer wife, Maria Jeritza; Allan Dwan; and Aileen Pringle. Without checking dates or adoption records, later gossips would insinuate that little Joseph was Joe Kennedy's illegitimate son.

Meanwhile, United Artists didn't like the proposed title of the new Swanson movie, and through the spring and early summer worked on Lance Heath to persuade his boss to come up with a more attractive moniker than *The Swamp*. But Gloria insisted it would have to stand, and UA had no choice than to list "Gloria Swanson in *The Swamp*, written and directed by Eric (sic) von Stroheim" among its coming attractions for 1928–29.

Predictably, theater owners reported back that the title of the new Swanson movie was sure to keep people away. They wanted it changed, especially in view of the ongoing success of *Sadie Thompson*. By the end of summer, Heath managed to refer to the new film as "tentatively entitled *The Swamp.*" Further than that, neither Kennedy nor Stroheim was willing to go.

The final script was pure Stroheim. The character of the dissolute prince, who would first be seen returning to the palace drunk, was a more fully developed reincarnation of the *Merry Go Round*'s young officer caught between a dominating fiancée and the innocent young girl he loves. Queen Helena was similar to a long line of sophisticated women, typically played by Maude George, and appearing in minor roles in almost every Stroheim movie. As written, she would read the Decameron and, completely disregarding the male servants and guards of her palace, stride around naked except for a white cat which she would carry in her arms. Stroheim had placed seminude women among the erotic decors of various bordellos in his previous films. Here, the queen would appear surrounded by a luxurious intimate decor and suggestive statuary. Whips would line her bedchamber wall, and Rodin's sculpture *The Kiss* grace a niche.

Kelly was a familiar Stroheim heroine—young, innocent, and religious. The "meeting cute" of Wolfram and Kitty was audaciously Stroheimian. No sooner has Kitty caught the eye of the prince, as she and the other girls are curtsying, than her bloomers drop down around her ankles and she has to struggle with her feet to step out of them. When the prince sees her predicament, he laughs. This so rouses her Irish temper that she wads her panties into a ball and throws them at him. Grinning, he catches them and stuffs them into his uniform jacket. When he orders his men to reverse direction and file past the novices again, Kitty pleads with her eyes for the prince to return her panties, and he playfully flips them back to her. Back in the convent, Kelly is told to pray for forgiveness by the mother superior. She kneels in the chapel and, with her face framed by burning candles, whispers, "Please make my wish come true—to see the Prince again."

The Hays office approved the script in general but made some cuts in the African sequences, turning the Dar es Salaam hotel from an obvious bordello into a halfway respectable dance hall–hotel. To avoid the wrath of the Ku Klux Klan, Hays suggested that a white, not a black priest, administer the last rites to Kitty's dying aunt. Stroheim objected that it was not totally illogical to have a black priest in Africa, and the matter remained unresolved while the director went to New York to cast his Wolfram. He didn't find an actor to play the dissolute prince and returned to Los Angeles. He told journalists he planned to introduce extraordinary realism into the scenes set in the jungle swamp. In a parody of Hollywood "style," he had the completed and revised screenplay delivered to the Kennedy office on a silver platter carried by two blacks clad as Nubian slaves in lion skins. Joe was eager to associate *The Swamp* with Stroheim's *The Wedding March*, scheduled to premiere in October and publicized by Paramount as a two-million-dollar wonder that had taken two full years to make.

Negotiations with Stroheim were hard. As with Henri's Pathé contract, the contractual language was drawn up for Gloria Productions by Pat

Sullivan. Sullivan wanted to minimize the up-front risk by making the initial payment for the screenplay modest. To keep the director's nose to the grindstone, the contract offered Stroheim a series of $10,000 bonuses as production went along. If he fell behind schedule or went more than fifteen percent over budget, the built-in bonuses were automatically eliminated. Stroheim complained he was being put "in a striped suit," but on May 9 he signed.

Gloria and Joe were having dinner on Rodeo Drive when Joe handed her a leather-bound copy of Stroheim's massive script and told her Robert Sherwood had finally read it and pronounced it the best film story ever written. Joe was like a college boy wanting to jump for joy but compelled to be serious by the matter at hand. Other knowledgeable literary people had also read the script and said it was great. "We have the star, the director, and the story now," Joe beamed. He was hiring two producers, Bill Le Baron and Ben Glazer, to keep Stroheim "on a tight leash and to see he doesn't take two years this time or spend two million again. They both read the script and they say it's far and away the best thing he's ever done. Oh, I tell you, Gloria, this is going to be a major, *major* motion picture."

The two overseers were already in Joe's employ. Le Baron was FBO's production chief, currently busy adding talking sequences to *The Perfect Crime,* to be released in August as FBO's first part-talkie. Benjamin Glazer was an Irish-born former theater and music critic, a screenwriter who at MGM had written several Greta Garbo–John Gilbert pictures, including their best romantic tragedy, *Flesh and the Devil.* He had authored Frank Borzage's current hit, *Seventh Heaven,* starring Janet Gaynor and Charles Farrell.

Stroheim found his Wolfram at the Goldwyn Studios. Walter Byron was one of Sam Goldwyn's European finds, a young Englishman perfectly suited to play the swaggering prince. Goldwyn had brought him to Hollywood a month earlier and matched him with Vilma Banky in *The Awakening,* directed by Victor Fleming. Gloria had her reservations, not about Byron, but about borrowing anyone from Goldwyn. The whole humiliating George Barnes episode was still seared in her mind—she, Barrymore, and a hundred other actors and crew members sitting idle on Catalina Island after Goldwyn pulled his loan-out cameraman off *Sadie Thompson.*

As a result, Sullivan demanded—and obtained—an ironclad contract stipulating that Goldwyn could not pull his young contract player off *The Swamp* in the middle of the shooting. That done, publicist Lance Heath could announce that Gloria's new leading man was Walter Byron. "Swanson and Von Stroheim consider Byron ideal for the wild and roistering German prince who plays opposite Queen Kelly, the Irish girl who Swanson has chosen to succeed *Sadie Thompson* on her list of outstanding screen portrayals," Heath's press release said. The picture would go into production "at an early date, possibly before the 1st of September."

Paul Ivano, a French-educated cameraman who had made his debut filming the *Ben-Hur* chariot race in 1924, was signed as director of photography. Stroheim wanted the Queen Helena palace and court to match his past Ruritanian splendors and managed to hire as his art director Harold Miles, who had replaced Paul Iturbe on De Mille's *King of Kings.*

Gloria and Joe finally made Stroheim relent on the title. Though no one had any immediate inspiration for a new title, the picture would *not* be called *The Swamp.*

Back to the Future

I cannot talk—I cannot sing,
Nor screech nor moan nor anything.
Possessing all these fatal strictures,
What chance have I in motion pictures.

—Photoplay, JANUARY 1929.

By starting their ambitious film as a silent four months after the release of the all-talking *Lights of New York,* producers Swanson and Kennedy and director Stroheim were extraordinarily careless, suicidal, or both.

Stroheim was not ready to begin filming by September 1. While he worked full-time supervising the authenticity of prewar German uniforms and the construction of Queen Helena's palace on the FBO backlot, silent films were being rereleased with synchronized scores and effects, and pictures that had gone into production as silents suddenly had talking sequences added. One was FBO's own *The Perfect Crime,* directed by Ben Glennon and starring the very British Clive Brooke. Released September 5, it was demolished by *The New York Times,* whose reviewer complained it was yet another silent stuffed with sound. Marquees across the country were trumpeting the first all-talking effort of one studio after another, followed by "The First 100% All-Talking Outdoor Picture," "The First All-Collegiate Comedy," and that mathematical absurdity, "The First 100% All-Talking, 100% All-Singing, 100% All-Dancing Musical." Movie attendance told the story. More and more Americans were flocking to the movies; by the end of 1928, attendance had doubled to one hundred million weekly admissions.

Apologists for Stroheim would claim that such late silents as Frank Borzage's 1927 *Seventh Heaven* and Victor Fleming's last silent, *The Way of All Flesh,* released in 1928, were box-office winners—conveniently omitting the fact that both were released with synchronized scores and some sound effects. By the fall of 1928—that is, one year after *The Jazz Singer's* sensational debut—silent movies were rapidly becoming unmarketable.

Most top directors had severe misgivings about the use of sound. They felt sound would both destroy a unique art form and lessen the commercial value of Hollywood movies in non–English speaking countries. None of them was anxious to rush into talkies, partly because they were afraid of losing their reputations, partly because they disliked the new technology. Like the stars and writers, they had to prove their talents again, and several directors of repute, such as Herbert Brenon, Edwin Carewe, and Fred Niblo, were having difficulty adjusting.

The free-flowing action and continuity was abruptly displaced by a static, stagelike technique, both because the cameras had to be immured in soundproof booths and because the microphone—"King Mike" and "Terrible Mike" to exasperated studio crews—was at first immovable and all action had to be geared to its location. Directors tore their hair in frenzy when their most cherished dramatic efforts were vetoed by their sound engineers, new despots trained by the telephone companies, whose only concern was that all conversation be conducted at one voice level. For a couple of nervous months, sound men with earphones plugged into black magic boxes lorded it over the movie sets. They concealed microphones in flowerpots, dictated where actors could stand in order to record, and yelled "Cut!" if any actor turned his head away from the mike. Since sound film ran at twenty-four frames per second instead of sixteen, twice as much light was needed to expose the same strip of celluloid. Already-nervous actors were soaked to the skin under the heat of added candlepower.

The studios solved the problem of disposing of millions of dollars' worth of silent merchandise as best they could by adding sound in some form to their remaining silents so theater owners could advertise that their attractions talked. Fans quickly became adept at deducing from the ads the degree to which silents had been made into audible pictures. "Sound effects and music" meant a recorded orchestral accompaniment plus various bell-ringings and door-knockings introduced into the otherwise silent action. "With sound and dialogue" usually meant that the players remained silent for five reels, became briefly loquacious in the sixth, then relapsed into silence in the seventh. After the final clinch in De Mille's *The Godless Girl,* Marie Prevost and George Duryea sat down on the curbstone and talked about the weather for ten minutes so that John J. Murdock could bill the picture as "part talkie."

If Stroheim was no more eager than Borzage, Vidor, De Mille, and other name directors to "go sound," what about Gloria and Joe? In retrospect they would blame each other—and Stroheim—for starting the film as a silent. But they were both fully aware of the coming change. Indeed, the whole thrust of Joe's merger with Sarnoff was predicated on the triumph of sound.

The list of stars playing the waiting game included Greta Garbo, Lillian Gish, and Norma Talmadge. The dashing John Gilbert was the first casualty of the microphone; Milton Sills, the first suicide. At Paramount, Thomas Meighan, Richard Dix, and Bebe Daniels were let go; the studio disdained even giving them a voice test. The theory that only actors with stage experience could deliver an acceptable accent was sweeping the nervous ranks. All of which might explain why Gloria didn't push the issue. Joe could have been more forceful, but it must be said in his defense that he pointed out to both Stroheim and Gloria that Photophone was at their disposal.

Trade-paper items show that they did think about it and that up to the last minute Gloria had reservations about starting the picture at all. *Variety* announced on September 5 that production of what was finally titled *Queen Kelly* might be delayed another three weeks so RCA sound equipment could be installed. Echoing the jitters among stars, the front-page story said, "Miss Swanson will appear in a few talking sequences and it marks the first time for her voice to be heard by the general public. She has never made any personal appearance tours nor has she ever spoken over the radio." A *Variety* item a week later announced that Ben Glazer, the overseer with Le Baron of the Stroheim project, was working on the screen treatment of FBO's first talkie, a film scheduled to go into production in ten days. Persistent rumors that Stroheim and Swanson did not see eye to eye on *Queen Kelly* were only laid to rest on November 5 when *Motion Picture News* reported that the film "went into actual production Thursday morning on location at the old Lasky ranch."

Gloria and Joe were not in Hollywood during the crucial last weeks before the start of production, when a decision to go sound *could* have been made. They were in New York, deeply involved in each other when Joe wasn't engineering the biggest takeover coup of them all.

For one week in August, he was special adviser in charge of production at First National Pictures, a move widely understood to mean that First National and its new president, Irving Rossheim, would be linked with the Keith Albee Orpheum chain, FBO, and Kennedy's other interests in a conglomerate going far beyond anything Sarnoff had ever had in mind.

The stellar roster at First National included Colleen Moore, Billie Dove,

Richard Barthelmess, Corinne Griffith, and Ken Maynard. Joe's contract
gave him an annual salary of $150,000 for five years. He immediately put
Derr in charge of management relations with First National stockholders
and told Glazer to drop supervising *Queen Kelly* and writing an all-talkie
screenplay to become First National production manager. After six days of
deliberations, however, the company board of directors reconsidered. Some
directors expressed second thoughts about granting such sweeping powers
to a man bent on a merger they might not like. Kennedy and his associates
might control Keith Albee Orpheum, FBO, and Pathé, but they had little
power among First National stockholders. A week after the KENNEDY
TAKES OVER FIRST NATIONAL headlines, he had no choice but to
resign. Rossheim's explanation to the press suggested that the company had
not "reached that state where artificial respiration was necessary."

Another setback followed. After huddling with Louis B. Mayer for a
month, De Mille signed an agreement to make three pictures at MGM, and
with his personal staff moved lock, stock, and barrel out of Mount Vernon
in early August. Whatever Joe's ultimate goal was in motion pictures, the
ability to hang on to powerful talent was not one of his obvious gifts.

Such defeats didn't prevent him from scanning wider horizons. Taking
Rose with him for her first European trip since her convent school year at
Blumenthal in 1909, Kennedy, with Murdock, went to London in August
to talk with English bankers about creating an international conglomerate
of American, British, and Continental holdings, and to attend a private
showing of Gaumont's first talking picture. The appeal of the French Gaumont process was its airtight patents, something that neither Photophone
nor the Western Electric system possessed.

Crossing the channel for a short holiday, Joe and Rose were greeted by
Henri in Paris. It was one of the hottest summers in memory in Europe,
and Henri took the Kennedys to the Atlantic Coast resorts of Deauville and
Biarritz, cooler than the sweltering Riviera. Lover, husband, and lover's
wife hit it off nicely. A snapshot dated September 12 and sent to Gloria with
the scrawled inscription, "Musqueteers in Biarritz," shows Joe and Henri
on the sand, Joe in a striped swimsuit, squinting without glasses toward the
camera, the slimmer Henri, showing half his chest and seemingly smiling
on request. Rose was charmed by the marquis. "Henri was very attractive,
charming, witty, a delightful man and a perfect consort for Gloria," she
would remember.

Alarming news from New York forced Joe to book immediate passage
back to America. Old Albee was trying to take back Keith Albee Orpheum.
Albee had allied himself with Marcus Heiman, the former president of the
Orpheum circuit, and the two were trying to persuade Warner Brothers to
knock off Kennedy and Murdock. Sailing ahead of Murdock, Joe rushed

back to prevent any rebellion among Keith-Albee-Orpheum stockholders and, on a personal note, to persuade Gloria to come to New York to be with him.

Perhaps not too inadvertently, Gloria had made Joe jealous for the first time. While Joe took his wife to Europe and, with Henri, enjoyed the French resorts, Gloria sat at home twiddling her thumbs. Although always intensely self-absorbed, she was never a person given to solitude, and she had invited Lois Wilson and Virginia Bowker to stay with her and the children for the summer. Late August was not the height of the Hollywood season, and Gloria was more than happy to receive an invitation to a Douglas Fairbanks–Mary Pickford affair for the visiting Prince George, the Duke of Kent.

The popularity of Mary and Doug was more official than real in the late 1920s, but nobody challenged their status as the film colony's first couple. An invitation to dine at Pickfair was a royal command. On this occasion, Mary sat on the right of the twenty-six-year-old prince, Gloria on his left. At one point, he leaned toward Gloria and whispered that he hoped he would be able to see a bit more of Hollywood's nightlife. His Royal Navy ship was moored in Santa Barbara, and he would have to join the vessel the next day. Couldn't they slip away for something a bit livelier?

Gloria whispered back that she couldn't see how. But after dinner, when a hundred lesser notables arrived for the dance, the prince gestured toward Chaplin and a handful of others and asked Gloria if they couldn't all make their excuses. She promised to try. Discreetly, she told the designated deserters to rendezvous at the Plantation Cafe, Fatty Arbuckle's in-spot in Venice. Protocol demanded that royalty depart first. Once Prince George had thanked host and hostess, Gloria apologized to Mary for having to leave early. She was expecting a call from Henri in Paris.

Going back to Crescent Drive to pick up a few bottles of champagne first, Gloria headed for Venice, soon followed by Chaplin and Lili Damita, who was the real reason for the prince's visit and the reason for the elaborate Pickfair party. To keep his son away from the sultry Lili, King George V had instructed his son to keep away from the picture colony. Being the guest of Doug and Mary apparently nullified the royal command.

When Gloria got to the Plantation Cafe, the prince and Lili were already there. The duke knew all the lyrics to the latest ditties and was a perfect dancer. They all stayed until three. When they were ready to leave, Gloria suggested they continue at her house.

Lois and Virginia couldn't believe their eyes and ears when the revelers arrived with half a dozen Plantation Cafe musicians. Gloria woke up the butler and got a breakfast organized. Chaplin entertained with skits in which he played all the parts. After breakfast, Prince George returned to the Roosevelt Hotel, where he was registered under the name Louis V. DuMorris. On her doorstep Gloria had everyone swear never ever to tell Doug and Mary. It was all in the papers the next day.

Joe called. He was furious at being on the wrong coast. He missed her, he said, and asked her to come to New York for a few days.

"I can't," she said. "The children."

"Bring them," he said.

"What about the picture?"

"He won't be ready to shoot for three more weeks. I just talked to him. You'll be back long before that. Please, Gloria."

To hear Joe say please was something. And she teased him back. He told her his birthday was coming up September 6.

"How old?"

"Forty."

"But deep down a frustrated adolescent."

"Running scared."

"What are you scared about?"

He laughed it off. He wanted her, he said. He was in love with her body and her independence.

A week after Joe's fortieth birthday she left for New York with little Gloria, Brother, Miss Simonson the governess, and a maid. Buddy was six years old and fascinated by trains. All across the continent he played engineer and conductor while his sister sat with Miss Simonson like a proper little lady, reading the stack of books they had brought along.

The autumnal hues of midwestern landscapes and the prospect of her own thirtieth birthday in six months made Gloria pensive. The dues exacted by society for illicit passion were high in manner-conscious America and exorbitant in the glasshouse movie industry, but in her case sexual passion was not pitted against maternal love. On the contrary. Her affair allowed her to be more of a mother. "In spite of the complications Joe Kennedy had brought into my life," she would remember, "he had nevertheless taken the business load off me for a year and allowed me hours every day to watch my children grow."

A few weeks shy of her eighth birthday, little Gloria was a tall girl with a smaller, prettier mouth than her mother's, sun-streaked blond hair, and deep hazel eyes. Her parents were civilized enough to speak to each other on matters that concerned her. Herbert's restaurant was flourishing, and he was a devoted father, picking up his daughter on the designated days and generous with gifts and attention. Gloria pretended not to know that father and daughter carried on an endearing correspondence of postcards and little notes.

Buddy was different—a ball of energy with big ears, quick brown eyes, and a broad grin. No absent father came to visit him or sent him greeting cards. To compensate, Gloria spoiled him. Yet in many ways, he was closer to Miss Simonson than Gloria, a fact that hurt Gloria. Even more than little Gloria's, Buddy's childhood would be spent in expensive boarding schools in England and Switzerland.

Joe was not on the Grand Central platform when the train pulled in. Instead, employees of his greeted them and took them to the hotel. Fifteen minutes later, Joe swept in carrying a stack of gifts for everybody. He was happy, noisy, smothering the children with attention. When he had a moment alone with Gloria, he called her the most desirable woman, held her gaze in his electric blue stare, and said he couldn't wait to take her out that evening. She told him they had to be reasonable; they couldn't be seen together. "We're business associates," he grinned.

"Business is done in the daytime if both associates are married," she said.

Others accused him of acting callously in business and personal relationships. He was often gossiped about as an upstart who simply didn't know the proper rules of behavior. Among well-bred sophisticates, a gentlemen might have discreet liaisons, but he never appeared at house parties or for weekends with a woman other than his wife. Gloria told him that if they wanted to go out they would have to be with other people.

He wanted to call one the horsemen. She said she'd get Sport Ward to join them.

Joe said he had been faithful to her.

"How can we be faithful, Joe. We're both married."

There had been no Kennedy baby that year, he told her. Fifty years later she would remember her own astonishment and then Joe saying it had been their year—it was almost a year ago that they had met at the Savoy Plaza. What he wanted more than anything, he said, was for the two of them to have a child.

Her reaction was one of shock. "You can't ask that of me," she said. "I refuse to discuss it. If you as much as mention it again, I will turn right around and go back to California tonight. You can't manipulate the public, Joseph. I would be finished tomorrow."

If anyone knew the cost of going against social conventions, it was Gloria. Coming less than three years after the Paris abortion, her brush-off was entirely in character. Yet, for decades, rumors would persist that

Kennedy did make her pregnant and that, at his insistence, she had had an abortion, that the reason for the delayed Stroheim film start was this abortion.

The evening with Sport Ward proved to be a soothing time out. The society lion teased Gloria by calling her Della Falaise, and he and Joe discovered they had a friend in common—Joe's Harvard classmate Robert Benchley, now editor of *Vanity Fair.* When Joe learned that Sport was a friend of Mayor Jimmy Walker, he opened up completely and told Ward about the complex merger talks with RCA's David Sarnoff. With a smile at Gloria, Joe said he knew both she and Mr. Von Stroheim felt sound reproduction still too crude to spoil a great picture. "Maybe next time," he smiled. "The important thing is to be ready to go if sound pictures become more than just a novelty. Well, I'm ready with Photophone. That's what our sound system is called."

Gloria marveled at Joe's sense of strategy. She knew no one in the industry who could plan ahead like him. Joe told the blasé Sport to join him in buying RCA stock when the right time came, telling him he could make himself a handy million on the stock market. When Joe momentarily left the table, Sport said, "Della Falaise, remove your spell from that poor man."

Gloria and Joe saw a lot of Sport over the next weeks as the battle for Keith Albee Orpheum reached its climax.

What might have given old Albee and Heiman the idea that with the help of Warner Brothers they could regain control were trade press reports that Joe was distancing himself from David Sarnoff. What was more, Photophone was suffering start-up difficulties that delayed the wiring of theaters and, *Variety* speculated on September 12, might lead to Western Electric winning the war. In reality, while Murdock was sailing back from Europe, Joe and the bankers were deep in negotiations with Sarnoff to buy Keith and FBO for $40 a share, a move that would give Keith a paper value of eighty million dollars and FBO an eight-million-dollar net worth.

On October 10, when Murdock reached New York, Keith's stock was selling at 32⅞. Two days later, when Gloria and Joe attended the opening of Stroheim's *The Wedding March* at the Rivoli, the stock reached 34. By Monday, October 15, it was rumored that the takeover could go either way, with RCA buying control by purchasing 510,000 shares at 38 a share, or Albee-Heiman wresting back control with the help of Warner Brothers and Fox at a slightly higher price. "Kennedy-Murdock are said to hold the whip hands," *Variety* reported on the seventeenth.

The Wedding March drew capacity crowds. Critical estimates varied. The *Daily News* awarded the film four stars, its highest tribute. The *New*

York Mirror said Stroheim certainly knew how to direct women. "He has done for the tepid and negative Fay Wray what he did for Mae Murray in *The Merry Widow*. She acts." *The New York Times*, the *Herald Tribune*, and the *Sun* gave the movie qualified endorsements.

Queen Kelly was set to start shooting on October 25 at the FBO studio on a ten-week schedule and a prestigious $285,000 budget. Gloria, however, was still in New York three days later when it all fell into place for Joe. Sarnoff exercised his option to buy enough of FBO to give RCA majority control. RCA Photophone was merged with Keith Albee Orpheum to create Radio-Keith-Orpheum, the future biggest little major of them all, RKO. Sarnoff came in as chairman, and Joe exchanged 75,000 Keith shares for an option on 75,000 shares of new RKO "A" stock at twenty-one dollars a share. He also pocketed a $150,000 fee for arranging the merger. Joe immediately set Michael J. Meehan, the Wall Street trader famous for sending RCA stock rocketing the previous spring, to put together a pool and whip up the new shares. Pathé Pictures was left out of the deal, and Joe stayed as Pathé's chairman of the board, with Murdock as president and E. B. Derr as vice president in charge of the West Coast studio.

However brilliant the masterstroke, it had one casualty—Joe's friendship with Guy Currier. The Harvard classmate who at critical moments had found the money that made the difference and had remained Joe's "silent" partner throughout the showbiz ascension forced a sale of the remaining Kennedy-Currier holdings in FBO for some five million dollars and bade an angry farewell. Joe had dealt with Sarnoff behind his back, and Currier felt betrayed.

Was Joe finished with the picture business? Cornered by reporters, he laughed off reports of his retirement. He would be on his way to Hollywood before the end of the week, he told *Variety*, not to take care of personal business but to get into things under the new regime. The trade weekly believed that the new regime he referred to meant Radio-Keith-Orpheum and that Sarnoff and Kennedy would be the active heads of the latest showbiz combination. The rapid consolidation caused jitters in the ranks that Sarnoff tried to still. "It is not our policy to remove anyone from an organization if they have proven their worth," he was quoted as saying in *Variety*'s October 31 lead story. "We expect to operate Keith's with the good men from within." On the West Coast, Paul Bern, a producer Joe had chosen as production head, crossed swords with Le Baron, Joe's appointed supervisor of FBO and Pathé. Le Baron preemptively moved into the George Washington office previously occupied by De Mille in the Mount Vernon building and announced he was Pathé's functioning production chief. Bern, who would marry Jean Harlow two months later and commit suicide in the biggest sex-murder scandal of the early 1930's, claimed *he* was the general production head and that Le Baron should only assume the supervision of productions to which Kennedy specifically assigned him, such as *Queen Kelly.*

Flushed with his triumphs, Joe felt nothing was impossible or out of the question, including having his wife and mistress meet.

Halloween was coming up, and he wanted Gloria and her children to come to Bronxville. He told Gloria he had promised Rose and his own children they would finally meet his movie star client and her daughter and little son. Gloria balked. She had no intention of meeting his wife. They argued. He said, "Please, I promised." She relented.

In her autobiography she would recall agreeing to a compromise. Little Gloria and Brother could go with Miss Simonson. All three were picked up by Eddie Moore, and Gloria would recall halfway regretting not following her costumed kids out the door and, instead, spending a miserable evening by herself. Her own daughter and Rose Kennedy remembered it differently: according to them, both Gloria and her children were house guests at Bronxville.

Joe was forty and pushing impatiently at his fate. For months he had primed his wife that Gloria was his most important business partner. The two women in his life played along. Echoing Joe's exact sentiments, Gloria told Rose she was grateful she had her husband to give her the right business advice because her affairs were a mess. Gloria would always wonder what exactly Rose knew, and she always watched for a remark, a glance, a gesture that would tell her whether Rose was a saint, a fool, or a better actress than she. There were moments she knew she was being tolerated, for Joe's sake, and moments when Rose must have been aware of the fatuously surprised face Gloria showed.

Rose willed herself to believe what her husband told her. She, they, had nothing in common with Gloria, no convictions, no sanctity. The mere fact of lying—if that was what Joe was doing—showed he respected that sanctity, the family they had created together, even if he had deserted their marriage bed. So to Rose, Gloria was a talented star, incipiently crucified by her own good looks, terribly lonely behind the put-on self-deprecation and blasé indifference to her own fame. Gloria was a woman married to an affable but untalented man and therefore desperately in need of Joe's solicitude and financial acumen.

Significantly, what Rose would recall was not a first private dinner, the film star's stories about friends and admirers, in-jokes, or I'm-just-a-person-like-everybody-else anecdotes, but what their children did. Probably confusing Kathleen and Patricia, Rose would write in her memoirs of Pat taking little Gloria down to show her the Bronxville public school, meet her classmates, and show off a little by introducing her house guest as "Gloria

Swanson's daughter." Nobody believed the girl, Rose would remember. "They just grinned, thinking it was a joke. After all Gloria Swanson was, to them, practically a supernatural being, so she couldn't be in Bronxville and wouldn't have a daughter, and Pat was doing some silly spoofing. I can't recall the exact details, but I do remember how completely indignant Pat was when she and Gloria's little girl came home and told us."

Rose remembered Pat as being around ten, the same age as little Gloria. Patricia was, in fact, four in 1928, while Kathleen and Little Gloria were both eight. Fifty-eight years later, Gloria Daly would recall the visit with her mother to the Kennedys. Which Kennedy daughter she played with she could no longer remember, but the pumpkins, the costumes, and the Halloween time stayed in her mind. She also couldn't get over the fact that one family could have eight children. Jack was impressed by who her father was. Gloria Swanson wondered why an eleven-year-old boy would be impressed with Herbert Somborn. When she asked her daughter, the answer was simple: "Because I told him Tom Mix goes to his restaurant for lunch."

From Hollywood word came that Stroheim had started *Queen Kelly* on the Thursday before Halloween. On Friday, November 2, Joe and Sport saw Gloria and her children off at Grand Central Station. Joe would follow with Eddie Moore and Ted O'Leary in a few days.

Queen Kelly

Authors should have more rights than producers,
and we should assert them more frequently.

—STROHEIM ad in *Motion Picture News.*

Almost one year after Erich von Stroheim told the story of Kitty Kelly to Gloria and Joe, *Queen Kelly* began filming on the former FBO, now RKO, lot. While the Paramount sound stages next door on Marathon Street went on twenty-four-hour work days (two eight-hour shifts for actual recording, with the remaining eight hours divided equally for time to erect and strike sets), and in New York thirteen out of fourteen Broadway film houses showed sound pictures, the Gloria Productions film began in the silent medium with which everybody was comfortable.

When Gloria got to Los Angeles, she sat in on the first week's rushes with Stroheim and cameraman Paul Ivano. What she saw in the projection room looked superb. The scenes of Walter Byron as Wolfram and Wilhelm von Brincken as his aide-de-camp racing back to the palace with a carriageful of demimondaines in satins and feathers after an all-night revel were dazzling.

To play Queen Helena, Stroheim had chosen Seena Owen. A native of Spokane, Washington, the thirty-four-year-old Owen had come to Hollywood as a teenager and worked with D. W. Griffith, Jacques Tourneur, Frank Borzage, and John Ford. She had been at Triangle at the same time as Gloria and costarred in one picture with Wallace Beery. Under Stroheim's direction she would play the mad queen with relish. When incensed, Queen Helena uncoils a most lethal bullwhip and flays the offending commoner as silent invective spews from her spittle-flecked mouth. Seena was not afraid of turning a juicy part into a romp. Sylvia Ashton, who ten years earlier had been a De Mille leading lady and had played Zasu Pitts's mother in *Greed,* was cast as Kitty Kelly's aunt in Dar es Salaam, and Tully Marshall as the old planter Jan Vooyheid. Marshall was an expressive actor who had costarred with Lois Wilson in *The Covered Wagon.* For Stroheim, he had played the degenerate foot fetishist in *The Merry Widow.* There was little doubt in the mind of Ivano that when it came to shooting the African wedding of the virgin Kitty and the loathsome Vooyheid, Stroheim would match the perverse incongruity of *The Merry Widow* wedding night.

Stroheim was in top form. In New York, *The Wedding March* had taken in $30,000 at the Rivoli box office by the end of its second week. There were financial constraints on *Queen Kelly,* but Stroheim had a handpicked cast and crew, a star who had high expectations, and a producer who stayed off his back. From the first day of shooting, he gave free rein to his flair for the erotic. He introduced Queen Helena sipping champagne in her bath, her nakedness covered by nothing more than a big white Persian cat, a motif of evil he had introduced in *The Merry Widow.*

Like Griffith, whom he adored, he was distant on the set. When Gloria visited the set before the filming of her own scenes began, he proudly walked her through the main decors—the palace grand hall, where over two hundred extras in pre-1914 splendor would toast the betrothal of Queen Helena and Prince Wolfram; the palace corridors; Wolfram's private chambers and bedroom. Still being hammered together out at the Pathé studio in Culver City was the two-story Dar es Salaam set, complete with a huge bar, tropical planetarium, and stairs leading to upstairs rooms. Never, he confided, had he felt so utterly confident. Absolutely nothing was wrong. He would be ready for her first scene in one week.

Stroheim was totally sincere. So much had gone wrong on the eight pictures that made up his tumultuous career that he was anxious to bring *Queen Kelly* in on time. During the second week, he put cast and crew on a twenty-four-hour schedule. His allotted ten weeks were twice as long as the average director's schedule for a feature, but he derisively referred to *Queen Kelly* as a "quickie."

Gloria first reported to work at the Lasky ranch, a stretch at the back of Griffith Park that would become the Forest Lawn Cemetery in the 1930s. A roadside crucifix and apple blossoms gave a touch of Mitteleuropa to the hillside trail where a double row of convent girls, shepherded by their nuns, passed a double file of cavalry on a drill. Although Gloria's novice's uniform was not the most intricate costume she had worn in her fifty-three features, she insisted that Ann Morgan, the dressmaker Joe's horsemen had eliminated in the housecleaning, be put back on the payroll. When Stroheim saw the English modiste on location one morning, he remarked on her angelic face and asked if she might play one of the nuns. Everybody agreed, and Ann donned a nun's habit.

Working with Stroheim was unlike anything Gloria had experienced before. The director was so painstaking that she lost all sense of time, hypnotized by his relentless perfection. A scene that Dwan or Walsh might wrap up in an hour took Stroheim all day. His obsessive care, however, paid off in the screening room. What Gloria saw of herself were images that looked like a master's painting of a girl she didn't quite know. Stroheim and Ivano peeled a dozen years from her face. And what she saw of Byron in his fiery uniform and pith helmet convinced her he would be Hollywood's next male star. After the outdoor filming at the Lasky ranch, Stroheim went on working at the studio at night, usually shooting scenes that didn't require his star's presence. The reason was the pressure of time. Caught in the crucible of his own artistic intransigence, he saw no other way of finishing the picture within the allotted schedule than to push himself, his cast, and his crew into fourteen-hour days. One morning they "wrapped" at 6:30. Another night he brought one actor "cold" into the picture, rehearsed him for an hour and a half for a single close-up, and at the end pronounced himself still not satisfied.

Joe Kennedy's arrival during the second week of November put an end to Stroheim's round-the-clock creativity. Informed that the *Queen Kelly* troupe was averaging fourteen hours' work a day, Joe walked on the set and saw hollow eyes and weary faces. Excessive overtime was ruled out on humane grounds.

What was happening to William Le Baron and Benjamin Glazer, who were supposed to make sure Stroheim didn't take two years to make the picture? Gloria would later say they were never there, and Joe would curse them. In fact, Le Baron was no longer theirs to command, while Glazer was on the Pathé lot, appointed Joe's chief of production.

Radio Pictures, RCA's newly formed production subsidiary, had grand designs for its new acquisition, and Le Baron figured largely in its plans. Kennedy did not. Whatever Joe's impression about the new regime may have been before he left New York, what Sarnoff needed was not a corporate raider but, rather, people who knew how to make smart movies. Joe had turned FBO around financially, but he had never made a movie of note. And he hadn't managed to hang on to FBO's biggest asset. When Fred Thomson's contract had run out in 1928, Zukor had outbid Joe and brought the cowboy star to the Paramount fold. RCA would be spending millions developing sound, and Sarnoff wanted to start off with something that commanded attention.

Against a background of flaring lightning bolts and flaming radio beacons, full-page ads in the trade papers proclaimed that Radio Pictures was "titanic in conception, titanic in development, titanic in reality, sweeping on to a mighty destiny." Musicals were Le Baron's first love, and music was what audiences loved about talkies. During a quick trip to New York, Le Baron snapped up Florenz Ziegfeld's hit musical comedy *Rio Rita.* Sarnoff was all for it and told Le Baron the challenge was to beat MGM's first all-talkie, *Broadway Melody,* set for a February 1929 release, and to compete with Universal's *Show Boat,* Paramount's *The Cocoanuts,* Fox's *Sunny Side Up,* and Warner's *The Desert Song.*

Queen Kelly, in the scheme of things, was an anachronism, a Gloria Productions film for United Artists, shooting on RKO stages because of its star's personal relationship with the *ancien régime* (Joe cleared out his office and moved his corporate self to Culver City on December 1), and with each passing week, wearing out its welcome.

Meanwhile, Pathé Pictures was celebrating its silver anniversary in the New World. Twenty-five years after Charles Pathé had sent J. A. Berst to America with a steamer trunk of films in 100- and 400-foot lengths (to be sold outright rather than rented in those pre-exchange days), Pathé was "old in years and wisdom," Joe told *Exhibitors Herald World,* but "young in energy, enthusiasm, absolutely independent and ahead with determination and confidence in the future." Not for publication was the cutting of overhead and salaries that he and Derr instituted, which after a streak of red ink resulted in a November net profit of $70,000.

Pathé had exchanges throughout North America, a laboratory in Jersey City, a building at 35 West Forty-fifth Street in New York, and in Culver City a studio complex that had been much improved during De Mille's tenure, which turned out features, shorts, and the weekly "Pathé News." The latter, under the supervision of Henri de la Falaise, was the only remaining connection with the once gigantic Pathé Frères in France. Pathé's biggest drawing cards were the rapidly climbing Constance Bennett, patrician Ann Harding, dramatic Helen Twelvetrees, and former De Mille actress Ina Claire. Among its young contractees were Mary Astor, Myrna Loy, Bill Boyd, and Eddie Quinlan. Its top directors were Tay Garnett, a World War I aviator who had started as a stuntman for Mack Sennett and Hal Roach and now specialized in action pictures; Leo McCarey, who gained fame directing Laurel and Hardy comedies; and newspaperman turned director Edward Griffith, who was no relation to D.W., but whose career would be almost twice as long.

Joe secured the use of RCA's Photophone for Pathé immediately and signed up Josiah Zuro, a former Broadway orchestra conductor, to handle the synchronization of all Pathé sound productions. Derr and Glazer were plenty busy gearing up for sound. *Sin Takes A Holiday,* starring Constance Bennett, was in the running to become Pathé's first talkie.

Gloria lost count of how many times "Von" shot the encounter of cavalry officers and convent girls on the Lasky ranch, how many times she curtsied and dropped her bloomers, how many times Byron laughed, how many times she rolled the knickers into a ball and threw them at him, how many times she pleaded with her eyes for him to return her panties, and how many times he playfully flipped them back to her before riding off with his men. In the evening, Gloria had Joe. During the day, she had Ann Morgan to keep her company.

When Ann told her that in one take the director had made Byron fondle the panties and pass them in front of his face before stuffing them into his saddle bag, Gloria decided to scrutinize the next day's rushes. Looking at the take in the projection room with Joe, Stroheim, and Ivano, she saw Byron sniff her panties.

As a sprightly eighty-two-year-old, Ivano would remember sitting between Stroheim and Gloria in the darkened screening room, and Joe Kennedy suddenly asking him what he thought of the scene.

"Photographically, it's beautiful," the cameraman answered diplomatically.

"But what's wrong with it?" Joe asked.

"I don't know if you'll be able to show it," Ivano admitted.

Stroheim kicked the cameraman in the shins one way, Gloria kicked him the other way, but he had already said it.

"All right," Joe allowed, "I guess we'll get away with it."

The idea of putting such a scene on the screen was so unthinkable that the Hays Code didn't even mention it. Gloria thought that might be the reason Stroheim believed he could get away with it. Since none of the men objected, she decided not to say anything. Byron's gesture *was* subtle.

In early December, Stroheim began shooting Wolfram and Kelly's midnight revels at the palace. Kelly's innocence was to be underlined with such intertitles as her saying, "Holy Mother of Patrick, I'm in my night shirt," as she refuses to take off the coat Wolfram has thrown over her after abducting her from the burning convent. Next, they filmed Queen Helena discovering the pair, and going after Kelly with a whip. To underscore the jealousy, Stroheim planned such intertitles as Kitty asking the queen, "He's going to marry you?" and her insane highness answering, "No, I'm going to marry him."

Stroheim was even more meticulous shooting in the studio than he had been filming on location. Gloria tracked the number of days it took to film one page and figured it would take four months to finish the whole script.

Derr could do the calculations in his head. At the present rate of progress, it would take 103 days, at $5,000 each, to get *Queen Kelly* in the can.

Joe set to work trying to persuade "Von" to eliminate half a dozen scenes, and to agree to let Glazer write new pages that would supersede the costly jungle-and-swamp chase sequence. To eliminate the expense of the coronation scene showing Wolfram, with Kitty at his side, ascending the Hesse-Nassau throne in the final fadeout, Kennedy and Glazer suggested the following: After rescuing Kitty in the East African swamps, Wolfram hears he is to be crowned. Because he fears Kitty will not make a suitable queen, he abandons her and goes back to Europe alone. Kitty goes mad and dies in an insane asylum. Stroheim balked. You couldn't end an epic with a shot of a wooden box in the ward of a madhouse.

He also resisted, at least halfheartedly, Joe's entreaties that they use sound, at least in part. In the end, though, the director finally agreed that sound could be introduced in at least three reels.

As Joe had done the year before, he went east to be with his family for Christmas and New Year's. And as he had done the year before, Henri came home from Paris. Gloria found her husband more attractive than ever and spent a happy, loving time with him. She would remember Joe calling several times and she warning him about the ever-slipping schedule. Joe told her he would speak to Le Baron and Glazer after the holidays.

Joe's Christmas gift was a surprise Gloria didn't get to enjoy until after New Year's—private star's quarters at the studio that outshone even the extravagant dressing-room villa Hearst had built for Marion Davies. Never mind that the bungalow was at a studio that was no longer Joe's; it featured a grand piano, a full kitchen, a private street entrance, and a private garage. The bungalow was jokingly called the Petit Trianon. (Ten years later Orson Welles would take over the Swanson quarters for himself during the making of *Citizen Kane*.) When Gloria saw it, she could only believe that Joe loved her. Her thanks had to be expressed over long distance, however. Just like the year before, when they had first become lovers in Palm Beach, Joe was taking a brief January vacation in Florida.

He could afford both to look over beachfront property and to give his working mistress a setside Trianon (even if it was at RKO, not Pathé). On Wall Street, Mike Meehan had done his job bullying up the new RKO stock. The 75,000 shares Joe had received in October at $21 a share were quoted in early December at $36, and speculated to be worth at least $45 if put on the market.

Besides playing golf and narrowing his house-hunting to North Ocean Boulevard, he met with Murdock and theater men from Cincinnati, Pittsburgh, and Texas to see if they could muscle back into Keith Orpheum. Murdock held a minority interest in nearly all the cinemas booked by the

Keith office but now owned by RCA. Old Albee was still angry at his former
deputy for having sided with Joe the previous summer, but he was not a
man to let feelings stand in the way of lucre.

Theaters that Albee personally owned in Providence and Pawtucket,
Rhode Island, and in Montreal, had never been part of the RCA deal, and
he now had the satisfaction of listening to Kennedy and Murdock pitching
the idea of a new transcontinental circuit in which the Rhode Island and
Canadian houses would form the nucleus. Joe would raise the money, some
forty million dollars, and Murdock would organize this inner circle within
the Keith circuit. If it didn't work, they could always sell out to Warner,
to Paramount's Publix, or even to Sarnoff. Everybody wanted choice theaters to wire for sound.

When Joe wasn't playing golf, looking at beachfront houses, or plotting
with Murdock (Sarnoff called them "brothers-in-crime"), he was with
Glazer, who, with Stroheim's grudging consent, was working on the part-
talking version of *Queen Kelly.* Joe liked the Belfast-born Glazer, who,
before becoming a screenwriter and a production chief, had earned a law
degree at the University of Pennsylvania and served as drama and music
critic at the Philadelphia *Press.* Joe loved classical music, but never told the
horsemen for fear it would make him seem "arty" or effeminate.

If Stroheim intended any message to emerge from the cynical Cinderella
story he was shooting, it was that man has little difficulty adapting himself
from civilization to barbarism. The theme belonged to the African second
half of *Queen Kelly,* and its illustration began during the second week in
January 1929 when work started in Culver City on the Dar es Salaam
sequence—rank, sordid, and, to Gloria, seemingly unrelated to the gay-
blade tenor of the European first half.

Reporting to the set, she realized that what, under prodding from the
Hays office, had been refined into a low-class sailor's dive had again become
a whorehouse. The establishing scene was an elaborate crane shot that
began with a sailor coming out of one of the upstairs rooms and, tidying
his trousers, going down to the huge bar to meet Jan Vooyheid.

Ivano would remember Tully Marshall the first day on the set as "a
strange character with a bottle of cognac in one pocket and a Luger
strapped to his other side, and shaking all over as someone suffering from
some horrible disease." They filmed Marshall going to the dying aunt and,
in a long scene, telling her he must marry her niece. Stroheim cast a
bespectacled black actor as the African priest, dressed him in white vestments, and had him perform the marriage as well.

The wedding in the bordello a few feet from the aunt on her deathbed
was pure Stroheim. Kitty's bridal attendant was a tubercular whore named

Coughdrops. The script called for Coughdrops to hand the unhappy Kelly a bouquet that recalls the flowers Kitty gave to Wolfram back at the palace. In a double exposure, the African minister would suddenly appear to her as Wolfram in vestments saying, "My lady of the orchids, wait for me."

Stroheim made Marshall's incarnation of Jan Vooyheid utterly repulsive. Not content to have the dying aunt marry off her niece to an old man, the director had Marshall play him as a leering, demented, twitchy lecher. Low-keyed lighting gave the bizarre scene a weird religious feeling, accentuated by the African priest and his altar boys.

On the third day of shooting the marriage, Stroheim began instructing Marshall, in his usual painstaking fashion, how to dribble tobacco juice on his young bride's hand so he could slip the ring onto her finger. It was the first week of February 1929, and then and there Gloria decided art had its limits. She excused herself to Stroheim, walked off the set, and went to her new bungalow.

There were to be several versions of what happened next. According to Gloria, she called Joe in Palm Beach. "You better get out here," she told him. "Our director is a madman! You and everybody tried to stop me from making *Sadie Thompson.* Believe me, Sadie is *Rebecca of Sunnybrook Farm* compared to what *Queen Kelly* is turning into. Now, are you coming out here and starting to make decisions or aren't you?"

There are indications Joe managed at least one patch-up on the long-distance phone before he hurried across the country. Shrewdly, he suggested that Gloria see her old mentor, De Mille, and at the same time he ordered Derr to keep a closer eye on the director. The intervention seemed to work. A telegram from Gloria to Joe on January 21 said, "VON TOEING THE MARK STOP DE MILLE INSPIRED CONFIDENCE AND COURAGE."

Chroniclers more charitable toward Stroheim would say it was not Marshall's drooling that broke the camel's back, but the irresistible triumph of sound—that Kennedy and Swanson had already agreed that a silent *Queen Kelly* would be unmarketable and that with almost half the picture in the can, reshooting the film as an all-talkie would be prohibitive. A February 6 *Variety* news item reporting the shutdown pending the arrival of Kennedy and Glazer mentioned "talker versions" in preparation, one by Glazer and one by Edmund Goulding, a number of actors being carried on the payroll in the interim. "Cost has amounted to around $700,000, but it is figured that if matters are straightened out again it can be finished within $1 million."

When Joe got to Los Angeles he found Gloria hospitalized in a state of near collapse, and he wrote in a letter to Henri that "her attitude towards the picture, and everybody connected with it, [is] quite hostile." Gloria would remember nothing of a hospital stay in her memoirs, but she did recall how Joe told her to come to the studio. When her chauffeur drove up to the gate, the guard told her Mr. Kennedy, Le Baron, Glazer, and several others were in the projection room. Mr. Kennedy's message was that he would join her in her bungalow.

An hour later Joe came in, alone, cursing Stroheim, Le Baron, and Glazer. He slumped into a deep chair and struggled to control himself, holding his head in his hands.

After a while he said, "I've never had a failure in my life."

Was he forgetting how Franklin Roosevelt had humiliated him back at Fore River twelve years ago, how the young assistant secretary of the navy had driven him to tears?

She would remember thinking that anyone who reached forty without a taste of failure might be considered deprived, when he sprang up and again raged at the people who had let if happen.

She felt she was more accustomed to crises that he, and began thinking of Mickey Neilan, Allan Dwan, Raoul Walsh—Jesse Lasky, even—people she could trust to come up with suggestions on how to salvage the picture.

Joe pulled her into his arms. She felt his tears on her face. "We'll try to save it," she said, holding him.

C H A P T E R · *16*

Eddie

> *"It is impossible to exaggerate about Hollywood and impossible to burlesque for it is the craziest place in the whole wide world."*
>
> —CECIL BEATON in *Vogue,* 1930

For the British it was India all over again, a century later. The decade before the emigrés from Hitler's Germany flocked to the shores of the Pacific, it had belonged to the English. They could, after all, speak the language and, as Madame Glyn proved, intimidate the parochial hostesses, offer lessons in deportment on Sunday afternoons, and keep a stern eye on any natives present. "Darling," a compatriot is reputed to have called out to Gladys Cooper at one gathering, "there seems to be an American on your lawn."

Edmund Goulding had no lawn, but he did have a marvelous stretch of beach at his Santa Monica house, where on Sundays he entertained a savant mix of compatriots and natives. It was at his housewarming party in 1926 that, while Mrs. Louis B. Mayer inspected the library, David Selznick first tried to kiss her daughter Irene on the terrace. It was also on the Goulding terrace that Noel Coward told of his 1929 drive along flat, straight boulevards with Gloria Swanson during which they discussed nothing but dentistry. And it was here that, two years later, Aldous Huxley patiently explained to Ivor Novello, brought over to adapt his stage success *The Truth Game,* that film was not a good medium for a writer to work in, "because you can't do it yourself. You depend on Jews with money, or 'art directors' or little bitches with curly hair and teeth, or young men who recommend skin food in the advertisements, or on photographers."

It was Allan Dwan who steered Gloria toward the thirty-five-year-old Goulding, a Noel Coward look-alike writer, director, bisexual, and idea man of wit and supreme self-confidence. Director of Garbo, Bette Davis, and Joan Crawford, he was, more immediately, cited in the *Los Angeles Record* as one of the ten best of that entirely new breed—dialogue writers. More to the point of any salvage operation for *Queen Kelly,* he was already thinking of what sound might mean to motion pictures. The previous summer in the *National Board of Review of Motion Pictures* magazine he had written that the silent movies accompanied by synchronized but wholly mechanical and artificial sound gave no inkling of what was to come. "The girl who in a close-up can sing a soft lullaby to her baby and whisper, 'Good night, my darling,' in such a way that the camera might be listening in through the keyhole—she will be the new star," he predicted.

A man of great flamboyance and elegance, Eddie Goulding had been a child actor in Britain and, after his arrival in Hollywood in 1925, gravitated toward the movies as a script author, working on Mae Murray vehicles and writing a superb screen adaptation of his friend Joe Hergesheimer's short story "Tol'able David." His debut as a writer-director had been fortunate. MGM had cast Joan Crawford, Constance Bennett, and Sally O'Neil as three flapper rivals in his backstage romance called *Sally, Irene and Mary.* Nobody had heard of O'Neil again, but Crawford was almost a star, Bennett was part of Hollywood's fast set, and Eddie became known for his flair for directing actresses.

He was also famous for his gifts as a storyteller. He had a magnificent voice and he knew how to use it, "writing with his voice instead of his hands," Jesse Lasky, Jr., would remember. The Laskys lived a few houses down the beach from Goulding, and fifteen-year-old Jesse was convinced Eddie was in love with his mother, Bess. That summer young Jesse got to sit in on a story conference with his father and Goulding. Lasky, Sr., was looking for a subject for Nancy Carroll, Paramount's new discovery, and while eating cracked crab by the Lasky swimming pool, Eddie came up with an idea. "He painted visions of scenes in a disconnected tone full of dramatic effects," Lasky, Jr., would remember. "He described a street in Prague. Of course, none of us had ever been to Prague; maybe neither had Goulding, but he engulfed us in moods: the rain on the dark street, patterns of lamplight in a deserted alley, the movement of night people among whom the heroine drifts like a displaced moonbeam, wonderfully detached, while the story grew around her—lurid and mysterious." At the end of the story, Lasky offered $25,000 for it. By Monday morning, however, when a Paramount stenographer was dispatched to Santa Monica to take down the screen treatment, Eddie had forgotten it.

Goulding was also a songwriter. He didn't know a note of music, but he could whistle and hum a tune. A studio arranger would take it down. Several became hits. People loved him. Louise Brooks, who first met him when she was seventeen, would call him an incomparable human being because when his friend the English dancer Marjorie Moss gave up her fight against tuberculosis in 1932, Eddie married her and filled the last two years of her life with beauty.

Goulding had been in on the *Queen Kelly* resuscitation before the production shutdown and hated everything he saw. With his agent, Phil Berg, he sat in on a screening of a rough-cut of the picture and decided that this mismatched love triangle set in a decadent Middle-European backwater and the squalor of an African bordello was not his cup of tea. Berg thought the footage just dreadful, and fifty years later would remember that one wit in the screening-room darkness suggested cutting the negative into mandolin picks as one way of getting some money back. In late February when Goulding met Gloria alone, he was both solicitous and brutally frank.

"Shelve it," he said. In a conspiratorial whisper he added, "And make a talking picture."

Joseph Kennedy should try to be among the avant-garde of sound producers, especially since Pathé had the rights to the RCA Photophone system, Goulding said. Did Gloria know that Bebe Daniels was Lee De Forest's second cousin, and that the inventor was on the set of *Rio Rita* for hours, fiddling with the microphones and reassuring the greenhorns there was life after sound? The technique of sound recording was constantly being improved. "Believe me, Chaplin, Garbo, and you are going to have to talk."

Her director friends were saying the same thing. Allan Dwan had told her that sound was something to lure the public away from that other novelty, radio. Dwan had finished *The Iron Mask,* his first part-talker, and was starting for Fox *Frozen Justice,* his first all-talker. He was running scenes in the screening room with the sound off to see if he was still making a movie. Mickey Neilan was writing the scenario and the dialogue of *The Fog,* his first effort at directing "a 100% sound" film, as he said in personal trade-paper ads.

The previous October, while *Sadie Thompson* was opening overseas, Raoul Walsh had lost his right eye. Driving through Cedar City, Utah, at night, he had frightened a jackrabbit, causing it to crash through the windshield of his car. When Gloria called to wish him a speedy recovery, he told her he had received letters from moviegoers in Paris, Yokohama, and Birmingham, England, who described themselves as being in the same trade as Sadie. Some of the letters had photos enclosed. One included an offer of free time on a tatami mat, while another voiced a professional opinion on the pitiful prowess of men of the cloth. A letter from Pago Pago offered him a carefree future with marital privileges if he cared to catch a boat.

Soon Raoul was back in action, shooting the first Hollywood all-talker in the great outdoors. Thanks to Movietone News, Fox had sound trucks, and Walsh persuaded the boss to let him take the trucks on location.

Filming *In Old Arizona* in the California desert, Raoul looked as dashing as ever with his black eye patch.

If *Sadie Thompson*'s worldwide success was an occasion for erotic fantasizing for Raoul, it was cause for new humiliations for Joe. The picture that Gloria had sold out to Joe Schenck and United Artists on his advice was not only a box-office hit, but her portrayal of the title role was now nominated for an award by the newly founded Academy of Motion Picture Arts and Sciences.

There were no surprises that first year of the "Oscars." The winners were known in advance. Gloria and Louise Dresser lost out to Janet Gaynor; Richard Barthelmess and Charlie Chaplin, to Emil Jannings. The best screen adaptation award went to Benjamin Glazer for *Seventh Heaven,* and the best picture was William Wellman's *Wings,* which had nearly cost Lasky his Paramount position. Gloria remembered Joe's enthusiasm for awards on their first date.

Sadie Thompson was such a sensitive subject with him, however, that she decided not to attend the awards dinner. The next day she chatted on the phone with Eddie Goulding, who had been at the Ambassador Hotel dinner. Academy president Doug Fairbanks had paid special tribute to the *The Jazz Singer,* Eddie reported, emphasizing his point that *Queen Kelly* was from the Stone Age.

But Joe refused to scrap what less than three months earlier had been their shining promise of a powerful movie. There was too much money and too much reputation at stake, he told Gloria. The money was more her debt to UA than his cold cash, although a part of the estimated $600,000 *Queen Kelly* had cost so far was his. What irked him more was the prestige, *his* prestige, if the film was not finished. Kennedys, he kept telling his sons, can't be losers.

The rough-cut filled twenty-two reels, or just under three and a half hours of silent screen time. Joe realized that without Stroheim, the picture lacked cohesion, and that all another director could do was save the furniture by reshaping and reediting the footage into a releasable movie. Joe floated the idea of reassigning "Von" to complete the silent version for foreign markets, while Glazer directed a talkie version for North American release. This would mean bringing Stroheim and Gloria together, and the biggest obstacle to that was not so much the director's haughty ego as Gloria's continued resentment.

"Maybe it's Von's exacting style you don't like, his taking you through the wringer," Joe grinned when they were alone. "Maybe that's why you're on the phone every other day with the fey little Englishman. He flatters you."

"Eddie thinks with your investments *you* should be the first one to want to join the future."

"How about paying off the present first?"

She hated *Queen Kelly,* she said, and everybody connected with it. He told her she owed him considerable money on the picture. She said she had called Lasky and offered to work for Paramount.

"Goddammit, are you crazy, Gloria?"

She was nervous, overwrought. "I should never have left Paramount."

"Yeah, but you did. And here we are."

"When I think I turned down a million a year for this."

"You were going stale, making formula pictures."

"I was making money."

Their argument grew uglier and ended with Joe insisting that some sort of resolution to *Queen Kelly* had to be found.

Gloria kept meeting with Goulding. People warned her that while the amusing and clever Eddie might be brimming with ideas, he had a hard time completing any of them. But new ideas were the tonic she needed. Would he like to direct her in a talkie, she asked on the phone one morning.

"Yes," he said. "In fact, I hoped you might take a hint."

"When?" she asked.

"The sooner the better."

Then, just as Joe was ready to admit that no one could save *Queen Kelly,* he met a Polish emigré who told him it could be done. Maybe.

At forty, Richard Boleslavsky, or Boleslawski, was a mountain of a man who had been an actor and an apprentice director in Moscow under the hypnotic theoretician of the theater Konstantin Stanislavsky. In the first flush of the October Revolution of 1917, Boleslavsky had made *Khleb* (Bread), a filmic hymn to the New Order. Still, he found it prudent to put some distance between Moscow and himself before Lenin found out that, as a Polish cavalry officer, Boleslavsky had fought against the Bolsheviks and, in novel and film, had exalted the valor of the Polish soldiers who stemmed the red tide at the Vistula River.

After working in Germany and France for the great Danish director Carl Dreyer, Boleslavsky had arrived in Hollywood full of theories about acting and elocution. Quick to see the opportunities the switch to sound might afford him, he added the knowledge of sound recording to his repertoire and advertised himself as a "show doctor," an appellation he would never outgrow. Although he would make fifteen Hollywood films under his own name, he remained the front office "hired hand" on other directors' movies, notably a number of Sam Goldwyn productions.

Discovering Boleslavsky pulled Joe out of his *Queen Kelly* funk. Gloria and he had dinner on Rodeo Drive the next night, and for the first time in weeks, he was in a happy, tender mood.

"I've been meeting with Eddie Goulding," she began.

"I've just met a crazy Polack."

"Joseph, I have a favor to ask you."

"What is it?"

"Eddie wants to make a picture with me. Just a light easy picture. It wouldn't take long. I told him I'd let him know. As long as we're stumped on *Kelly* for the moment, I think I should work with this man while I have a chance."

"Maybe we're not stumped on *Kelly,* after all," he smiled.

"What do you mean?"

Joe told her he had shown the *Queen Kelly* rough-cut to this Richard Boleslavsky, who was willing to work on it on condition they give him a month by himself to go through the miles of footage. "And now I come to the part you're not going to like. This Boleslavsky and I agree that we can save the film if we add sound to it. Now, Gloria, you may not think much of sound as it's been up to the present, but—"

With a yelp she interrupted him. "Joseph, I'm ten minutes ahead of you for once. Darling, the picture I want to make is a talking picture, and I think I can be done with it before Boleslavsky is ready to go to work."

She would remember how, for the first time in a month, Joe dissolved into peals of laughter and whacked his thighs, how she ran behind his chair, hugged him and felt the curse of *Queen Kelly* melt away.

They struck a bargain. If she and Goulding could come up with an exciting script in the month Joe was in New York, Joe and she would produce her first talkie together. Boleslavsky, in the meantime, could continue working on the Stroheim footage. The two of them would then use what they'd learn from making of the Goulding talkie to finish *Queen Kelly* with style and elegance. "This Polack tells me that a few songs, some dialogue, and a happy ending will work wonders," Joe reported back to Gloria after Boleslavsky had taken a look at the footage.

For Gloria, Goulding was the miracle worker.

After the two months spent with Stroheim's tortured themes and work methods, the weeks she spent with Eddie and Laura Hope Crews coming up with a clever little art-deco tearjerker-comedy in the breakfast room at Crescent Drive passed like a charm.

Eddie knew no one with a better ear for the spoken word than his friend Miss Crews, and since they were going to do sound, they'd better have a script with plenty of rich, convincing dialogue. A native Californian, the thirty-nine-year-old Crews had been a child actress of note and had graduated to adolescent and leading lady roles opposite such stars as John Drew and Henry Miller. At the height of her stage fame, she had turned her

146-acre Connecticut farm into a home for a dozen orphan boys and girls, and given them an education and her name. Business reverses, however, had made her accept Goulding's offer to come to Hollywood, not as a player but as a drama coach and adviser in the selection of stories for talkies.

Gloria knew she couldn't afford to fluff the battle with King Mike. At Goldwyn's suggestion, she signed Crews to a one year, $1,000-a-week-contract—an unheard of sum for a character actor that prompted dozens of Crews's Broadway colleagues to hurry west. The opportunities presented by Hollywood stars with uncultured and untrained vocal cords resulted in a second California gold rush.

Photoplay published monthly surveys of its readers' reactions to talkies. By April 1929, when there were 1,600 theaters equipped for sound, one reader said talkies had allowed audiences to focus their attention on characters and the plot—in contrast to silents, which obscured storylines under a wealth of elaborate technical effects. By mid-1929, ninety percent of the people surveyed were in favor of good talkies.

Eddie said they should write an original story. Gloria was all for it, but warned they only had a month. Laura moved into the Crescent Drive guest house for the duration, and Gloria hired a court stenographer. Working days and evenings, the trio, with the shorthand secretary taking down practically everything they said, came up with the story of Marion Donnell, a fast, modern yarn full of adroit anticlimaxes. Marion is a Chicago legal secretary who meets, marries, and has a baby with the son of a wealthy Lakeshore Drive family. The groom's father tries to break up the marriage, succeeds, and moves to gain custody of his grandson. To keep the baby, Marion has to accept favors from her former boss, which puts her respectability in question and leads to complications before a suitably surprising finale.

The stenographer came in handy when Eddie dropped verbal pearls and forgot them in the heat of pursing different tacks. "One minute the three of us praised each other," Gloria would recall, "the next we fought like savages, and the demure stenographer took it all down—script dialogue, gossip, arguments and sandwich orders." After ten days of confinement and anxiety, a particularly terrible row caused Laura to leave in tears. She couldn't take it anymore. The same evening she called to ask if Eddie and Gloria had solved the problem that had caused her misery. They had, and she moved back into the guest house.

The Trespasser, as they called Marion's story, was finished by the time Joe returned from New York. Gloria invited him over for a reading. At the appointed hour, Eddie Moore showed up instead. Joe was detained, they should go ahead without him. Before the audience of one horseman, Gloria read Marion's part; Laura, the other women's parts; and Goulding, the men's roles plus the camera directions. When they were through, Moore called the boss, who invited them all to lunch at Rodeo Drive. Here, Gloria discovered yet another side of her lover. He hadn't been detained during the morning, he told her, he had just feared she would fail, that the two of them were somehow jinxed. Only when Eddie Moore called to say the script had sounded as good as anyone could wish had Joe become himself again.

During lunch, Goulding provoked a crisis. There was a terrible hole in the middle of *The Trespasser,* he announced. "The audience can't just see Marion, out of the blue, dressed in gorgeous clothes in a deluxe apartment with her former boss," he said, looking accusingly at Laura and Gloria. "It happens much too fast. The mood's not right. In fact, it's awful."

Before anyone could object, he came up with his own answer. "So we have to establish the new mood and let the audience figure it out. And since it's a sound picture, we should—yes—do it with music. Marion could sing him a love song. Gloria, can you sing?"

"She sings beautifully," Joe exclaimed like a proud parent. "Why, Gloria wanted to be an opera singer when she was young. She's told me so many times."

Joe tried to borrow a songwriter from William Le Baron, but RKO was deep in *Rio Rita* and had no composers or lyricists to spare. Goulding rose to the occasion and came up with a song himself. "Keep whistling," Gloria told him. "Laura, hum it with him while I find someone to write it down." She called a friend who called a friend who sent an old violinist over to write down the whistling and humming. Eddie spoke to Elsie Janis and got her to write the lyrics. They called the song, "Love, Your Magic Spell Is Everywhere."

For the part of Jack Merrick, the financier's son who twenty-four hours after eloping with Marion finds his way back to his father's fold, the Pathé casting director suggested they test Clark Gable. But in white tie and tails Gable just didn't have it. And he spoke like a private eye—something that wouldn't have mattered six months earlier. Both Gloria and Eddie had wanted to introduce someone new, and they finally settled on Robert Ames, the Paramount player who had starred opposite Pola Negri, but for whom *The Trespasser* was also a talkie debut.

In the midst of all this, Joe's father suddenly suffered a heart attack. P.J. was living with his daughter Margaret and her husband, Charles Burke, and had aged into a mellow, pink-faced seventy-one-year-old when he suffered a coronary and was taken to the Deaconess Hospital. Joe rushed to Boston, but P.J.'s condition seemed to improve. When the doctors agreed the crisis had passed, Joe went back to California, where the *Queen Kelly* situation demanded his attention. On May 18, the day after Joe's return to Los Angeles, P.J. died.

To the hundreds of telegrams of condolences, Joe answered that P.J. had been a great man and a great father. Joe decided not to go to the funeral but to stay in California. Rose and Joe Jr., a strapping youth of nearly fourteen, attended with Honey Fitz, congressmen and state legislators, city councilmen, and hundreds of men and women from East Boston. Young Joe, his mother would remember, behaved with dignity at the funeral and wake. Two weeks later, Joe wrote to his son, "I have heard such lovely reports about you at Grandpa's funeral. I am more than proud to have you there as my representative. Help mother out and I'll be there as soon as possible."

The Trespasser was ready to go into production. While Joe struggled with *Queen Kelly,* he got Goldwyn to loan George Barnes to *The Trespasser.* This time, an ironclad contract stipulated that the cameraman could not be pulled off the picture midway. Goulding wanted more than one cameraman, and Greg Toland, the future cinematographer of *Citizen Kane,* joined the crew.

Before the first day of shooting, Goulding had the whole picture rehearsed on a bare stage by both cast and crew. The biggest adjustment for Gloria was knowing where the microphones were and then forgetting about them. As they went through the script, the cameramen and sound engineer figured out where lights, sets, and microphones would be. The film editor sat in on the rehearsal, stopwatch in hand, timing everything. To muffle their sound, the cameras were encased, along with their human operators, in shack-sized blimps that could not be moved. For scenes in which the characters moved from one room to another, as many as twelve cameras rolled simultaneously. The cameras covering the exit from one room could not be turned off as the characters moved out of view into the next room because that would provoke an electrical surge through the studio's primitive power grid, causing the motor speed of the other cameras to increase in midshot. Ten changes of gowns and five styles of headdress kept Gloria fashionable and up to date in the contemporary society setting.

The Trespasser was in the can in twenty-one days. Gloria lost twenty pounds and came close to another mental and physical breakdown. Because the editor had been in on the shooting from the rehearsal on, the editing and scoring—with Eddie's "Love, Your Magic Spell Is Everywhere" becoming the theme song—were a cinch. Just over three months passed between the first day at Gloria's breakfast table and delivery of the completed film to UA. It was the cheapest picture she had made since becoming a star.

But there was still *Queen Kelly.*

While Joe spent the summer back east, E. B. Derr was in charge in Culver City, overseeing a three-features-a-month production schedule as well as Boleslavsky's progress with the Stroheim footage. In New York, Joe attended the July 30 opening at the Globe Theater of Radio Pictures' first release, *Street Girl,* with David Sarnoff and a bevy of Westinghouse and General Electric directors. He didn't bother to go the premiere of Pathé's *Paris Bound* four days later because he was with his family in their new summer house at Hyannisport. Still, via long-distance telephone, he hired more *Queen Kelly* help. Sam Wood, Gloria's director at Paramount before she escaped to New York, and a young writer named Delmer Daves were put to work on a new screen treatment, while Laura Crews was assigned to write new dialogue. In the new version, Kitty Kelly would be the rightful heir to the Hesse-Nassau throne and fool everybody in the end.

Costs kept climbing. Gloria would eventually claim *Queen Kelly* reached an astronomical $800,000 in 1929 dollars. In self-defense, Stroheim would maintain that only $400,000 had been spent by the time production was halted, that he had used $100,000, and that the remaining $300,000 had gone to Gloria. She had indeed paid herself weekly salary installments since the reorganization of her corporation in January 1928. Ironically, both might be right. Gloria's figures would include almost a year's extra expenses, while Stroheim conveniently forgot the cost of Boleslavsky's attempted salvage job.

Screening *The Trespasser,* meanwhile, convinced UA salespeople in New York that they had a winner. Joe Schenck wanted the Swanson talkie released as soon as possible. The Rialto, UA's flagship theater on Broadway, was booked until early November, however. In a flurry of transcontinental and transatlantic telephone calls, a September 9 world premiere in London was decided on, and Gloria was asked to attend. She was thrilled when they called. She would let them know the next day.

Before she could call Joe, he was on the phone to her. He was ecstatic. "E.B. told me about the London premiere."

"But if I go away in September, won't that interfere with *Queen Kelly?*" she asked.

"No," he replied.

They had been there before. Boleslavsky and the writers needed time, he explained. He wanted her, and he wanted to go to London with her. They'd be back before Boleslavsky would be ready to reshoot a few sequences. "Nobody's going to keep me from attending my first London premiere."

When she objected that the two of them couldn't sail to Europe together, he suggested she go to Paris and pick up Henri for the London premiere.

"You and I cannot travel on the same boat going over even if we're going to meet my husband," she came back.

"We won't be alone." As if he were addressing a nervous patient, he told her Rose would be coming. Conveniently forgetting their trip the year before, he told Gloria that Rose had never been to Europe.

Gloria refreshed his memory.

"I've promised her this trip," Joe came back.

Again, Gloria protested.

Joe said his sister Margaret would be coming too. "You and Rose will never have to be alone together."

She still resisted, knowing he would "out-argue" her. Subtle civility was not his strong point. Over the phone came dates and suggestions for side trips. Everything would be fine; she had no idea how happy she would make him. E.B. would arrange for the tickets.

Did she think of the previous Halloween, when he had first wanted to reconcile the opposites in his life? Was he getting more careless, ready to flout conventions? Was he more deeply in love with her than before? In her autobiography, she would recall how she got him to arrange for an extra ticket before she gave in, how she called Virginia Bowker in Chicago and invited her to London.

Before they left for Europe—Gloria and her old friend traveling aboard a Cunard liner that sailed a week before the French liner carrying Joe, Rose, and his sister Margaret—Gloria spent a long weekend at Hyannisport with the family. It was a weekend that would prove traumatic for twelve-year-old John Kennedy, but would go unmentioned in the Swanson memoirs. By the time she wrote her story, Joe's second son had become a tragic figure in American history and what happened to him that day on Nantucket Sound was, in the hindsight of a lifetime, too portentous, too embarrassing, and perhaps too silly.

Hyannisport

Her arrival was flamboyant. Instead of coming by train or automobile, Gloria landed in the harbor on August 10 in full view of the gathering Saturday crowd. Joe had rented the Curtiss amphibian plane that flew her up from the Hudson River at New York City, and after the aircraft circled the harbor and glided down for a landing, summer residents in tennis frocks, linen knickers, and white flannels gaped from the breakwater as she came to shore in a launch piloted by Joe himself. For the next few days, Hyannis followed her every move as if she were visiting royalty.

If she was now easier to "out-argue" than she had been the previous October, it was partly because she depended on Joe more than ever. Between last year's Halloween and this summer's New England resort season lay the beached monster called *Queen Kelly*. The production that was supposed to showcase her talent and vault Joe to the top in Hollywood was a shambles of celluloid in editing bins in a Pathé studio cutting room. Whatever she thought of her lover's sexual exuberance, of his need to show her off and to include her in his family circle, she was ready to grin and bear it because only he had the means to undo the disaster.

Queen Kelly could be explained away as a fumble, a setback of an ambitious producer who was on the verge of recouping nicely on his first talking picture. But that was not good enough for Joe. He had to prove himself to Gloria. If he couldn't win this one, he was just another Boston businessman—a crass mick. What she had going for her was his desperate ambition.

The period before *The Trespasser* launching was a depressingly vacant time for Gloria. Henri was in France making money as a Joe Kennedy appointee. Gossip columnists were beginning to say that Henri and she were separated. In her eyes, they were compromised as man and wife by their need to believe in Joe, in his ability to extricate her from the *Queen Kelly* mess and to make Henri rich (he was writing to her that he had bought a country home in France). The irony was that while she was over half a million dollars in the hole to Joe Schenck and United Artists—and had little chance of getting out from under the debt unless *Queen Kelly* was revived (or *The Trespasser* made her the first of the genuine made-in-Hollywood dramatic stars to triumph in the new medium)—Joe Kennedy had become a millionaire.

She was not good at being alone with her responsibilities, her debt, Schenck's growing insolence. Also, her future and her career were being evaluated with an odd new sobriety in the usually gushing queen of the fan magazines.

Two weeks before she said yes to Joe's summons to Massachusetts, *Photoplay* came out with a probing piece that told how Gloria was living apart from Henri, how she was in deepening financial trouble, and how all her hopes were riding on *Queen Kelly*. Written by the usually reliable Katherine Albert, the article in the July issue spoke of restless years for Gloria, years of misery and ecstasy, of careening from bottom to top and back down again since she had become her own producer. "To produce her own pictures," Albert said, "that has hurt more than one star. Gloria has the final word on story, direction, photography, clothes, casting. It isn't practical. Neither is Gloria."

Calling Swanson "still a significant and startling figure in the intricate design of Hollywood," Albert, who had been an actress herself before becoming *Photoplay*'s investigative reporter, asked what had happened to Gloria's lavish penthouse in New York and to the Westchester County estate. She also revealed that the Crescent Drive mansion itself might have to revert to the Gillette family, which carried the mortgage on the property. Albert had checked with Gillette officials, who refused to either confirm or deny that the safety-razor king might foreclose. How could Gloria stay at Crescent Drive? "It all depends on you and *Queen Kelly,*" Albert told her readers. "We who know her, hope it will be the beginning of a happier era."

The Cape Cod vacation was preceded by publicity interviews in New York and a novelty of the new era—cutting a record. At a news conference, Gloria announced that after *The Trespasser*'s opening in London and swings through Brussels, Berlin, and Paris for the continental premieres, she would return to Hollywood during the first week in October to turn *Queen Kelly* into an all-talking picture.

To the press she explained the production halt as a consequence of an impasse over story treatment and character development in the final dialogue scenes. Production had merely shut down after the expiration of Erich von Stroheim's eleven-week contract. To explain why *The Trespasser* got finished before *Queen Kelly,* she told *The New York Times* that one set of screenwriters had gone to work revising *Kelly* while other scenarists began writing *The Trespasser.* Whichever finished first would go before the cameras first; *The Trespasser,* as it were, was ready for the sound stages, and so it was made prior to the completion of *Queen Kelly.*

"Off screen one finds Gloria Swanson again the vivacious person she was before worries incidental to independent production of pictures gave her a constantly serious mien," the *Times* wrote in its Sunday, August 18, edition. "She chats about her nine-year-old daughter, Gloria, who cried when her mother left Los Angeles, who can play Mendelssohn's 'Spring Song' on the piano, who has seen her mother on the screen once and does not go to the movies. Miss Swanson has had a private sound film record made of her daughter and of her adopted son—Buddy, she calls him—playing a piano duet."

On the Saturday morning before she flew to Cape Cod, she was at the RCA Victor studio, recording Eddie Goulding's *Trespasser* theme song, now simply called "Love," and Toselli's "Serenade," the other song she sang in the picture. "I love the talking pictures," she told newsmen. "I would like to make more. I would do Shakespeare in the films but would not modernize him. No, I do not take voice culture lessons. I was once in musical comedy, you know. Talking pictures are so much harder than the silent kind."

Rose and the children were on the front lawn when Joe came up with their houseguest. Everybody had grown. Joe Jr. was a robust, easygoing fourteen-year-old now. The slight willowy Jack was less sociable. He had been sick a lot, it was explained. Nine-year-old Kathleen was all toothy grins, as was eight-year-old Eunice. Eunice spent a lot of time with the little ones, five-year-old Pat and four-year-old Bobby. Jean, now a year and a half, was with her nurse, and so was Rosemary.

Gloria had found out about Rosemary, and about how guilty the child's parents felt about her, two months earlier. A few days before Joe had left for the east, she had walked in on him in the middle of a phone call. He had seemed upset and she had gestured that she could wait in the next room, but he had waved her toward a chair. What she overheard of the conversation made her realize that he was talking to a hospital official and had offered to donate an ambulance but wanted assurances that the hospital could cure his daughter. When he hung up, she suggested her Dr. Bieler, and for the first time saw herself become the object of his anger. He had taken Rosemary to the best doctors in the east, he explained in a rising crescendo, and he didn't want to hear about any three-dollar doctor in Pasadena who recommended zucchini and string beans for everything. And while he was at it, he'd appreciate it if she'd stop touting that quack to people with serious problems. People would think her unhinged if she suggested grave illnesses could be treated with squash.

She had protested, but he had risen in fury. "I don't want to hear about it," he had snarled. "Do you understand me?" He had quickly calmed down, touched her arm, and motioned for her to wait outside. When he joined her a while later, he was himself again, and for the rest of that evening was considerate and charming. After he left California, she had asked Eddie Moore what was wrong with Rosemary. Eddie had looked unhappy, then tapped the side of his head with the top of his index finger and softly said, "She's . . . not quite right."

Joe was the proud new proprietor all that Saturday afternoon. Rose, the kids, and he had spent several summers in Hyannisport renting a house that was then called the Malcolm cottage. Now he owned it. Very little land was available for building, and like most latecomers, he had had to content himself with buying an existing house and spending almost an equal amount renovating it. All spring, he had had the original builder remodel and double the size of the Malcolm house, built in 1903. It now had fifteen rooms, all comfortable though not elegantly furnished, and nine baths, and as she could see, it sat on a bluff overlooking two and a half acres of lawn, the beach, and Nantucket Sound beyond. Before it was too late, he had hastily revised the plans to include, at a cost of $15,000, the first private talking picture theater in New England. Mr. Culcahy, the film booker at the Maine–New Hampshire Theater chain, had orders to bring out one fresh film suitable for young audiences every Saturday.

The rambling white frame house was not the largest summer residence, but its location was the prettiest. The lawn was both football field and baseball diamond. The beach served as an arena for swim meets, and the Sound was the scene for celebrated sailing races. Flaming youth was at a disadvantage in Hyannis, outnumbered by a conservative population addicted to fan-tan, the new craze for bridge, pingpong, and evenings spent playing records on a Victor arthophonic record player. The neighbors, said

Joe, were the Falveys, the Harringtons, the Prendergasts, "Pittsburgh steel money."

From the moment Gloria Swanson alighted from the Kennedy launch—petite, chic, and flawlessly coiffed despite the breeze—she set the resort on its ear. She was reported seen at the beach, but not bathing. She was spotted at the nearby Craigville Beach Club dining room. The *Barnstable Patriot* and the *Sippican Sentinel* told of her visit to the "clubhouse" of an informal girls' club that Kathleen shared with playmates. Gloria obliged the girls by scrawling her autograph on the wall. "We were thrilled, of course," one eyewitness would remember. "Her name stayed on that garage wall for years." Normally, the biggest excitement came after supper when the evening mail was available for pickup at the post office. Children, maids, chauffeurs, bicycles, and dogs converged on the narrow corner post office. Now, there was Gloria Swanson to talk about.

Gloria saw a new aspect of her lover. The house reverberated with Kick, Eunice, and the toddlers, and in the middle of it all was Joe, apparently aware of what his children were up to all the time. He never went anywhere without one child tagging along. The boys listened intently to his every word, as if they knew they had to take advantage of his presence because it might be cut short any moment. Young Joe and Jack wanted to be with their father, to talk with him. They knew he was leading a glamorous life.

They also knew that the next week their parents and Miss Swanson would be off to Europe. As a treat, or a compensation, Rose had arranged for her parents to visit. It would be Josie and John Fitzgerald's fortieth anniversary, and Joe Jr., Jack, and their sisters and brothers would attend a dinner at a rented summer house in West Hyannisport, to be followed by a private screening of a new movie at the Kennedy house.

Gloria got to meet Rosemary. In the big house, nurses and Rosemary's sisters looked after her, watched out that she didn't spill things on her clothes. Rosemary loved compliments, Eunice explained. If you told her she had the best teeth, the prettiest smile in the family, she would be happy for hours. Because of Rosemary's special situation, Kick enjoyed the status of eldest daughter. And, it seemed, she had all the gifts. Happy and carefree, bright and secure, she got along with everybody and fit into any situation. She was the favorite companion of Jack, the most self-absorbed of the children. It was not difficult to see that Young Joe, Jack, and Kick were their father's favorites.

Joe was gruff, dour, and difficult to please. He didn't want his love to overwhelm his children, he told Gloria one evening. High expectations were in everything the family did. They might be Catholic, but there was no

"boys play, girls pray" distinction. Friends of the girls were equally ferocious. The Kennedys organized everybody. Vistors had to play.

Gloria's presence altered little in Rose's routine. As Gloria would remember, "If she suspected me of having relations not quite proper with her
husband, or resented me for it, she never once gave me any indication of
it." When Joe and Rose took their guest out for dinner, it was as if Joe dared
his wife to say anything. The attraction that summer was the former barken-
tine *Fairhaven,* which had been brought to Hyannis's railroad wharf and
remodeled into an elegant new supper club named La Goleta. The evening
Joe took his wife and Gloria, Rose saw her husband introduce Miss Swanson as his most important business associate and Rose's friend. Every
morning without fail, Rose attended early mass at St. Francis Xavier on
South Street, returned to have breakfast with her oldest children, and
imposed her own version of the facts on her world.

Joe had planned an evening at the West Beach Club, but so many eager
summer acquaintances had pressed forward to meet the Kennedys' celebrity houseguest at La Goleta that the second outing was abandoned. A need
for a few hours of privacy with Gloria before she went back to New York
gave Joe the idea of taking her where absolutely nobody would see them—
sailing on the Sound.

No record was kept of the size, class, or category of the *Rose Elizabeth,* the first of what would be a series of Kennedy sailboats. Acquired in
1927, the *Rose E* had been christened by Young Joe and Jack after their
mother, and that first summer, when they had been only twelve and ten,
they had actually won a race in the boat. Better than that, they had rescued an exhausted man, clinging to the bottom of his overturned boat.
The *Boston Post,* perhaps prodded by Grandpa Honey Fitz, had referred
to the deed as a "daring rescue" and to the boys, apprentice sailors at
best, as "champions."

Joe was no great yachtsman. Young Joe and Jack knew that. It is
possible that, when Joe announced he was taking Miss Swanson for a cruise,
the boys offered themselves as deckhands. It is possible that Gloria joked
about how she couldn't swim and Joe bragged about his athletic prowess
as a swimmer. It is likely that Kennedy declined the boys' offer and that,
in any case, Young Joe had better plans for the afternoon than going sailing
with his father, Gloria Swanson, and his kid brother. Did Jack think it his
duty to transgress the paternal command because he knew how poor his
father's seamanship was and that Miss Swanson couldn't swim? Did he
imagine a sudden thunder squall roiling the sea and fantasize himself leaping from a hideaway in the hold, righting the boat, and in one searing glance

of gratitude from his father, earning equal status, if only for an afternoon, with his big brother? Did his mother tell him to sneak on board? We will never know, but when Joe pushed the *Rose Elizabeth* from the slip, Jack was below deck.

Alone, at last. Whether Gloria and Joe had in mind an afternoon of love in the cabin, a last tryst until they met again in Europe, or whether they merely longed for a couple of hours by themselves, a moment to redeem the distances that stood out so much more clearly here in the bosom of his family than in their lives in California, we can imagine them, in their bulky sweaters and practical deck shoes, throwing each other a wink and a smile of complicity as they heard the seagulls screech overhead and watched the breakwater recede in a diminishing perspective.

They had been lovers since little Jean had been born, passion to each other in the desert of his marriage, in the slipping certainties of hers. He possessed no gift for fidelity or tolerance, but had a natural capacity for emotions and sensuality. The year and a half had given her a sense of personal time. Beyond her "style," her independence and fierce privacy, he had discovered tenderness, playfulness, and a keen sense of the feminine self. She was, to him, personality through choice, moments of rebuff and moments of want, a game of renewal, the delicious shock of reexperience. To her, he was initiative, cupped hands protecting a match being lit close to her face and illuminating them both.

Did the boy mean to come up once they were off and, with a wrinkled grin, beg their forgiveness? Was he stopped by what he heard, words he didn't grasp but understood were not meant to be overheard? He was twelve years old and desperate to be seen as an equal of Young Joe. He was in love with his too absent father, off again in a few days; he was the number two son who lived in the shadow of his big brother. As the minutes passed, the adult talk above turned perhaps toward sentiments that confused him, perhaps toward a review of the woman's impression of his brothers and sisters, of *him,* interspersed with his father's caustic comments. Things were said that he apparently knew would provoke paternal anger if his father found out he was being spied upon, because Jack stayed in the hole.

Somewhere out on the Sound, Joe trimmed the sails and threw the anchor over the side. It was a gorgeous day and, within sight of the Cape Cod coastline, the *Rose Elizabeth* bobbed prettily at anchor, allowing the skipper to abandon the helm and, with his guest, to remove sweaters, look for snacks and refreshments, and stretch out on the warm deck.

Was it a prolonged silence above that drove Jack toward the stairs? Was it hunger, thirst, a need to pee, an unbearable urge to be discovered, to be forgiven? What he saw when he peeked up was too unexpected, too startling, too awful for anyone to live with. We will never know exactly what it was because the harbormaster's suppressed report only dealt with the consequence—boy overboard!

In the leap of a wounded animal, the kid was over the side and swimming away, out to sea. Away. Rather drown than have to live down the shame of what he had seen.

"Jack!"

On deck, Joe shouted, tore his own trousers and glasses off, and jumped after the boy. Nonswimmer Gloria stood at the railing, dumbfounded, her mind reeling.

Joe had always refused to acknowledge his second son's condition as being as serious as his medical record suggested, but swimming after the boy, he must have blessed his own powerful physique and Jack's frail health. It didn't take long for Joe to reach the boy, to grab him, turn him over, and press him against his breast, and with one arm begin backstroking back toward the boat. Jack had never been so humiliated, never in all his strange episodes of pain and lethargy so ready to die as now. Joe held the boy in the vise of his arm, felt the sniffles, the hurt in the skinny body, his own guilt. The boy had wanted to commit suicide.

He shouted up to Gloria to drop the rope ladder, trod water until she found it and got it over the side. Together they lifted the boy up, wrapped him in towels, talked, explained, shivered, exchanged glances. The boy sat slumped in the towels. His father cajoled, threatened, demanded explanation, and ended up holding him and the tiller at the same time. There was more adult talk on the way in, more explanations, postures. Jack must have mumbled his agreement to whatever his father told him to say when they got back.

Gloria rushed back to New York the next morning; Joe and Rose began preparing their own departure.

The incident was hushed up with Kennedy money and Kennedy influence. The story seeped out through the neighbors' children, one of whom would retell it in vivid detail by the time Jack had finally captured the mantle. The incident was retold while presidential helicopters used the front lawn, the beach was patrolled by the Secret Service, and Jack was out sailing with a lady who was not his wife. Specific points got magnified, distorted and, when challenged, fluffed back into bare facts.

What happened out on Nantucket Sound that August afternoon in 1929, however, would remain as an explanation of traumatic beginnings and randy proclivities, of the family's inner story.

Triangles

Eenie, Meenie, Minie, Mo
Stars, they face the mike with woe.
If they holler watch 'em go.
Eenie, Meenie, Minie, Mo.

—MOTHER GOOSE OF
HOLLYWOOD, 1929.

In dockside interviews in New York, Gloria told reporters she had two reasons to go to Europe: to attend the several premieres of her first talking picture, and to bring back her husband. "No more of these uncompanionable marriages for me," she said. "I want Hank to be with me, not separated from me."

If Joe, Rose, and Gloria had formed a triangle sufficiently odd to be noticed by Cape Cod summer residents—Joe got abusive on their evening out and ordered a man to stop staring and mind his own business—there was another triangle that gossip columnists had no qualms about mentioning. Henri de la Falaise, they reported, was not pining away in Paris by himself, but was to be found increasingly in the company of Pathé Pictures' rising star, Constance Bennett. Could it be that Swanson was heading to Europe not just to put an end to an uncompanionable marital arrangement but to snatch back her husband from the arms of a glamorous twenty-two-year-old who was not deep in debt, but rather a brand-new millionaire?

"Ask a question of any one of these three and their oh so opaque glances will tell you that gossip is just one of those dear, quaint things people will indulge in," wrote Ruth Waterbury in *Photoplay*. "Surely, say their glances, there's nothing to it if a titled husband stays some six thousand miles away form his stellar wife. Really, murmur their voices, it's ridiculous to notice that Miss Bennett and the Marquis got off the same train arriving at Berlin."

How stupid, gesture their hands, to think there's any meaning in Henri's and Connie's staying at the same German hotel. How innocent, shrug their shoulders, Hank's being a witness to Connie's new Pathé contract."

Twice married and twice divorced like Gloria, Constance Bennett was the eldest daughter of the distinguished stage actor Richard Bennett, whose Manhattan apartment Gloria had rented for the making of *Zaza* seven years ago. A girl with big liquid eyes, a gift for self-perfection (and an annulled marriage to a University of Virginia student behind her), she had been a climbing ingenue of nineteen when she had married the wealthy Philip Morgan Plant, given up her career, and with her husband, moved to Europe. Their idyll lasted four years.

With a divorce and a million-dollar settlement, Connie was back. She told reporters that between working all the time and "drifting" all the time, she preferred working. She had signed with Pathé and spent July and August filming *Rich People* with Edward Griffith. Her glazed smartness, everybody at Pathé believed, was sure to please feminine audiences who had a hard time identifying with the underworld or the "gutter" where Helen Twelvetrees was usually seduced and abandoned. If audience response showed women believed in her, Griffith predicted feminine martyrdom would be the essential ingredient in a developing pattern that might be called confession films.

Gloria and Virginia Bowker sailed aboard the *Olympic* in the company of Broadway musical director Busby Berkeley and his wife. A week later, Joe, Rose, and his sister Margaret followed aboard the *Ile de France*. Joe got off in Southampton to go to London to arrange the premiere details, while Rose and Margaret sailed on to Cherbourg. As they docked, Henri raced up the gangplank with bouquets of flowers.

Much too cultivated to let his wife suspect anything, Henri had booked rooms, arranged tours, and planned dinner parties and visits to the couture houses. Instinctively, both Gloria and Henri avoided being alone together, and Rose, her sister-in-law, and Virginia were with them on a trip to Deauville.

Gloria talked about her home, her children, and her career in that order when she was with Rose. Children were the safest subject, and Rose herself talked endlessly about hers. When it came to Jack, she told how the boy cried when she packed her bags until he realized his crying irritated her and made her withdraw from him.

When Gloria and Henri were alone, she almost told him everything. He seemed on the verge of saying what he really felt. She either didn't know the rumors about Connie Bennett or chose not to believe them. Sometimes his gestures seemed to ask for forgiveness for what she might read in his eyes. At one point, she sensed that if, then and there, he asked her to quit everything and live with him on the farm he now owned in Normandy, she would do it. He didn't ask.

Joe was between them—Joe's promises of enduring security that Henri wanted as much as she. Henri was Henri, attentive to her moods. He understood she had three hectic months behind her and was facing grueling premieres in four European cities before facing American opening audiences. He recalled the *Madame Sans Gêne* tour, the adulation she surely was glad to have survived. He understood her paralyzing dignity, her giddy, mounting nervousness about the new ordeal. They ate dinner at midnight and breakfast at 4 P.M. She decided to postpone any decision, not that she knew what to do. She didn't want to know about Connie or face the fact that what her husband was doing was nothing more than tit for tat.

From Deauville, they all rushed back to Paris, where Gloria endured days of fittings with Rose at Lucien Lelong's. It was Rose's first exposure to dazzling haute couture. "I was fascinated as the beautiful mannequins slinked and slithered the length of the ornate salon showing M. Lelong's creations," she would write. "And, of course, being with Gloria magnified the experience, for the *vendeuses* and management hovered around her, attentive to her every whim, and both the girls and the customers kept stealing glances at her. She was the great celebrity. I, by comparison, was a nobody, just the wife of the producer. But it was fun being with her and sharing in the excitement she generated." From there, it was on to London, flying from Le Bourget to Croydon aerodrome and motoring to Claridge's.

Gloria was a wreck before her British Broadcasting Corporation appearance. The London officials of UA and Pathé, Henri, and Joe had never seen anyone in such a state of dangling nerves as Gloria was after singing "Love, Your Magic Is Everywhere" over the BBC airwaves. Lavish bouquets, congratulatory telegrams, parties, and banquets increased her nervous euphoria before the opening night.

The British press treated the first Gloria Swanson talking picture as an event, and the September 9 premiere at the New Gallery Theater matched the *Madame Sans Gêne* galas in New York and Los Angeles four years earlier. Police had to form a flying wedge to clear a way through the crowd of thousands for the star and her entourage. Inside the theater, the audience applauded Gloria's arrival at her mezzanine seat at the start and gave her a standing ovation at the end. She was led to a microphone on the stage so she could speak to the audience that had just heard her recorded self for the first time. At a press party, journalists told her *The Trespasser* was certain to be her most successful movie.

An emergency popped up the next day when several newspapers questioned whether Gloria Swanson's singing voice was actually hers. She had spoken from the New Gallery stage, but she had not sung. Why? Joe got on the phone and arranged for her to sing a song in the middle of someone else's recital at Queens Hall several nights later.

A more dramatic crisis followed their arrival in Paris, when they checked into the Ritz Hotel. Whatever Gloria had chosen to believe, or not believe, about Henri and Connie Bennett, the truth was suddenly revealed in black and white and in a fashion as melodramatic as any Gloria had played in scores of marital romances. Whether the feminine "e" was missing or was fudged, Gloria opened an envelope addressed to the Marquis—not the Marquise—de la Falaise, and stumbled on a love letter from Bennett that made it abundantly clear she and Henri were having an affair.

Furious, Gloria told Henri and Joe and the rest of them that she was suing for divorce immediately and that Henri could not escort her or be seen with her at the opening, or at any of the other openings. Henri retreated to other quarters at the Ritz; Gloria's attitude was one of cold, regal rage.

When emotions cooled, Joe huddled with seasoned veterans of publicity and studio diplomacy. Both he and Gloria had a lot of money in *The Trespasser,* and the question was whether a sensational divorce would hype the box office or cause an offended public to stay away. Joe didn't think they should take any risks. He ordered Henri and Gloria to act as if they were man and wife, and to appear at the Paris gala as a devoted and glamorous couple. They did as they were told.

Joe was stunned. More in love with Gloria than ever, he became possessive and oversolicitous. Rose joined right in. Poor Gloria, constantly on public display, was married to a man who was charming and witty but knew little about business, finance, or the complexities of film production. Rose could understand why Gloria needed Joe to run her business.

Joe might have started the affair to show himself he had outgrown his Irish-Catholic narrowness, that he was a man of the world, making his own rules, getting what he wanted, and ready to indulge without guilt in bracing adultery. Gloria might have let him seduce her because she knew she needed his predatory magnetism more than her husband's tony diffidence to save the life-style to which she had become accustomed. There had been no doubt that she had needed him more than he need her when they tumbled onto her bed at the Poinciana Hotel.

Now Joe might be a movie millionaire and she a star hobbled in worse debt than when they met, but their roles were changing. Increasingly, he needed her. It was ironic, but he had little talent for the business in which he had chosen to make his fortune. He had made money by manipulating film companies, not by scoring at the box office. It stared them in the face.

Queen Kelly, his important film, in which he had not wanted Gloria to do anything but act, was a heap of intractable celluloid. *The Trespasser,* her off-the-cuff effort of a few months, was a hit.

In the back of his mind, Joe began formulating a scheme to sell off Pathé as he had done with FBO. In the meantime, there were decisions only he could make, judgments that called for a sense of what goes, of shifts in popular longings, truths, and fantasies. E.B. was a capable administrator, and the studio producers ranged from De Mille's former manager William Sistrom to Benjamin Glazer, but when it came to contracting or dismissing screen talent, they pushed Joe to call the shots. Before they left Paris, Joe asked Gloria to help him make decisions that demanded what she had, a hunch for talent, an instinct for what made for show-biz success.

"Who do you think I should keep?" he asked her, handing her a list of Pathé contract players.

Her heart wasn't in it, but looking over the names, she told him to hang on to, among others, Ann Harding and Carole Lombard. Tartly, she also suggested he put Connie Bennett in another picture right away.

Henri stayed in Paris. The Kennedys, Gloria, Virginia, and Joe's sister sailed back to America, this time on the same ocean liner. In her own way, Gloria loved Henri, and in her memoirs she would claim that her deepest wish was that they would somehow overcome their trials and tribulations. "I had to trust Joe would either salvage *Queen Kelly* or find some other way to make us all successful, because he had the clear ability to do so," she would write, "and I prayed that Henri would have the patience and love to wait until I could simplify my life again. For the moment, however, our three lives were tried in a complicated knot, and there was no way I could untie it. I, too, had to wait and hope."

Joe might have raged and cried and Gloria might have been ready to sacrifice her pride, her marriage, to get out from under *Queen Kelly,* but Stroheim was merely biding his time. Although vexed by his dismissal—it was, of course, not the first time he had been fired from a picture—he was hoping to return and complete the film as soon as his star was through with *The Trespasser.*

Stroheim was not ostracized by Hollywood. There was no collective gasp, no urge to run him out of town. *Queen Kelly* was one of 641 movies made in Hollywood in 1928. It was business as usual between Stroheim and United Artists. Joe Schenck bought *East of the Setting Sun,* a story and screenplay by Stroheim, and wanted Stroheim, Walter Pidgeon, George Fawcett, and Josephine Crowell to star in it. "Von" planned to direct it. In the meantime, James Cruze offered him the starring role in his first all-talker. Written by Ben Hecht, *The Great Gabbo* was the story of a self-destructive megalomaniac, a vaudeville ventriloquist whose ego drives him to ruin and madness.

Cruze was an admirer of Stroheim, and although neither Gloria's memoirs nor any of Stroheim's biographers would mention any move by Cruze to aid Stroheim in his efforts to finish *Queen Kelly*, it is entirely possible that the director of *Covered Wagon* tried to help. Cruze was married to Betty Compson, the star of RKO's *Street Girl*. Compson might have relayed a word to Le Baron or to E. B. Derr. However, if Joe still harbored hopes of bringing Von and Gloria together to finish *Queen Kelly*, Derr was by now totally against Stroheim. In any case, Stroheim accepted Cruze's offer, and the sound test was perfect. Stroheim's voice, which revealed that English was not his mother tongue, was good and—what was not the case with a lot of actors—it matched his physique.

Whatever Joe thought of Eddie Goulding's aversion to *Queen Kelly*, he agreed with Gloria and E.B. that the exciting Englishman was too good to let go. There were times when Eddie either had fifty ideas a minute or none for a whole month. He was either earning a fortune or he was flat broke, but the summer of 1929 was not one of his off-seasons. While his producer and star were opening *The Trespasser* in European capitals, he was making $3,000 a week in Culver City, shooting another winner. The story and the music of *The Grand Parade* were Eddie's. The stars—Helen Twelvetrees and Fred Scott—were Pathé's. And since Laura Crews had months to go on her personal contract with Gloria, she was told to divide her time between writing *Queen Kelly* dialogue for Richard Boleslavsky and teaching film elocution to Radio Pictures' youngest hopeful, Irene Dunne.

The Kennedys, Gloria, Virginia, and Margaret reached New York as the trade reviews came out. "Seeing *The Trespasser* with Gloria Swanson talking and singing with the picture itself, it's easy to understand the smash it is in London," *Variety* glowed. "For it's one of those cinch money pictures. A holdover." United Artists pressed for a monstrous opening at the Rialto November 1, and Gloria was asked to stay until the premiere and also to attend the Chicago premiere on her way back to California.

While Rose went home to Bronxville, Joe moved into the Waldorf-Astoria, and Gloria was put up at the Plaza Hotel. Joe spent much of his days at the uptown branch of Halle and Steigletz on Madison Avenue and Fifty-second Street, watching the stock market and sending most of his short orders outside the brokerage firm to friends in the offices of J. H. Oliphant and of Bache and Company. Gloria spent her days submitting to UA's publicity barrage. Her suite was a bedlam of journalistic clamor as newspeople were rushed in and out.

"Miss Swanson, in simple, unadorned black, gyrated through the symphony with arms outstretched, guiding her interviews, welcoming her guests, conducting the afternoon as a leader might his music," effused a nameless reporter with an affection for musical metaphors in the Sunday, September 29, edition of the *Times*. "The score was written in the air and harmony arose from an incongruous mixture of telephone bells, the synthetic, full notes of an electric phonograph and a series of discordant questions coming from a battery of baritone interviewers."

Did she like being interviewed?

"Well, we actresses feel that newspapermen always think us dull."

How about a musical?

"Of course I shall make one to be shown on an enlarged screen in color."

Engineers from a radio station were setting up for an evening program that would feature Gloria singing. The phonograph played "Love, Your Magic Spell Is Everywhere" as she took telephone questions from reporters in Buffalo and Los Angeles. Her hair, braided, Lorelei-fashion, around her head, came loose. "Oh dear, I won't last at this rate," she sighed sitting down next to one interviewer. Nobody, apparently, had the nerve to ask what happened to the husband she had said she was bringing home from Europe.

Laura Crews came to New York with the new dialogue for *Queen Kelly*. She sat in on other interviews and interrupted newsmen with, "Isn't she divine. Isn't she lovely. Wonderful voice." Gloria returned the compliment by explaining how Crews, her director, and she had talked endlessly about the story line, about the veracity of the situation, about whether a young woman would do this or that under such and such circumstances.

Schenck decided against putting Stroheim's *East of the Setting Sun* into production. *The Great Gabbo* came out, and it was such a hit that Warner Brothers asked Stroheim to star in an espionage melodrama, possibly to be followed by a writing-directing-acting contract. There was talk of a Gloria Swanson stage debut in a new play being written by veteran Eugene Walter, famous for his 1908 sensation, *The Easiest Way*. On the long-distance telephone, Gloria discussed a new picture with Goulding.

But Eddie was unhappy. He wanted to know about his theme-song royalties and a $10,000 bonus Joe Kennedy had promised him. Before leaving Hollywood, Joe had promised to make a deal with the music publisher for "Love, Your Magic Spell Is Everywhere." Nonchalantly, Eddie now admitted he had signed two contracts that someone at Pathé had shoved in front of him while they were all in Europe. One was for the release of *The Trespasser*, the other for the release of "Love."

"You see," he told Gloria, "I've discovered that in signing the second piece of paper I made the whole song, with all royalties, etcetera, over to you and Kennedy."

It was explained to Goulding that if he would remake *Queen Kelly* as an operetta, he would get his bonus, half the royalties, and $3,000 a week in salary until next March 1. He read the new *Queen Kelly* script, written by Laura Crews and Lawrence Eyre, ran the Boleslavsky rough-cut in the screening room once more and, by telephone, told Joe he wouldn't touch it. Next, he advised his boss that he had agreed to make pictures for Paramount, that *Devil's Holiday*—a well-worn plot about a gold-digging manicurist transformed by true love—would be his first.

Fred Thomson, De Mille, now Goulding. Hanging on to talent was not Joe's forte.

Black Tuesday

Birds do it, bees do it.
Even educated fleas do it.
Let's do it.

—COLE PORTER

Four million shares a day, five million, six million.

Stock tapes were installed aboard the *Leviathan* and *Ile de France* to inform passengers of the additional money they would be able to spend when they reached Europe. For the convenience of those staying at home, Western Union announced plans to spend four million dollars to increase the rate of stock tickers to 500 characters a minute. All the old markers by which the price of a promising common stock could be measured had long since passed. Stocks were being bought for a marginal down payment of as little as ten percent, with the bulk of the purchase financed by the broker's credit.

Housewives were more interested in the price of RCA stock, the speculative favorite, than the price of roast beef. Waitresses and men's room attendants in fashionable clubs, gardeners with an opportunity to loiter behind hedges on Long Island estates, taxi drivers, charwomen, anyone who could snoop, peep, or eavesdrop had a tip. Everybody had heard about the chauffeur who had made a killing on Wall Street and retired to a country estate. Now *his* chauffeur was doing it. Brokerage houses came up with a wondrous proliferation of holding companies and investment trusts that existed to hold stock in other companies, and these companies often existed to hold stock in yet other companies. Pyramiding, it was called.

There had been a couple of nasty scares in the spring after Republican Herbert Hoover became the thirty-first president. To cool the market, the Federal Reserve Board tightened its own lending to member banks so that they in turn would dampen speculative credit. Stock prices fell for several days when, on March 26, the interest rate for "call money," or speculative credit, jumped from 12 percent to 15 percent, then to 17 and finally to 20 percent. Another dizzying drop in prices followed, and the turnover in stocks reached 8,246,000 shares in one day. Demand for more margin, more credit, shot up. Once again the bull market seemed on its last legs.

But several New York banks decided to come to the rescue. Whatever they thought of the Federal Reserve's new policy, they saw a panic brewing, and anything was better than a panic. The next day Charles E. Mitchell, president of National City Bank, announced that his bank was prepared to lend twenty million dollars on call, of which five million dollars would be available at 15 percent, five more million at 16 percent, and so on up to 20 percent. A slap in the face of the Federal Reserve, Mitchell's action served to peg call money at 15 percent, and stocks not only ceased to slide, they cheerfully recovered. The lesson was plain: The public simply would not be shaken out of the market. Prices rose out of all proportion to the earnings of the companies that issued the stocks, indicating the market's willingness, in Max Winkler's phrase, to discount not only the future but the hereafter.

Time and again the economists and the forecasters had cried wolf, and the wolf had made his most fleeting visit. Time and again the Federal Reserve had expressed fear of inflation, and inflation had failed to bring a recession. The arguments against the doubters were so overwhelming that the majority of sober financial leaders were won over. Investment trusts were multiplying, and by the fabulous summer of 1929, branch offices of the big Wall Street houses blossomed in every city. Three hundred million shares were estimated to be carried on margin.

While the Kennedys, Gloria, and their entourage were premiering *The Trespasser* in London, the stock market reached a new peak. RCA's stock, which had been quoted a year earlier at 101, stood at 505 on September 3, but Joe was no longer holding his 75,000 Radio shares. As Mike Meehan had pushed the price up during the previous winter, Joe rode for a while, then sold out at 50, clearing a two-million-dollar profit. On October 3, when the RCA stock slumped from 114¼ to 82½, he repeated his old adage to a friend, "Only a fool holds out for the top dollar."

The following weeks seemed to prove him—and Bernard Baruch, who also got out—wrong. National City's Mitchell declared the correction had done "an immense amount of good by shaking down the market." On October 22, Mitchell had new reassuring words: "I know of nothing fundamentally wrong with the stock market or with the underlying business and credit structures." A week later, the giant edifice of prices, honeycombed with speculative credit, crumbled under its own weight. The roar of voices rising from the stock exchange floor became a roar of panic. Sixteen million shares were dumped on Tuesday, October 29, the "Black Tuesday" that would haunt a generation.

The president of Union Cigar, stunned when his company's stock plummeted from \$113 to \$4, fell or jumped to his death from the ledge of a New York hotel. Tales of suicide became standard fare in the mythology of the Crash. By mid-November, the RCA stock Joe had sold out at 50 stood at 28. Market-wise reporters struggled to describe the horror on the stock exchange floor. With a measure of irony, broker Fred Schwed was to write, "Like all life's rich emotional experiences, the full flavor of losing important money cannot be conveyed by literature."

Sitting on a fortune while the rest of Wall Street was in ruins made Joe realize it would be easier for less fortunate people to forgive his riches if he claimed it was a hunch that had saved him, not his ability to analyze a situation in the most clearheaded way, his sticking to Galen Stone's old advice of judging a stock by its earning power and dividends, and his refusal, as Rose would say, to be swept along on the tides of opinion. Shrewdly, he began telling of how, elbowing his way into a broker's office during the summer, he momentarily gave up and surrendered instead to a shoeshine boy in the lobby. "The boy who shined my shoes didn't know me," Joe would tell *Newsweek* the year John F. Kennedy became president. "He wasn't looking for a market tip, but he told me precisely what was going to happen to various stocks on the market that day. I listened silently as I looked down on him and when I left the place I thought: 'When a time comes that a shoeshine boy can tell you what's going to happen in the market and be entirely correct, there's something the matter with me or the market.' And I got out."

Joe mentioned no shoeshine boy on November 1, when he, Rose, and Gloria were driven to the Rialto for the *Trespasser* premiere. Gloria, "stunning in a golden wrap," as *Variety* described her, got nervous when she saw the entire block between Forty-second and Forty-third streets blocked by people. As the limousine edged toward the curb, the crowd surged forward. Gloria was afraid someone might break the car window and cut her face. It had happened once to a friend of hers, she told Rose.

Policemen opened the car door. Joe spotted Ted O'Leary and several of his employees, and ordered two of them to grab Gloria under the arms while he and the others began elbowing forward. Gloria felt her feet leave the ground. A thousand faces cheered and massed toward her. When she felt someone behind her step on her train she panicked. She screamed to O'Leary to pick her up. He yanked her so forcefully that she slipped. Arms held on to her on both sides, and she was carried into the lobby horizontally, headfirst, face down, like a battering ram. As they set her down, people on the mezzanine level applauded rapturously. Gloria would remember her entrance as being worthy of Mack Sennett. This time they stayed for the performance, and at the end of the feature Gloria took the rostrum with a few words of thanks. "An applause reception, lasting over a minute, said more than the new talking star possibly could," *Variety* reported. "She twiddled her thumbs like a dumbfounded child—but what a kid!"

The raving reviews ranged from the *New York Mirror*'s "Glorious Gloria as she never was before" to the *Tribune*'s "She is improved by the arrival of the microphone. Audiences will delight in it and bring it enormous popular success." They mirrored Hollywood optimism during the first weeks after Black Tuesday. The new profits for 1929 would be euphoric. The talkies were making big money for everybody. Warner led the pack with seventeen million dollars in profits; even Pathé would declare net earnings of $554,000.

Joe was profoundly shocked and uneasy about the future, even as he continued to make money during the market's dazed descent. Stories of his short-selling exploits put his profits "anywhere from a plausible one million dollars to a wildly improbable $15 million," Whalan would write in *The Founding Father.* When Joe wasn't at Pathé Pictures' Forty-fifth Street office, he was at the desk he maintained at Halle & Steigletz on Madison Avenue and Fifty-second Street, following the mood of near-total demoralization. Since his Old Colony Reality days, when he had taken over defaulted mortgages on Boston tenements, he had been an expert at buying at distress prices. On November 13, Wall Street skidded to its lowest level in 1929. In less than two months, thirty billion dollars' worth of securities had gone down the drain.

For amusement stocks, the box score of the havoc was mixed. Wall Streeters didn't much care for Fox Film's idea of selling stock to its theater patrons, while Warner's situation was called clouded as the company denied rumors of a merger with Paramount. RKO's stock snapped back, declined slowly, then moved forward again on bullish talk. Pathé's securities rallied from a Black Tuesday low of 5 to 10½ because it was associated with hopeful gossip about RKO. Market observers pointed out that popular-priced entertainment always prospered in times of stress and public calamity. Gloomy communities always sought cheer in theaters. The next few months would no doubt witness a public vogue for comedies.

There was to be no record of when Joe got the audacious idea of driving the worth of Pathé *down,* or of whether David Sarnoff was in on it from the beginning, but it is likely that the scheme to weaken Pathé in order to allow RCA to buy it at distress prices began taking form at the depth of the abyss. The week before Black Tuesday, Joe almost had a deal to merge with the Shuberts' legitimate theater organization. An agreement was reached with William Phillips, but the Shuberts' stock slumped further than Pathé's.

The Trespasser grossed $67,000 in its first week at the Rialto (with the top seats priced at two dollars), the best record on Broadway. The picture was hailed as one of the best talkies so far and would be noted, in the historic perspective, as an early example of the fluent use of sound.

The success should have impelled Gloria and Joe to fly into each other's arms in a delirious embrace. They weren't jinxed. There was no curse. On the Rialto screen, soon on a thousand screens, the credit crawl proclaimed *The Trespasser* to be: "A Joseph F. Kennedy production; United Artists release." What more could they want? With a deep bow to Eddie's slightly manic romanticism and insouciant talent, the film and its rewards were theirs.

When they were alone, however, Joe refused to take his own billing seriously. He had not considered the picture important enough to care when Gloria, Eddie, and Laura had started it; now his pride forbade him from taking credit. The picture might be a smash hit—the second week at the Rialto, it took in a hefty $48,700—but to him it was still a society tearjerker. After more than three years in the movies, he couldn't look beyond content to form, couldn't see the sparkle with which Eddie had visualized a test in three dimensions. He graded movies according to what they said, not *how* they said it, according to their social values, their lofty messages, their budgets. He wanted to present Gloria in something important, and by that he meant a film with a grand humanistic theme. He wanted to present her in something that was *his,* something that had originated with him.

In the meantime, there was *Queen Kelly,* the crippled child of his first initiative, the first blush of his infatuation for her. Boleslavsky was almost ready to start filming the new scenes, and while Gloria stopped over for the *Trespasser* premiere in Chicago, Joe rushed to Los Angeles to get everything ready for the start-up.

A few days before Gloria was ready to set out for Chicago and follow Joe west, Ted O'Leary called to say an important person wanted to see her. The horsemen had orders never to mention names on the phone, and Gloria assumed it was a routine interview. Usually, it meant meeting someone Joe wanted to impress or do business with.

In the late afternoon, O'Leary picked her up at the Plaza. On the way to another Manhattan hotel, she asked who she was going to see.

"His name is O'Connell." When O'Leary saw his answer annoyed her, he added, "A friend of the Kennedys."

They took the elevator to an elegant suite. A young man with a clerical collar opened the hotel door and thanked her for coming. Before she could turn to O'Leary for an explanation, Boston's William Cardinal O'Connell stepped forward and dismissed both the cleric and O'Leary.

Feeling tricked, she faced the smiling old man whose robes smelled of incense and whose eyes behind the glasses seemed not to be there. He thanked her for coming and asked her to sit down.

Somewhat stiffly, she sat on the edge of a chair and listened to the cardinal's compliments on her success. She didn't like his tone and figured that with the exception of *Sadie Thompson,* he had probably never heard of any of her films.

In a cool, pert voice, she thanked him, hoping he would get to the point.

He looked across at her for a moment, then said he would like to talk to her about her association with Joseph Kennedy.

She answered that her association with Mr. Kennedy was a business association, the details of which were handled by Mr. E. B. Derr, who held the powers of attorney from her and acted in her name.

With some bluntness, the cardinal said it was rather her personal association with Mr. Kennedy that he wished to speak of.

She got up and made a movement toward the door. O'Connell stepped in front of her. "You are not a Catholic, my child. Therefore, I fear that you do not grasp the gravity of Mr. Kennedy's predicament as regards his faith."

"That is true," she answered, "but Mr. Kennedy is a Catholic. Shouldn't you be talking to him?"

O'Connell was roused to his full ecclesiastic hauteur. "I am here to ask you to stop seeing Joseph Kennedy. Each time you see him, you become an occasion of sin for him!"

Her knowledge of Catholic transgressions was limited, and she felt herself at a disadvantage. Angrily, she answered that if Joe had told his eminence in confession that seeing her was an occasion of sin for him, "then you have no right to discuss it. And if he didn't then you have nothing to discuss."

In firm tones, O'Connell told her that Joe had spoken of his relationship with her with some of the highest representatives of the church. Since there was no possibility of dissolving his marriage under church law, Joe had sought official permission to live apart from his wife and maintain a second household with her. Furthermore, as a prominent Catholic layman, Joe was exposing himself to scandal every time he so much as appeared in public with her.

"Then tell him so," she answered, stunned by what the cardinal had just said.

O'Connell asked if she had no feelings for Joe's family. She replied that of course she did, just as she had for her own children. He said that as a Catholic there was no way Joseph Kennedy could be at peace with his faith and continue his relationship with her.

"Please consider that very carefully," he added.

"I shall. But I repeat, it's Kennedy you should be talking to."

She put on her gloves. The audience was over.

Downstairs, O'Leary was waiting for her. "Why didn't you warn me?" she asked.

"I knew if I did, you wouldn't come. I'm sorry. Orders."

"Joe's orders?"

Joe knew nothing about it, O'Leary answered. "All I can tell you is that it was Cardinal O'Connell who contacted me."

Who then? Rose? Honey Fitz? Joe's sister?

Kennedy biographers, especially Catholics, would tend to disbelieve that Gloria met the Cardinal. Doris Kearns Goodwin would claim the Boston Archdiocese archives contain no indication O'Connell was in New York at the time Gloria claimed the meeting took place, adding that the cardinal was a proud and imperious man who held himself aloof from the everyday problems of his parishioners. But the Kennedys and the Fitzgeralds were no ordinary parishioners—Joe would leave a substantial legacy to the archdiocese—and although in the hindsight of the family saga it would seem shocking that Joe might have contemplated leaving Rose and the children, at least one witness would remember his threatening to do so.

Geraldine Hammon, Rose's niece, would recall overhearing a heated argument that summer at John Fitzgerald's house. Honey Fitz had confronted his son-in-law and told him that unless he stopped the affair with his movie star, he would tell Rose. Undaunted, Joe threatened in turn that if Honey Fitz did tell his daughter, Joe would, goddammit, divorce Rose and marry Gloria Swanson.

Bravura or anger at having a man living in a glass house throw stones? A garbled version of the father-in-law's threat reached the ears of the ever-prying Hedda Hopper. The former Boston mayor, the columnist reported, ordered Joe Kennedy to wind up his film affairs and get out of Hollywood by a certain date, or certain secrets would burst into the open. Brave words from a man whose association with a cigarette girl had forced him out of politics. Of course, Fitzgerald hated to see Joe humiliate his favorite daughter. By this time, however, he was sucking up to Joe and accepting financial handouts from his daughter's husband, who now bridled at being introduced as the "mayor's son-in-law."

Gloria would remain convinced that Rose and her father were behind the cardinal's rebuke. She would never know whether Rose had asked her father to seek the prelate's help or whether Fitzgerald had acted on his own.

As for the substance of O'Connell's remonstrance over Joe's soliciting church permission to live apart from Rose, it was already a fact. Since 1926, Joe had spent more time away from his wife than with her. For the last year, they had not slept together.

Even if Joe had not made up his mind to leave his family, one can imagine him wanting to console Gloria, devastated over Henri, by giving their liaison a future. If she were to lose Crescent Drive in a foreclosure, he might indeed have suggested they find a house together. Also, women friends of Rose would report that she had put her foot down at about this time. Even a devoted Kennedy worshiper like Pearl S. Buck would comment that it was only in public that Rose maintained her proud silence. To save her marriage, it would not have been out of character for a devout Catholic woman of Rose's generation and upbringing to seek the intercession, through her father or on her own, of the archbishop and family friend who fifteen years earlier had pronounced Joe and her man and wife.

Aboard the 20th Century Limited to Chicago, Gloria had time to measure her regained star status (Clara Bow, Elinor Glyn's "it" discovery, was the latest casualty of the sound barrier) against the complications of her life. She tried never to talk about Henri to Joe, because Joe was the cause of her and Henri's estrangement, and because Henri was in Joe's employ. She sensed her marriage sliding, perhaps beyond repair, but she didn't know whether she had the will to do anything about it. Whatever her own guilt, to lose Henri to a younger woman hurt.

The Chicago premiere, which Virginia Bowker attended with Gloria, was no less triumphant than the New York opening. Before *The Trespasser* lit up the screen, the management showed *Elvira, Farina and the Meal Ticket,* the two-reeler Gloria had made with Gerda Holmes at Essanay in 1915. It brought the house down. Gloria and Virginia laughed until they cried and spent the rest of the evening reminiscing about the studio on Argyle Street, and Lightning Hopper directing them and Wallace Beery in Sweedie comedies. Catty talk of a sadistic streak and one sensational lawsuit, eventually dropped, for the alleged seduction of Mexican beauty Juanita Montayana, had kept Beery's name in the gossip columns. But he, too, had survived the arrival of sound, costarring with Florence Vidor in William Wellman's *Chinatown Nights,* and was now a $2,000-a-week Paramount star.

Gloria called Joe in Los Angeles. He told her to hurry back. Boleslavsky was getting ready to shoot the new *Queen Kelly* sequences. She said she was bringing Virginia with her.

"Have them write in one extra talking nun, will you?" she asked. "I'd like Virginia to be in the picture."

He said, "Fine!"

When Gloria got to Los Angeles, new sets had been built on the Pathé lot. Seena Owen and Walter Byron were back to shoot the added scenes with dialogue, and Joe had borrowed Vincent Youmans from RKO to write several songs for Gloria.

In her memoirs, Gloria would say she did not mention meeting Cardinal O'Connell to Joe but looked for some nuance in his behavior, some hint that he knew. There was none.

Three million Americans were out of work by December, and the evenings at Rodeo Drive turned gloomy during the last weeks before Joe's annual return east for Christmas and New Year's. When the horsemen joined Gloria and Joe, the conversations turned toward the multitude of economic ills that had passed unnoticed or been glossed over during the stock market euphoria. Derr would remember the general agreement around the table that the Coolidge-Hoover boom was dead, that prosperity was more than an economic condition, that the bull market had been the climax of a cycle in mass thinking and emotions. Joe usually offered the bleakest outlook. He admitted that he dreaded tomorrow's headlines. No matter what President Hoover and the soothsayers of high finance proclaimed, he believed Americans were facing new realities.

On December 9, Boleslavsky yelled "Action!" for the first time. Starting up *Queen Kelly* galvanized Gloria and Joe. The new ending would have Kitty Kelly succeed in her suicide attempt, with Prince Wolfram swearing eternal love at her grave. As soon as they saw the first rushes, however, the accumulated excitement evaporated. The new scenes had neither the mood nor the texture of Stroheim's work. The actors took differently to Boleslavsky's direction. Even the sets clashed.

Two days later, Joe sent the actors home and suspended production. There was no anger, no despair at this time, only resignation. No need to throw good money after bad, he said.

A Cadillac for a Playwright

*I was dealing less with a declining social order
than with a dissolving moment in time.*

—ELLEN GLASGOW

Henri wrote that it would be easier if he stayed in Paris this year. Coming after the terminal exhaustion of *Queen Kelly* and where that left her financially, Gloria didn't want to speculate on whether Henri's letter meant the final collapse of their marriage. To dispel the gloom and avoid too much solitary introspection, she asked Virginia Bowker to stay and help make Christmas festive for the children. There *were* things to be thankful for. Gloria wouldn't face a humiliating foreclosure on Crescent Drive; there would be no lurid headlines of SWANSON LOSES GOLDEN BATHTUB. *The Trespasser* was seeing to that.

Joe arrived in Bronxville as the older children came home from various boarding schools for the holidays. Returning from Canterbury School in New Milford, Connecticut, Jack had to admit he hadn't heard about the market slump. President Hoover was proclaiming that "conditions"—in the repeated phrase of the day—were "fundamentally sound," and Treasury Secretary Andrew Mellon predicted a revival in the New Year. Nonetheless, the decline in business activity was becoming alarming, and it was an especially bitter pill for the Republican Party, which had persuaded itself that prosperity was a Republican invention.

Gloria was baffled to see gifts arrive for little Gloria, Brother, and herself from the Kennedys. The same Rose Kennedy who had set her up with Cardinal O'Connell also sent Christmas gifts. Gloria could only respond in kind and a few days before Christmas called her New York secretary and told her to go shopping for the Kennedys. Eddie Goulding mentioned a miniature billiard table that was all the craze that season, and Gloria gave instructions to have one of them sent from little Gloria,

Brother, and their mother to the whole family. Unfortunately, miniature billiard tables were sold out everywhere in New York. Individual gifts were sent to Bronxville instead.

Joe called Gloria so often from New York that he ran up the largest private telephone bill in the country in 1929. His New Year's Eve call allowed them to exchange their one ardent wish for 1930: to come up with a success together. He was learning, he said, that to take her independence as a challenge would be the sure way for him to lose her. She told him that in a few days their romance would enter its third year.

To start the new year and the new decade on a high note, Joe returned to Hollywood in mid-January and assigned Josephine Lovett, a successful scenarist, to write a sparkling *Trespasser* follow-up. Tentatively entitled *Purple and Fine Linen,* the comedy was penciled into Pathé's production schedule (as a Gloria Productions film for United Artists release) for August. Vincent Youmans was signed to compose the songs, and his agent was sure he would deliver tunes as memorable as his "Tea for Two" and "No, No, Nanette." Constance Bennett was not on the lot. Nobody would tell Gloria where she was, only that she wasn't scheduled to start *In Deep* until May because Ed Griffith was directing Ann Harding in *Holiday* first.

Goulding's *The Grand Parade* was Pathé's first 1930 release, and in an April 11 letter to the stockholders, Joe Kennedy reported that the company had behind it "the most prosperous year in its history." Substantial progress had been made in reducing expenses and boosting the studio's efficiency. The chairman of the board's report was accompanied by a revised release schedule that listed eighteen features for the first half of 1930.

Wall Street corrected itself. Stocks had not lost their lure, and during the first three months of 1930, a little bull market gave a plausible imitation of the big stampede of the previous golden summer. Leading stocks actually regained more than half the ground they had lost. In April, however, the bubble burst. Commodity prices began to slide, industrial output slumped, and the stock market took a new series of painful tumbles.

As a distraction from the depressing headlines, Gloria had herself painted by Geza Kende, a portraitist in the manner of van Dongen. The artist came to the house every day, and the result was a wall-sized canvas showing Gloria stand in a floor-length mauve gown. Joe loved the painting, and Gloria had Kende do portraits of little Gloria and Brother. To fill the void of Henri's prolonged absence, she had Virginia stay on. More than spinster aunt to the children, more than solicitous presence for Gloria, Virginia was an eminently sane person coming to terms with the fact that she would never be an outstanding actress. Living at Crescent Drive for a while sidestepped the tedium of being single and impecunious.

One evening in early March while Gloria and Joe were having dinner at Rodeo Drive, he solemnly kissed her and presented her with a leather-bound copy of Josephine Lovett's screenplay.

At home later that night, Gloria and Virginia read the script together. They were aghast. The story of an American widow in Paris was just dreadful. Gloria spent a sleepless night. More than anything, Joe wanted to produce a successful picture and to know that his name on the screen credits was authentic. He had no imagination and, worse, he had no knack for picking people who did. The point of making movies was not to defeat expectations but to outdo them.

To make sure it wasn't just Virginia and she who were blind to Lovett's brilliance, she called Joe in the morning and asked if he'd mind her showing the script to Allan Dwan. Go right ahead, he said. She had the script sent over to Dwan's residence, and that evening jumped when her maid announced Mr. Dwan on the phone. His verdict confirmed her worst fears.

"It stinks," he said. He was a true friend, she realized, when he added that he'd have no qualms telling Joe Kennedy to his face what he thought of *Purple and Fine Linen*.

Gloria arranged a meeting at her dressing room at Pathé the next day. She watched the blood drain from Joe's face as the director told him the Lovett script was awful. "Don't buy it," Allan added.

"It's already bought," Joe snapped. "I commissioned it."

Gloria didn't want another *Queen Kelly* to creep up on them, and signaled Allan frantically. "Why don't you take it home," she said, "read it again, and see if you can't come up with some ideas to liven it up."

Dwan threw her an angry glance and said he couldn't promise anything. "Try," she implored.

When he called her that night, he said it was hopeless.

"Please, Allan," she pleaded. "Remember, we started with nothing a couple of times at Paramount."

"Nothing would be preferable."

"Look, it means everything to Joe Kennedy to succeed with an idea that started out as his. Even if nothing is left of the idea by the time the picture's finished, let's try to give him that. Try, Allan."

The intelligence that Dwan could bring to bear on idiot projects was considerable, but this story of a young woman with a five-million-dollar inheritance, determined to have everything except another husband, defeated him. Gloria managed to entice him to come to another meeting at her Pathé dressing room.

In a voice not much more cheerful than a raven's croak, she would remember, Allan advanced a couple of ideas. Soon he had Joe chuckling and congratulating him.

Turning to Gloria, Joe said, "You see? Just a few changes and it will be fine."

"You'll need a different title, too," Allan sighed.

"Don't you like the title?" Joe's voice was disappointed.

"I hate it."

Joe swallowed and asked what they should call it.

"Let's make it first and then name it," Alan said. "It'll be less confining that way."

"Oh, I think we should name it now," Joe said.

Gloria would remember her heart sinking. They were back to *The Swamp.*

"Well, I don't," Allan said.

Joe yielded and wanted to discuss money. Allan said it was too early for that. Gloria's leggy fragility and effortless elegance softened the two men's repartee as she sat between them, legs crossed and cigarette poised, eager, soothing, and making the point that it was her photographed profile, her big blue eyes, her screen beauty they were talking about. By the end of the meeting, Dwan had agreed to work up a few scenes with actors. If Joe liked them, they could maybe draw up a contract then.

While Allan and Gloria got some actors together and began improvising funny situations, Joe assigned a pair of scenarists from the Pathé writers' building to the project. James Gleason was a writer-actor who specialized in action stuff directed by Tay Garnett. He had written *Oh Yeah,* starring Robert Armstrong and himself, and was working on *Visiting Fireman* for Armstrong, Eddie Quillian, and himself. James Seymour was the scripter of Helen Twelvetrees's last two films, an author who knew how to write big women's scenes. Joe was sure the combined talents of the two Jims would work miracles on the Lovett material.

The scenes Allan, Gloria, and the actors put together had Joe and the horsemen laughing until they said their sides ached. "You've done wonders," Joe sighed. "Go ahead and start the picture. I'll have the studio give you anything you want. One thing, though, I'd feel much better if we had a title. Now."

Dwan eyed the Pathé boss suspiciously, but didn't remind Joe that they had agreed to worry about what to call it later.

To make Joe happy, Gloria organized an evening of title search. All kinds of new writing talent was coming to Hollywood. Playwrights who knew how to write dialogue were especially in demand, and in addition to Joe, Allan, and the two Jims, Gloria's dinner guests included Elmer Rice and Sidney Howard, a pair of Broadway transplants who, with Frances Marion, Robert Sherwood, S. N. Behrman, and Charles MacArthur, made up Sam Goldwyn's "eminent authors."

Gloria and Allan told their guests the story of the youthful widow, innocent in the ways of the world, who is left five million dollars when her sixty-year-old husband dies. Her lawyer informs her about her wealth in his Manhattan office, but New York isn't big enough for this widow who wants everything except another husband (nursing one sixty-year-old baby was enough), and off she goes to Paris. What a woman can do with five million and no man to cramp her style was the core of the comedy, and Gloria and Allan read bits of dialogue from scenes with the widow in dress and hat shops and on a masseuse workout table, and others involving three men who pop up—an attorney from the New York law office sent to France to spy on her, a Russian violinist, and, to work in those Vincent Youmans tunes, a singer-dancer.

"What a widow!" one of the assembled writers exclaimed, grinning.

Turning to Joe, Allan exclaimed, "There's your title."

"Find out who said that and give him a Cadillac," Joe roared. "I mean it."

The winner turned out to be Sidney Howard, a native California playwright who had won a Pulitzer Prize for *They Knew What They Wanted,* a social drama set in Napa Valley and later turned into the musical *The Most Happy Fella.*

While the two Jims punched up the script with Allan—and wrote in a part for Virginia Bowker to compensate for the *Queen Kelly* role she never got—Gloria received a long letter from Henri that never mentioned Joe but suggested a quiet divorce. What should not have happened had come to be, he wrote. "How it happened? Why it happened? Who started it? Let's pretend we don't know." He proposed they remain friends while they faced the decision that could only become more awkward the longer they delayed it.

> So, darling, let's face it. I ask you please to make it public that we are separated. Later on in a very quiet way a divorce should come but only when and the way you will want it. Please let me hear from you so I can give out the exact same statement. And we should both refuse to talk about any other issues.
>
> If you will be sweet enough to do that, darling; it will make things much easier for both of us, in case I would have to go to the States. It would avoid a lot of nasty and very unnecessary publicity.
>
> There is lots, lots more I could say to you, Gloria, and would like to say—but what's the use? If you have kept some of my old letters, you may read them. Their only fault is that they did not, could not,

express half of what I felt for you. That kind of feeling never dies, Gloria, but sometimes it is better to pretend to forget about it.

I am going to seal this letter without rereading it, because if I did I wouldn't send it—and I must.

Goodbye, darling—it's all, all over.

Henri

Writing her autobiography fifty years later, she would say she always loved the handsome marquis, indeed, that she loved him more that spring day in 1930 than at any time in their five-year marriage, that she loved him more than "I could ever love the man on whose account we were separating."

A few weeks later, when she arrived for dinner with Joe and Youmans at Rodeo Drive, she all but tripped over Constance Bennett smoking a cigarette in the hallway.

They exchanged frosty hellos.

Gloria couldn't resist asking one question: "Have you been in Paris recently?"

The younger woman eyed her coolly. "Yes, I have."

"Staying for dinner?"

"No."

Gloria went into the library, assuming Bennett's laconic answers meant she was either embarrassed to be seen there or disconcerted with Gloria's familiarity with the house. She heard the front door open and close. Joe joined her. What was Connie Bennett doing there?

"Going out with one of the boys," Joe grinned. With a hint of sauciness that intimated Connie had tried her charms on him first, he added, "She couldn't hook the boss, so she settled for one of the boys."

His grin must have made Gloria wonder, if only for a second, whether her lover was capable of cheating on her with her husband's mistress. Bennett was fast becoming Pathé's biggest attraction. *Rich People,* the film she had made with Edward Griffith, was Pathé's winter 1929–30 success, and now that she was back from France, Griffith was set to direct her. After that, she would star for Paul Stein, who was screen-testing Gilbert Roland and Joel McCrea for the role of her leading man in a comedy to be called *Adam and Eve.*

Bennett was very sophisticated and, having been married to Phil Plant, was used to a lot of money. McCrea, who was Paramount's handsome teenage star, would remember her taking him home to his parents' house in Brentwood in her huge Cadillac, driven by a black chauffeur also named

Bennett. "She couldn't lose. She was a hit." Joe signed her to a contract that kept her a Pathé property until 1934.

The company was barely making money. No picture was started in March, and only two in April, but for May and June eight pictures were announced, including two Bennett vehicles. The flurry of activity set off rumors of merger, and RKO bought considerable amounts of Pathé stock.

On May 8, when the Federal Reserve Board admitted the country was in "what appears to be a business recession"—*appears to be* was as far as the Hoover administration seemed willing to go—Joe resigned as Pathé's president. At the request of Elisha Walker and John Murdock, he retained the title of chairman of the board. The subsequent management shuffle, which saw E. B. Derr become the acting head of Pathé, was supposed to signal that Kennedy was done with the movie business.

Nobody believed this "retirement." Joe and his associates were said to have fifteen million dollars still invested in Pathé. If anything, he was rumored to be engineering a merger. The rumors were correct; he tried to sell the company to Howard Hughes.

Not yet twenty-five, the orphaned Texas millionaire was leaping into national prominence with his finally finished *Hell's Angels.* Hollywood Boulevard was blocked off and street cars rerouted for the opening of the picture (billed as the most expensive movie in history) at Grauman's Chinese Theater. Kennedy was not the only one wooing the young man in the leather flight jacket who always wore a fedora rakishly tilted across his forehead and had a succession of striking actresses on his arm. Joe Schenck was after him, too.

Gloria called Hughes "just a kid" who didn't move in the same circles as she. Joe was more receptive to the flamboyant young Texan. There was to be no conclusive evidence that the two ever met, because Schenck was faster than Kennedy. Though Hughes wanted a studio, Schenck discouraged him from going after Pathé. The UA boss knew the Kennedy finances through Gloria Productions Inc., and he told Hughes that whatever Joe wanted for Pathé it was too much. Hughes joined the UA fold.

On May 28, President Hoover predicted that business would be normal by fall. A thousand banks caved in, unemployment grew steadily, and by early summer over four million Americans were out of work. Joe railed against Washington, saying Hoover was blind to the necessity for a new social approach to economic problems. What the country needed was a man of action, someone who could give orders and worry about his authority to do so afterward.

Henri arrived in July as Gloria announced they were separating. "Henri and I have decided to continue living apart, as we have lived for the last year and a half," she told the Associated Press. "We have found it possible to maintain separate establishments and still be the best of friends." It took the press only two weeks to report that the Marquis de la Falaise was the constant companion of Constance Bennett.

Gloria and Milton Cohen made up. The lawyer who in January 1928 had wired her "WISH ALWAYS TO BE YOUR FRIEND BUT NEVER YOUR LAWYER" would handle her divorce proceedings against Henri.

Joe and Allan Dwan pulled out all the stops to make *What a Widow* a sophisticated romantic comedy. The final Gleason-Seymour script was a staccato romp. It gave the professional singer-dancer a cheating wife and invented six handsome young men who tailed the widow everywhere.

Smartly named Tamarind Brooks, the widow, is resolved to spend her fortune in the pursuit of life, liberty, and Paris fashions, so after crossing the Atlantic aboard the *Ile de France,* she goes on a buying spree at couturier houses. She has her first massage, her first taste of champagne, takes violin lessons from a Russian and singing lessons from a Spanish baritone, all the while falling for Gerry, the chaperon lawyer from the New York office who thinks she is falling for Victor, the permanently sloshed male half of the married song-and-dance combo of Victor and Valli. Meanwhile, Tam thinks Gerry is smitten by Valli. It gets complicated when Valli objects to the attention the Russian is paying to Tam and Tam resents what she believes is Valli's flirting with Gerry.

To satisfy the Hays Code and give the story a new spin, Gerry manages to get Victor and Valli a divorce, but when he hears Tam is going to Monte Carlo with Victor, he decides to leave for home in a hurry—booking a berth on the next available zeppelin. Tam and Victor don't get to go anywhere. In his apartment, the already soused Victor plies the widow with cocktails until she's drunk enough to be dragged to the bedroom. Victor staggers back into the living room to sleep off his stupor. In the morning, Tam takes the worst for granted and decides Victor will have to marry her. On the way to secure a marriage license, the suddenly sober Victor tells her nothing happened last night. She drops him in the middle of the street and dashes for the Dornier DO-X airplane to be in New York when Gerry's airship lands.

Transatlantic aviation was a chic idea whose time had almost come. The Dornier DO-X was set to attempt an Atlantic flight from Cadiz to New York via the Azores and Bermuda, and Joe persuaded the Fokker Aircraft Corporation not only to give him footage of the DO-X in flight over Lake Constance, Switzerland, but to lend Pathé Pictures a model of the interior to show Tam flying to New York. He also hired the pilot who hoped to fly the sixty-five-passenger plane to America to play himself walking down the mock-up aisle.

Dwan chose Owen Moore, Mary Pickford's first husband and a Paramount contract player, for the part of Gerry. Selecting Lew Cody to play Victor was type-casting. An urbane bon vivant who had been Gloria's second husband in *Don't Change Your Husband,* Cody was, off camera, an alcoholic who never went to bed sober. He was very much in the news, having buried Mabel Normand, his wife of four years, in February. Margaret Livingston, who had finished *Innocents of Paris* with Maurice Chevalier, got to play Valli. Allan sent out word he wanted six gorgeous young men to play the widow's lovesick swells. Sam Wood sent over Joel McCrea, but Gloria vetoed the handsome newcomer when she heard Connie Bennett was also considering him.

One stage over, Paul Stein and Connie Bennett were filming, not *Adam and Eve,* but the much-delayed *Sin Takes a Holiday.* Started the same day as *What a Widow,* the Robert Milton–Dorothy Cairns screen story was terribly close to the Lovett-Gleason-Seymour effort. Set in sophisticated Manhattan with sojourns in Paris, Monte Carlo, and St. Moritz, *Sin* had Bennett as a divorce lawyer's Cinderella secretary. Played by Kenneth MacKenna, the lawyer finds himself accused of adultery by the husband of one of his clients and decides to make his secretary his wife in name only so as to be safe from the intentions of the would-be divorcee. Put under contract and given $5,000 for the year the sham marriage is supposed to last, Sylvia, the secretary, is miffed when her in-name-only husband evinces no interest in her. She goes to Paris, where couturiers transform her into a princess and one of the lawyer's philandering friends, played by Basil Rathbone, falls for her, and knowing the reasons for her marriage, wants her to marry him as soon as the year is up. When Sylvia returns to New York, her stunning appearance in the newest fashions so astonishes her husband that he drops his pursuit of a divorcée and falls in love with his wife.

The woes of the larger world intruded on the film industry and on Gloria and Joe's private lives. Although Hollywood's big crisis wasn't to come until 1932, Joe was convinced that the crash had written finis to a chapter of American history. The one thousand bank failures concerned him as much as the ever rising unemployment because they showed the banker in him that the recession would be prolonged and painful. Falling factory output and commodity prices sent stocks careening down once more until the panic levels of the previous November looked positively bullish by comparison. The capitalism that had made him rich was dragging millions of families down toward hunger and want. Resentment was building against the unfairness of the system, against the rich. Despite the obvious distaste of the country for socialism, radicals on soap boxes demanded punishment for the "fat cats."

Joe never told Gloria how rich he was. He never told his wife, either. In fact, estimates of his profits from the crash alone, the result of short-selling stocks like Anaconda and Paramount, ranged as high as fifteen million dollars. His net worth at the time was at least $100 million in 1930 dollars. Still, he managed to escape the congressional furor that saw his Wall Street pals M. J. "Mike" Meehan, Bernard (Sell 'em) Smith, and Harry Sinclair stutter and suffer convenient lapses of memory. National City's Charles Mitchell was fired, and Richard Whitney, president of the New York Stock Exchange, was convicted of embezzlement.

What scared Joe were the strident calls for wholesale political and social reorganization. There were evenings when he was especially gloomy. He would gladly give up half his wealth, he said, if he could be sure of keeping, under law and order, the other half. To cheer him up, Gloria repeated the setside joke of the day or the newest wrinkle on how Sidney Howard had come by his Cadillac. The anecdote was all over Hollywood, aided and abetted by Lance Heath. The story was a publicist's dream for establishing a movie title.

While a second unit filmed an actual departure of the *Ile de France* from New York, Dwan's principal photography group in Culver City progressed at a painful pace. Putting farce on film had never been easy, and there were days when Gloria thought herself back in Chicago shooting Sweedie two-reelers. There were also days when she and Allan thought they were back in Astoria shooting *Manhandled.* "The hardest of the arts happens to be comedy, *the* essence of acting," she would remember. "Anybody can be a character actress, that's easy. But to play a perfectly insane woman in a drawing room is the hardest. What are you doing? You have no props to use, you're so natural that it doesn't mean anything. . . .

"Polishing silly, spontaneous madness is difficult and Allan had a number of handicaps to cope with. Owen Moore was not well at the time, and Lew Cody could not remember his lines, so we had to reshoot many of the scenes, and each time we did, we lost some of the original bounce."

Youmans composed three tunes, with J. Russel Roberts and George Waggner adding the lyrics: "You're the One," "Love Is Like a Song," and "Say 'Oui' Cherie."

The camera was an engine for imposing types, and while Gloria, Allan, and the other actors tried to make the antics funny, she was keenly aware of the changing *Zeitgeist.* On the evidence of *The Trespasser,* her screen personality still stimulated and excited interest even as new faces like Joan Crawford, Marlene Dietrich, Norma Shearer, Jean Harlow, and Carol

Lombard were imposing themselves. Women were no longer copying the flat-chested, spindle-legged, carefree flapper. Not only were the skirt lengths coming down with the stock prices, a measure of formality was returning. *Vogue* was writing about "the new economy," advertising Vogue Patterns on its cover, and reporting that Gloria Swanson was among the readers who sent in for them.

Every star contributed some new look or fashion—Garbo her hollow eye sockets and plucked eyebrows, Dietrich her sucked-in cheeks, Crawford her bow-tie mouth. Morals were being made over, too, and the code of behavior was in a flux. With soup lines stretching around city blocks, entertainment concerned solely with whether two people went to bed or not seemed frivolous if not downright offensive. Joe's Harvard classmate Robert Benchley expressed a growing feeling when he wrote in his column in the *New Yorker* that he was ready to announce that sex, as a theatrical property, was as tiresome as the Old Mortgage. "I am sick of rebellious youth and I am sick of Victorian parents, and I don't care if all the little girls get ruined or want to get ruined or keep from getting ruined. All I ask is: Don't write plays about it and ask me to sit through them."

If Gloria had anything to be grateful for it was *The Trespasser.* Figures from United Artists indicated her melodrama about Marion, the plucky Chicago secretary, would more than pay for the *Queen Kelly* losses. Better still, the picture allowed her to enter the sound era with her own production company, giving her more control over her fate than any star.

What the public wanted, of course, were brash musicals to cheer them up or gangster flicks to thrill them. *Rio Rita* grossed $2.5 million, and William Le Baron continued the song-and-dance routine at RKO while spending $1.5 million filming Edna Ferber's 1929 best-seller, *Cimarron.* Even De Mille was doing a musical as his second of three pictures for MGM. Yet another Jeanie Macpherson story about a dull wife trying to recapture her husband by disguising herself as a sultry French vamp, *Madame Satan* featured dance numbers aboard a zeppelin and, for a spectacular ending, an airship disaster from which the entire cast parachuted to safety.

The driving force behind the gangster genre at Warner Brothers, which as a result of the takeover of First National owned nearly a quarter of the country's screens, was former FBO gag writer Darryl Zanuck. Second in command to Jack Warner, the wiry Zanuck made sure directors, writers, and actors all contributed to the violence, tension, big-city cynicism, and knock-out action that audiences loved. *Little Caesar,* filmed under the First National banner, was the first and most famous of the gangster flicks. It was directed by Mervyn Le Roy, a thirty-year-old cousin of Jesse Lasky, and starred Edward G. Robinson in a daring caricature of Al Capone. With his squat build, frog mouth, and heckling voice, Robinson was the kind of actor no studio would have put in a starring role a year earlier.

Despite Dwan's talent and hard work, there were days when Gloria had the sinking feeling there might be no audience for *What a Widow.* As an actress whose career had been intimately linked to the intoxicating allure of fashion, she was much more conscious than Joe of the relentless pressure to invent something new.

To give the film an extra boost, Joe saw to it that it was given snappy opening credits. Gloria suspected he wanted to make sure nobody missed the "Joseph P. Kennedy Presents" title. Dudley Murphy, Gloria's less than outstanding cameraman on *The Loves of Sunya,* filmed the elaborate animated titles, while Pathé's musical director, Josiah Zuro, scored the picture. Although finished first, *Sin Takes a Holiday* was set for release in mid-November, a month after *What a Widow.* "The Swanson pictures always had precedence over Pathé's interests, even on Pathé's own ground," wrote accountant William Brooks to RKO's president Hiram S. Brown in late September. Joe was less than two months away from making his deal with David Sarnoff, way over Brown's head.

After dinner one evening, Joe told Gloria he had a surprise to show her. He led her into the library and, pointing to the wall, said, "What do you think?"

Facing them on the wall was a Geza Kende painting, a portrait he had commissioned of himself.

"I've been posing for weeks, secretly," he smiled, sitting down on a couch across from the canvas.

Gloria didn't know what to say. The oil painting was very much the portrait of the chairman of the board, severe and elegant. The eyes staring out of the canvas gave the impression of great expectations. She smiled and watched Joe watch his idealized self. He must have told the artist he wanted to look like this.

She felt dwarfed, standing in the library of this rented house and watching Joe watch himself looking down on them. It was three years ago that they had met at the Savoy Plaza. The picture spoke very directly and it occurred to her that his dream of power extended far beyond being the president of some huge conglomerate. As if he managed to read her thoughts, he said he was thinking of opening an office in Washington. Maybe he would build or buy a house there, at the center of the country's real power.

A Shabby Ending

*In art there are no generations, only individuals;
all times have been modern.*

—NADIA BOULANGER

United Artists set the *What a Widow* opening for October 9, 1930, at New York's Rialto Theater. Joe Schenck wanted Gloria to attend. Before she left California, Lance Heath set up interviews with New York reporters via long-distance telephone. No, despite offers from Florenz Ziegfeld, A. H. Woods, Lee Shubert, and other Broadway producers, she was not following Colleen Moore, Vilma Banky, and Lillian Gish to the stage. Nor was she going on a singing tour. She had an outstanding invitation to do a nation-wide singing tour for the National Broadcasting Corporation but that, too, had to wait until after her next picture. As yet untitled, it would be a serious story like *The Trespasser,* nothing like the romantic comedy *What a Widow.*

Joe didn't try to "out-argue" her about not going with her to New York this time. Business would keep him in Culver City, and more important, he was not well. He was in agony with new flare-ups of his ulcers, and he was visibly losing weight. A doctor suspected neuritis and dyspepsia, and told him to cut back on his workload and his smoking.

The first trade review of *What a Widow* sounded promising. *Variety* predicted men would like the second Swanson talkie and women would love it. "Whether it is the big money getter *The Trespasser* was depends upon the theatermen," the trade paper said. "Dwan has given an unusually fast tempo to the entire production. He weaves everything in and out. Miss Swanson, as the joy-seeking widow, has plenty of scope for airy playing. Often she is very cute in her panto and sallies, greatly aided of course by the apt dialog, while her naturalness in the role is something to wonder at."

The competition was decidedly mixed on Broadway that first week of October. D. W. Griffith had rediscovered his epic inspiration in *Lincoln,* with Walter Huston in the title role. John Barrymore could be seen in Lloyd Bacon's adaptation of *Moby Dick* with an incredible happy ending in which Ahab slays the big white whale and returns to New Bedford for a fadeout clinch with his beloved Joan Bennett. A second Lloyd Bacon film, *The Office Wife,* with Joan Blondell, was playing at the Winter Garden. Edward Everett Horton could be seen in *Once a Gentlemen* at the Beacon, and George Arliss was in *Outward Bound* at the Hollywood. The critics had called De Mille's *Madame Satan,* released two days before *What a Widow,* a slow, dull, and unfunny flop, but declared Frank Borzage's adaptation of Ferenc Molnar's *Liliom* a wonderful success.

Despite the encouraging *Variety* notice, *What a Widow* failed to impress the regular critics. "A farce that sinks into slapstick," complained *The New York Times.* "Frequently the attempts to be funny are rather pathetic, but here and there the actions of the players possess a spirit of mirth." The box-office returns matched the tepid reviews, and if Gloria had steeled herself, the disappointment sent the ulcer-ridden Joe into another emotional tailspin.

The picture might never have been at the level of his ambitions, but it was he who had commissioned the Josephine Lovett script. It was he who had brushed aside the misgivings of star and director, he who had insisted they go forward, he who had ordered fancy screen titles so no one would miss the "Joseph P. Kennedy Presents" credit. Now the film formed, with *Queen Kelly,* the bookends to her *Trespasser.* Worse, *Queen Kelly* and *What a Widow* stood as flops between *Sadie Thompson* and *The Trespasser* because everybody in Hollywood said Gloria was sure to receive an Oscar nomination for her Marion, the Chicago secretary, while Eddie Goulding got one for directing.

Would Joe *ever* get it right?

Not that Gloria was able to escape the finer ironies of their tangled lives. A month after Milton Cohen announced she was beginning divorce proceedings against Henri de la Falaise, and three weeks after the Academy of Motion Picture Arts and Sciences gave Norma Shearer the best actress award for *The Divorcee* and Lewis Milestone the best director Oscar for *All Quiet on the Western Front, Sin Takes a Holiday* opened to smash reviews and solid box office. Constance Bennett "gives an easy and intelligent performance, Basil Rathbone is capital and Kenneth MacKenna does well," *The New York Times* wrote.

If Milton Cohen had insinuated himself into Gloria's life again, so had Irving Wakoff, the accountant to the stars. Pat Sullivan wrote and signed the Gloria Productions checks, including the $7,000 salary that was transferred to her personal account every week. Wakoff handled her personal funds and her taxes.

Shortly after her return from New York, Wakoff called and asked why Sidney Howard's Cadillac had been charged to her personal account. "It should be charged to the budget of the picture, shouldn't it?" he asked.

"Of course it should," she answered. "I'll ask."

On December 6, the news exploded in the trade press that Pathé was being sold to RKO for five million dollars. "RKO is assuming the leases on the Pathé exchanges throughout the country, Pathé News, the laboratory at Jersey City, the building at 35 West 45th Street, the studio in Culver City, and all product, features and short subjects, beginning with *Sin Takes a Holiday,*" the *Motion Picture News* announced in its cover story. "Radio also acquires the services of Constance Bennett, Ann Harding and Helen Twelvetrees as the three biggest Pathé drawing cards, and contracts with Bill Boyd and Eddie Quinlan. Directors involved are Tay Garnett, Paul Stein, Edward H. Griffith, Russell Mack, Joseph Santley and Howard Higgins." Not part of the sale was the forty-nine-percent stake Pathé had in the DuPont-Pathé Company, a raw stock and laboratory firm estimated to be worth five million dollars.

Stockholders were furious and the film industry was stunned. Joe's glib explanation to the press that Pathé was "sufficiently established to continue without my executive aid" satisfied no one. Pathé was losing in the merger, Hollywood executives told the *Motion Picture News,* because of its plans and recently completed productions that "will make the company worth a great deal more next year." Pending the liquidation, Joe kept his own men in command, Derr as president, O'Leary as sales chief, and Pat Scollard handling the New York end of the company's affairs.

Joe knew Pathé would end 1930 with a $2.6 million loss. In the meantime, he was coming out with a substantial amount of cash. Stockholders charged mismanagement, deceit, fraud, steamroller tactics, and illegally obtained proxies. Joe answered that management had tried to sell Pathé to Paramount, United Artists, and Howard Hughes but that all had declined. Dissident stockholders claimed the company was worth twenty-five million dollars, not five million dollars.

RKO stockholders were also unhappy. The only property RKO obtained that it didn't already have was a newsreel service. And to get that, its management "practically emptied the RKO treasury," as New York congressmen William I. Sirovich would charge.

Joe was suffering a new acute attack of inflamed ulcers and felt miserable. In a letter to John Murdock on December 9, he said he believed all this was taking five years off his life. "I am going to stay around until the stockholders' meeting in January and if there is anything left of me then, I am going to go away for three or four months."

The dinners on Rodeo Drive turned lugubrious. Derr, O'Leary, Sullivan, and Moore were there almost every night, but Gloria no longer played Snow White to the their Seven Dwarfs. Though Eddie remained the boss's indispensable shadow, Derr and Sullivan were outgrowing their subservient roles. Joe never gave any of the executives who helped make him a fortune a piece of the action, though he paid them decent salaries. E.B. and Pat Sullivan, the two money wizards, resented it. If Joe was pulling out of the movie game, it was clear they had no intention of following him.

One evening when they were all there, one of the horsemen happened to mention Sidney Howard. That reminded Gloria of her accountant's query.

"By the way, Irving Wakoff tells me I paid for Sidney Howard's Cadillac out of my personal account," she said, fixing Joe with a look. "How come? You gave Sidney the car, I didn't. He thanked you for it, not me. So I think it's only fair that you pay for it."

He stared back at her across the table, hurt and angry.

In her memoirs, she would say she was joking, that she assumed the whole thing was a bookkeeping error. But Joe became agitated and choked on his food. His eyes bulged. "He looked at me the way he had looked the day I suggested he take his daughter Rosemary to Dr. Bieler. When he regained composure, he stood up and without a word left the room."

They continued the dinner in awkward silence. Gloria felt tricked, cheated of an answer. When Joe didn't return after half an hour, Eddie suggested he drive her home. It was only a three-block drive, but long enough for Gloria to ask what was the matter with Joe. Eddie was nervous and ducked her question.

It was too silly.

The next day Gloria expected to hear Joe's cheery Boston voice on the phone, acknowledging he had been childish, apologizing, and perhaps explaining the pressure he was under. She was quite ready to forgive because she cared deeply for him. "How could I not care for the man for whom I had given up a marriage and a title," she would ask in retrospect, "the man I still trusted to effect important changes in the motion picture business, the man who always managed to intrigue me, even when we disagreed, with his courage and energy, the scope of his vision and daring."

She spent the day at home, staring unseeingly at familiar landscapes. In hindsight, it was clear that her return from France and *Madame Sans Gêne* had been her peak. Paramount had put up the biggest sign Times Square had ever seen and laid on a transcontinental train and a brass band to greet her in Los Angeles, while all of UA—Mary and Doug, Chaplin and

Schenck—stood waiting at the station. And all the familiar faces had surrounded her at the premiere at Sid Grauman's theater. She couldn't remember whether it had been Henri or Addie who had asked why she was so sad after the premiere. "This should be the happiest night of your life."

She had answered that all this was happening not because she was a good actress, but because she was Cinderella who had married the prince, Lazarus risen from the grave, the prodigal daughter returned. Where could she possibly go from here? she had wondered.

Life had become difficult, and interesting. She had no regrets. The incident of the night before ran through her mind again. How could she have known Joe would take such offense? Her brisk tongue only matched his salty outspokenness. That was the way they were—looking for openings, putting the onus on the other, sending each other sarcastic telegrams. She had always joked about difficult predicaments and provocative situations.

He didn't call. Not even Eddie called with some lame excuse.

It was not long before Christmas and their annual separation. As the days passed without a word from Joe, she realized her sally had stung deep in his psyche. He didn't like to have his judgment questioned. Still, she couldn't imagine he would leave for the east without seeing her.

But he did.

She only *heard* he had left. A few days later, the power of attorney she had signed early in their relationship was returned by mail.

Ducking out was crude. Joe was leaving her in the lurch. He knew it, and he felt like a heel. His excuse to himself was his illness.

He left Los Angeles bereft beyond his calculations, trapped in his own bad faith and exhaustion. Were dramatic scenes any better than sneaking out of town? Weren't all good-byes insincere, unfair? Sentiments and money matters were all mixed up in this retreat, Gloria riding him with her sarcasm and her digs, Pathé a stick of dynamite. His mood matched the wintry landscape and the prostrate country through which the train was crossing; it reflected the burning eyes of men staring back from freight cars on sidings, and the Hoovervilles of tarpaper shacks at the edges of cities where the homeless warmed themselves with coal tossed to them by sympathetic locomotive brakemen. The number of unemployed had reached six million.

He was thirty pounds lighter, smoking heavily, and in such pain from his ulcers that he checked himself into Boston's Lahey Clinic convinced that, like his mother, he had stomach cancer. He told Rose to stay with the children in Bronxville and celebrate Christmas with them. He wanted no visitors.

Midlife crisis, time for sobering introspection and new resolutions? In his hospital bed on New Year's Eve, he thought of all the things he had wanted too soon, emotional and financial quagmires, the things he had achieved, the things that were important. It had all happened. The hospital bed meant being detached from reality. It meant waiting for the verdict of incurable disease.

The stomach disorder was diagnosed as being noncancerous. It gave him a new lease on life, and the first things he could think of were to see his family and to get to that goddamn stockholders' meeting in New York. The cancer scare had reduced ideas to their essentials. At forty-two, maybe all anyone had left was one future.

Afterimages

The January 8, 1931, Pathé stockholders' meeting was stormy. From the floor, charges were hurled thick and fast that the company's sickly finances were the result of a management conspiracy to weaken Pathé in order to sell it off at a bargain price.

Joe stood up, pale and irritable, and told the meeting that RKO's offer was about six hundred thousand dollars more than the book value of Pathé's assets. Hoots of derision greeted his remarks.

"Management hopes to retire six million dollars in bonds and probably the preferred stock," he continued. "Even if par is paid for the preferred, the company still has its forty-nine-percent interest in Du Pont-Pathé."

"We want our dividends," someone shouted.

Joe pressed on. "RKO intends to continue Pathé for some time to come. RKO assumes leases for ten years on the Pathé home office building at an annual rental of one hundred and five thousand dollars. It also assumes leases on Pathé exchanges. And all Pathé personnel except the company officers are being retained."

The opposition from the floor centered around Joseph Conn, a theater owner from Providence, and his lawyer, Joseph B. Kaufman. Somebody whispered to Joe that Conn and Kaufman's allies numbered 115 and that their "unfriendly" interests represented more than 20,000 shares of common, preferred, and Class A stock.

"The deal will not lessen but, on the contrary, will increase competition in the industry," Joe said. "It's my opinion that RKO will make more pictures in the future than the two companies did separately in the past."

"We're gonna sue you," a voice around Conn and Kaufman shouted.

"Of the twenty pictures on the current schedule," Joe continued, "eleven have been released and four are in the works. The company has no further production plans after completion of the four films now being made with RKO financing, but I anticipate that RKO will produce the remaining five films on the schedule."

Joe knew he was lying. RKO wanted to abandon a good part of Pathé's lineup. Joe and E.B. had had an angry confrontation over this. After this meeting Joe was going to fire Derr.

Conn stood up and offered to buy Pathé for six million dollars. He needed time to put together his financing and asked that the meeting be adjourned to consider his proposal.

Joe gaveled. Somebody offered a motion to adjourn. The chair refused. Joe began reading the company losses, $386,000 in the last quarter of 1930 alone.

Shouts and boos greeted his figures.

The meeting ended with a defeat for the dissidents. Holders of two-thirds of the common and preferred stock voiced approval of Kennedy's deal. Conn said he would try to make the Department of Justice block the merger. After the meeting, the dissidents formed a committee of seven to raise funds for a lawsuit. An injunction would be filed in three days, they told the press. To finance their court battle they assessed themselves twenty-five cents a share.

At the end of January, Lee Marcus, an RKO vice president, became the interim president of the combined RKO-Pathé. Constance Bennett was quickly put to work in *The Easiest Way,* directed by Gloria's old admirer Jack Conway. Derr and Sullivan found themselves looking for work.

Joe felt they had betrayed him and in an odd display of vengefulness he warned Louis B. Mayer not to hire them. The Kennedy warning practically guaranteed their joining MGM, because Mayer thoroughly disliked Joe. Before the two able executives were hired, they had to listen to Mayer explain how he had turned down Kennedy's invitation to speak at that Harvard symposium.

The RKO-Pathé merger rankled equally with RKO stockholders, who saw not only their company's treasury emptied in order to buy duplicate plants and services but new debt loaded on to finance the takeover. Because RCA owned twenty-two percent of RKO, its cooperation was necessary. A refinancing plan favorable to RCA was accepted after RKO management made it clear that the alternative was for RKO to begin bankruptcy proceedings.

RCA emerged controlling sixty percent of the combined RKO-Pathé. David Sarnoff, Elisha Walker, Kennedy, and Lehman Brothers all got richer while the small investors felt swindled. Sarnoff had recently been elevated to the presidency of RCA. Excavation was beginning for Radio City, a midtown Manhattan project that would place RCA in Rockefeller Center and give Radio-Keith-Orpheum an "international music hall" flagship house with the biggest-ever screen and the last word in RCA Photophone sound reproduction.

On January 26, 1931, *Cimarron* premiered at the Globe Theater, reaping praise and going on to collect two Academy Awards. But the two years of RKO's "titanic" efforts had yielded a total loss of half a million dollars. Sarnoff was not pleased, and Le Baron was fired. His replacement was twenty-nine-year-old David Selznick.

Production was consolidated at the Gower Street lot and the Culver City studio was closed. Russell Birdwell, Selznick's small, gimlet-eyed publicity chief, who would dream up the *King Kong* campaign and the search for a Scarlett O'Hara stunt for *Gone with the Wind,* moved into the Gloria Swanson bungalow. In the ceiling of the dressing room, he found a primitive bugging device. The lover who had built the Petit Trianon had spied on his mistress.

The dissident stockholders' lawsuit charged Kennedy and his management with negligence, waste, and the transfer of Pathé's assets to RKO. Conn, the champion of the lost cause, denounced directors of companies who quit without considering their obligations to the stockholders who had elected them. He predicted the suit would never come to trial. "They wouldn't dare to have this mess stirred up," he told the *Motion Picture Herald,* revealing he had already been approached with a substantial settlement "to keep my mouth shut."

Prudently, Joe went on an extended vacation. A mood of permanent depression was descending on the country, but Palm Beach, where Joe showed up in February, was fun and games as usual. To forestall questions about his future, he announced he was returning to Wall Street in association with Elisha Walker. Walker, too, had just been through a merger, his Blair and Company investment house linking up with Bank of America's subsidiary, Transamerica Corporation.

When Joe returned to Rose it was not as a guilty penitent but as a man who would never again submit to the constraints of conventional morality.

He had broken unspoken ethical rules in other areas of his life. Sexual conquests were just another form of self-vindication.

Rose asked no questions, since she pretended nothing had ever happened. She was committed to marriage, family, church, and the life-style of a rich man's wife. Joe was seen in Palm Beach with Nancy Carroll, the Paramount star who, at a distance at least, looked so much like Gloria that society gossip had Kennedy and Swanson back together again. Starlets and showgirls were the women he seduced, but he also chased friends of the family, the wives and daughters of business associates, and later, his daughters' schoolmates and his sons' girlfriends. He maintained a suite at the Ritz in Boston and an apartment at New York's Waldorf-Astoria.

While he officially denied the liaison with Gloria, he talked freely—and often graphically—of their relationship when he was with "the boys." To Mary Pitcairn, who dated John Kennedy and later married Senator Kenneth Keating, he spoke of how wonderful Gloria was and how he kept in touch with her. Once, he telephoned Gloria in front of the young woman. "She was at the Plaza Hotel in New York," Pitcairn would remember. "He said, 'I'm going to call her up and make a date for tomorrow night,' or something. Which he did."

Rose was forty-one and gratified by the turn of events. The paterfamilias was home again, commuting to Wall Street during the week, as the other men in Bronxville did, and ordinarily home at nights and during weekends. She was sure Joe's maturity, and his increasing interest in the question of how the torch would be passed on to the next generation, would make it unlikely that he would fall in love with any of his young distractions to the point where he would tear up his family. In her memoirs Rose would call this period the happiest of her life, a time of an affectionate maturing of their seventeen-year marriage. After lunch on Sundays the two of them got into the habit of taking long walks, whether it was in the Bronxville woodlands or along the Cape Cod shore. As their daughter Pat would say, "Those Sunday walks were *their* walks. It indicates something about their relationship. They were interested in each other, they enjoyed each other, they wanted to talk with each other." Visiting relatives saw endearing winks and teasing banter. Tenaciously serene, Rose tried to be attentive and loving.

They resumed their sex life. Once again, Rose became pregnant.

The spring of 1931 found Gloria with a mountain of bills, divorce proceedings, and little energy to resume independent production. She hired lawyers and more accountants, who all confirmed what Irving Wakoff had told her: She had some property, but she was by no means rich.

There were painful discoveries. Sidney Howard's Cadillac was not the only gift debited to her private account. A fur coat that Joe had supposedly given her also had been charged, as had the private star's bungalow that he had built at RKO as her 1928 Christmas present.

The Kennedy office in Transamerica's Los Angeles building was less than helpful. It would take a year to sort out the accounts.

Though she had herself and two children to support, she was not eager to return to work. "Once again, I had misjudged people and had been deceived by someone I had totally trusted and I was stunned and in pain. In spite of my reputation for will and stamina and pluck and durability, all I wanted was to call for my mother or to hold my babies in my arms and sob for a month, or a year for that matter, and claim for once my natural right as a woman to feel nothing but vulnerable."

Still, she decided she had to act while Hollywood's collective memory of *The Trespasser* and her Academy Award nomination was still fresh. She decided to talk to Mayer and Irving Thalberg to see if they were interested in having MGM produce the remaining pictures on her United Artists contract. Mayer and the small, pale Thalberg ruled with equal power—and equal hostility toward one another. Somehow MGM thrived on their differences; as Paramount entered a period that, in retrospect, would be called its "civil wars," MGM was becoming the most prestigious of all Hollywood studios.

Gloria got to see Mayer and, like Derr and Sullivan, had to hear him tell her how much he loathed Joe Kennedy. The source of the deep dislike was the years the immigrant son of Orthodox Russian Jews had spent in Boston and the latent anti-Semitism he had sensed in Joe.

Gloria told the MGM boss her affairs were in a shambles. She had neither the time nor the energy to resume producing her own films. Would MGM be interested in producing her movies for UA release?

Mayer was used to dealing with rebellious actresses, not with stars as independent producers. He was impressed, and he admitted he had tried several times to merge MGM with UA. Largely because of Charlie Chaplin's opposition, he had never succeeded. What kind of money was she talking about?

It took several discussions to get to that. After one such meeting, E. J. (Eddie) Mannix, Mayer's burly righthand man, while walking her to the street entrance suddenly burst out, "Your friend is sure carrying a torch for you."

They were outside on Grant Avenue when Mannix told her that Joe Kennedy was putting pressure on Mayer not to make a deal with her. After that, she heard of other incidents where Joe's long arm had reached out to try and control her. It was both galling and touching. He still wanted to influence her life.

She wanted $250,000 a picture, she told Mayer at their next meeting.

He said he wanted a commitment for four pictures from her. They shook hands on a deal. He would have a contract drawn up.

When the papers were ready for her signature, he called and suggested she see Joe Schenck before committing herself. She knew that meant the two had been talking. She expected the worst from a meeting with Schenck, whom she had resented since *Sadie Thompson,* but she agreed to see him. When they met, though, he was his old charming self, treating her like a long-lost child and raving about *The Trespasser.*

"I don't want you to leave United Artists," he smiled, leaning over his desk and lighting her poised cigarette. "I'll match whatever L.B. is offering you."

She blew smoke toward the ceiling. It felt nice to be wooed.

Schenck carried on. "I can think of a lot of properties for which you'll be absolutely right. I want to see to it that you stay right on top."

She felt herself being swayed. However, he had taught her to negotiate like an Armenian rug dealer, and she added new conditions.

"Let's let bygones be bygones, Gloria," he smiled. "Rudy's gone. And Norma's retired. Griffith's . . . well. We should stick together."

Appeals to loyalty tugged at her heartstrings. She added silly little conditions. He said she had something he wanted.

"What?"

"*Rain,* darling."

She couldn't believe it.

"I'm serious. Lewis Milestone is the hottest director since his Oscar for *All Quiet on the Western Front.* And wait till you see his *Front Page* with Pat O'Brien, Adolphe Menjou, Edward Everett Horton. A classic, produced by Howard Hughes. Joan Crawford will play Sadie, Walter Huston the reverend."

"And Mr. Hays?"

Schenck lowered his voice and knocked the ash off his cigar. "The Depression has sobered the Hays office. We'll sail through like a breeze."

She sold him *Rain,* and a week later signed a million-dollar contract for four UA films. From Mannix she learned the terms were better than anything Mayer would have offered.

The title of Gloria's first film under her new UA contract was promising; the result, a disaster. *Indiscreet* was based on soap opera material: Gloria's kid sister falls in love with Gloria's former lover, a writer and man-about-town. To show the infatuated girl he is worthless, big sister sacrifices her reputation and her own happiness by encouraging the man to make advances to her again. The ending swings wildly from near-slapstick, as Gloria behaves crazily at a dinner party to show insanity runs in the family and thus prevents her sister's marriage, to high drama, as Gloria compromises herself in the arms of her ex-lover in the presence of the man she really loves.

The director was Leo McCarey, the Hal Roach two-reeler graduate who was just one film away from directing his smash hit, the Marx Brothers' *Duck Soup.* On *Indiscreet,* he was totally off, directing this, his sixth sound picture, as if it were his first, with clumsily paced dialogue and awkward pauses. In order to keep Gloria from backing out of the project, Joe Schenck and Sam Goldwyn hired Ben Lyon as her leading man.

The final product was so coarse Schenck thought it might be smart to use *The Trespasser* formula and premiere *Indiscreet* in London. To cheer her up, he told her their next picture would be the screen adaptation of David Belasco's latest Broadway hit, *Tonight or Never.* Coco Chanel would design the dresses, and while Gloria was in Europe, she could spend a month or two in Paris being fitted for a fabulous wardrobe.

Gloria took her children, Virginia Bowker, and a governess with her. In New York, Sport Ward saw to it that she met a lot of new people. One was Jeff Cohen, a wastrel who promptly proposed marriage and asked her to share his beautiful, empty house in Paris. She declined marriage, but accepted use of the Paris house on condition he let her pay rent.

After depositing Virginia and the children in Paris, Gloria went to London, where Noel Coward met her. United Artists was throwing a grand dinner at Claridge's. The guests would include Lady Louis Mountbatten, known for the height of her heels and the brilliance of her smile; Sylvia Hawkes, who had become Lady Ashley in the teeth of his lordship's family opposition; Harold Lloyd; Eddie Goulding; "And, my dear, Doug Fairbanks, without Mary."

She didn't quite know how to interpret the significance of Mary Pickford's not being with Doug.

"And King Alfonso of Spain."

"Really?"

"Couldn't be more convenient. He's just arrived in exile."

Gloria especially enjoyed Lady Ashley. A former fashion model and chorus girl, Sylvia was tall, slender, with fair hair and a lisp. She was the perfect English rose. They hit it off immediately and in the course of a few hours behaved like old friends.

The London reviews of *Indiscreet* were sufficiently polite to justify carrying the celebration to Paris. Sylvia couldn't come, but Coward and Goulding joined her at the Ritz at the place Vendôme, around the corner from Coco Chanel's salon. During the day, Gloria had fittings with Chanel, whose new lover was Paul Iribe, the set designer who had made *The Affairs of Anatol* so dazzling to look at. At night, Gloria and Virginia went out with their two Englishmen. "Eddie and Noel were two of the most amusing men in the world," Gloria would remember. "After several years of dinners mostly with Joe Kennedy and the horsemen and a few discreet friends, I felt in their company as if I had suddenly run away and joined the circus."

In a nightclub on the Champs Elysées one night, Coward and Goulding introduced Gloria to Michael Farmer, a handsome thirty-year-old strong silent type, whom Noel described as a moody playboy who spent his time fishing, hunting, and sailing in season. Gloria thought he had the physique of Henri and the chiseled face of Craney Gartz. He ordered drinks and downed his own in a matter of minutes.

A week later the foursome was in Cannes boarding Farmer's comfortable yacht for a Mediterranean cruise. They and their congenial host spent all of July aboard the boat or at parties in Cannes, Nice, and Monaco. On the deck one starry night, Michael kissed Gloria and announced he loved her. She suggested he find someone else to love because he was two years younger than she, and she was not yet legally divorced. The last thing he'd want was to cope with a divorced actress with two children. He insisted he wanted to marry her.

Their summer flirtation continued. One night, anchored in the Baie des Anges, as the lights of the Cannes shoreline glittered outside the porthole, they became lovers. It was a sweet quick tryst that was only repeated twice before Gloria rushed back to Paris to resume the Chanel fittings.

She found a cyst on her right breast and went to see the doctor who had saved her life after the 1925 abortion. He took a biopsy sample and had her spend an uneasy twenty-four hours before calling her back for a second consultation.

He performed a thorough examination, and when he was finished his face lit up. The lump, he told her, was not malignant. He also told her she was pregnant. "But this time, my dear Marquise, you must not interrupt the pregnancy. You would risk your life if you did."

The shock and confusion on her face forced her to admit she was divorced from Henri. The doctor was visibly embarrassed. She said she didn't want an abortion. Since she didn't have cancer, she was going to have the baby.

It was too ironic. After trying to have a child with Henri, after successfully avoiding having one with Joe, a near one-night stand with a playboy who looked like a cross between Henri and Craney had left her pregnant.

She swore Virginia and Eddie to secrecy. Her plan was to hurry back to Los Angeles, make *Tonight or Never* before she started to show, then go on an extended vacation, perhaps to some obscure New England village— they could tell Joe Schenck she was having a nervous breakdown or was on a religious retreat—have the baby, and announce she was adopting it.

"Inasmuch as I've already adopted one baby, nobody will be surprised if I'm crazy enough to do it again as soon as I become single."

At her first fitting after the July holiday, the forty-eight-year-old Chanel found Gloria plump. "Take off the girdle and lose five pounds," the designer snapped. "You have no right to fluctuate in the middle of fittings."

Gloria wasn't sure she could lose five pounds.

"Why not?"

"Reasons of health, maybe." But why couldn't the House of Chanel make a pair of underpants that would keep her slim for two months of filming?

Since World War I, Chanel's name had stood for a fashion that repudiated the corset, a fashion that stressed an elegance of ease and comfort.

"Look, just *try* it," Gloria pleaded. "If not, I will lose five pounds."

Chanel was the exception to the rule that artistic temperament rarely goes hand in hand with financial acumen. Her horror of being dependent on anyone gave her a shrewd and provident approach to money. The in-house specialist in undergarments sewed surgical elastics into a panty girdle. It took three assistants to get Gloria into it, but the result was stunning.

As Gloria was about to leave for Hollywood with trunks of Chanel clothes and a stack of sturdy elastic panties, Eddie convinced her to have dinner with the father of her unborn baby. She agreed that it was the least she could do, since she had decided never to see Michael again. When they met, he was pouting and drinking until she told him to leave his glass empty for a while. Instead of resenting her remark about his alcohol intake, he pushed his glass aside and said he loved her and wanted to marry her.

She had had three unsuccessful marriages, she explained. Henri, for one, had told her it was impossible to be married to her because she was a businesswoman first and a wife second. "Perhaps he was right. In any event, I don't really want to be married again. I'm not even sure I believe in marriage anymore."

"Don't you think that's a bit selfish?" he asked. "To live on my boat until I fall in love with you and then walk away scot free?"

When she told him that she was walking away anything but scot free, that she was pregnant, by him, he insisted she marry him. She refused. He called the next day to say that he had booked passage aboard the *Mauretania* in the name of Mr. and Mrs. Martin Forster; they would arrive in New York August 15 and get married the next day.

She said no.

He threatened to tell the press.

"How dare you!" she asked.

"Because I love you. How many times do I have to tell you? And you love me too, if for no other reason than because you're pregnant by me. Please, Gloria."

She introduced him to little Gloria and Brother. The children didn't run away screaming, but she was still unsure. Virginia offered to sail to New York with the children on a separate ocean liner while "Mr. and Mrs. Forster" kept their *Mauretania* reservations. Gloria agreed to the arrangement.

The sea air cleared her thoughts. On August 16, 1931, they were married before the mayor of Elmsford, New York. It was an area of Westchester County that Gloria knew well. Elmsford was five miles from Bronxville. She wasn't sure the marriage was legal—that she was totally divorced from Henri. In any case, the newlyweds traveled to California as Mr. and Mrs. Forster. In Los Angeles, Michael moved into the Beverly Hills Hotel across from Crescent Drive.

Chanel came to Hollywood for *Tonight or Never.* Thirteen million Americans were out of work, but Goldwyn was sure people down to their last pennies would not always choose a piece of bread over a ticket to a show. This was no time for caution. Glitz was what people wanted. Chanel hated the whole thing and rushed back to Paris, saying she had met only one star worth the bother of going to California to see. Who? Erich von Stroheim.

Constance Bennett became the second Marquise de la Falaise de la Coudraye in November. In quick succession, RKO had put her in two more pictures after *The Easiest Way,* both stories in which she was seduced and abandoned. Her marriage was celebrated at the home of director George Fitzmaurice, with her father and sister Joan in attendance. Instead of a honeymoon, the bride spent her ten-week vacation from RKO farming herself out to Warner Brothers at $30,000 a week.

When informed that taxes on such a salary would be ruinous, she told Jack Warner, "Oh, then you will have to pay the tax for I must have thirty thousand clear."

Michael Farmer came out into the open. He and Gloria eloped to Yuma, Arizona, for a much publicized marriage. Joe Schenck and Sam Goldwyn reveled in the controversy when the mayor of Elmsford announced he had already married Swanson and Farmer.

The film colony embraced Michael as it had accepted Henri, and the Farmers were deluged with invitations.

For Gloria, filming *Tonight or Never* strapped into the rubber corset under Chanel's subdued designs was uneventful. Mervyn Le Roy, who had directed six pictures since *Little Caesar,* told Gloria he had had a crush on her nine years ago when he was Sam Wood's assistant. Ferdinand Gottschalk was cast as the aging nobleman to whom Gloria, a concert singer, is engaged. Melvyn Douglas played the young impresario who captures the singer's heart. Gloria was four months pregnant when Le Roy shouted "Cut!" for the last time. Before Louella Parsons and the rest of the gossip columnists could start counting months on their fingers, Michael, Gloria, and her children sailed the long way to Europe via the Panama Canal.

Lawyers for UA threatened to cancel the last two pictures on Gloria's contract. To avoid being served papers, she went into seclusion and evolved an elaborate code to communicate with Irving Wakoff and Gloria Productions' New York secretary.

They spent Christmas in Paris. Visiting Lady Ashley at her Ritz hotel suite, Gloria saw photographs of Douglas Fairbanks everywhere. "I thought you knew," Sylvia explained. "After all, you introduced us, remember, at the dinner party with King Alfonso. It's frightfully complicated." Sylvia was still married to his lordship; Doug was still wedded to Mary.

Gloria and Michael decided to spend the winter in the Swiss Alps.

Rose and Joe's ninth child was born in February 1932. It was a boy. He was christened Edward Moore Kennedy after Joe's ever loyal Eddie Moore. The family called him Ted.

Young Joe was going on seventeen and on his way to Harvard. He was tall, powerful, quick, and quite handsome, with his father's flashy smile and steely look. Jack was fifteen, chronically underweight, and finally diagnosed at the Lahey Clinic as having a congenital malformation of the spinal column. He was a boarder at Choate, the prep school Joe Jr. had been attending. When Jack came home for spring break that year, two friends picked him up at the Bronxville station. In a much repeated family anecdote, he said, rather sarcastically, that he wanted to stop by the house to check the nursery "and see if there's anybody new in the family." He came out a while later and said, "By God, there is."

Kathleen, who looked more and more like her mother, was getting ready to begin her first year at the Noroton School of the Sacred Heart Convent, three miles from Choate, in Connecticut. Noroton was Rose's solution to what she regarded as Kick's excessive popularity with boys. She was on the phone with boys for hours and was constantly invited to Saturday afternoon movies. Eunice and Patricia attended local schools, while Rosemary struggled with tutors, who first suggested that, given her limitations, she was doing quite well but later came to believe that she would never progress beyond a fourth-grade level. Bobby was about to begin school. He was a puny boy who tried to play with his big brother Jack and idolized Young Joe. Jean was three, chubby, and still eating at the "little table" with a governess. The age differences and the fanning out to different schools helped each child become his own person, but family life was still intrusive and judgmental.

For those with money, the Depression brought its own opportunities. Joe enlarged his holdings in blue chip stocks after they hit rock bottom. For $100,000, he also picked up a third estate, a sixteen-room winter residence on Millionaires Row in Palm Beach. Built by the Gold Coast's celebrated architect Addison Mizner, the Spanish villa with its red-tile roof sat on two acres facing the Atlantic on North Ocean Boulevard.

The country expected little, even in this election year, from politics and politicians. Cynicism and hopelessness prevailed. Voters in Chicago had thrown out the notorious Mayor William Thompson only to see municipal politics develop along the lines of New York City's Tammany corruptions. The general attitude was "What's the use?" Racketeers flourished, as did bootleggers, rumrunners, and the Prohibition issue. Even after Franklin D. Roosevelt's spectacular 1930 election as governor of New York, progressives and intellectuals found him weak because he sidestepped Republican demands that he use his powers to oust corrupt Democrats in New York City. President Hoover created a two-billion-dollar Reconstruction Finance Corporation to make loans to banks, insurance companies, farm associations, railroads, and other industries, but the demands on the depleted treasury continued.

Joe was rich. Politics ran in his blood. His fear that hyperinflation would ultimately rob him of his wealth made him forget moneymaking for a while and plunge into Democratic politics.

Joe had seen Roosevelt in action at the Bethlehem shipyard on the Fore River, and he had met his old nemesis at the governor's mansion in Albany in 1930. FDR had bested him back in 1917, but Joe now believed the fifty-year-old Roosevelt had the resources, the talent, and the personality to bring about a fundamental shift in the political order. Joe was ready to put his money where his mouth was, to contribute solidly to the election campaign, but if he joined the Roosevelt for President bandwagon he expected to become something more than a distributor of leaflets at Roosevelt rallies.

True to his billiard instincts, Joe didn't head for Warm Springs, the Georgia resort where Roosevelt joined other polio victims once a year for therapeutic swims in the healing waters, but went instead to California to talk to that real kingmaker, William Randolph Hearst.

The sixty-nine-year-old publisher, whose newspaper empire was being undermined by the Depression, was an isolationist. "Unless we Americans are willing to go on laboring indefinitely merely to provide loot for Europe," he had said over the NBC radio network, "we should personally see to it that a man is elected to the presidency this year whose guiding motto is 'America First.' " Hearst didn't trust Roosevelt's lukewarm repudiation of internationalism, and was already working for House Speaker John Nance Garner. The Texan opposed foreign entanglements and the canceling of war debts, and he was to Hearst's liking on finance and tariffs. A glowing biography of "Cactus Jack" Garner was running in the Hearst papers.

The California delegation to the Chicago Convention in June would be controlled not only by Hearst but also by William Gibbs McAdoo, a tall, lanky San Franciscan who had served as treasury secretary under Woodrow Wilson, whose hooded eyes gazed at the world with amused skepticism. McAdoo was for New York's Al Smith, FDR's old enemy. Kennedy had Hearst's undivided attention when he told him Roosevelt was "the hardest trader" he'd ever run up against, a man even tougher than Joe himself. Joe's arguments didn't persuade the publisher, but when Joe arrived at the Roosevelt camp in Warm Springs a week after Garner won the California primary, the political press—and Roosevelt's aides—found it significant that he was just back from talks with Hearst. In a swipe at fellow-millionaire Bernard Baruch, who favored Maryland governor Albert Ritchie, Joe told the press, "I'm the only man with more than twelve dollars who's for Roosevelt."

The candidate was gracious. Joe was affable, outspoken, and he slapped his thighs when he laughed. He was the kind of self-made man Roosevelt loved to have on board, someone who was willing not only to contribute but also to raise money for the campaign. Rexford Tugwell, a handsome and brilliant economics professor who from his Columbia University windows could see a Hooverville spreading across from the campus, and Harvard economist Adolf Berle formed the inner circle, or Roosevelt "brain trust." They were as eager to discuss radical solutions to the Depression as they were leery of associating their candidate with Wall Streeters. Still, they were ready to look at ideas on their merits. When Joe said the time of big business was yielding to an era of big government, they listened. Tugwell had spent two months in Soviet Russia in 1927 with a delegation of unionists and intellectuals, and he was impressed by the renewal of Soviet agriculture.

They all talked about economics, about the disastrous 1924 Democratic convention that had taken 103 ballots to nominate John W. Davis and led to disaster at the polls. They also discussed the other Democratic presidential hopefuls—Smith, Garner, Ritchie, and former Cleveland mayor and secretary of war Newton D. Baker. Columnist Walter Lippman, who called Roosevelt "dangerous," was promoting Baker, while Baruch said that the conservative, distinguished Ritchie was the only Democrat he would support with any contribution.

Late at night when Roosevelt and Kennedy got together alone, they talked for hours. Their laughter floated through the open windows and could be heard in nearby resort cottages.

Gloria had doubts about her fourth husband's emotional stability during the months in St. Moritz. Though her pregnancy made her increasingly ungainly, Michael was insanely jealous. If she as much as talked to a waiter, he flew into tantrums, poking her in the side until she feared he might hit her. When she announced one morning that she was leaving him, he churlishly answered that as long as all the passports were in his possession, she wasn't going anywhere. She locked the door to her room. He stood outside sobbing and asking for forgiveness. For a week after that, he was all kindness and consideration.

She felt she would be safer in London, where she had friends. She found boarding schools for little Gloria and Brother, left the governess with them in Switzerland, and went with Michael to England.

She refused to have the baby in a hospital. She had delivered little Gloria at home twelve years earlier and again wanted to give birth in private surroundings. Lady Thelma Furness, Gloria Vanderbilt's twin sister, who had introduced her friend Wallis Simpson to the Prince of Wales, graciously lent the expectant movie star her charming town house on Farm Street near Berkeley Square. The house would be empty for the next two months, Lady Thelma said. Moving in, Gloria and Michael discovered that the most recent occupant had been Mrs. Simpson, and that the Prince of Wales had been a frequent if furtive visitor. His ascension to the throne, abdication, and marriage to Simpson were still four years away.

Sylvia Ashley promised to try and arrange for the midwife of the royal family to attend to Gloria. Elinor Glyn came for a visit, telling Gloria that if she exercised her face by contorting jaw, ears, and scalp she would keep wrinkles away. Lady Ashley and Doug Fairbanks came by, bringing with them Major Norton, one of the heads of United Artists in London. When they got around to talking movies and the two films Gloria owed UA, Doug suggested she make one right here. She was British by marriage and could therefore form a British production company. Gloria wondered what she should do with Michael.

"Involve him," Sylvia said without hesitation.

Fairbanks agreed. When they brought up the subject with Michael at dinner, he loved the idea. While Gloria had their baby, he would help Fairbanks and Norton raise production funds through UA investors. There were soon scenes of jealousy, with Michael suspecting Gloria of flirting with Norton.

Gloria got together with a writer to collaborate on the story of marital misunderstandings among the upper crust. The sessions on Farm Street were only a pale reflection of the creative seances with Eddie Goulding and Laura Crews on Crescent Drive three years earlier. In desperation, Gloria telegraphed Eddie in Hollywood and asked him if he would write and direct her. He was too busy shooting *Grand Hotel* with Greta Garbo, John Barrymore, Wallace Beery, Tully Marshall, and Ferdinand Gottschalk at MGM. Instead, he suggested Cyril Gardner, their editor on *The Trespasser.* Gardner had collected one film with George Cukor and was anxious to become a full-fledged director.

They called the script *A Perfect Misunderstanding.* Norton raised pre-production money, and when Gloria asked Noel Coward to suggest someone for a Ronald Colman–type role, she was told she couldn't do any better than Laurence Olivier, a young actor Coward had taken to New York to play the second lead in *Private Lives.* Olivier was twenty-five and looked twenty-one, Gloria decided when she saw him. She suggested he grow a mustache for the role.

Norton, not young Olivier, was the object of Michael's jealousy. Gloria was walking through Hyde Park with her husband one afternoon when he suddenly told her he didn't want her to have lunch alone with Norton anymore.

"What are you talking about?" she said. "He's helping me raise money for the picture."

"I know what he's up to," Michael sneered, "and I never want you to be alone with him again. If I catch you two together—ever—I'll kill him! I'm not joking."

To make his point, he took her hand and thrust it into his jacket pocket. She felt a revolver.

In early April, she went into labor. Sylvia arrived with the royal midwife and two obstetricians. When Gloria came out of a slight dose of anesthesia, she saw Sylvia at the foot of the bed with the baby in her arms. It was a girl. The newborn child was beautiful and unmistakably Michael's, Gloria thought as she took the infant and held her to her breast. They called her Michelle.

The Republican convention was held in Chicago's vast new stadium from June 14 to June 16. It was, H. L. Mencken opined, "the stupidest and most harrisome ever heard of . . . a convention of country postmasters, federal marshals and receivers in bankruptcy. Unemployment and depression were seldom mentioned." The Democrats followed the Republicans into the stadium on June 27—"to carry on their quadrennial suicide pact,"

Mencken wrote in reference to the party rule demanding a two-thirds majority to win presidential nomination. They were 3,210 delegates and 30,000 spectators.

Joe was in the smoke-filled rooms and on the floor of the convention, working uncommitted delegates and, with FDR's convention chief James A. Farley, trying to persuade McAdoo to release his California delegates soon enough to prevent too many deadlocked ballots. Roosevelt himself was in Albany, sitting by the radio in shirtsleeves and chain-smoking as he heard the results of the first ballot—666 votes for him, 203 for Al Smith, and 90 for "Cactus Jack" Garner. Roosevelt was carrying the South, losing New York to Smith, but winning the Farm Belt, the Rocky Mountain states, and the Pacific Northwest. The next two roll calls saw Oklahoma switch to Garner. Farley got desperate and before the July 1 session tried to persuade Garner's delegates to switch to Roosevelt.

Joe got on the telephone to Hearst in San Simeon, California.

"W.R., do you want Baker?" he asked, knowing Hearst loathed the former secretary of war.

Hearst groaned.

"If you don't want Baker, you'd better take Roosevelt, because if you don't, you're going to take Baker."

"Could I get Ritchie?"

"No, I don't think so. I think if Roosevelt cracks on the next ballot, it'll be Baker."

"I'll get back to you."

Before the fourth ballot, Hearst had persuaded Garner to accept the vice-presidential slot. Baker had picked up Mississippi. When the roll call came on the fourth ballot, McAdoo asked for permission to speak from the platform. "California came here to nominate a president of the United States," he began. "She did not come here to deadlock this convention, to engage in another desolating contest like that of 1924."

The Roosevelt delegation stood up and cheered. "And so, my friends," McAdoo yelled into the microphone, "California casts forty-four votes for Franklin Delano Roosevelt!"

The candidate decided to break with tradition and flew to Chicago to deliver his acceptance speech. Roosevelt's flight refueled in Buffalo and Cleveland, fought headwinds, and took nine hours to get to Chicago.

Gloria and Michael were asleep in Farm Street, with the door to the nursery open, when the phone rang. Gloria fumbled in the darkness, found the light switch, and picking up the phone, saw it was 4 A.M. The operator said it was a transatlantic call from Chicago. Gloria immediately feared her mother was ill, or worse.

It was Virginia Bowker, speaking from a very noisy place or over a terrible connection. Gloria managed to understand that Addie was all right before Virginia yelled there was someone who wanted to speak to her.

"Who?"

Gloria only heard static. A man's voice came on, shouting, "Hello Gloria, this is Joe."

She recognized the Boston accent immediately. Emotions flooded over her. Now, he called, a year and a half late.

"It's four o'clock in London," she shouted back. "I'm nursing a new baby. What do you want?"

"I read about the baby," he shouted. "We just had one, too. We named him after Eddie Moore. That isn't why I called."

"I should hope not," she yelled back. "Why did you call?"

Michael was awake by now; so was the baby.

"Do you know who's here with me, Gloria? The next president of the United States, Gloria! He just won the Democratic nomination. I want you to say hello to him."

She thought Joe was so blatantly opportunistic that she shouted back, "How dare you!"

Joe was his old self. "Seriously, Gloria. He wants to say hello to you. Wait a second while I—"

"Don't bother! I don't want to talk to him and I don't want to talk to you!"

She slammed down the phone, angry, confused.

"Who's that?" Michael's voice was suspicious.

"The next president of the United States, presumably. But I hung up on him."

The Shadows We Cast

*I don't know how it is that you start working
at something you don't like, and before you
know it, you're an old man.*

—HERMAN MANKIEWICZ

Erich von Stroheim never directed another film.

While Joe Kennedy liquidated Pathé Pictures and Gloria Swanson starred in *Tonight or Never,* Stroheim's old nemesis Irving Thalberg consented to let "Von" star opposite Greta Garbo in *As You Desire Me,* a screen version of Pirandello's new play, *Come tu mi vuoi,* if George Fitzmaurice directed. Garbo and Stroheim were sensational as the amnesiac and the man she is never certain is her husband.

Winfield Sheehan, the Fox producer who attended the baptism party Joe Kennedy had thrown for Gloria's five-year-old son in 1928, was enough of a rebel against the anti-Stroheim hysteria promoted by Thalberg and Mayer at MGM and Carl Laemmle, Jr., at Universal to give Von a chance to direct again. The property was *Walking Down Broadway,* the story of two girls rooming together in New York. Zasu Pitts, Stroheim's favorite actress, was cast along with Boots Mallory.

Stroheim wanted to disprove the legends about his extravagance, and worked quickly in a harmonious and friendly atmosphere. Sheehan was proud of having hired Stroheim, and when Eleanor Roosevelt, the new first lady, came to Hollywood, he conducted her with pride to the set.

"I want you to meet the greatest director in the world," the producer beamed.

Stroheim bowed and clicked his heels.

Mrs. Roosevelt smiled and said, "Yes, I know."

Business, unfortunately, called Sheehan to New York. In his absence,

Sol Wurtzel, the studio production manager, screened the *Walking Down Broadway* rough-cut and found it strange and unpleasant. Stroheim thought Wurtzel was stupid and destructive; Wurtzel believed the director was crazy. Wurtzel told Stroheim he would leave the decision to the public. Stroheim thought this meant the film would be released, or at least presented at a preview. But only Fox personnel were summoned to give their opinion. Since the word had already gone out that Wurtzel hated *Walking Down Broadway,* most of his underlings wrote on the opinion cards that the film was muddled and morbid. Alfred Werker, a director of westerns, remade the picture and Fox released it as *Hello Sister!*

At Universal, at Paramount, at MGM, at United Artists, and now at Fox, Stroheim was finished as a director. Reduced to seeking employment in quickies that traded on his name and fame, he wrote a novel called *Paprika* in the hopes of capturing the attention of film producers. After its publication, Sam Goldwyn was vaguely interested, and invited Stroheim to his home. But Goldwyn's interest in *Paprika* was fleeting.

Clarence Brown, who was directing his third Garbo picture, got Stroheim a job supervising costumes on *Anna Karenina,* and realizing Von's financial plight, took up a discreet collection to present to him as a Christmas gift in 1934. Louis B. Mayer gave fifty dollars, others considerably more. Then personal tragedy of the kind that belonged in a Stroheim picture struck Valerie, Von's wife of nearly fifteen years. She was being given a dry shampoo with a highly volatile product at a hair salon, when a hairdresser lighted a curling iron over a gas flame. The fumes of the shampoo burst into flames, igniting Valerie's hair. Shrieking, she covered her eyes, saving her sight, while the hairdresser grabbed a fur coat on the rack to smother the flames. "Not with my coat!" a client shouted. The attendant ignored the coat's owner and flung it over Valerie.

Taken to the Queen of Angels hospital, she was near death for weeks, her face and torso blackened by the fire. Before she was well enough to leave, the Stroheims' twelve-year-old son was taken to the same hospital suffering from polio. Von took a room at the hospital.

When Valerie recovered, she became a recluse, refusing to show herself in public. Thalberg hired Stroheim as a writer, and for several months "Von" labored in a cubbyhole at MGM, where he had once been a feared tyrant. He sent telegrams to Sergei Eisenstein in Moscow, offering his services to the triumphant Soviet cinema, but Joseph Stalin's purges were making intellectuals fearful. A French production company offered him a part in *Koenigsberg,* and he left for Paris in 1936. He had always been a cult figure in France, and the *Koenigsberg* part led to Jean Renoir and to his classic role in *Grand Illusion.*

With the exception of the World War II years, Stroheim spent much of the rest of his life in Maurepas, outside Paris, with Denise Vernac, a young journalist. He had the discipline to take directions from directors less famous and less gifted than he, and for a thousand dollars a day and a bottle of whiskey delivered to his dressing room would appear in any film. The rise of Nazism gave him juicy parts and a revival of the sobriquet "the man you love to hate."

In 1942 Von was in Philadelphia playing a roadshow engagement of *Arsenic and Old Lace*. He was in his dressing room, removing his stage makeup, when there was a soft knock on the door. A tall, elderly gentlemen with a gaunt face entered. The man almost floated in his too-big clothes. Rheumy eyes fixed on Stroheim, who turned white, clicked his heels, and kneeled at the feet of the visitor he not seen for a quarter century: David Wark Griffith.

When the touring company reached Chicago, Gloria was a backstage visitor. She told Stroheim he looked grand. *Queen Kelly* was forgiven.

Griffith lived at the Knickerbocker Hotel on a Hollywood Boulevard slowly going seedy, cadging drinks from people from the past. One of his frequent barstool companions was Marshall Neilan. There was no bitterness in Mickey. He laughed and joked about the turn of his fortune and said he was sure he'd be on top again. Griffith died in 1948, forgotten; Mickey, ten years later. Mary Pickford, it was said, paid for Mickey's funeral.

Joe Schenck, who went senile at the end, formed Twentieth Century with Darryl Zanuck in 1933, then merged it with Fox Films. Norma Talmadge divorced Schenck a year later. Although he was linked romantically with Merle Oberon, he never remarried.

As chairman of Twentieth Century-Fox, Schenck was instrumental in settling disputes between the studios and the Screen Actors Guild in 1937, but in the early 1940s he fell prey to labor racketeers muscling in on the lush film industry. He was charged with offering labor racketeer Willie Bioff a $100,000 bribe to convince stagehands to cross the picket lines that a loose coalition of painters, draftsmen, plumbers, grips, and other film craftsmen had thrown up around the Fox studios on Pico Boulevard. The federal prosecutor artfully brought Schenck to trial before Bioff and got the sixty-three-year-old Fox chairman convicted and sentenced to three years in prison. After a week at Alcatraz, Schenck told authorities, "I'll talk, gentlemen."

After Schenck's testimony helped send Bioff away for ten years, President Truman pardoned the studio boss. Fox reinstated him as chairman, and Schenck applauded Screen Actors Guild president Ronald Reagan's decision to let his members cross the craftsmen's picket line. In 1947 Schenck sat on the management-organized kangaroo court that blacklisted writers who refused to tell the House Un-American Activities Committee if they had ever been members of the Communist Party.

Schenck, the Russian emigrant boy who had risen from being a $4.50-a-week New York factory worker to become one of the most powerful figures in the film industry, gave away much of his fortune to charity. He spent his last years in a state sometimes called "confused" at his Beverly Hills estate, and died at the age of eighty-three. Anita Loos eulogized him by saying, "One of the best Christians I've ever known was a Jew."

Irving Thalberg, the boy genius with a weak heart, died three months after his thirty-seventh birthday in 1936. The funeral at the B'nai B'rith synagogue was the closest thing to a national rite of mourning Hollywood had ever seen. The ushers who escorted the mourners to their seats were Clark Gable, Fredric March, Douglas Fairbanks, Sam Wood, Cedric Gibbons, and Harry Carey. The Barrymore brothers, the Marx Brothers, Chaplin, Walt Disney, Howard Hughes, Carole Lombard, Gary Cooper—all were there. Even Stroheim came to pay his respects to his old enemy. During the service, every studio observed a five-minute silence.

MGM fell apart in the 1950s. Stockholders became restive, noticing dwindling profits and the inability of tired old men—Nicholas Schenck (Joseph's older brother) at the presidency of Loew's Inc., and Louis B. Mayer at the studio—to revitalize the companies. Mayer schemed against the new people, tried a coup d'état, and was routed at a 1957 stockholders' meeting. Two weeks after the meeting, the humiliated and drained Louis B. died. The Mayer house on the Santa Monica beach was sold to Pat Kennedy and Peter Lawford and later served as a West Coast base for President Kennedy.

In an attempt to recoup at least a little of the $800,000 investment in *Queen Kelly,* Gloria and Stroheim's longtime editor Viola Lawrence put together a complete version in 1931. Surprisingly faithful to the original script, the only addition to the so-called "Swanson version" was the two scenes closing the film. Instead of Stroheim's powerful ending, which left the audience with the image of Kitty as a travesty of the murdered queen, Gloria had Kitty happily seated next to King Wolfram. Adolph Tandler composed a score.

This *Queen Kelly* was released in a few European theaters. The change to sound, however, was not merely technological. Even the stylized

Ruritanian revels of a film like *Queen Kelly* were passé, and were spurned by audiences who preferred the slangy contemporaneity of all-talking movies.

In the late 1970s, when Gloria was writing her memoirs, she impulsively called Raoul Walsh from her New York apartment one night. Raoul was in his early nineties and living on his ranch in Santa Susana, in the Simi Valley of southern California, with his horses and young wife.

Gloria wanted to clear up one thing: Was it Raoul or Henri who had suggested making a film of "Rain" that first day the three of them had breakfast on the Crescent Drive terrace?

"We both did," Raoul told her. He remembered everything and asked when she'd come and see him. After the book was finished, she promised. She was ready to hang up when he said, "Hey, wait a minute. Let's hear you say it."

With her best throaty Sadie Thompson voice, she gave it to him the way she snapped at Lionel Barrymore back in 1927: "You'd yank the wings off butterflies and claim you were saving their souls, you psalm-singing sonofabitch!"

"That's it. Good night, Sadie."

Walsh, who used to wear a white eyepatch on Oscar nights and directed his last picture for Jack Warner when he was seventy-seven, lived to be ninety-three.

Only one copy of the original *Sadie Thompson* exists. It is in the vault at the Eastman Archives in Rochester, New York. The last reel is missing.

Joe Schenck might have talked Howard Hughes out of buying Pathé Pictures from Joe Kennedy in 1930, but seventeen years later Hughes became the owner of RKO. He toured the Gower Street studio and the Culver City lot where successive Sarnoff hirelings had supervised the making of Fred Astaire–Ginger Rogers musicals, *King Kong,* and *Citizen Kane.* Hughes's famous comment after touring his new acquisition was "Paint it!"

His years at RKO were erratic. He canceled projects, fired some eight hundred employees one Saturday, ordered the company to pay $100,000 to Hughes Tool Company for the services of Jane Russell, and in a brilliant stroke of casting, put her opposite the undernourished Frank Sinatra and a leering Groucho Marx in *It's Only Money.*

He lured crack production teams from Warner Brothers, but left them dangling on vital decisions or woke them up in the middle of the night for rambling conference calls until, in frustration, they left. Deficits and stockholder lawsuits piled up. In 1954 he tried to merge RKO into his mammoth Hughes Tool Company to use it as a tax write-off, but then sold it to General Tire and Rubber Company. Six years later he lost his beloved Trans World Airlines and began his descent into total seclusion and madness.

Constance Bennett never worked for Hughes. Noel Coward was supposed to write a big picture for her in 1932, but RKO dropped her after Gregory La Cava directed her in *Bed of Roses,* in which she played a golddigger who sells her body with a coldbloodedness seldom seen even in this farce genre. Though Warner Brothers reduced her salary from $100,000 a film to $225,000 a year, her sophisticated appearance set standards of beauty and fashion. Slender as a sylph, and with a Parisian taste in clothes, her pompadour hairdo and surprised-looking face carried her into the 1940s, to be best remembered for her portrayal of the bewitching and sultry ghost in the *Topper* film series, in the first of which she played opposite Cary Grant.

She also showed a good head for business. Said her investment adviser of her, "I used to think Mary Pickford was the smartest, but she can't hold a candle to Constance. She knows the earning power and dividend record behind every bond and every share of stock she owns."

Her marriage to Henri lasted nine years. It was a repeat of Henri's union with Gloria: no children and long separations. Forever elegantly slim, handsome, and with a mocking glint in his blue eyes, Henri was a lady killer. He remained in Europe for long periods while Connie led her own life, mostly with matinee idol Gilbert Roland. As a couple, Henri and Connie grazed Hollywood news columns only once when, in 1933, an immigration crackdown on aliens in the film colony found the marquis still to be "visiting" as the husband of Gloria Swanson. Henri and Connie embarked on a cruise ship and, via the Panama Canal, sailed to Europe so he could return with a reentry permit listing him as the right lady's husband.

Henri spent much of the late 1930s in Britain, shooting grouse in Scotland with Lord Throckmorton and chasing wealthy ladies in elegant London. His pied à terre was at 20 Grosvenor Square; his hunting grounds, the aristocratic Club 400. Connie divorced him in 1940 in Reno, charging desertion, and a year later she married Roland. They had two daughters and divorced in 1944. Connie's fifth husband was Brigadier General John Theron Coulter, who saw to it that after she died of a cerebral hemorrhage in 1956 she was buried at the Arlington National Cemetery.

Eddie Goulding telephoned Gloria in 1936. Would she sell the rights to *The Trespasser* to Warner Brothers? He had interested Bette Davis in the story and he was sure Warner would pay good money for the property.

Gloria called Irving Wakoff, who told her the rights were controlled by

Joe Kennedy. She couldn't believe it. Wakoff was positive. Gloria's secretary found out that Joe was on his way to Europe aboard the *Normandie*.

Gloria sent a shore-to-ship telegram: "DEAR JOE WILL YOU PLEASE GIVE ME THE STORY RIGHTS TO THE TRESPASSER BECAUSE I WISH TO REMAKE IT CABLE ADDRESS GLORISWAN BEVERLY HILLS BON VOYAGE YOU LUCKY DOG." His answer came the following day: "DELIGHTED GIVE YOU ALL ASSETS CORPORATION INCLUDING STORY HAVE YOUR LAWYER ACCOUNTANT TO WHOM WE SENT FIGURES ADVISE YOU THEN CORPORATION COULD BE DISSOLVED DONT RELINQUISH STORY GRATIS SEVERAL WANT IT GOOD LUCK JOE."

A wistful smile creased her lips. The two telegrams ended the collaboration that was supposed to have made them both millions and changed the history of the cinema.

Goulding and Davis remade *The Trespasser* under the title *That Certain Woman.* It was a flop.

Warner Brothers rematched director and star in two more heart wrenchers. *Dark Victory* was memorable, but *The Old Maid* was marked by such a succession of monstrous fights between Bette and Miriam Hopkins that Eddie feigned a heart attack so he wouldn't have to direct Davis again.

After World War II, Goulding went to Fox to remake *Of Human Bondage,* this time with Eleanor Parker and Paul Henreid. He also directed Maugham's uncinematic *The Razor's Edge* and contributed the moody background melody that became famous with Mack Davis's lyrics, "A Small Cafe, Mam'selle." Tyrone Power, who played the searching American opposite beautiful Gene Tierney, became the double-crossing heel in Goulding's *Nightmare Alley,* a tough-minded treatment of telepathy, sleazy ambition, failure, and degradation.

Goulding directed four films in the 1950s and died at the end of the decade.

Allan Dwan was still making pictures in the early 1960s, still hustling scripts when he was in his nineties and at his modest house on Stanley Avenue in the flatlands of West Hollywood, receiving highbrow movie buffs, ambitious newcomers like Peter Bogdanovich, and would-be directors like Steven Spielberg and George Lucas. The new generation saw in Dwan the durable, ideal filmmaker for whom beauty was function and narrative flair a matter of visual density. When Dwan moved the camera, it was not to follow the action, but to define the meaning of it.

Bogdanovich wrote a monograph on Dwan and, with the anecdotes Allan told him about his early years, wrote and directed *Nickelodeon,* the story of a bumbling lawyer who accidentally becomes a director for a movie troupe making westerns in the early 1910s. Dwan lived long enough to see Ryan O'Neal play him in *Nickelodeon*. He was ninety-six when he died.

Riding the Roosevelt Special in 1932 was the happiest time in Joe's life.

A month after the Chicago convention, FDR invited Kennedy to join the campaign train on its 9,000-mile, coast-to-coast-and-back-again journey. With Eddie Moore, Joe boarded the train in Albany on September 13, and to his intense satisfaction discovered that he and Eddie were in Car D, the combined sleeper-parlor car that carried the candidate's closest advisers and friends. Campaign manager James Farley was there. So were speechwriter Raymond Moley; the patrician Brenkinridge Long of Kentucky, floor manager at the convention and now southern election strategist; and the delicately attractive Marguerite "Missy" LeHand, FDR's secretary and mistress for the past twelve years.

Under a scorching sun in Topeka, Kansas, Roosevelt spoke to farmers about crop control. In Salt Lake City, he promised more government help to railroads. In Sioux City, he castigated the Hoover administration for spending. In the cool autumn of Seattle on September 20, he spoke "in the name of a stricken America and a stricken world."

The Special was nearly a dozen cars long. After the dining and lounge cars came the car for the candidate and his family, which included twenty-six-year-old Jimmy Roosevelt and his young wife, Betsy Cushing, the daughter of an eminent Boston physician. Behind Car D were two coaches for cameramen, broadcasters, and the rolling telegraph offices. There was a separate car for newspaper reporters and a special coach for what Moley called "visiting firemen"—dignitaries who boarded for a day or two of jaunting with FDR.

Kennedy fitted marvelously into the late-night conviviality in which Farley, Moley, Long, and a dozen others regaled each other with stories. Their laughter drifted up toward the head of the train. Young Jimmy Roosevelt would call Joe "a rather fabulous figure." When the Special reached Yuma, Joe chartered a fleet of buses to take everybody to the Grand Canyon. In Chicago, he pulled strings with Cubs (and Catalina Island) owner William Wrigley to get a block of tickets that allowed everybody on the train to see Babe Ruth and Lou Gehrig lead the Yankees to a seven-to-five victory over the Cubs in the third game of the World Series. In each city, Joe slipped away from the rostrum seeking out local financial leaders to explain to them why Roosevelt was the man to save capitalism and to solicit pledges from them. Figures would vary, but besides his own $50,000, it is estimated he raised $150,000 for Roosevelt. In a letter two years later to his reporter friend Louis Ruppel, Joe would say, "I have had a lot of fun in my life and met a lot of fine people, but none finer or a greater crowd than I met on that train."

On October 25, FDR gave his "four horsemen" speech in Baltimore. "Destruction, delay, deceit, and despair" were the horsemen of the Republican leadership. Hoover was so unpopular that mounted police had to protect him in Detroit. Traveling in a fleet of limousines provided by Henry Ford, the presidential party drove down streets lined with glum and silent people. The difference between the two candidates was now established— Hoover wanted to use the government's powers sparingly, while Roosevelt was ready to intervene directly to redress the situation. Two weeks before the election, the polls had Roosevelt winning forty-four out of forty-eight states.

He carried forty-two. The popular vote was 22.8 million for Roosevelt to 15.7 million for Hoover. Hoover wired his congratulations; Hearst, still less than overwhelmed, sent his best wishes via Joe, who was throwing a victory party at the Waldorf-Astoria.

Celebrations continued in Florida, where the president-elect enjoyed a cruise on Vincent Astor's yacht. Joe was aboard, and at one of the shore parties managed to get his in-laws invited. Honey Fitz beamed and Josie told people her son-in-law had made FDR president.

The triumphant Roosevelt and his "brain trust" didn't know what to do with Joe, and ended up treating him rather shabbily. A banker with wide experience and contacts in the worlds of finance and film, Joe expected to be named secretary of the treasury, a cabinet post that would have allowed him to keep an eye on the country's money—and his own. He was bitterly opposed by Frederic Howe, who, according to his biographer, "didn't care for Mr. Kennedy for reasons known only to himself." Less partisan opinion had it that the eccentric Howe told his boss that, since Democrats had vowed to chase the moneychangers out of the temple, it would be unwise to admit a Wall Street sharpie of Kennedy's repute to the treasury. Roosevelt wanted Carter Glass, the irascible seventy-four-year-old Virginia senator who had been Woodrow Wilson's secretary of the treasury and the architect of the Federal Reserve Bank Act, but Glass elected to stay in the Senate, and FDR settled on William H. Woodin, president of the American Car & Foundry Company and a $10,000 contributor to the Democratic campaign.

Joe was a proud man. Instead of telephoning Hyde Park, he returned to business. Making America "wet" again by repealing Prohibition was one of Roosevelt's campaign promises. In anticipation of repeal, Joe took Jimmy Roosevelt with him on a trip to England, where for a reported $118,000 he cornered the U.S. franchise for Gordon's gin and Haig & Haig, King Williams, and John Dewar whiskies. A *Saturday Evening Post* story a few years later would assert that young Roosevelt had been instrumental in opening doors for Joe among British distillers, a charge Joe would vehemently deny. In any case, he somehow wrangled Customs permits to import big quantities of Scotch and gin for "medical purposes." When the bars were legally opened, the Kennedy warehouses were bulging. Eleanor Roosevelt didn't like seeing her son used to help Joe with the Scotch deal, and in rancor she held out against John Kennedy at the 1960 Chicago convention.

Roosevelt took office on March 4, 1933, a month after Adolf Hitler became Reich chancellor of Germany. The next day, the new administration decided to stop the run on banks and the hoarding of gold by proclaiming a three-day bank holiday and calling for a special session of Congress to convene on March 9.

Tackling the economic issues finally gave Joe an appointment. At the recommendation of Bernard Baruch and Moley, Roosevelt made Joe the chairman of the newly-created Securities and Exchange Commission. "A grotesque appointment," *The New Republic* complained. Howe complained that assigning Kennedy to police Wall Street was akin to setting a cat to guard the pigeons, and stockbrokers regarded Joe as a Judas strangling the business in return for prestige. But FDR saw the appointment as a brilliant stroke. Who would be better to clamp down on illicit practices than an insider who had made his pile?

Unlike many New Dealers, Joe got things done, and the SEC soon became the glamour spot in the new administration. The best and the brightest of the young attorneys who flocked to Washington wanted to work there—among them, a young Canadian economics professor named John Kenneth Galbraith and a future Supreme Court justice named William O. Douglas.

Like the rest of the New Dealers, Joe put in excruciating hours and in his first year on the job flew 25,000 miles on nascent puddle-hop airlines. The rules he put into effect stabilized markets and protected the investing public from fraud and corruption. ("It takes a thief to catch a thief," someone at the White House was supposed to have commented.) Joe even attacked selling short. It was slow and tedious work. Joe didn't see much of the president, the massive figure behind his desk, his cigarette and cigarette holder rising at a jaunty angle, telling everybody how important the work they were doing was. To Henry Morgenthau, Jr., Roosevelt complained that "Joe calls up and says he is hurt because I have not seen him."

Joe rented Marwood House, a twenty-five-room Maryland estate overlooking the Potomac.

Except for weekends, when Rose and the children came down, it was the Rodeo Drive style of clubhouse living again. Eddie Moore occupied a part of the rambling house, and other cronies lived there, too. Joe took care of his health. He was up early enough to go horseback riding or take a swim in the pool before sitting down at his desk at 7:30. In the summer, he liked to work on the huge veranda in the morning to the accompaniment of Beethoven or Brahms on the record player. Marwood had a projection room, and the former movie mogul entertained a few lieutenants, influential journalists, and an occasional girlfriend in the evening with dinner and a screening. Any young lady who might visit left early enough to allow the master of the house a full night's sleep.

Roosevelt came to Marwood a couple of times with Missy LeHand, SEC general counsel John Burns, and Tommy Corcoran, the energetic Irishman from Rhode Island who served as a presidential assistant. Joe would get the mint juleps mixed, organize a dinner and a movie, and sit down with the president on the veranda. The *New York Times* columnist Arthur Krock, who became a lifelong friend of Joe, would remember a summer evening on the veranda with the mint juleps. Corcoran got out his accordion and the merriment went on past midnight, with FDR and Joe singing along, and the president trying the accordion himself.

Over the next few years, Henry Luce ordered up two cover stories on Kennedy in *Time,* and for the first time in his life Joe became something of a national figure. To help the 1936 reelection campaign, he turned author, writing a slim volume called *I'm For Roosevelt.* The book argued in favor of a planned economy and berated businessmen for foolishly opposing FDR when they should be on their knees thanking him for saving their fortunes. As the first millionaire to have put his energy behind Roosevelt, Joe was no longer just a quick-buck artist but a friend and confidant of the president, a member of the heady crew that was shaping the course and destiny of the nation.

Under his SEC administration, Wall Street began to breathe again. Joe did so well, in fact, that in 1936, when Roosevelt needed a chairman for the Maritime Commission, he turned again to Joe. And again Joe gave him a smooth, efficient performance.

During the summer of 1936 the lure of Hollywood beckoned Joe once more.

The "civil wars" at Paramount were almost too tempting. Two of the KKKs—the ruthless Sam Katz and the brilliant Sidney Kent—had engineered the downfall of Jesse Lasky and were moving in on Adolph Zukor. The crafty Hungarian managed to hang on to the chairmanship, but the situation was chaotic. The second quarter of 1936 saw Paramount report a six-million-dollar loss, while factions made war in the boardroom. Zukor got hold of his Wall Street banker, Elisha Walker, who suggested that Joe Kennedy be hired to go to California for an in-depth look at the situation.

As the country's highest-paid financial consultant, Joe spent May and June on Marathon Street around the corner from his old Gower Street haunts. His recommendations were bruising: put an end to Wall Street backseat driving, to exorbitant executive salaries, and to trashy movies. In a thinly veiled takeover threat, he wrote that if his suggestions were not acted upon, it might be difficult to explain "such inaction to litigious stockholders or to enquiring congressional committees." To the acute embarrassment of the Paramount board, Kennedy insisted that his exposé be made public. "Thalbergs and Zanucks cannot be bought or manufactured," his report said. It added that Paramount, one of the finest properties in the industry, had "gone into eclipse" while being steered by "the best downtown business brains." There was talk of making Kennedy president of a "new" Paramount.

In Washington, however, he was too good a target for lawmakers out to make a splash for themselves. When disgruntled Paramount stockholders asked Congressman Adolph J. Sabath to inquire, the Illinois Democrat suggested that not only Paramount be investigated but also RKO's takeover of Pathé Pictures and the subsequent capital restructuring. Sabath was the oldest member of Congress, and his committee investigating bondholders' reorganizations had already found evidence of collusion in bankruptcy proceedings leading to the default of hundreds of bond issues. The committee, he said, was alarmed by charges that the new Paramount management was engaged in an insidious program of wrecking the company "for the purpose of consummating a merger with RKO."

In a lengthy telegram from Hollywood, Joe suggested a postponement of congressional hearings. Once back in Washington, he got the White House to persuade Sabath to drop the subject.

With the Kennedys spending their summers at Hyannisport and their winters at Palm Beach, and with the older children away at school, Joe decided the Bronxville mansion was perhaps one house too many. The decision to sell the house plunged him into a new vocation, real estate. He asked New York's leading realtor, John J. Reynolds, to sell the Bronxville property for him.

"Do you think I could make some money in real estate?" he remarked casually to Reynolds.

"We both could," Reynolds replied.

The second Roosevelt term brought Joe a triumph. In December 1937 Roosevelt appointed him ambassador to the Court of St. James's, the most prestigious of all diplomatic posts. The press reaction was universally favorable, and paper after paper retold the story that began in East Boston and

made Joseph P. Kennedy into the Irish-American Rockefeller, the Frank
Buck of the business world. Never mind that Joe and his family were more
Anglo snobs than Irish ethnics, the press loved the image of Irish Joe as
ambassador to Great Britain. The Boston Irish didn't know what to think
of P.J.'s boy, all dressed up in satin knickers and bowing to the king and
queen. Joe was delighted, and as he and Rose and the family sailed in stages
for England, no one could foretell how catastrophic the appointment would
be for the now forty-nine-year-old Joe, his country, and the Anglo-Ameri-
can alliance in the face of rising totalitarianism.

Most of London greeted the colorful new envoy, and later his charming
wife and nine children, with delight. At his first press conference, the
ambassador deliberately shocked the British newsmen by planting his feet
on the desk. "You can't expect me to develop into a statesman overnight,"
he winked. Convinced that London would be dreary at times, he persuaded
the Hays office in Hollywood to transfer his old friend Arthur Houghton
to its London office. Back in 1927, Joe had brought Houghton to FBO for
a while to keep him posted on who was on the way up, who was slipping,
and who was sleeping with whom. When it came to finding agreeable
women, Arthur always knew where to look.

Rose arrived shortly after Joe, bringing all the children except Joe Jr.
and Jack, who were at Harvard, and Rosemary, who was attending a special
school in New York. Going on eighteen, Kick was no longer a schoolgirl,
and she soon made acquaintances in London's exclusive social circles.
Eunice, Pat, and Jean entered a convent school in Roehampton, while
Bobby and Teddy went off to prep school each morning. As soon as Rose
found a school in Hertfordshire for retarded children, Rosemary was
brought over. Some of the aristocrats smiled at the way Joe would insist that
Kick be properly chaperoned at Wimbledon and then disappear into the
crowd himself with a blonde, but he was soon on first-name basis with the
foreign policy establishment.

But not all Englishmen were amused. Colonel Josiah Wedgwood, an
outstanding Liberal member of Parliament, let it be known in Washington
that the Roosevelt administration should have sent its best man and not "a
great publicity seeker who is apparently ambitious to be the first Catholic
President of the United States." The White House was perfectly aware of
Joe's political ambitions. In fact, FDR sent Joe to London to get him out
of the way and prevent him from lending his talents to the conservative wing
of the party.

The Roosevelt administration's view of Europe was uncertain at best.
It didn't know what to think of a problem like Czechoslovakia, created as
a result of the breakup of the Austrian empire and the 1919 Versailles
Treaty, with a German minority clamoring to be German again. Many

senior State Department professionals saw Bolshevism as a greater threat than Adolf Hitler, and were not overly concerned with the persecution of Jews. Roosevelt didn't trust the State Department professionals, not even Cordell Hull, his secretary of state, preferring to rely on cables from his ambassadors. This was a situation tailor-made for Kennedy.

As fate would have it, Joe became a personal friend of Prime Minister Neville Chamberlain. Although twenty years older than Joe, Chamberlain was also a self-made businessman and a pragmatist. He had met Hitler and didn't like him, but he felt the führer was guided by no more than self-interest and a desire for a new Bismarckian "place in the sun" for Germany—that is, economic progress and freedom from the shackles of the Versailles Treaty.

Joe also fell in with the far-right "Cliveden set." Chamberlain's most clamorous support came from the Astor family, dominated by the often outrageous American-born Lady Astor. Soon Rose and Joe were mingling at the Astors' magnificent Cliveden country estate, listening to the likes of Charles Lindbergh (who gave the most fearsome assessment of Herman Göring's Luftwaffe,) William Bullitt (FDR's ambassador to Paris, who inveighed against the impotence of French Prime Minister Edouard Daladier's government), and George Bernard Shaw, the eighty-two-year-old playwright and critic of all social and moral theories. It was in this atmosphere of genteel, eccentric defeatism that Joe decided to undertake the one crusade in his life—to keep the United States out of war.

The summer of 1938 saw Joe attend Young Joe's graduation at Harvard, visit the president at Hyde Park, and make a trip to Los Angeles. While Rose entertained her parents in London, Joe called up Gloria, saying he was just across the street at the Beverly Hills Hotel. He came over, and Gloria invited six people for a dinner party. She thought he was the same old Joe.

He brought Joe Jr. and Jack to England and, with them and Eddie Moore, made his first visit to Ireland. The family went to southern France in August as Hitler pressed the Czech question.

The political situation brought Joe back to London ahead of Rose and the children for what would be the toughest six weeks of his ambassadorship. Chamberlain was not about to take Britain to war, and in September he flew to Munich with Daladier to meet the führer. In thirteen hours of talks with no Czech representative present, Germany, France, Italy, and Great Britain agreed to Germany's annexation of the Sudetenland—the richest part of Czechoslovakia. Joe was in the diplomatic gallery in Parliament when the returning Chamberlain reported the Munich agreement had brought "peace in our time." In private talks with Joe, the prime minister said he realized the rape of Czechoslovakia would be put on his shoulders but that he could live with that since the alternative was war.

Lindbergh gave Joe his assessment of Europe's military forces, a dismal picture of German might and Anglo-French weakness, and over the next weeks, Joe defended the Munich deal in speeches at all available forums. He also pressured Will Hays to censor the views of dissenting Englishmen in a Paramount newsreel on the Sudeten agreement, and he told German ambassador Herbert Von Dirksen that he would go to Berlin only if he could meet Hitler. American reaction to a Kennedy telling a Royal Navy League dinner that Munich had proved it was possible to "get along" with dictatorships was harsh. The White House was flooded with telegrams and phone calls, many asking if American foreign policy had changed. Back at Harvard, Jack wrote to his father that "while it seemed to be unpopular with the Jews, etc.," the speech was considered "to be very good by everyone who wasn't bitterly antifascist."

The Nazi attack on Jewish property that became known as Kristallnacht provoked Joe to offer a solution to Germany's Jewish question: Hailed in *Life* magazine as a plan that might carry Kennedy to the White House, the proposal called for the resettlement of Germany's 600,000 Jews in sparsely inhabited parts of Africa and the Americas. Cordell Hull greeted the Kennedy plan with sarcasm, and in a direct rebuke of Joe, the White House announced that Myron C. Taylor would henceforth speak for the United States on refugee matters. By the winter of 1938–39, Joe's optimism that a settlement could be made turned to utter gloom. Again and again, he warned Washington that 1939 would be a year of war. As the backlash against the Munich pact grew in England, the U.S. ambassador became the object of a whispering campaign. The grinning, cussing Kennedy, whom many Britons had found endearing, was now accused of being on the payroll of the film industry, of strong-arming shipping space for his Haig and Haig cargo on scarce transatlantic transport, and of selling Czech securities on the London stock exchange just before the German invasion of the Sudetenland and winding up with a £20,000 profit.

The Soviet-German nonaggression pact in August 1939 shocked him. "I have done everything that I can think of, Joe," the prime minister told him as they waited to see if Hitler would attack Poland. The waiting ended on September 1, when German Panzer divisions crossed the Polish border. Joe had tears in his eyes when he heard Chamberlain on the radio telling his people Britain and France had declared war on Germany.

Joe's diplomatic career came to end in November 1940. Back in Boston, on his way to Washington to report to Roosevelt, he gave an interview to Louis N. Lyons, a reporter for the *Boston Globe*. Kennedy made indiscreet remarks about Britain, the British government, and Congress. Later, Joe said he expected Lyons would use his judgment and protect him in his capacity as ambassador. But Lyons simply quoted him as saying such things as that democracy "is finished in England. It may be here," and "England isn't fighting for democracy. That's bunk. She's fighting for self-preservation just as we will if it comes to us." When the interview appeared, Joe told another reporter: "He has destroyed me as an ambassador. There's nothing left for me to do but resign."

Joe's presidential ambitions had one last gasp. Early in 1940 his name was put forward as a possible Democratic candidate by a group of admirers who wanted to enter him in the Massachusetts primary. He declined, and after a confidential chat with FDR, endorsed Roosevelt for a third term. Joe and Rose were in Palm Beach on December 7, 1941, when the news of Pearl Harbor came. He fired off a telegram to the White House: "IN THIS GREAT CRISIS ALL AMERICANS ARE WITH YOU. NAME THE BATTLE POST. I'M YOURS TO COMMAND."

As in 1932, Joe waited and waited. No call ever came. He sat out World War II, lost Young Joe, and after it was all over, decided Jack should go into politics. Jack had played with the idea of becoming a journalist or a teacher, but agreed to enact the family dream. In 1948 Joe and Rose lost Kathleen in a plane crash in France. Joe unashamedly put the weight of his fortune behind his remaining sons and watched with pride as Jack was elected first to the House of Representatives, then to the Senate.

With Jack moving into the public arena, Joe thought it was time to put down his own story. He hired James Landis, a former dean of the Harvard Law School, to help him write his autobiography, but his old journalist friend Arthur Krock, to whom he showed a draft, told him it was for the most part "a tedious repetition of the public record." Krock advised Joe to do a "frank" apologia for his life, the picaresque tale of his rise, but Jack's political career made it impossible to tell the true story.

A year into the JFK presidency, Joe was overcome by a stroke at Palm Beach. Therapy was painful and slow, and his fight for recovery was an uphill battle. He was so ill in 1963 that the family waited a full day to tell him Jack had been assassinated in Dallas. He steeled himself to watch the funeral on television. When Bobby was murdered in Los Angeles in 1968, Joe overheard Ted breaking the news to Rose, who was in Europe.

Pain clouded Joe's eyes and fear took hold as the years passed. In the spring of 1969, when former President Eisenhower died, he watched the television coverage of the funeral, making sounds and gestures indicating that he thought Ted had been shot, too, and was being buried without his having been told. Cardiac arrests became more frequent, and it is believed he never knew of Ted's car accident, in July 1969 on Chappaquiddick Island, that killed secretary Mary Jo Kopechne and blocked the presidential ambitions of Joe's only surviving son.

Joe died on November 18, 1969, having outlived four of his nine children.

Gloria's star faded after *Perfect Understanding* became the third flop in a row made under her four-picture UA contract. The fourth movie was never made. Life with Michael Farmer was difficult. They quarreled all the way to Hollywood in 1933. Louella Parsons called Gloria to tell her Mary Pickford blamed her for the breakup of her marriage to Doug. Gloria had introduced him to Sylvia Ashley, after all.

Gloria then called the now alcoholic Mary to tell her Sylvia was, for one thing, a marvelous friend, and that, for another, marriages ended not because a third party introduced a spouse to someone else but because they were ready to fall apart. "I'm in a marital mess myself," she told Mary, "but I've got nobody to blame. I tell myself that every day."

Gloria discovered another lump in her breast and made another trip to Paris. The lymph node proved to be benign. "After that I seemed to be floundering, traveling back and forth to Europe without purpose," she would remember. "Months passed, until I realized one day to my horror we were already into 1934. For the first time in my life I felt that time was slipping away, unproductively." She could not remember when she had last been happy.

In Los Angeles, Herbert Somborn's lawyer called to say her former husband wanted to see her. Since he had been a devoted father, she assumed he wanted to discuss their daughter's next return from school in Switzerland. In fact, he was dying.

"He doesn't have much time, Miss Swanson," his doctor said.

He looked awful when she saw him at the Mount Sinai Hospital the next day. "You're the only woman I ever loved," he whispered. He asked whether it was true he was dying of cancer.

She patted his arm and told him doctors had said *she* had cancer. "It doesn't matter what they say, Herbert."

Gloria's marriage to Michael Farmer ended as she began an affair with Herbert Marshall, the distinguished 1930s leading man. Women, Norma Shearer said, fell for Marshall because his face expressed tenderness and silent suffering. He had lost a leg in World War I but had mastered walking on an artificial limb without limping. The quiet-spoken Bart, as his friends called him, was married to actress Edna Best, but she preferred to live in England. Before becoming involved with Gloria, Bart had conducted discreet, civilized affairs with Kay Francis and Miriam Hopkins.

Lois Wilson and Allan Dwan told Gloria to get back to work. She said she would, but dreaded making the first calls. Irving Thalberg said it was time to start preparing an MGM picture for her, and Frances Marion was assigned to develop a story. It was decided Gloria would be marvelous in a remake of Elinor Glyn's torrid *Three Weeks*. Thalberg ordered up a fresh script from Frances Marion.

Before Marion's screenplay was halfway finished, Erich Pommer, the most famous executive of the German cinema to leave Germany when Hitler came to power, called up Gloria and offered her the starring role in *Music in the Air,* a tender, romantic musical that had warmed Broadway's heart during the winter of 1932 with such Jerome Kern–Oscar Hammerstein songs as "I've Told Every Little Star," "One More Dance," "We Belong Together," and "There's a Hill Beyond the Hill."

Now a producer at Fox, Pommer was the grand seigneur, the former head of UFA. When Gloria met him in his office, she told him she was nominally committed to Thalberg. "Well, in that case," Pommer said, "we can announce that you are on loan to Fox from MGM." They signed a contract the next day.

The film script for *Music in the Air,* the story of two temperamental opera singers in Munich too busy fighting with each other to realize they are actually in love, was to be written and directed by two other refugees from Berlin, Billy Wilder and Joe May. Wilder was an underworked screenwriter who didn't mind jumping fully clothed into Pommer's swimming pool to amuse Pommer's guests (as long as Pommer paid him the eighty dollars he had offered for the stunt). May was a veteran director of schmaltz.

For the picture, Fox built an entire Bavarian village as well as reproductions of the Munich zoo and opera house on the backlot, and commissioned René Hubert to create a fabulous wardrobe for Gloria. As leading man, Pommer and May cast John Boles, Gloria's choice for *The Loves of Sunya* seven years earlier.

Everybody was confident that, with the lovely score, the gorgeous sets, and Swanson and Boles in the starring roles, they had a winner. But the reviews were no more than polite, with *The New York Times* noting that "the years have not scarred Miss Swanson's loveliness." The box office returns were disastrous. Gloria would remember the country ignoring *Music in the Air* and rushing instead to see six-year-old Shirley Temple in a musical called *Stand Up and Cheer.*

The failure of *Music in the Air* caused Thalberg to reconsider remaking *Three Weeks.* He was looking for the "right" property for Gloria, he said. Before it could be found, he died.

Gloria next wanted to do the film version of a Broadway play to which David Selznick owned the film rights. She staged an emotional reading of the story to persuade Columbia Pictures' Harry Cohn to buy it for her. He said no, uttering one of Hollywood's more memorable lines: "If Selznick wants to sell it, it means it can't be any good."

Eddie Goulding and Bette Davis did the picture for Warner Brothers. It was *Dark Victory.*

After that, Gloria moved to New York, where she surveyed her assets. They totaled $250,000—once her price for a single film—most of the money earnings from *The Trespasser* and its remake, *That Certain Woman.*

She found a huge ground-floor apartment with a courtyard garden at Fifth Avenue and Seventy-third Street, kept up her Dr. Bieler-inspired regime (there was one refrigerator with ingredients for her diet, another with the food for the help), founded a cosmetics line, designed budget-priced clothes under the label Forever Young, starred in comedies on the straw-hat circuit, and made sculptures of wealthy people for a $5,000 fee.

In 1938 she went back to Paris. Henri came to meet her at the Hotel Crillon, where they had first met fourteen years earlier. They embraced. Little Gloria, she told him, was now a college junior at Stanford, Brother was at boarding school in Rhode Island, and Michelle, whom he had never seen, was starting school. Before she left Paris, Henri introduced her to Emmita Rodriguez Maldonado, a blue-eyed twenty-seven-year-old Colombian coffee heiress. Gloria thought the wealthy and cosmopolitan Emmita, who had spent most of her life in Europe and was courted by artists, aristocrats, and Howard Hughes, would be a perfect match for Henri.

September 1939 found Gloria in California, crying at little Gloria's wedding, and Henri trying to go to war. Emmita tried to dissuade him. After all, he was forty years old. "We have always paid the blood tax," he answered. "It's the only privilege left for the nobility." His command of English won him an assignment to the joint French-British army headquarters at Laval in Brittany, where Emmita visited him on weekends in her new Fiat Topolino. When Germany invaded Denmark and Norway, pushed through Holland and Belgium, and trapped 350,000 British and French soldiers at Dunkirk, Henri was one of the survivors who crossed the channel in small boats to land at Dover. The ragged remnant of the uniform on his back was all he had.

Ambassador Kennedy lent Henri money to buy himself clothes and approved U.S. visas for him and Emmita. Henri, meanwhile, sent urgent telegrams to Emmita telling her to escape to Spain. Getting no reply, he volunteered to go back to collapsing France with the last contingent of liaison officers. Logic, instinct, and premonition made Henri and Emmita look for each other at the last place they had been together. Tooling around Normandy in her Fiat and asking retreating regiments where she could find the Anglo-French liaison unit, Emmita stumbled on Henri in a village café.

He had only ten minutes before his unit pulled out. They decided to meet in twenty-four hours in a hotel in Vannes, but the Wehrmacht got to Vannes before they did. Radio bulletins announced that the Germans had reached Le Mans and were closing in. Looking for Henri among disintegrating columns of fleeing soldiers, Emmita saw an officer standing at a crossroads with his service revolver drawn. It was Henri. All she could ask was what he was doing there. Waiting for the Germans with just his pistol? No, he had an infantry brigade hidden behind the hedgerow.

The German war machine overran them separately, made Henri a POW and Emmita one of the thousands of women who showed up at the barbed wire to look for their men. A gallant kommandant not only issued a travel permit to this errant South American lady, but, after a Wehrmacht vehicle backed into her Fiat, had the sports car repaired. Henri and Emmita finally escaped to Biarritz and crossed into Spain. In Madrid, where Henri borrowed a thousand pesetas from the doorman at the Palace, they managed to obtain visas to Portugal. Money wired by Emmita's mother bought them passage west, at enormous prices, aboard a Portuguese freighter. The eight other passenger cabins were occupied by wealthy East European Jews. All nine cabins were infested with lice. After a three-week zigzag across the Atlantic to avoid German U-boats, they reached New York in July 1941. They camped in Gloria's apartment to catch their breath, then headed for California. After Henri's divorce from Connie became final, the marquis and the heiress were married.

Gloria also went to Los Angeles that summer. RKO had asked her to costar with Adolphe Menjou in *Father Takes a Wife,* a comedy about a temperamental actress who marries a shipping tycoon. The director was Jack Hively, famous for *The Saint* series. Prerelease publicity focused on Gloria's knack with clothes ("You Will Swoon Over Her Trunkfuls of Stunning Fashions"). But Pearl Harbor turned Americans' minds from glamour and fashion to war and uniforms, and *Father Takes a Wife* was a flop. Gloria was back in New York in December when the United States entered the war. So were Henri and Emmita. Together with Gloria and her old friend Sport Ward, they rang in 1942 at the Copacabana.

Brother was called up in 1944. From Camp Breckinridge in Kentucky, where he went through basic training, he asked his mother if she would ask Joe Kennedy to help him get transferred to a different company. Joe did. Buddy wrote a long thank you letter, which pleased the former ambassador. Unlike Joe Kennedy, Jr., Lieutenant Joe Swanson came home from the war.

William Davey became Gloria's fifth husband in 1945. A bespectacled, affable, and wealthy stockbroker, he had only one fault, which she discovered too late. He was an alcoholic who drank secretly and in the process underwent a complete change of character. Though it was an embarrassment to explain to friends and family, she divorced him after just over a month.

After *Music in the Air*, Billy Wilder had found steady employment in the writers' pool at Paramount. The elfin Viennese had been teamed with a suave Yankee named Charles Brackett, and over the next fourteen years, the two would make movie history with their stories about millionaires, chambermaids, drunkards, smart-alec cabdrivers, and *nouveaux riches*. Their most famous screenplay was *Ninotchka* for Ernst Lubitsch.

By the mid-1940s, when Wilder began directing their joint efforts, they were known for their ability to work in barbers' chairs and at parties, and for their reluctance to put anything down on paper ("in self-defense," so no one could mess with their scripts). Their scripts were "talked" into existence, with a secretary taking down their prose at the last possible moment. By 1948, they were talking up the idea of doing a movie about Hollywood. They decided it would be the story of a silent-day queen and a young man—she, living in the past, refusing to believe her days as a star are gone, while plotting her comeback; he, a screenwriter, a nice guy who can't make the grade in Hollywood. Here, Wilder and Brackett got stuck for months until one day when they were discussing Balzac's *Le Père Goriot*, one of them remarked "Suppose the old dame shoots the boy?"

Gloria arrived in Los Angeles in January 1949 to be interviewed by Wilder and Brackett. They wouldn't show her a script. The story, Brackett told her, was about an ex-movie queen who persuades a younger writer to work with her so she can return to pictures. There was a murder in it.

"Who murders whom?" Gloria wanted to know.

"We honestly aren't sure," Wilder lied.

A contract was signed, and Gloria rented a house on Mulholland Drive. Montgomery Clift was offered the part of the writer, but he refused to play love scenes with an older woman. According to the script, Joe Gillis, the young writer, was twenty-five, while Norma Desmond, the movie queen, was fifty, exactly Gloria's age. William Holden, who was then thirty-two, was also reluctant but signed on. To play Max von Mayerling, Norma Desmond's butler-chauffeur, formerly her director-husband, they cast Erich von Stroheim. Cecil B. De Mille would also be in the picture, Wilder said, playing himself.

Stroheim arrived from Paris in April. Gloria hadn't seen him since the *Arsenic and Old Lace* tour in 1942. With Wilder adroitly steering the conversation, they began to reminisce about *Queen Kelly*. At the right moment, Wilder asked Gloria if she would let him use a clip from *Queen Kelly* in the picture. Since practically no one had ever seen it, she thought it was a brilliant idea.

Sunset Boulevard became the cinema's most famous self-portrait, a gnawing, haunting ruthless film that was called everything from a piece of dry ice to a pretentious slice of Roquefort. Portraying contemporary Hollywood as stupefyingly vulgar, small, smart, and smug, the film granted the silent era a kind of barbarous intensity. Wilder let the actors dig into themselves. Gloria played Norma Desmond viciously, without regard for sympathy. Holden knew how to register a mixture of pity, guilt, and nausea in his love scenes with the crazy, demanding woman. Both are washouts—she, the forgotten, totally passé movie queen; he, a self-admitted failure who succumbs to being a kept man. Around them spins a galaxy of rejects and has-beens; even Joe Gillis's wholesome girlfriend is the daughter of a family that *was* in the movies. Norma's French-Italianate Sunset Boulevard mansion has rats in the swimming pool and the wind moans in the organ pipes. Wilder and the art directors talked Gloria into lending mementos from her past to dress the sets. Scores of stills in old frames decorate the tables and her full-length Geza Kende portrait adorns the salon of the moldering mansion.

Cruel scenes abound. Stroheim plays out his own degradation, saying, "In the early days there were three directors of great promise: D. W. Griffith, C. B. De Mille, and Max von Mayerling." The hack writer squirms as he sits through the running of Norma's old movies in the mansion's projection room. It is while screening a clip from *Queen Kelly*—Kitty kneeling in a chapel, softly lit, her face framed by burning candles, praying she will see the prince again—that Gillis recognizes her for the first time and says, "You used to be in pictures. You used to be big." Standing up in the murderous glare of the projector, she utters the famous line: "I *am* big. It's the pictures that got small."

Norma's fortnightly bridge game with her old cronies, played by Anna Q. Nilsson, H. B. Warner, and Buster Keaton, is classified as "the waxworks" by Gillis. To amuse her bored and pampered lover, Norma does her parasol-twisting takeoff of a Mack Sennett bathing beauty and impersonates Charlie Chaplin. It is at this moment that Max von Mayerling chooses to let her know that Paramount is on the phone. The mustache and bowler-hat remain, but Chaplin vanishes; the Medusa mask comes back on her face and she says: "Paramount! Ha! Let 'em wait. I've waited long enough!" In fact, De Mille is calling to ask if he can rent her leopard-upholstered Isotta-Fraschini automobile. But Norma is persuaded that De Mille wants her, not her car, and no one dares tell her the truth.

The story grinds on until, inevitably, it ends in a head-on collision between illusion and reality, in violent death and glint-eyed madness. Feeling her young lover leaving her, Norma kills him. Then, faced by a barrage of reporters, police, and newsreel cameras, she literally goes mad, and descends the grand staircase in her house believing she's acting Salome in one of her own movies.

The filming went smoothly except for Stroheim's endless suggestions. Wilder listened patiently, but even he found such ideas as Max von Mayerling washing and ironing Norma's underwear too audacious. The bridge party sequence gave Gloria and the other 1920s stars the creeps. Warner had been her leading man in *Zaza* and played Christ in De Mille's *King of Kings.* "Waxworks is right," Buster Keaton deadpanned. When Wilder shouted "Print it!" for the last time, Gloria burst into tears. She didn't want the filming to be over. She had planned a wrap party at the Mulholland Drive house; instead cast and crew gave her one right on the set.

She was paid a mere $33,000, hardly her price in the old Paramount days, for this, her sixty-third feature. But by the time the studio screened it for her and a hundred invited guests—Louis B. Mayer was there, and Gloria caught a glimpse of Mickey Neilan—they knew they had a blockbuster. *Newsweek* put *Sunset Boulevard* on its cover, and the film made Gloria Swanson famous all over again. Offers of pictures—mostly ripoffs of *Sunset Boulevard*—came in. Together with Bette Davis, who had played an aging actress in *All About Eve,* and Judy Holliday in *Born Yesterday,* Gloria was regarded as the leading contender for the 1950 Academy Award for best actress. She spent Oscar night in a Manhattan nightclub with Addie, Michelle, William Holden, *Born Yesterday* director George Cukor, Celeste Holm, and José Ferrer. The competition was intense, and the best-actress Oscar went to Judy Holliday for *Born Yesterday.*

The release of *Sunset Boulevard*—and Gloria's Oscar nomination—revived interest in *Queen Kelly.* With Gloria in attendance, New York's Museum of Modern Art gave the ninety-minute Swanson version its U.S. premiere in July 1950. Thirteen years later, two edited reels of the African sequence were rediscovered in, of all places, the garage of Dudley Murphy, the *Loves of Sunya* cameraman. Kino International acquired the rights to *Queen Kelly* from the Swanson estate and began to rehabilitate it into a version as close to the Stroheim original as possible. Gloria's print was in mint condition—perhaps the finest preserved film from the silent era. Shown for the first time in New York, Los Angeles, and Paris in the fall of 1985, the painstaking ninety-six-minute restoration, incorporating stills, explanations, and outtakes, and with Adolph Tandler's period score, revealed all of Stroheim's barbaric splendor and reckless flamboyance, his wry sexual fetishism, and his fascinations with aristocratic excess. Wrote *Le*

Monde, "Even incomplete, *Queen Kelly* can radically question today's movies. The point is not to go back fifty years, of course, but to measure what we have lost, even if it entails reinventing everything."

In 1951 Gloria made her Broadway debut with José Ferrer in a revival of the Charles MacArthur–Ben Hecht hardboiled farce, *Twentieth Century.* The next year she made *Three for Bedroom C.,* a romantic film about a famous star and her daughter traveling by train from Chicago to Los Angeles. Critics were disappointed that the film wasn't *Sunset Boulevard,* and Gloria gave up on scripts calling on her to play eccentric actresses. Her next movie was *Nero's Mistress,* an Italian production costarring Vittorio de Sica, Brigitte Bardot, and Alberto Sordi. The film was so bad it took six years for it to find an American distributor.

At parties given by Aristotle Onassis, Gianni Agnelli, Gunther Sachs, the Aga Khan, and the Duke of Otrante, Gloria occasionally ran into Henri and Emmita. The la Falaises lived in Paris, a stone's throw from the Bois de Boulogne. They had restored Henri's ancestral manor (Emmita insisting on electricity, hot water, and telephone), bought a home on Majorca, and were sought-after guests at Lord Throckmorton's enclosure at Ascot, at Prince Bismarck's boar chases in Sachsenwald, and at the white-tail deer hunts that Cantinflas and his Russian wife organized in the hills above Acapulco. As the Washington houseguests of Barbara Hutton in 1960, they met Joe and Rose Kennedy. Emmita thought that Joe was a force of nature with the personality of a gangster and that Rose was smarter than anyone suspected. Young John had a way with women, Rose told the marquise during a tête à tête, but the presidency would keep him out of trouble.

Gloria spent much of the 1960s in France and Italy with a long line of companions, suitors, and escorts. All of them were younger than she. Addie died in California in 1966. Little Gloria divorced and remarried. Michelle became the wife of a French diplomat and lived in Paris. They gave her six grandchildren. Buddy died in 1975.

Henri died in Spain of a heart attack in 1972 after he and Emmita celebrated their thirtieth anniversary. He had defended France in two wars, but with the exception of two months as Gloria's secretary in 1924 and his brief stint at Pathé, he had never worked a day in his life. Emmita and he were childless. To keep the la Falaise name attached to the patriarchal home in St. Florent des Bois, she gave it to Henri's nephews, but they planned to sell it to developers.

Quintessential symbol of movie glamour, maker and spender of millions, Gloria Swanson, like Norma Desmond, never got small. The public knew her best in her later years as a tireless advocate of natural foods. She credited her regime of diet and exercise with keeping her in the sort of condition that prompted people to describe her as youthful, slender, and chic well into her seventies. She maintained she never had a face lift, although she admitted that a young Roman lover of hers had persuaded her to have her eyes done.

In the 1970s she and a very pregnant little Gloria were having lunch at the Ritz Hotel in Paris when a lady came over to the table. It was Rose Kennedy. They chatted about the joys of grandmotherhood, and Rose gave little Gloria a Kennedy half-dollar as a keepsake for the baby.

"The mess I made of marriage was all my fault," Gloria said in interviews. Her sixth husband was William Dufty, a writer several years her junior. Dufty was the author of *Sugar Blues,* and the two of them waged a crusade against the use of sugar. He helped her write her autobiography; she sculpted a bust of him.

She played herself in Jack Smight's *Airport 1975,* a cheap sequel to the hit 1970 thriller *Airport.* To reporters, she talked of her sixty years in movies, how she owed it all to the public. The new feminism didn't mean much to her. "I've always been liberated, and I need a man above me, someone I can respect."

Her advice to young actresses. "Not too much success all your life. Those who only know success don't grow very much."

And the future of movies? "Poetry and romance. I think people will always need a dream."

She died of a heart ailment in New York Hospital on April 15, 1983, a week after her eighty-fourth birthday.

Bibliography

Allen, Frederick Lewis. *Only Yesterday: An Informal History of the 1920s.* New York: Harper & Row, 1931.

Beschloss, Michael. *Kennedy and Roosevelt, The Uneasy Alliance.* New York: W. W. Norton, 1980.

Bessy, Maurice. *Erich von Stroheim.* Paris: Pygmalion, 1984.

Birmingham, Stephen. *The Grandes Dames.* New York: Simon & Schuster, 1982.

Bogdanovich, Peter. *Allan Dwan.* New York: Praeger, 1971.

Clinch, Nancy Gager. *The Kennedy Neurosis.* New York: Grosset & Dunlap, 1973.

Collier, Peter, and Horowitz, David. *The Kennedys: An American Drama.* New York: Simon & Schuster, 1984.

Coursodon, Jean-Pierre, and Sauvage, Pierre. *American Directors.* New York: McGraw-Hill, 1983.

Curtiss, Thomas Quinn. *Von Stroheim.* New York: Farrar, Straus & Giroux, 1971.

Davis, John H. *The Kennedys: Dynasty and Disaster, 1848–1984.* New York: McGraw-Hill, 1984.

De Mille, Cecil B. *The Autobiography.* Englewood Cliffs, NJ: Prentice-Hall, 1959.

Everson, William K. *American Silent Film.* New York: Oxford University Press, 1978.

Finler, Joel W. *Stroheim.* Berkeley: University of California Press, 1968.

Galbraith, John Kenneth. *A Life in Our Times.* Boston: Houghton Mifflin, 1981.

Gilbert-Fountain, Leatrice. *Dark Star: The Untold Story of the Meteoric Rise and Fall of the Legendary John Gilbert.* New York: St. Martin's Press, 1985.

Goodwin, Doris Kearns. *The Fitzgeralds and the Kennedys.* New York: Simon & Schuster, 1987.

Griffith, Richard, and Mayer, Arthur. *The Movies.* New York: Simon & Schuster, 1957.

Higham, Charles, *Cecil B. De Mille.* New York: Scribner's, 1973.

Jenkins, Alan, *The Twenties.* New York: Universe Books, 1974.

Kennedy, Joseph P. ed. *The Story of the Films.* Chicago: A. W. Shaw, 1927.

Kennedy, Rose. *Times to Remember.* New York: Doubleday, 1974.

Kirkpatrick, Sydney D., *A Cast of Killers.* New York: Dutton, 1986.

Koskoff, David E. *Joseph P. Kennedy: A Life and Times.* Englewood, NJ: Prentice-Hall, 1974.

Koszarski, Richard, *The Man You Love to Hate: Erich von Stroheim vs. Hollywood.* New York: Oxford University Press, 1983.

Kotsilibas-Davis, James. *The Barrymores: The Royal Family in Hollywood.* New York: Crown, 1981.

la Falaise, Emmita, Marquise de. *Les Années magnifiques.* Paris: Editions premières, 1986.

Lanchester, Elsa. *Herself.* New York: St. Martin's Press, 1983.

Lasky, Betty. *RKO: The Biggest Little Major of Them All.* Englewood Cliffs, NJ: Prentice-Hall, 1984.

Lasky, Jesse L. Jr. *Whatever Happened to Hollywood.* New York: Funk & Wagnalls, 1973.

Lasky, Victor. *J.F.K: The Man and the Myth.* New York: Macmillan, 1963.

Loos, Anita, *Cast of Thousands.* Grosset & Dunlap, 1977.

Marion, Denis, ed. *Stroheim.* Paris: Etudes cinématographiques, 1966.

Martin, Ralph G. *A Hero for Our Time: An Intimate Story of the Kennedy Years.* New York: Macmillan, 1983.

Moore, Colleen. *Silent Star.* New York: Doubleday, 1968.

Morgan, Ted. *Maugham.* New York, Simon & Schuster, 1980.

———— *F.D.R.: A Biography;* New York: Simon & Schuster, 1985.

Rhode, Eric. *A History of the Cinema.* New York: Hill & Wang, 1976.

Sadoul, Georges. *Histoire du Cinéma mondial.* Paris: Flammarion, 1949.

Schickel, Richard. *D. W. Griffith: An American Life.* New York: Simon & Schuster, 1984.

Sennett, Mack. *King of Comedy.* Garden City, NY: Doubleday, 1954.

Steichen, Edward. *A Life in Photography.* Garden City, NY: Doubleday, 1981.

Stiles, Lela. *The Man Behind Roosevelt: The Story of Louis McHenry Howe.* Chicago: World, 1954.

Swanson, Gloria. *Swanson on Swanson: An Autobiography.* New York: Random House, 1980.

Talmey, Allene. *Doug and Mary and Others.* New York: Macy-Masius, 1927.

This Fabulous Century: 1920–30. Alexandria, VA: Time-Life Books, 1969.

Tulard, Jean. *Dictionnaire du Cinéma.* Paris: Robert Laffont, 1982.

Wagenknecht, Edward. *The Movies in the Age of Innocence.* Norman, OK: University of Oklahoma Press, 1980.

Walsh, Raoul. *The Life Story of a Director.* New York: Farrar, Straus & Giroux, 1974.

Whalen, Richard J. *The Founding Father: The Story of Joseph P. Kennedy.* New York: New American Library, 1964.

Wolf, George, and DiMona, Joseph. *Frank Costello: Prime Minister of the Underworld.* New York: Morrow, 1974.

Index